READING FOR CHANGE

PERFORMANCE AND ENGAGEMENT ACROSS COUNTRIES

RESULTS FROM PISA 2000

Irwin Kirsch
John de Jong
Dominique Lafontaine
Joy McQueen
Juliette Mendelovits
Christian Monseur

OECD
ORGANISATION FOR ECONOMIC CO-OPERATION AND DEVELOPMENT

ORGANISATION FOR ECONOMIC CO-OPERATION AND DEVELOPMENT

Pursuant to Article 1 of the Convention signed in Paris on 14th December 1960, and which came into force on 30th September 1961, the Organisation for Economic Co-operation and Development (OECD) shall promote policies designed:

- to achieve the highest sustainable economic growth and employment and a rising standard of living in Member countries, while maintaining financial stability, and thus to contribute to the development of the world economy;
- to contribute to sound economic expansion in Member as well as non-member countries in the process of economic development; and
- to contribute to the expansion of world trade on a multilateral, non-discriminatory basis in accordance with international obligations.

The original Member countries of the OECD are Austria, Belgium, Canada, Denmark, France, Germany, Greece, Iceland, Ireland, Italy, Luxembourg, the Netherlands, Norway, Portugal, Spain, Sweden, Switzerland, Turkey, the United Kingdom and the United States. The following countries became Members subsequently through accession at the dates indicated hereafter: Japan (28th April 1964), Finland (28th January 1969), Australia (7th June 1971), New Zealand (29th May 1973), Mexico (18th May 1994), the Czech Republic (21st December 1995), Hungary (7th May 1996), Poland (22nd November 1996), Korea (12th December 1996) and the Slovak Republic (14th December 2000). The Commission of the European Communities takes part in the work of the OECD (Article 13 of the OECD Convention).

The Centre for Educational Research and Innovation was created in June 1968 by the Council of the Organisation for Economic Co-operation and Development and all Member countries of the OECD are participants.

The main objectives of the Centre are as follows:

- *Analyse and develop research, innovation and key indicators in current and emerging education and learning issues, and their links to other sectors of policy;*
- *Explore forward-looking coherent approaches to education and learning in the context of national and international cultural, social and economic change; and*
- *Facilitate practical co-operation among Member countries and, where relevant, with non-member countries, in order to seek solutions and exchange views of educational problems of common interest.*

The Centre functions within the Organisation for Economic Co-operation and Development in accordance with the decisions of the Council of the Organisation, under the authority of the Secretary-General. It is supervised by a Governing Board composed of one national expert in its field of competence from each of the countries participating in its programme of work.

FOREWORD

Compelling incentives for individuals, economies and societies to raise levels of education have been the driving force behind the concern of governments to improve the quality of educational services. The prosperity of OECD countries now derives to a large extent from its human capital and the opportunities for its citizens to acquire knowledge and skills that will enable them to continue learning throughout their lives.

The OECD Programme for International Student Assessment (PISA) was set up to measure how well young adults near the end of compulsory schooling are prepared to meet the challenges of today's knowledge societies. PISA is forward-looking, focusing on young people's ability to reflect on and apply their knowledge and skills to meet the challenges of adult life in the real world.

PISA is conducted once every three years, and is organised around three domains: mathematical literacy, reading literacy and scientific literacy. In each three-year cycle one of these three domains is the major focus of data collection. In 2000, when the first PISA data collection occurred, reading literacy was the major domain, accounting for over two thirds of the testing content. Reading literacy is not only seen as a necessary foundation for performance in other subject areas within an educational context, but it is also a prerequisite for successful participation in most areas of adult life. Today's world calls for citizens to become life-long learners. To meet this goal, students must be prepared to handle the variety of printed and written information that they will encounter throughout their lives.

A report presenting the first results of PISA 2000 was published in 2001 (OECD, 2001*b*) covering results in all three domains and looking at the relationship between student performance in these areas and selected characteristics of individuals, families and schools. This report refines and extends the discussion of the reading literacy results contained in the first report.

The title of this report, *Reading for Change*, intends to capture two major messages. The first refers to achievement in reading literacy: PISA results suggest that changing and improving students' reading proficiency could have a strong impact on their opportunities in later life. The second message refers to engagement in reading: levels of interest in and attitudes toward reading, the amount of time students spend on reading in their free time and the diversity of materials they read are closely associated with performance in reading literacy. Furthermore, while the degree of engagement in reading varies considerably from country to county, 15-year-olds whose parents have the lowest occupational status but who are highly engaged in reading obtain higher average reading scores in PISA than students whose parents have high or medium occupational status but who report to be poorly engaged in reading. This suggests that finding ways to engage students in reading may be one of the most effective ways to leverage social change.

Even in countries in which there is generally a high level of reading proficiency, there are substantial numbers of 15-year-olds who are not proficient readers which is likely to limit them in their choices and opportunities in their future life. How much reading literacy is enough or what single point on the combined reading literacy scale indicates a degree of literacy that will guarantee success is not a question that can be answered from this report in general terms. Policy implications will therefore have to be derived at the country level, each country carefully evaluating its own particular pattern of characteristics and their associations with the reading literacy of students. Remedies to shortcomings will differ from country to country, depending on the educational structure and other country-specific variables. However, the analyses provided in this report suggest that all countries would be well advised to seek means to raise the level of interest in reading among students, and especially among boys.

Reading literacy as measured in PISA requires students to demonstrate their skills in dealing with a wide range of texts, drawn from different situations and approached from a number of perspectives. One major focus of this report is to present in some detail the construct of reading literacy that underpins PISA, and to show the connections between this construct and countries' results. The report does that by presenting results not just in terms of means and distributions of performance on the combined reading literacy scale, but also in terms of five subscales that are defined with respect to two text formats (continuous and non-continuous) and three approaches to, or "aspects" of, reading: retrieving information, interpreting and reflecting.

Though many users of international surveys are first and foremost intent on spotting the relative positions of countries on some overall reporting scale, differences in student performance within countries are significantly larger than differences in the average performance of countries. On the combined reading literacy scale, the difference between the most and least able students (represented by the 90th and 10th percentiles) ranges, within each country, between two and a half and four and a half PISA levels indicating a high and concerning degree of inequality in some countries. In some countries the difference between boys and girls is much larger than in others, some countries show a bigger disadvantage for students from low-income families, and the educational structure of some countries seems to have a stronger impact on differences among students.

A further difference between countries lies in their relative strengths on the reading literacy subscales. In some countries students are better in retrieving information from texts than in reflecting on these texts. In these countries students tend also to do better on non-continuous texts than on continuous texts. By contrast, in countries where students are better at reflecting than at retrieving information students generally do better on continuous texts. But there are also countries that show quite different patterns with respect to the different aspects and text formats used in the PISA reading literacy survey.

PISA is a collaborative effort, bringing together scientific expertise from the participating countries, steered jointly by their governments on the basis of shared, policy-driven interests. Participating countries take responsibility for the project at the policy level through a Board of Participating Countries. Experts from participating countries serve on working groups that are charged with linking the PISA policy objectives with the best available substantive and technical expertise in the field of international comparative assessment of educational outcomes. Through participating in these expert groups, countries ensure that the PISA assessment instruments are internationally valid and take into account the cultural and curricular contexts of OECD Member countries, that they provide a realistic basis for measurement, and that they place an emphasis on authenticity and educational validity. The reading functional expert group, which guided the development of the reading literacy assessment framework, oversaw the construction of the assessment tasks, and helped in conceptualising the shape of this report, consisted of members from nine countries selected for their various backgrounds and expertise in reading and measurement. A list of the members is contained in the back of this report. Test developers from the Australian Council for Educational Research (ACER) and CITO group (Netherlands) selected texts that were culturally diverse and developed a pool of items that mapped closely to specifications outlined in the framework.

Wolfram Schulz from ACER contributed to the data analysis for Chapter 7. Kentaro Yamamoto from Educational Testing Service (ETS) performed the analyses that resulted in placing the PISA students on the prose literacy scale used in the International Adult Literacy Survey, as reported in Chapter 8. Our thanks are also extended to Marylou Lennon for her comments on early drafts of individual chapters and to Lynn Jenkins for her careful editorial work on the full report. We also acknowledge the valuable feedback from Aletta Grisay, Eugene Johnson and from members of the PISA Board of Participating Countries.

This report represents a true collaboration among the authors who are members of the reading expert group or of the PISA consortium. Credit, should any accrue, needs to be shared with the various individuals and institutions mentioned.

Irwin Kirsch
John de Jong
Dominique Lafontaine
Joy McQueen
Juliette Mendelovits
Christian Monseur

TABLE OF CONTENTS

INTRODUCTION TO PISA AND READING LITERACY

This monograph is concerned with…the interests, attitudes, and skills that enable young people and adults to meet effectively the reading demands of their current lives (and)…to take full advantage of the many opportunities now available to make life richer and more satisfying through reading.

William S. Gray and Bernice Rogers
Maturity in Reading, 1956

Although these words were written almost half a century ago, they reflect the basic principles of the framework for reading literacy that underlies the Programme for International Student Assessment (PISA), an international survey of reading, mathematical and scientific literacies among 15-year-olds. The focus of this framework is on the application of reading skills across a range of situations for a variety of purposes and not on the mechanics of knowing how to read. Hence, the framework recognises that reading literacy plays an important role in people's lives, from public to private, from school to work, from citizenship to lifelong learning. Literacy enables the fulfilment of individual aspirations – defined goals such as successfully completing initial education or gaining employment as well as goals which are less defined and less immediate but nevertheless enrich one's personal life and growth. Not surprisingly, reading literacy is an important component in the concept of human capital, which is linked to both the social and the economic fate of individuals and nations (OECD, 2001*a*).

The overall educational attainment of the world's population is constantly increasing: more young adults attain higher levels of education each decade. But at the same time, the growing importance of knowledge in modern economies has resulted in a change in the demand for labour from lower to higher levels of skills. Educational expansion has not been able to keep up with this growing demand for skilled workers, and countries are experiencing increased unemployment among those with lower levels of skills.

This first chapter discusses the origins and background of PISA and how PISA differs from other international school-based surveys. In addition, we explain why reading literacy is fundamental in modern society, how the definition and framework for the assessment of reading literacy were developed, and what steps were taken to ensure the comparability of measurement across languages and cultures. Finally, we lay out the focus and organisation of this report.

Aims of the PISA study

Improving the quality of education is a major policy initiative in Member countries of the Organisation for Economic Co-operation and Development (OECD). This stems, in part, from the growing recognition that the prosperity of a nation derives to a large extent from its human capital and the opportunities for its citizens to learn and acquire knowledge on a continuing basis.

Since 1985, the OECD has gathered comparable data on a number of indicators including the human and financial resources invested in education, access to, progression in and completion of education, and the operation of education and learning systems. Since the early nineties the OECD has published these data in annual reports entitled *Education at a Glance*.

To complement this information, PISA was set up to measure how well young adults, at age 15, who are at or near the end of compulsory schooling, are prepared to meet the challenges of today's knowledge societies. Rather than looking backward at the extent to which young people have mastered a specific school curriculum, PISA looks forward, focusing on young people's ability to reflect on and apply their knowledge and skills to meet real-life challenges, whether they plan to continue education and eventually pursue an academic career, or are preparing to start work.

PISA is a collaborative effort between the governments of the Member countries of the OECD, representatives of those countries jointly steering the project through a Board of Participating Countries. The first PISA survey was conducted in the year 2000 in 32 countries (28 OECD and four non-OECD countries), using an assessment that took the form of written tasks for reading, mathematics and science, carried out under test conditions in schools. The survey will be repeated every three years with varying areas of focus and is designed primarily to enable interested parties to monitor the development of national education systems by looking closely at outcomes over time.

A report presenting the first results of PISA 2000 was published in 2001 (OECD, 2001*b*) covering results in reading literacy, mathematical literacy and scientific literacy. In addition, variables such as interest in reading were presented as outcomes of learning. This report focuses on reading literacy, the main assessment domain in the first PISA cycle. Other thematic reports based on data obtained in the first cycle of PISA will also be published.

PISA aims to inform parents, students, the public and those who run education systems about whether young people reaching the end of compulsory education have acquired the necessary skills and knowledge to meet the challenges of our present-day society. More specifically, PISA aims to assess whether students are sufficiently prepared to continue developing their knowledge and skills to keep up with changes that are bound to occur in the future. Therefore the skills within PISA are defined in relation to real-life challenges, *i.e.*, as necessary intellectual equipment for students' futures as working and learning adults. PISA will provide this information in a regular cycle, monitoring standards not only across countries but also over time.

How PISA differs from other international surveys

There have been a number of other international studies of reading achievement. Two studies conducted by the International Association for the Evaluation of Educational Achievement (IEA) were the Reading Comprehension and Literature sections of the IEA 1971 Six Subject Study (Walker, Anderson and Wolf, 1976) and the IEA 1991 Reading Literacy Study (IEA/RLS) (Elley, 1992; 1994). The first assessed 10 and 14-year-olds; the second assessed the grades attended by the majority of 9 and 14-year-old students. The International Adult Literacy Survey (IALS) measured the literacy skills of adults 16 to 65 years of age in 23 countries (OECD and Statistics Canada, 2000). The current Adult Literacy and Lifeskills (ALL) survey will measure the literacy, numeracy and problem-solving skills of adults 16 to 65 years of age in participating countries.

A major difference between PISA and the two IEA reading literacy studies is that PISA began with the development of a detailed framework outlining the theory, domain organisation and methods of assessment that would be a blueprint for the test instrument. The frameworks for PISA reading, mathematical and scientific literacies were widely circulated to participants, critiqued, modified and finally adopted by OECD governments, before the assessments were developed (OECD, 1999; 2000). No such documents were disseminated for the two IEA studies mentioned above, although "it is likely that previous studies drew up that type of working document for internal use" (Lafontaine, 1999). A framework document was developed for IALS and is part of the documentation for the ALL survey (Kirsch, 2001).

Another major difference between the two IEA studies and PISA is evident in the item formats used. The IEA Six Subject Study and IEA/RLS were composed of multiple-choice items and, in the case of the latter, some short, objective-response items. In PISA, almost half of the items require students to construct a response, often relating the reading material to their own knowledge and experience.

A third IEA study, Progress in International Reading Literacy Study (PIRLS), was conducted in 2001 to assess the grade attended by the majority of 9-year-old students and to link back to IEA/RLS. Like PISA, PIRLS began with a comprehensive framework (Campbell, Kelly, Mulis, Martin and Sainsbury, 2001), and like PISA, PIRLS adheres to an interactive theory of reading. Despite strong similarities, there are also significant differences between the two studies, in part as a result of their aims of sampling different populations. Since its target population was at the end of early reading instruction, PIRLS focused on investigating the relationship between reading achievement on the one hand, and reading curriculum and instructional practices on the other. By contrast, "reading" per se is not a curriculum item for most 15-year-olds and, therefore, the factors associated with the level of reading proficiency among the PISA population cannot be so directly related to the reading curriculum and reading instruction. Perhaps more importantly, PISA makes the assumption that 15-year-olds need to know not only how to read but how to apply their knowledge and skills in everyday settings as they begin to make the transition to adult life. PISA focuses on assessing reading literacy in the context of everyday situations.

Reading literacy as a foundation skill

Among the increasing demands placed on the educational development of citizens, reading literacy is fundamental. The emergence of the telephone and television gave rise to the belief that oral and visual modes of communication would soon replace the printed word (Birkerts, 1994; 1998; Coover, 1992). Contrary to these expectations, the written word has gained in importance as a means of communication.

According to Halloway (1999), reading skills are essential to the academic achievement of lower and upper secondary-school students, but after seven or eight years of elementary education, many students still lack sufficient proficiency as readers, and many adolescents continue to perform at unacceptable levels.

Olson (1997a; 1997b) actually claims that in our present-day society literacy introduces a bias, in the sense that it advantages those who have the necessary skills at the required level. Literacy provides access to literate institutions and resources, and has an impact on cognition (Olson, 1994), shaping the way in which we think. Likewise, Elwert (2001) advances the concept of "societal literacy" referring to the way in which literacy is fundamental in dealing with the institutions of a modern bureaucratic society. Law, commerce and science use written documents and written procedures such as legislation, contracts and publications that one has to be able to understand in order to function in these domains. Some years earlier

Freire and Macedo (1987) wrote that literacy is power to the people. They saw literacy as a process of "conscientisation" which involved "reading the world" rather than just reading the "word".

In our literate societies reading is a prerequisite for success in life. But not just reading. Literacy skills apply to learning, working and living. Moffett and Wagner (1983) contend that reading comprehension is not distinct from general comprehension. The skills required for comprehending texts – such as identifying the main idea, recalling details, relating facts, drawing conclusions, and predicting outcomes – are important in everyday life. One has to be able to identify a general pattern, to recall details, to see relationships, and to draw conclusions from experiences all the time in dealing with everyday issues. Reading experience adds to our own experience and thus advances and enhances the process of learning to live in our society.

The International Adult Literacy Survey (IALS: OECD and Statistics Canada, 1997) shows that after controlling for educational qualifications the level of literacy has a net direct effect on pretax income, on employment, on health, and on participation in continued education. This study also shows that people with lower levels of literacy are more likely to depend on public assistance and welfare and to be involved in crime. Kirsch, Jungeblut, Jenkins and Kolstad (1993) report similar findings from a study of adult literacy in the United States. They conclude that literacy can be thought of as a currency in our society. In addition to the personal consequences, such as the lower likelihood of being employed full-time and the greater likelihood of living in poverty, limited overall literacy skills reduce a country's resources and make it less able to "meet its goals and objectives, whether they are social, political, civic, or economic" (p. xix).

Lewis (2002) claims that some states in the United States use third-grade reading statistics to determine how many prison beds they will need in 10 years' time. Though this might seem far-fetched, it has been reported that half of all adults in U.S. federal prisons cannot read or write at all. The typical 25-year-old male inmate functions two or three grade levels below the grade actually completed (Bellarado, 1986).

The United Nations Educational, Scientific and Cultural Organization considers that literacy is a good yardstick for measuring educational achievement and estimates that it may be a better measure of education than enrolment, especially among young people in developing regions, since it usually reflects a minimal level of successfully completed schooling (UNDP, 2002). In this same publication, the UNDP points out that there is a strong correlation between level of literacy and achievement in society. This was also found in the International Adult Literacy Survey (OECD and Statistics Canada, 2000).

Reading is a prerequisite for successful performance in any school subject. By incorporating the three literacy domains of Mathematics, Reading and Science, PISA 2000 provides information on the relationships between the domains. The correlation between the Reading and Mathematics scores in PISA is 0.81, and the correlation between Reading and Science scores is 0.86. Both these correlations are slightly higher if they are computed for girls and boys separately.

Reading therefore is not merely a goal; it is also an important tool in education and individual development, both within school and in later life. In the European Union, the European Commission (2001) recognises that reading skills play a central role in an individual's learning at school: "*The ability to read and understand instructions and text is a basic requirement of success in all school subjects. The importance of literacy skills does not, however, come to an end when children leave school. Such skills are key to all areas of education and beyond, facilitating participation in the wider context of lifelong learning and contributing to individuals' social integration and personal development.*"

It can be concluded that the ability to read and understand complicated information is important to success in tertiary education, in the workplace, and in everyday life. Achievement in reading literacy is therefore arguably not only a foundation for achievement in other subject areas within the education system, but also a prerequisite for successful participation in most areas of adult life (see, for example, Cunningham and Stanovich, 1998; Smith, Mikulecky, Kibby and Dreher, 2000). It is now generally acknowledged that learning in school is not enough. But in order for students to become lifelong learners, their education must have prepared them to handle print adequately and comfortably, in whatever form it comes to them.

The task of addressing the gap between the literacy achievement of students of diverse disadvantaged backgrounds and their mainstream peers has been identified as a particular challenge for education systems in the new millennium (Au and Raphael, 2000). Revealing how literacy skills are distributed among young adults, and discovering the network of relationships between these skills and student background variables, are necessary first steps towards remedying lack of sufficient skills by the time young adults leave compulsory education.

Background of the reading literacy framework

Inherent in the words of Gray and Rogers cited at the beginning of this chapter is the view that reading literacy is a dynamic rather than a static concept that needs to parallel changes in society and culture. The reading literacy skills needed for individual growth, economic participation and citizenship 20 years ago were different from what is expected today and in all likelihood will be different from what is expected 20 years from now. We live in a rapidly changing world, where both the number and types of written materials are increasing and where growing numbers of people are expected to use these materials in new and sometimes more complex ways.

The industrial society merely required skilled and literate workers who had achieved some degree of knowledge and skills during their education. Individuals were expected only to master relatively discrete and simple tasks that they performed repeatedly, relying chiefly on knowledge and skills acquired during their education. In the incipient Information Age, businesses are constantly innovating and customising their products. As the average person changes career every five to 10 years, lifelong learning has become critical to the success of every individual. The goal of education has ceased to be the collection of static information and has been replaced by the need to acquire skills in processing, synthesising and evaluating information.

In the United States, the report from the Secretary's Commission on Achieving Necessary Skills (SCANS, 1991) suggests that the workplace of the future will require the ability to "acquire, organize, interpret, and evaluate information and use computers to process it." Therefore, the report defines a skilled reader as someone who "locates, understands, and interprets written information in prose and documents – including manuals, graphs, and schedules – to perform tasks; learns from text by determining the main idea or essential message; identifies relevant details, facts, and specifications; infers or locates the meaning of unknown or technical vocabulary; and judges the accuracy, appropriateness, style, and plausibility of reports, proposals, or theories of other writers." This, as we will see in Chapter 2, comes very close to the PISA definition of reading literacy.

Reading has pervaded human life for centuries, but the set of skills required for successful reading changes continuously. Looking up information on the Internet is becoming an everyday activity for a growing number of people and provides a clear example of a context in which reading requires skills that go far beyond decoding. Traditionally, printed material goes through a process of scrutiny and editing by a number of persons before it reaches the reader. Information on the Internet, however, shows a more diverse quality. Though some of it has been edited, a significant proportion has not, and readers will have to rely on their own critical skills in deciding whether and how to use the material. Furthermore, the sheer volume of the information available necessitates the use of selection criteria. To gather information on the Internet requires the ability to scan and skim through large amounts of material and immediately judge its merit. Critical thinking has therefore become more important than ever in reading literacy (Halpern, 1989; Shetzer and Warschauer, 2000; Warschauer, 1999). Warschauer (in press) concludes that overcoming the "digital divide" is "not only a matter of achieving online access, but also of enhancing people's abilities to adapt and create knowledge using ICT". The correlation between data on the proportion of national populations in OECD countries using the Internet (CIA, 2001), and overall PISA 2000 reading literacy scores for those countries, is 0.53. As people consult the Internet more frequently, they will probably become more adept. Education systems can, however, boost the process by equipping students with the appropriate reading skills.

The Internet is only one example of an information source. The ability to access, understand and reflect on all kinds of information is essential if individuals are to be able to participate fully in our knowledge-based society. A framework for assessing the reading literacy of students towards the end of compulsory education, therefore, must focus on reading skills that include finding, selecting, interpreting and evaluating information from a wide range of texts associated with situations both within and beyond the classroom.

The curriculum, whether defined at the national or the local level, is not the only factor influencing achievement in reading literacy. Student engagement (Guthrie and Wigfield, 2000) and access to printed materials (Neuman and Celano, 2001) are among a number of variables that have been shown to correlate with reading achievement. A strong predictor of reading comprehension is the amount of time students spend on reading (Anderson, Wilson and Fielding, 1988). If students read well they tend to read more and, as a result, they acquire more knowledge in all domains (Cunningham and Stanovich, 1998). Students with poor reading habits often find reading material too difficult (Allington, 1984), and develop a negative attitude to reading (Oka and Paris, 1986). They end up in a vicious circle, because by reading less they have fewer opportunities to develop reading comprehension strategies (Brown, Palincsar and Purcell, 1986), and so they fall further behind in all subjects, because reading is required for all academic areas (Chall, Jacobs and Baldwin, 1990).

This, however, does not mean that there is no hope for change. Parents, teachers and communities can dramatically affect how much children read (Gambrell, 1996). Moreover, recent studies suggest that knowledge of metacognitive strategies is closely correlated with reading achievement and, most importantly, can be taught effectively (Cornoldi, 1990; Mokhtari and Sheorey, 2001; Paris and Winograd 1990; Winn, 1994).

Multivariate analyses of the data will allow us to study how background and attitudinal data can help to explain differences in reading literacy at the student level. In addition, this report explores the amount of variability that may be contributed by schools and the complex relationships that exist between student background and school characteristics. Thus, it may provide policy-makers with new information on the differences in achievement between students which will allow them to define more effective strategies for countering these effects.

The PISA definition of reading literacy evolved in part from the IEA Reading Literacy Study (Elley, 1992) and from the International Adult Literacy Survey (IALS). It reflects the emphasis of the latter study on the importance of reading skills in active and critical participation in society. It is also influenced by current theories of reading which emphasise its interactive nature (Dechant, 1991; McCormick, 1988; Rumelhart, 1985), by models of discourse comprehension (Graesser, Millis and Zwaan, 1997; Kintsch and van Dijk, 1978; Van Dijk and Kintsch, 1983), and by theories of performance in solving reading tasks (Kirsch, 2001; Kirsch and Mosenthal 1990).

Apart from these procedural aspects, PISA takes into account different reading contexts because it specifically aims at measuring the reading abilities which 15-year-olds will require in order to function as future citizens, workers and lifelong learners. The European framework for languages (Council of Europe, 2001) distinguishes four major domains of language use: the personal or private, the public, the educational, and the occupational. Reading tasks in PISA address these different domains because they call for different types of reading, for example "reading to learn" from educational texts or "reading to do" in work-related texts (Sticht, 1975; Stiggins, 1982).

Development of the reading literacy framework, measurement instrument and student background questionnaire

Given the perspective described in the preceding paragraphs, the definition of reading literacy in PISA did not start from an interpretation of reading as a simple one-dimensional skill that could be represented adequately by a single scale or a single point along a scale. Different perspectives on the number and composition of scales defining reading literacy were taken into account in the development stage of PISA. This report presents information about the performance of countries on a single composite reading literacy scale as well on a set of subscales that are based on important components taken from the framework. Results are reported on these subscales in an effort to investigate the complexities of the reading process and to explore the possibility that reading skills may vary between countries.

The framework was developed collaboratively by the Reading Functional Expert Group (RFEG), an international committee of reading experts convened to provide intellectual leadership for the study. Draft versions of the framework were circulated to Member countries for comment, and refined in response to the feedback received. Since the framework served as a blueprint for the development of the reading literacy tasks, the RFEG also played a major role in guiding the selection of texts to be used in the assessment, the development of questions asked about these texts, and the creation of marking guides for the constructed-response items to ensure that they reflected what was intended by the question or directive.

The PISA Consortium invited participating countries to submit reading tasks operationalising the specifications of the framework developed by the reading expert group. From these submissions and additional material selected by test developers in Australia and the Netherlands, about 800 constructed-response and multiple-choice items were drafted and piloted in Australia and the Netherlands. The pilot functioned as an initial check on the suitability of the reading tasks, and also served to gather examples of students' answers to the constructed-response items. These sample answers were used to refine the marking guides and served in the training of markers. After several rounds of feedback from national panels, 372 of the redrafted items, including a number of items drawn from the International Adult Literacy Survey (IALS), were field-tested in participating countries. After extensive analysis of the field-trial results and further consultation with national panels, 141 items, including 15 items from IALS, were retained for the main study.

PISA also gathered information about students through questionnaires. Two sets of questions in the student questionnaire were designed to assess reading practice and reading attitudes. In the case of reading practice, a list of different kinds of reading material was provided, and students were asked to estimate their frequency of reading each. For reading attitudes, a set of 10 statements about reading was compiled. Students had to indicate whether they agreed or disagreed with each statement. Positive and negative statements about attitudes towards reading were balanced in order to avoid compliance effects. In addition, students were asked to indicate how much time they spent each day reading for enjoyment. These questions were combined to form an index of engagement in reading.

Quality and comparability

The measurement of reading literacy across a range of cultures and languages is an ambitious undertaking. Meaningful measurement requires the instruments to be culturally and linguistically equivalent for all participating groups. A detailed account of the range of strategies adopted to ensure equivalence is set out in the *PISA 2000 Technical Report* (OECD, 2002*b*). Here we present some of the main elements intended to ensure comparability.

Because of differences between countries in the structure of the education system, it is impossible to draw up an internationally comparable definition of school grades. Valid international comparisons of the yield of education systems must therefore define their populations with reference to a target age. PISA covers students who are 15 years of age at the time of the assessment, irrespective of the grade level or type of institution in which they are enrolled and whether they are in full-time or part-time education. However, it excludes 15-year-olds not enrolled in school. In general, at least 95 per cent of this target population was covered by the actual samples used in PISA 2000, and in the majority of countries even higher percentages were attained. This high degree of coverage contributes to the comparability of the assessment results. (For further details on the PISA population and sample coverage, see *PISA 2000 Technical Report* (OECD, 2002*b*)).

More than a quarter of a million students, representing almost 17 million 15-year-olds enrolled in the schools of the 32 participating countries, worked on paper-and-pencil assessments lasting two hours for each student. In this first cycle students spent, on average, 85 minutes on reading tasks. Rigorous rules were applied for sampling from the target student population in each of the participating countries to ensure the representativeness of the national samples.

In an international comparative study, it is important that the sources for various tasks cover a wide range of cultures and languages. Therefore, at the start of the PISA 2000 test development process, the OECD called for item submissions from participating countries in accordance with a set of submission guidelines. In particular, the guidelines described PISA's literacy orientation and its aim of assessing *students' preparedness for life*. Countries were specifically encouraged to submit authentic materials. Almost two-thirds of all participating countries submitted materials (see Annex A1.1 for a list of countries and organisations that contributed items to PISA).

Admittedly, reading material originating in one particular country risks being culturally unfamiliar to students from other countries. One may argue, however, that 15-year-old students can be expected to read material drawn from countries other than their own, or representing other cultures. The guiding principle adopted in assembling the instruments was to balance three key components of the framework for reading literacy: situation, text structure, and nature of the question or directive associated with a text (OECD, 1999). In this way, PISA focused more on the construct of reading literacy and less on the issues of content and familiarity. Nevertheless, the collection of materials from participating countries was an important way of ensuring that as many cultural perspectives as possible were represented in the reading material.

Other means of maximising cultural relevance and the appropriateness of tasks to all countries and subgroups included the following (see Annex A1 for quantifiable indices to ensure cultural appropriateness for PISA 2000).

- The appropriateness of the materials received from the range of participating countries was controlled through an extensive item review process that took place before the field trial, which included national reviews in each country and close scrutiny by the international team of translators. Ratings were obtained from national subject-matter experts for each item and stimulus according to students' exposure to the content of the item, item difficulty, cultural concerns, other bias concerns, translation problems, and an overall priority for including the item. A database was established which tracked comments on each reading literacy task that was developed. This became an additional source of information that was used to revise and select items for the final assessment.

- Texts and items were reviewed by an international cultural review panel. This international panel met to review and discuss the set of reading literacy items used in the field trial along with the marking guides and the set of item analyses that were computed for each task. The feedback from the panel was used along with other information to revise and select the final set of tasks used in the assessment.

- Cultural equivalence was further enhanced by using the field trial data to provide a wider range of sample responses from the participating countries in the marking guides. The field trial data were also used to decide whether to exclude from the main study items that had shown unacceptable levels of interaction between item difficulty and country, language, gender or socio-economic background.

- Quality and comparability issues were addressed by extensive and rigorous translation procedures. All materials were developed in two source versions: an English and a French version. Some cultural issues and potential translation problems were discovered at an early stage through the preparation of the parallel source versions in two languages. These materials were then sent to participating countries, along with extended translation guidelines (pertaining to intended measurement issues, vocabulary and sentence structure, common translation traps, acceptable or non-acceptable adaptations, etc.) to be translated from both language sources and reconciled into a national version. Then translated materials were sent back for verification by a team of translators appointed by the Consortium and trained in checking the equivalence between the source and national versions. Countries were permitted to make limited adaptations to the material to improve its cultural and linguistic appropriateness for that country/language where these were judged by the international consortium not to change what was being measured.

- To minimise changes in the difficulty of items as a result of the translation process, the test developers provided translation notes where appropriate. In these notes they drew attention to potential translation problems and possible misinterpretations. To further ensure that the intentions of the questions remained unchanged, test developers provided a summary of these intentions and the key processes that the items were testing. During the translation process, the test developers adjudicated on lists of country adaptations in order to ensure that the changes did not alter what the items were testing.

- Markers from participating countries were trained centrally both for the field trial and for the main study. A set of marking guides was prepared, containing all items requiring manual marking. The marking guides contained a large number of sample answers covering the range of available scores for each item. Participating countries had extensive input into the marking guides during the training of markers. Care was taken in developing these guides to reflect what was intended from a measurement perspective. The marking guides emphasised that markers were required to "code" rather than "score" responses. That is, markers' subjectivity was reduced because markers were not asked to evaluate the quality of an answer, but to decide which of the stated categories best fitted that response. The actual scoring was done after the analyses of the field-trial data, which provided information on the appropriate "scores" for each different response category.

- The international consortium provided an online marker query system which helped to ensure that each country and each marker was interpreting and applying the marking guides in a similar way. Both within-country and between-country data were collected and analysed to ensure scoring comparability. Data from this study are reported in the *PISA 2000 Technical Report* (OECD, 2002*b*).

- The length of each test form was controlled so that students with limited experience of taking tests within time constraints would not be disadvantaged (the word limit was based on rates of omission in field trial data).

- A statistical index called *differential item functioning* (DIF) was used to detect items that worked differently in some countries. These items were suspected of cultural bias and reviewed in consultation with national experts. As a result, some items were excluded from scaling as if they had not been administered in that particular country.

Focus and organisation of this report

This report provides a detailed look at the construct of reading as defined and operationalised for PISA. A set of sample items used in PISA that cover important components of the framework is also presented. Each item used in the assessment is an important source of evidence for making inferences about the knowledge and skills of students in participating countries. Information about why these items were constructed and what they measure is important for understanding the results and for drawing implications for policy-makers and educators. *Chapter 2* presents the framework for reading literacy along with the notion of described proficiency scales that explore what performance along each scale means. It also introduces the subscales that are used to report results. *Chapter 3* presents the set of sample items and maps them back to the framework.

While the initial report (OECD, 2001*b*) provides extensive information on how countries performed on the composite reading literacy scale, it says relatively little about the subscales that were created to examine possible interactions between countries. *Chapter 4* focuses on the ranking of countries and variation in literacy skills both within and between countries on each of two sets of subscales. Significant differences between countries on these subscales are highlighted. Moreover, participating countries will be concerned not just about the overall performance of their students, but also about the amount of variation that exists between high and low performers. This chapter also discusses statistics that reveal the degree to which inequality exists within countries.

A unique contribution of this report is the prominent role it gives to the concept of engagement in reading. Information on the distribution of engagement in reading among students in participating countries and on how this relates to performance on the reading literacy scales is presented in **Chapter 5**. The relationship of reading engagement to selected student background characteristics is also an important part of this chapter.

Chapter 6 continues the exploration of how reading literacy relates to selected background characteristics. This chapter examines group differences within and between countries with respect to the relationship between individual, family, home and school characteristics on the one hand, and performance on each of the reading literacy subscales and engagement in reading, on the other.

Chapter 7 takes a multivariate look at the impact of student background characteristics on performance. A multilevel multivariate regression model is selected that provides the best fit among the participating countries. This chapter examines the significance of each student characteristic after taking all other variables into account. These analyses are conducted for the combined reading literacy scale as well as for each subscale. Interesting interactions between the subscales are noted.

Chapter 8 reports on the relationship between PISA findings and those of the International Adult Literacy Survey (IALS) by means of an analysis of the 15 prose literacy items from IALS that were embedded in the PISA reading literacy assessment. IALS explicitly studied the relationship between adults' reading literacy skills and their social, cultural and economic characteristics. The analyses presented in Chapter 8 provide an opportunity to estimate the prospects in adult life of 15-year-olds in relation to their reading literacy.

Chapter 2

THE CONSTRUCT OF READING LITERACY FOR PISA

KEY POINTS

- This chapter lays out the framework that served as a blueprint for selecting PISA assessment texts and constructing tasks based on those texts. Each reading literacy task administered in the assessment provides evidence about the skills and knowledge of PISA students and is used to support the kinds of inferences we want to make about how well they can understand and use information contained in a wide range of texts associated with both academic and non-academic environments.

- One element of the framework is the definition of reading literacy. It is noted that definitions of reading and reading literacy have changed over time in parallel with changes in society, the economy and culture. The concept of learning, and particularly the concept of lifelong learning, has expanded views of reading literacy and the demands made on it. Literacy is no longer considered an ability only acquired in childhood during the early years of schooling. Instead, it is viewed as an expanding set of knowledge, skills and strategies which individuals build on throughout life in various situations and through interaction with their peers and with the larger communities in which they participate.

- In addition to presenting an overview of the framework and the tasks that were constructed to measure reading literacy, this chapter also provides a discussion about how the results of PISA reading literacy are reported. The set of reading literacy tasks used in PISA 2000 are summarised along a composite reading literacy scale and in terms of five subscales consisting of three aspect scales (retrieving information, interpreting texts and reflection and evaluation) and two format scales (continuous texts and non-continuous texts).

- The reading literacy scale not only summarises proficiency, but also reflects the pool of tasks used to measure proficiency by characterising them along the same dimension. Just as students within each country are sampled from the population of 15-year-old students within the country, each reading literacy task represents a class of tasks from the domain of reading literacy defined here. It is noted that the progression of items along the composite scale and each of the subscales represents a range of text types and task requirements, suggesting growing complexity. This progression is discussed in terms of some of the processes that are required of students and the proficiencies that they need to demonstrate in order to respond correctly to these tasks.

This chapter highlights key components of the reading literacy framework that were used to select reading texts and construct tasks to accompany those texts. Each item constructed for PISA was intended to provide evidence about the status of reading literacy among 15-year-old students in participating countries. The overall purpose of developing a reading literacy framework for PISA was to improve measurement by moving away from the interpretation of survey results in terms of discrete tasks or a single numerical outcome (*e.g.*, the average percentage correct) and towards a more meaningful interpretation, identifying levels of performance that were sufficiently generalisable to be valid across groups and over time. The intended result was an enhanced degree of measurement (Messick, 1989). While the chief benefit of developing a framework for reading literacy would be improved measurement, a number of other potential benefits were also seen as important:

- A framework provides a common language and a vehicle for discussing the definition and assumptions surrounding it.

- Such a discussion provides a mechanism for building a consensus around the framework and the measurement goals that grow from it.

- A better understanding of what is being measured results from the process of developing a framework and then linking it to the evidence collected through the assessment tasks.

- This understanding, and its connection to what we say about students, provides an important link between public policy, assessment and research which, in turn, enhances the usefulness of the data collected.

Along with presenting key components of the framework for reading literacy, this chapter also introduces the manner in which student performance across one or more sets of reading literacy tasks is summarised and reported to the various constituencies that read this monograph.

Characterising the PISA reading literacy framework[1]

Definitions of reading and reading literacy have changed over time in parallel with changes in society, the economy and culture. The concept of learning, and particularly the concept of lifelong learning, has expanded perceptions of reading literacy and the demands made on it. Literacy is no longer considered an ability only acquired in childhood during the early years of schooling. Instead, it is viewed as an expanding set of knowledge, skills and strategies which individuals build on throughout life in various situations and through interaction with their peers and with the larger communities in which they participate.

Through a consensus-building process involving the Reading Functional Expert Group (RFEG) and the PISA advisory groups, the following definition of reading literacy was adopted for the survey.

> *"Reading literacy is understanding, using and reflecting on written texts, in order to achieve one's goals, to develop one's knowledge and potential and to participate in society."*

This definition goes beyond the notion of reading literacy as decoding and literal comprehension; it implies that reading literacy involves understanding, using and reflecting on written information for a variety of purposes. It thus takes into account the active and interactive role of the reader in gaining meaning from written texts. The definition also recognises the full scope of situations in which reading literacy plays a role for young adults, from private to public, from school to work, from active citizenship to lifelong learning. It spells out the idea that literacy enables the fulfilment of individual aspirations — from defined aspirations such as gaining an educational qualification or obtaining a job, to those less immediate goals which enrich and extend one's personal life. Literacy also provides the reader with a set of linguistic tools that are increasingly important for meeting the demands of modern societies with their formal institutions, large bureaucracies and complex legal systems.

Readers respond to a given text in a variety of ways as they seek to use and understand what they are reading. This dynamic process involves many factors, some of which can be manipulated in large-scale assessments such as PISA. These include the reading situation, the structure of the text itself and the characteristics of the questions that are asked about the text (the test rubric). All of these factors are regarded as important components of the reading process and were manipulated in the creation of the items used in the assessment.

In order to use *situation, text* and *test rubric* in constructing the assessment tasks, and later in interpreting the results, these factors had to be operationalised. That is, the range for each of these components needed to be specified. This allowed for the categorisation of each task so that the weighting of each component could be taken into account in the final assembly of the survey.

Situation

The manner in which situation was defined was borrowed from the Council of Europe's (2001) work on language. Four situation variables were identified: *reading for private use, reading for public use, reading for work* and *reading for education.* While the intention of the PISA reading literacy assessment was to measure the kinds of reading that occur both within and outside classrooms, the manner in which situation was defined could not be based simply on where the reading activity is carried out. For example, textbooks are read both in schools and in homes, and the process and purpose of reading these texts differ little from one setting to another. Moreover, reading also involves the author's intended use, different types of content and the fact that others (e.g., teachers and employers) sometimes decide what should be read and for what purpose.

Thus, for the purpose of this assessment, situation can be understood as a general categorisation of texts based on the author's intended use, on the relationship with other persons implicitly or explicitly associated with the text, and on the general content. The sample texts were drawn from a variety of situations to maximise the diversity of content included in the reading literacy survey. Close attention was also paid to the origin of texts selected for inclusion in this survey. The goal was to reach a balance between the broad definition of reading literacy used in PISA and the linguistic and cultural diversity of participating countries. This diversity helped to ensure that no one group would be either advantaged or disadvantaged by the assessment content.

The four situation variables taken from the work of the Council of Europe can be described as follows:

• *Reading for private use (personal):* This type of reading is carried out to satisfy an individual's own interests, both practical and intellectual. It also includes reading to maintain or develop personal connections to other people. Contents typically include personal letters, fiction, biography and informational texts read for curiosity, as a part of leisure or recreational activities.

- *Reading for public use:* This type of reading is carried out to participate in the activities of the wider society. It includes the use of official documents as well as information about public events. In general, these tasks are associated with more or less anonymous contact with others.

- *Reading for work (occupational):* While not all 15-year-olds will actually have to read at work, it is important to assess their readiness to move into the world of work since, in most countries, over 50 per cent of them will be in the labour force within one to two years. The prototypical tasks of this type are often referred to as "reading to do" (Sticht, 1975; Stiggins, 1982) in that they are tied to the accomplishment of some immediate task.

- *Reading for education:* This type of reading is normally involved with acquiring information as part of a larger learning task. The materials are often not chosen by the reader, but assigned by a teacher. The content is usually designed specifically for the purpose of instruction. The prototypical tasks are those usually identified as "reading to learn" (Sticht, 1975; Stiggins, 1982).

Figure 2.1 shows the distribution of reading literacy tasks in the assessment across all four situations. While the reading tasks could have been distributed evenly across the four situations, the occupational situation was given less weight because of the likelihood that 15-year-olds would be relatively unfamiliar with this category of text. It was also important to reduce the potential dependence on specific occupational knowledge that might result when occupational texts were selected.

Figure 2.1
Distribution of reading literacy tasks by situation

Context	Number of tasks[1]
Educational	39
Occupational	22
Personal	26
Public	54
Total	**141**

1. Included in assessment instrument.

Texts

A key distinction made between texts that is at the heart of the PISA assessment is their classification into continuous and non-continuous texts.

- *Continuous texts* are typically composed of sentences that are, in turn, organised into paragraphs. These may fit into even larger structures such as sections, chapters and books. The primary classification of continuous texts is by rhetorical purpose, or text type.

- *Non-continuous texts,* or documents as they are known in some approaches, can be categorised in two ways. One is the formal structure approach used in the work of Kirsch and Mosenthal (1989-1991).[2] Their work classifies texts by the way in which underlying lists are put together to construct the various non-continuous text types. This approach is useful for understanding the similarities and differences between types of non-continuous texts. The other method of classification is by everyday descriptions of the formats of these texts. This second approach is used in classifying non-continuous texts in PISA.

Continuous texts

Text types are standard ways of organising continuous texts by content and author's purpose.[3]

- *Narration* is the type of text in which the information refers to properties of objects *in time*. Narrative texts typically provide answers to *when*, or *in what sequence*, questions.

- *Exposition* is the type of text in which the information is presented as composite concepts or mental constructs, or those elements into which concepts or mental constructs can be analysed. The text provides an explanation of how the component elements interrelate in a meaningful whole and often answers *how* questions.

- *Description* is the type of text in which the information refers to properties of objects *in space*. Descriptive texts typically provide an answer to *what* questions.

- *Argumentation* is the type of text that presents propositions as to the relationship between concepts, or other propositions. Argumentative texts often answer *why* questions. Another important sub-classification of argumentative texts is persuasive texts.

- *Instruction* (sometimes called *injunction*) is the type of text that provides directions on what to do and includes procedures, rules, regulations and statutes specifying certain behaviours.

- A *document* or *record* is a text that is designed to standardise and conserve information. It can be characterised by highly formalised textual and formating features.

- *Hypertext* is a set of text slots linked together in such a way that the units can be read in different sequences, allowing readers to follow various routes to the information.[4]

Non-continuous texts

Non-continuous texts are organised differently from continuous texts and so require different kinds of reading approaches. The reader should refer to the work of Kirsch and Mosenthal for a discussion of the structural approach. According to their work, lists are the most elementary non-continuous texts. They consist of a number of entries that share some property(ies). This shared property may be used as a label or title for the list. Lists may have their entries ordered (*e.g.*, the names of students in a class arranged alphabetically) or unordered (*e.g.*, a list of supplies to be bought at a shop). Classifying non-continuous texts by their format, as shown below, provides a familiar means of discussing what types of non-continuous texts may be included in the assessment.

- *Charts and graphs* are iconic representations of data. They are used for the purposes of scientific argumentation, and also in journals and newspapers to display numerical and tabular public information in a visual format.

- *Tables and matrices*. Tables are row and column matrices. Typically, all the entries in each column and each row share properties and thus the column and row labels are part of the information structure of the text. Common tables include schedules, spreadsheets, order forms and indexes.

- *Diagrams* often accompany technical descriptions (*e.g.*, demonstrating parts of a household appliance), expository texts and instructive texts (*e.g.*, illustrating how to assemble a household appliance). It is often useful to distinguish procedural (how to) from process (how something works) diagrams.

- *Maps* are non-continuous texts that indicate the geographical relationships between places. There is a variety of types of maps. Road maps mark the distance and routes between identified places. Thematic maps indicate the relationships between locations and social or physical features.

- *Forms* are structured and formatted texts which request the reader to respond to specific questions in specified ways. Forms are used by many organisations to collect data. They often contain structured or pre-coded answer formats. Typical examples are tax forms, immigration forms, visa forms, application forms, statistical questionnaires, etc.

- *Information sheets* differ from forms in that they provide, rather than request, information. They summarise information in a structured way and in such a format that the reader can easily and quickly locate specific pieces of information. Information sheets may contain various text forms as well as lists, tables, figures and sophisticated text-based graphics (headings, fonts, indentation, borders, etc.) to summarise and highlight information. Timetables, price lists, catalogues and programmes are examples of this type of non-continuous text.

- *Calls and advertisements* are documents designed to invite the reader to do something, *e.g.*, to buy goods or services, attend gatherings or meetings, elect a person to a public office, etc. The purpose of these documents is to persuade the reader. They offer something and request both attention and action. Advertisements, invitations, summonses, warnings and notices are examples of this document format.

- *Vouchers* testify that their owner is entitled to certain services. The information that they contain must be sufficient to show whether the voucher is valid or not. Typical examples are tickets, invoices, etc.

- *Certificates* are written acknowledgements of the validity of an agreement or a contract. They are formalised in content rather than format. They require the signature of one or more persons authorised and competent to bear testimony of the truth of the given statement. Warranties, school certificates, diplomas, contracts, etc., are documents that have these properties.

The distribution and variety of texts that students are asked to read for PISA are important characteristics of the assessment. Figures 2.2a and 2.2b show the distributions of continuous and non-continuous texts. It can be readily seen that continuous texts represent almost two-thirds of the tasks or items contained in the assessment. Within this category, the largest number comes from expository materials (31 tasks) while the smallest number of tasks is from injunctive texts (9 tasks). The remaining tasks based on continuous texts are roughly equally distributed between narrative, argumentative and descriptive texts. Tasks based on non-continuous texts represent about one-third of the items in the reading literacy assessment. The majority are based on asking students to read either tables or charts and graphs. The remaining non-continuous tasks are based on maps, advertisements, schematics and forms that 15-year-olds are expected to be able to read and use.

Figure 2.2a	
Distribution of reading literacy tasks by text type: continuous texts	
Text type	**Number of tasks based on continuous texts**
Narrative	18
Expository	31
Descriptive	13
Argumentative/Persuasive	18
Injunctive	9
Total	**89**

Figure 2.2b	
Distribution of reading literacy tasks by text type: non-continuous texts	
Text type	**Number of tasks based on non-continuous texts**
Charts and graphs	16
Tables	15
Schematics	5
Maps	4
Forms	8
Advertisements	4
Total	**52**

Test rubric

There are three sets of variables that make up the test rubric: questions or directives, which set out the task for the examinee; response formats, which set out the ways in which examinees are asked to demonstrate their proficiency at the task; and rules for marking, which specify how examinees' answers are to be evaluated. Each of these will be discussed in turn, though the first requires considerably more attention.

Questions and directives – Five aspects

In an effort to simulate authentic reading situations, the PISA reading assessment measures the following five aspects associated with achieving a full understanding of a text, whether the text is continuous or non-continuous. Examinees are expected to demonstrate their proficiency in all these aspects:

• forming a broad general understanding,

• retrieving information,

• developing an interpretation,

• reflecting on and evaluating the content of a text and

• reflecting on and evaluating the form of a text.

The full understanding of texts involves all of these aspects. It is expected that all readers, irrespective of their overall proficiency, will be able to demonstrate some level of competency in each of them (Langer, 1995). While there is an interrelationship between the five aspects – each may require many of the same underlying skills – successfully accomplishing one may not be dependent upon successful completion of any other. Some view them as being in the repertoire of each reader at every developmental level rather than forming a sequential hierarchy or set of skills.

Figure 2.3 identifies the key distinguishing characteristics of the five aspects of reading measured in PISA. While this figure necessarily oversimplifies each aspect, it provides a useful scheme for organising and remembering the relationships between them. As depicted in this figure, the five aspects can be distinguished in terms of four characteristics. The first deals with the extent to which the reader is expected to use information primarily from within the text or to draw also upon outside knowledge. A second distinguishing characteristic involves the extent to which the reader is asked to focus on independent parts of the text or on the relationships within the information contained in the text. Sometimes readers are expected to retrieve independent pieces of information while at other times they are asked to demonstrate their understanding of the relationships between parts of the text. Focusing on either the whole text or on relationships between parts of the text is the third distinguishing characteristic. The fourth characteristic relates to whether the reader is asked to deal with the content or substance of the text rather than its form or structure. The five aspects of reading are represented in the last line of Figure 2.3 at the ends of the various branches. By starting at the top of the figure and following each branch one can see which characteristics are associated with each aspect.

In the following discussion, an initial attempt is made to define each aspect operationally and to associate it with particular kinds of questions and directives. Although each aspect is discussed in terms of a single text, it should be understood that each can also apply to multiple texts when these are presented together

Characteristics distinguishing the five aspects of reading literacy

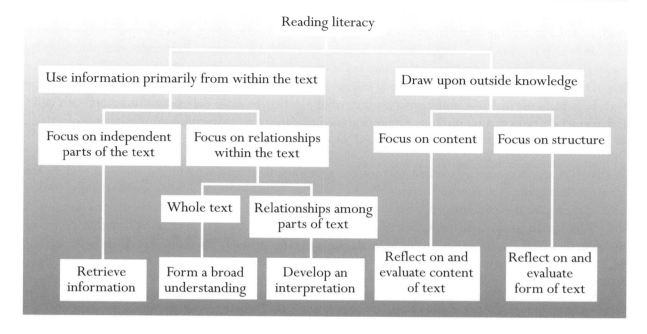

as a unit within the test. The description of each aspect has two parts. The first provides a general overview of the aspect, while the second describes particular ways in which the aspect might be assessed.

Retrieving information. In the course of daily life, readers often need a particular piece of information. They may need to look up a telephone number or check the departure time for a bus or train. They may want to find a particular fact to support or refute a claim someone has made. In situations such as these, readers are interested in retrieving isolated pieces of information. To do so, readers must scan, search for, locate and select relevant information. The processing involved in this aspect of reading is most frequently at the sentence level, though in some cases the information may be in two or more sentences or in different paragraphs.

In assessment tasks that call for retrieving information, examinees must match information given in the question with either identically worded or synonymous information in the text and use this to find the new information called for. In these tasks, retrieving information is based on the text itself and on explicit information included in it. Retrieving tasks require the examinee to find information based on requirements or features specified in questions or directives. The examinee has to detect or identify one or more essential elements of a question or directive: characters, pace/time, setting, etc., and then to search for a match that may be literal or synonymous.

Retrieving tasks also can involve various degrees of ambiguity. For example, the examinee may be required to select explicit information, such as an indication of time or place in a text or table. A more difficult version of this same type of task might involve finding synonymous information. This sometimes involves categorisation skills, or it may require discriminating between two similar pieces of information.

The different levels of proficiency associated with this aspect of comprehension can be measured by systematically varying the elements that contribute to the difficulty of the task.

Forming a broad general understanding. To form a broad general understanding of what has been read, a reader must consider the text as a whole or in a broad perspective. There are various assessment tasks in which readers are asked to form a broad general understanding. Examinees may demonstrate initial understanding by identifying the main topic or message or by identifying the general purpose or use of the text. Examples include tasks that require the reader to select or create a title or thesis for the text, to explain the order of simple instructions, or to identify the main dimensions of a graph or a table. Others include tasks that require the examinee to describe the main character, setting or milieu of a story, to identify a theme or message of a literary text, or to explain the purpose or use of a map or a figure.

Within this aspect some tasks might require the examinee to match a particular piece of text to the question. For example, this would happen when a theme or main idea is explicitly stated in the text. Other tasks may require the examinee to focus on more than one specific reference in the text – for instance, if the reader had to deduce the theme from the repetition of a particular category of information. Selecting the main idea implies establishing a hierarchy among ideas and choosing the most general and overarching. Such a task indicates whether the examinee can distinguish between key ideas and minor details, or can recognise the summary of the main theme in a sentence or title.

Developing an interpretation. Developing an interpretation requires readers to extend their initial impressions so that they develop a more specific or complete understanding of what they have read. Tasks in this category call for logical understanding; readers must process the organisation of information in the text. To do so, readers must demonstrate their understanding of cohesion even if they cannot explicitly state what cohesion is. In some instances, developing an interpretation may require the reader to process a sequence of just two sentences relying on local cohesion, which might even be facilitated by the presence of cohesive markers, such as the use of "first" and "second" to indicate a sequence. In more difficult instances (*e.g.*, to indicate relations of cause and effect), there might not be any explicit markings.

Examples of tasks that might be used to assess this aspect include comparing and contrasting information, drawing inferences, and identifying and listing supporting evidence. "Compare and contrast" tasks require the examinee to draw together two or more pieces of information from the text. In order to process either explicit or implicit information from one or more sources in compare and contrast tasks, the reader must often infer an intended relationship or category. Tasks that require the examinee to make inferences about the author's intention and to identify the evidence used to infer that intention, are also examples of tasks that assess this aspect of comprehension.

Reflecting on and evaluating the content of a text. Reflecting and evaluating on the content of a text requires the reader to connect information found in a text to knowledge from other sources. Readers must also assess the claims made in the text against their own knowledge of the world. Often readers are asked to articulate and defend their own points of view. To do so, readers must be able to develop an under-standing of what is said and intended in a text and must test that mental representation against what they know and believe on the basis of either prior information, or information found in other texts. Readers must call on supporting evidence from within the text and contrast that with other sources of information, using both general and specific knowledge as well as the ability to reason abstractly.

Assessment tasks representative of this category of processing include providing evidence or arguments from outside the text, assessing the relevance of particular pieces of information or evidence, or drawing comparisons with moral or aesthetic rules (standards). The examinee might be asked to offer or identify alternative pieces of information that might strengthen an author's argument, or to evaluate the sufficiency of the evidence or information provided in the text.

The outside knowledge to which textual information is to be connected may come from the examinee's own knowledge, from other texts provided in the assessment, or from ideas explicitly provided in the question.

Reflecting on and evaluating the form of a text. Tasks in this category require readers to stand apart from the text, consider it objectively and evaluate its quality and appropriateness. Knowledge of such things as text structure, genre and register play an important role in these tasks. These features, which form the basis of an author's craft, figure strongly in understanding standards inherent in tasks of this nature. Evaluating how successful an author is in portraying some characteristic or persuading a reader depends not only on substantive knowledge but also on the ability to detect nuances in language – for example, understanding when the choice of an adjective might colour interpretation.

Some examples of assessment tasks characteristic of reflecting on and evaluating the form of a text include determining the utility of a particular text for a specified purpose and evaluating an author's use of particular textual features in accomplishing a particular goal. The examinee may also be called upon to identify or comment on the author's use of style and what the author's purpose and attitude are.

Figure 2.4 shows the distribution of reading literacy tasks by each of the five aspects defined above. The largest category of tasks is represented by the two branches of Figure 2.3 which ask students to focus on relationships within a text. These 70 tasks require students either to form a broad understanding or to develop an interpretation. They have been grouped together for reporting purposes into a single aspect called interpreting texts. The next largest category is made up of 42 tasks which require students to demonstrate their skill at retrieving isolated pieces of information. Each of these aspects – forming a broad understanding, retrieving information and developing an interpretation – focuses on the degree to which the reader can understand and use information contained primarily within the text. The remaining 29 tasks require students to reflect on either the content or information provided in the text or on the structure and form of the text itself.

Figure 2.4
Distribution of reading literacy tasks by aspect of reading literacy

Aspect	Number of tasks
Retrieving information	42
Interpreting (combines developing an interpretation and gaining a broad understanding)	70
Reflecting on and evaluating content and form	29
Total	**141**

Response formats

Figure 2.5 indicates that 63 of the 141 reading literacy tasks in the PISA assessment are constructed-response items which require judgement on the part of the marker. The remaining tasks consist of constructed-response tasks that require little subjective judgement on the part of the marker, as well as

Figure 2.5
Distribution of constructed-response and multiple-choice tasks by aspect of reading literacy

Aspect	Number of multiple-choice tasks	Number of complex multiple-choice tasks	Number of closed-constructed response tasks	Number of open-constructed response tasks
Retrieving information	10	2	10	20
Interpreting texts	43	3	5	19
Reflection and evaluation	3	2	0	24
Total	**56**	**7**	**15**	**63**

simple multiple-choice items, for which students choose one of several alternative answers and complex multiple-choice items, for which students choose more than one response.

This figure also reveals that while multiple-choice and constructed-response items are represented across the aspects, they are not distributed evenly. That is, a larger percentage of multiple-choice items are associated with the two aspects dealing with interpreting relationships within a text. This is shown in the second row of Figure 2.5. In contrast, while there are 29 reflection and evaluation tasks, only five are multiple choice. Twenty-four are constructed-response tasks that require judgement on the part of the marker.

Marking

Marking is relatively simple with dichotomously scored multiple-choice items: the examinee has either chosen the designated answer or not. Partial-credit models allow for more complex marking of items. Here, because some wrong answers are more complete than others, examinees who provide an "almost right" answer receive partial credit. Psychometric models for such polytomous scoring are well-established and in some ways are preferable to dichotomous scoring as they utilise more of the information that is in the responses. Interpretation of polytomous marking is more complex, however, as each task has several locations on the difficulty scale: one for the full-credit answer and others for each of the partial-credit answers. Partial-credit marking is used for some of the more complex constructed-response items in PISA.

Scaling the reading literacy tasks

In total, some 141 reading literacy tasks were constructed and administered to nationally representative samples of 15-year-olds in participating countries to ensure that the assessment provided the broadest possible coverage of reading literacy as defined here. However, no individual student could be expected to respond to the entire set of tasks. Accordingly, the survey was designed to give each student participating in the study a subset of the total pool of tasks, while at the same time ensuring that each of the tasks was administered to nationally representative samples of students. Summarising the performance of students across this entire pool of tasks thus posed a challenge.

One may imagine these 141 reading literacy tasks arranged along a continuum in terms of difficulty for students and the level of skill required to answer each item correctly. The procedure used in PISA to capture this continuum of difficulty and ability is Item Response Theory (IRT). IRT is a mathematical model used for estimating the probability that a particular person will respond correctly to a given task from a specified pool of tasks. This probability is modelled along a continuum which summarises both the proficiency of a person in terms of their ability and the complexity of an item in terms of its difficulty. This continuum of difficulty and proficiency is referred to as a "scale".

Reporting the results

The results of the reading literacy assessment were first summarised on a single composite reading literacy scale having a mean of 500 and a standard deviation of 100. In addition to the single composite scale for PISA, student performance is also represented on five subscales[5] – three aspect subscales (retrieving information, interpreting texts and reflection and evaluation) and two format subscales (continuous texts and non-continuous texts). These five subscales make it possible to compare mean scores and distributions between subgroups and countries by various components of the reading literacy construct. Although there is a high correlation between these five subscales, reporting results on each subscale allows for the possibility that interesting interactions may appear among the participating countries. Where such features occur, they can be examined and linked to the curriculum and teaching methodology used. In some countries, the important question may be how to teach the current curriculum better. In others, the question may not only be how to teach but also what to teach.

Figure 2.6 summarises the various text types and the associated tasks along the two format scales. The 89 continuous tasks were used to create the continuous texts subscale while the 52 non-continuous tasks were used to create the other text format subscale. Organising the data in this way provides the opportunity to examine the extent to which countries differ with respect to abilities in these two areas.

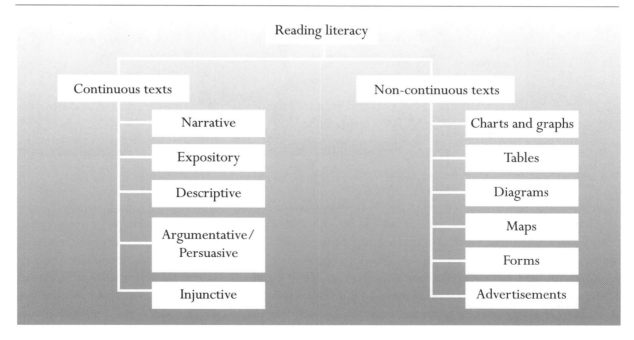

Figure 2.6

Relationship between the reading literacy framework and the reading literacy subscales by text type

Figure 2.7 summarises the 141 reading literacy tasks in terms of three aspects. There are two reasons for reducing the number of aspect scales from five to three. The first is pragmatic. In 2003 and 2006 Reading, as a minor domain, will be restricted to about 30 items instead of the 141 that were used in 2000. The amount of information, therefore, will be insufficient to report trends over five aspect subscales. The second reason is conceptual. The three aspect subscales are based on the set of five aspects shown in Figure 2.3. *Developing an interpretation* and *Forming a broad understanding* have been grouped together because information provided in the text is processed by the reader in some way in both: in the case of Broad understanding, the whole text and in the case of developing an interpretation, one part of the text in relation to another. *Reflecting on and evaluating* the content of a text and *reflecting on and evaluating* the form of a text have been collapsed into a single "reflection and evaluation" scale because the distinction between reflecting and evaluating on form and reflecting on and evaluating the content, in practice, was found to be somewhat arbitrary.

Figure 2.7

Relationship between the reading literacy framework and the reading literacy subscales by aspect of reading literacy

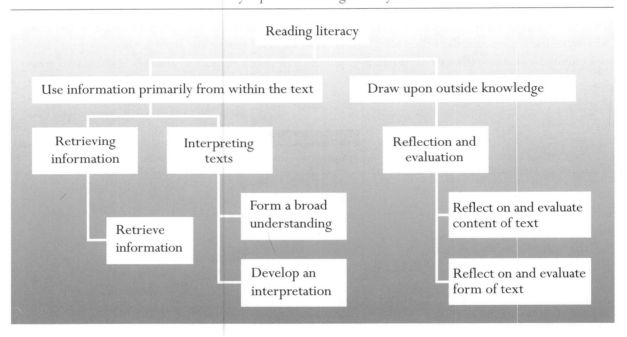

The scores on the composite scale as well as on each of the five subscales represent varying degrees of proficiency. A low score indicates that a student has very limited knowledge and skills while a high score indicates that a student has quite advanced knowledge and skills. Use of IRT makes it possible not only to summarise results for various subpopulations of students, but also to determine the relative difficulty of the reading literacy tasks included in the survey. In other words, just as individuals receive a specific value on a scale according to their performance in the assessment tasks, each task receives a specific value on a scale according to its difficulty, as determined by the performance of students across the various countries that participated in the assessment.

Building an item map

The complete set of reading literacy tasks used in PISA varies widely in text type, situation and task requirements and hence also in difficulty. This range is captured in Figure 2.8. This item map provides a visual representation of the reading literacy skills demonstrated by students along the composite scale and the five subscales. The map contains a brief description of a selected number of released assessment tasks along with their scale values. These descriptions take into consideration the specific skills the item is designed to assess and, in the case of open-ended tasks, the criteria used for judging the item correct. An examination of the descriptions provides some insight into the range of processes required of students and the proficiencies they need to demonstrate at various points along the reading literacy scales.

An example of how to interpret the item map may be useful. In Figure 2.8, an item at 421 on the composite scale requires students to identify the purpose that two short texts have in common by comparing the main ideas in each of them. The score assigned to each item is based on the theory that someone at a given point on the scale is equally proficient in all tasks at that point on the scale. It was decided that "proficiency" should for the purposes of PISA mean that students at a particular point on the reading literacy scale would have a 62 per cent chance of responding correctly to items at that point. This means that students scoring 421 on the composite reading literacy scale will have a 62 per cent chance of correctly answering items graded 421 on the scale. This does not mean that students receiving scores below 421 will always answer incorrectly. Rather, students will have a higher or lower probability of responding correctly in line with their estimated score on the reading literacy scale. Students having scores above 421 will have a greater than 62 per cent chance of responding correctly while those scoring below 421 will be expected to answer an item of that level of difficulty correctly less than 62 per cent of the time. It should be noted that the item will also appear on an aspect subscale and on a format subscale as well as on the combined reading literacy scale. In this example, the item at 421 is an interpretation item and thus appears on the interpreting texts scale as well as on the continuous texts scale.[6]

Levels of reading literacy proficiency

Just as students within each country are sampled from the population of 15-year-old students within the country, each reading literacy task represents a class of tasks from the reading literacy domain. Hence, it is indicative of a type of text and of a type of processing that 15-year-old students should have acquired. One obvious question is, what distinguishes tasks at the lower end of the scale from those in the middle and upper ranges of the scale? Also, do tasks that fall around the same place on the scale share some characteristics that result in their having similar levels of difficulty? Even a cursory review of the item map reveals that tasks at the lower end of each scale differ from those at the higher end. A more careful analysis of the range of tasks along each scale provides some indication of an ordered set of information-processing skills and strategies. Members of the reading expert group examined each task to identify a set of variables that seemed to influence its difficulty. They found that difficulty is in part determined by the length, structure and complexity of the text itself. However, they also noted that in most reading units (a unit being a text and a set of questions or directives) the questions or directives range across the reading literacy scale. This means that while the structure of a text contributes to the difficulty of an item, what the reader has to do with that text as defined by the question or directive interacts with the text, affecting overall difficulty.

A number of variables were identified that can influence the difficulty of any reading literacy task. The type of process involved in retrieving information, developing an interpretation or reflecting on what has been read is one salient factor. Processes range in their complexity and sophistication from making

Figure 2.8
PISA item maps

Item difficulty on PISA scale	Nature of tasks	Retrieving information	Interpreting texts	Reflection and evaluation	Continuous texts	Non-continuous texts
822	**HYPOTHESISE** about an unexpected phenomenon by taking account of outside knowledge along with all relevant information in a **COMPLEX TABLE** on a relatively unfamiliar topic. (score 2)			O		O
727	**ANALYSE** several described cases and **MATCH** to categories given in a **TREE DIAGRAM**, where some of the relevant information is in footnotes. (score 2)		O			O
705	**HYPOTHESISE** about an unexpected phenomenon by taking account of outside knowledge along with some relevant information in a **COMPLEX TABLE** on a relatively unfamiliar topic. (score 1)			O		O
652	**EVALUATE** the ending of a LONG NARRATIVE in relation to its implicit theme or mood. (score 2)			O	O	
645	**RELATE NUANCES OF LANGUAGE** in a **LONG NARRATIVE** to the main theme, in the presence of conflicting ideas. (score 2).		O		O	
631	**LOCATE** information in a **TREE DIAGRAM** using information in a footnote. (score 2)	O				O
603	**CONSTRUE** the meaning of a sentence by relating it to broad context in a **LONG NARRATIVE.**		O		O	
600	**HYPOTHESISE** about an authorial decision by relating evidence in a graph to the inferred main theme of **MULTIPLE GRAPHIC DISPLAYS.**			O		O
581	**COMPARE AND EVALUATE** the style of two open **LETTERS.**			O	O	
567	**EVALUATE** the ending of a **LONG NARRATIVE** in relation to the plot.			O	O	
542	**INFER AN ANALOGICAL RELATIONSHIP** between two phenomena discussed in an open **LETTER.**		O		O	
540	**IDENTIFY** the implied starting date of a **GRAPH.**	O				O
539	**CONSTRUE THE MEANING** of short quotations from a **LONG NARRATIVE** in relation to atmosphere or immediate situation. (score 1)		O		O	
537	**CONNECT** evidence from **LONG NARRATIVE** to personal concepts in order to justify opposing points of view. (score 2)			O	O	
529	**EXPLAIN** a character's motivation by linking events in a **LONG NARRATIVE.**		O		O	
508	**INFER THE RELATIONSHIP** between **TWO GRAPHIC DISPLAYS** with different conventions.		O			O
486	**EVALUATE** the suitability of a **TREE DIAGRAM** for particular purposes.			O		O
485	**LOCATE** numerical information in a **TREE DIAGRAM.**	O				O
480	**CONNECT** evidence from **LONG NARRATIVE** to personal concepts in order to justify a single point of view. (score 1)			O	O	
478	**LOCATE AND COMBINE** information in a **LINE GRAPH** and its introduction to infer a missing value.	O				O
477	**UNDERSTAND** the structure of a **TREE DIAGRAM.**		O			O
473	**MATCH** categories given in a **TREE DIAGRAM** to described cases, when some of the relevant information is in footnotes.		O			O
447	**INTERPRET** information in a single paragraph to understand the setting of a **NARRATIVE.**		O		O	
445	Distinguish between variables and **STRUCTURAL FEATURES** of a **TREE DIAGRAM.**			O		O
421	**IDENTIFY** the common **PURPOSE** of **TWO SHORT TEXTS.**		O		O	
405	**LOCATE** pieces of explicit information in a **TEXT** containing strong organizers.	O			O	
397	Infer the **MAIN IDEA** of a simple **BAR GRAPH** from its title.		O			O
392	**LOCATE** a literal piece of information in a **TEXT** with clear text structure.	O			O	
367	**LOCATE** explicit information in a short, specified section of a **NARRATIVE.**	O			O	
363	**LOCATE** an explicitly stated piece of information in a **TEXT** with headings.	O			O	
356	**RECOGNISE THEME** of an article having a clear subheading and considerable redundancy.		O		O	

simple connections between pieces of information, to categorising ideas according to given criteria, and critically evaluating and hypothesising about a section of text. In addition to the type of process called for, the difficulty of retrieving information tasks is associated with the number of pieces of information to be included in the response, the number of criteria which the information found must satisfy, and whether what is retrieved needs to be sequenced in a particular way. In the case of interpretative and reflective tasks, the amount of a text that needs to be assimilated is an important factor affecting difficulty. In items that require reflection on the reader's part, difficulty is also conditioned by the familiarity or specificity of the knowledge that must be drawn on from outside the text. In all aspects of reading, the difficulty of the task depends on how prominent the required information is, how much competing information is present, and whether or not it is explicitly stated which ideas or information are required to complete the task.

In an attempt to capture this progression of complexity and difficulty, the composite reading literacy scale and each of the subscales were divided into five levels:

Level	Score points on the PISA scale
1	335 to 407
2	408 to 480
3	481 to 552
4	553 to 625
5	more than 625

Tasks within each level of reading literacy were judged by expert panels to share many of the same task features and requirements and to differ in systematic ways from tasks at either higher or lower levels. As a result, these levels appear to be a useful way to explore the progression of reading literacy demands within each scale. This progression is summarised in Figure 2.9.

Interpreting the reading literacy levels

Not only does each level represent a range of tasks and associated knowledge and skills, it also represents a range of proficiencies demonstrated by students. As mentioned previously, the reading literacy levels were initially set by PISA to represent a set of tasks with shared characteristics. These levels also have shared statistical properties. The average student within each level can be expected to successfully perform the average task within that level 62 per cent of the time. In addition, the width of each level is in part determined by the expectation that a student at the lower end of any level will score 50 per cent on any hypothetical test made up of items randomly selected from that level.

Since each reading literacy scale represents a progression of knowledge and skills, students at a particular level not only demonstrate the knowledge and skills associated with that particular level but the proficiencies associated with the lower levels as well. Thus the knowledge and skills assumed at each level build on and encompass the proficiencies laid down in the next lower level. This means that a student who is judged to be at Level 3 on a reading literacy scale is proficient not only in Level 3 tasks but also in Level 1 and 2 tasks. This also means that students who are at Levels 1 and 2 will be expected to get the average Level 3 item correct less than 50 per cent of the time. Or put another way, they will be expected to score less than 50 per cent on a test made up of items drawn from Level 3.

Figure 2.9

Reading literacy levels map

Retrieving information	**Interpreting texts**	**Reflection and evaluation**
5 Locate and possibly sequence or combine multiple pieces of deeply embedded information, some of which may be outside the main body of the text. Infer which information in the text is relevant to the task. Deal with highly plausible and/or extensive competing information.	Either construe the meaning of nuanced language or demonstrate a full and detailed understanding of a text.	Critically evaluate or hypothesise, drawing on specialised knowledge. Deal with concepts that are contrary to expectations and draw on a deep understanding of long or complex texts.

Continuous texts: Negotiate texts whose discourse structure is not obvious or clearly marked, in order to discern the relationship of specific parts of the text to its implicit theme or intention.
Non-continuous texts: Identify patterns among many pieces of information presented in a display which may be long and detailed, sometimes by referring to information external to the display. The reader may need to realise independently that a full understanding of the section of text requires reference to a separate part of the same document, such as a footnote.

4 Locate and possibly sequence or combine multiple pieces of embedded information, each of which may need to meet multiple criteria, in a text with unfamiliar context or form. Infer which information in the text is relevant to the task.	Use a high level of text-based inference to understand and apply categories in an unfamiliar context, and to construe the meaning of a section of text by taking into account the text as a whole. Deal with ambiguities, ideas that are contrary to expectation and ideas that are negatively worded.	Use formal or public knowledge to hypothesise about or critically evaluate a text. Show accurate understanding of long or complex texts.

Continuous texts: Follow linguistic or thematic links over several paragraphs, often in the absence of clear discourse markers, in order to locate, interpret or evaluate embedded information or to infer psychological or metaphysical meaning.
Non-continuous texts: Scan a long, detailed text in order to find relevant information, often with little or no assistance from organisers such as labels or special formatting, to locate several pieces of information to be compared or combined.

3 Locate, and in some cases recognise the relationship between pieces of information, each of which may need to meet multiple criteria. Deal with prominent competing information.	Integrate several parts of a text in order to identify a main idea, understand a relationship or construe the meaning of a word or phrase. Compare, contrast or categorise taking many criteria into account. Deal with competing information.	Make connections or comparisons, give explanations, or evaluate a feature of text. Demonstrate a detailed understanding of the text in relation to familiar, everyday knowledge, or draw on less common knowledge.

Continuous texts: Use conventions of text organisation, where present, and follow implicit or explicit logical links such as cause and effect relationships across sentences or paragraphs in order to locate, interpret or evaluate information.
Non-continuous texts: Consider one display in the light of a second, separate document or display, possibly in a different format, or combine several pieces of spatial, verbal and numeric information in a graph or map to draw conclusions about the information represented.

2 Locate one or more pieces of information, each of which may be required to meet multiple criteria. Deal with competing information.	Identify the main idea in a text, understand relationships, form or apply simple categories, or construe meaning within a limited part of the text when the information is not prominent and low-level inferences are required.	Make a comparison or connections between the text and outside knowledge, or explain a feature of the text by drawing on personal experience and attitudes.

Continuous texts: Follow logical and linguistic connections within a paragraph in order to locate or interpret information; or synthesise information across texts or parts of a text in order to infer the author's purpose.
Non-continuous texts: Demonstrate a grasp of the underlying structure of a visual display such as a simple tree diagram or table, or combine two pieces of information from a graph or table.

1 Locate one or more independent pieces of explicitly stated information, typically meeting a single criterion, with little or no competing information in the text.	Recognise the main theme or author's purpose in a text about a familiar topic, when the required information in the text is prominent.	Make a simple connection between information in the text and common, everyday knowledge.

Continuous texts: Use redundancy, paragraph headings or common print conventions to form an impression of the main idea of the text, or to locate information stated explicitly within a short section of text.
Non-continuous texts: Focus on discrete pieces of information, usually within a single display such as a simple map, a line graph or a bar graph that presents only a small amount of information in a straightforward way, and in which most of the verbal text is limited to a small number of words or phrases.

Figure 2.10 shows the probability that individuals performing at selected points along the combined reading literacy scale will give a correct response to tasks of varying difficulty – one is a Level 1 task, one is a Level 3 task, and the third task receives two score points – one at Level 4 and the other at Level 5. It is readily seen here that a student who is estimated to be below Level 1 with a score of 298 has only a 43 per cent chance of responding correctly to the Level 1 task that is at 367 on the reading literacy scale. This person has only a 14 per cent chance of responding to the item from Level 3 and almost no chance of responding correctly to the item from Level 5. Someone in the middle of Level 1 (with a proficiency of 371) has a 63 per cent chance of responding to the item at 367, but only slightly more than a one in four chance of responding correctly to the task at 508 and only a 7 per cent chance of responding correctly to the task selected from Level 5. In contrast, someone who is at Level 3 would be expected to respond correctly to tasks at 367 on reading literacy scale 89 per cent of the time and to tasks at 508, near the middle of Level 3, 64 per cent of the time. However, they would only have just over a one in four chance (27 per cent) of correctly responding to items from the middle of Level 5. Finally, a student who is at Level 5 is expected to respond correctly most of the time to almost all the tasks. As shown in Figure 2.10, a student having a score of 662 on the combined reading literacy scale has a 98 per cent chance of answering the task at 367 correctly, a 90 per cent chance of answering the item at Level 3 (308) correctly and a 65 per cent of responding correctly to the task selected from near the centre of Level 5 (652).

Figure 2.10

Probability of responding correctly to selected tasks of varying difficulty for students with varying levels of proficiency

	Level 1 item at 367 points	Level 3 item at 508 points	Level 4 item at 567 points	Level 5 item at 652 points
Below Level 1 (Proficiency of 298 points)	43	14	8	3
Level 1 (Proficiency of 371 points)	63	27	16	7
Level 2 (Proficiency of 444 points)	79	45	30	14
Level 3 (Proficiency of 517 points)	89	64	48	27
Level 4 (Proficiency of 589 points)	95	80	68	45
Level 5 (Proficiency of 662 points)	98	90	82	65

Figure 2.10 also introduces a further matter for discussion. This relates to the highest and lowest designated levels. Even though the top of the reading literacy scale is unbounded, it can be stated with some certainty that students of extremely high proficiency are capable of performing tasks characterised by the highest level of proficiency. There is more of an issue for students who are at the bottom end of the reading literacy scale. Since Level 1 begins at 335, there is a certain percentage of students in each country who are estimated to be below this point on the scale. While there are no reading literacy tasks with a scale value below 335, it is not correct to say that these students are without any reading literacy skills or are "totally illiterate". However, on the basis of their performance in the set of tasks used in this assessment, they would be expected to score less than 50 per cent on a set of tasks selected from Level 1. They are classified, therefore, as performing below Level 1.

Since comparatively few young adults in our societies have no literacy skills, the PISA framework does not call for a measure of whether or not 15-year-old students can read in a technical sense. That is, PISA does not measure the extent to which 15-year-old students are fluent readers or how competent they are at word recognition tasks or spelling. It does, however, reflect the contemporary view that students should, upon leaving secondary school, be able to construct, extend and reflect on the meaning of what they have read across a wide range of continuous and non-continuous texts commonly associated with a variety of situations both within and outside school. While we are unable to say what knowledge and skills students performing below Level 1 may possess with regard to reading literacy, their level of proficiency indicates that these students are unlikely to be able to use reading as an independent tool to assist them in acquiring knowledge and skills in other areas.

Notes

1. This section of the paper draws heavily from the PISA Framework for Assessing Reading Literacy that was prepared by the Reading Functional Expert Group (RFEG) and approved by the the Board of Participating Countries (BPC). It is available on the PISA website. The reader is referred to this document for a longer and more detailed discussion of some of the issues presented in this part of the paper.

2. The Kirsch and Mosenthal model was set out in detail in a series of monthly columns called Understanding Documents published in the *Journal of Reading* between 1989 and 1991.

3. This section is based on the work of Werlich, 1976. Category names in parentheses are alternative ways of labelling the class.

4. Note that the continuous text types *document/record* and *hypertext* and the non-continuous text types *information sheets, vouchers* and *certificates* were not represented in the PISA 2000 assessment.

5. Each subscale was developed by holding the item parameter fixed and re-estimating the distribution of ability for each country on that subset of reading literacy tasks.

6. Since each subscale was developed by holding the item parameter fixed and re-estimating the distribution of ability for each country on that subset of reading literacy tasks, each reading literacy task is shown in Figure 2.8 in terms of where it is placed on the composite scale as well as on one of the three aspect subscales and one of the two format subscales.

Chapter

3

SAMPLE TASKS

Implicit in the definition of reading and the framework developed for PISA is the idea that young adults in modern developed countries should be able upon leaving school to construct, extend and reflect on the meaning of what they have read across a wide range of continuous and non-continuous texts associated with situations found both inside and outside school. Each assessment task constructed to represent the reading framework provides a piece of evidence about the nature and extent to which students in participating countries have developed these skills.

This chapter presents a small selection from the tasks used in the reading literacy assessment for PISA 2000. The majority of these 141 tasks are being held secure by the OECD so that they can be used in future cycles of PISA to measure trends in reading proficiency over time. However, a subset of 45 tasks has been published and these can be found in *Sample Tasks from the PISA 2000 Assessment – Reading, Mathematical and Scientific Literacy* (OECD, 2002*a*) and on the PISA website at *www.pisa.oecd.org*. The 19 tasks selected for this chapter are drawn from the released set, and are presented with a discussion that aims to explain the way in which individual tasks contribute various kinds of evidence of reading proficiency.

Selection and organisation of the sample tasks

The texts and tasks chosen for this chapter cover the range of difficulty associated with each of the three aspect subscales and the two format subscales outlined in the previous chapter. Of the 19 tasks included in this selection, 13 are marked dichotomously, as either full-credit or no-credit (scores of 1 and 0 respectively), and six are marked polytomously, as full-credit, partial-credit or no-credit (scores of 2, 1 and 0). Both full-credit and partial-credit scores give information about the degree of difficulty of a task. Hence there are 25 "task difficulties" derived from the 19 tasks. Of these, four fall within Level 1, five within Level 2, seven within Level 3, three within Level 4 and six within Level 5. Each of these tasks is shown in Figure 2.8, Chapter 2.

In PISA 2000, reading literacy was assessed using a series of texts, with a number of tasks attached to each text or to a set of connected texts. A text or texts and the associated tasks are described as a unit. This chapter presents selections from six units: three units based on continuous texts, followed by three units based on non-continuous texts.

The texts that constitute the stimulus for each unit are reproduced in the following pages much as they appeared to the students who were in the PISA sample. This is to give as accurate a sense as possible of what was tested. The way a text is presented – for example, its layout, print size, headings and accompanying illustrations – can affect its impact on the reader and, therefore, the results of any tasks based on it in an assessment. The texts are introduced with a brief description of how they reflect the framework components and why they were selected for the reading instrument.

Each task is introduced with a description of the features thought to contribute to its overall difficulty. These features are also what help to distinguish between tasks in terms of level and subscale.

As mentioned in Chapter 2, about 55 per cent of the tasks in PISA Reading 2000 were multiple-choice questions or tasks that required minimal judgement on the part of the marker. The remaining 45 per cent were constructed-response tasks that required markers to make judgements. During the marking process the constructed-response tasks were accompanied by marking guides describing the kind of response required for each scoring category, and giving examples of responses in that category, mostly drawn from student answers collected during the international piloting and field trials of the questions. All markers undertook an intensive training programme, and the entire marking process was strictly monitored. Details of the scoring methodology can be found in the *PISA 2000 Technical Report* (OECD, 2002*b*).

Each item presented in this chapter is classified according to situation, text format, aspect, level and PISA scale score. For example, the following information states that the item is from an educational situation, using a non-continuous text. It is a retrieving information task of Level 2 difficulty, with a PISA scale score of 460.

> **Situation:** *Educational*
> **Text format:** *Non-continuous*
> **Aspect:** *Retrieving information*
> **Level:** *2*
> **PISA scale score:** *460*

Runners

The first text is a piece of expository prose from a French-Belgian magazine produced for adolescent students. It is classed as belonging to the educational situation. One of the reasons for its selection as part of the PISA 2000 reading instrument is its subject, which was considered of great interest for the PISA population of 15-year-olds. The article includes an attractive cartoon-like illustration and is broken up by catchy sub-headings. Within the continuous text format category, it is an example of expository writing in that it provides an outline of a mental construct, laying out a set of criteria for judging the quality of running shoes in terms of their fitness for young athletes.

The tasks within this unit cover all three aspects – retrieving information, interpreting texts and reflection and evaluation – but all are relatively easy, falling within Level 1.

Two of the four *Runners* tasks are reproduced below.

Feel good in your runners

For 14 years the Sports Medicine Centre of Lyon (France) has been studying the injuries of young sports players and sports professionals. The study has established that the best course is prevention ... and good shoes.

Knocks, falls, wear and tear...

Eighteen per cent of sports players aged 8 to 12 already have heel injuries. The cartilage of a footballer's ankle does not respond well to shocks, and 25% of professionals have discovered for themselves that it is an especially weak point. The cartilage of the delicate knee joint can also be irreparably damaged and if care is not taken right from childhood (10–12 years of age), this can cause premature osteoarthritis. The hip does not escape damage either and, particularly when tired, players run the risk of fractures as a result of falls or collisions.

According to the study, footballers who have been playing for more than ten years have bony outgrowths either on the tibia or on the heel. This is what is known as "footballer's foot", a deformity caused by shoes with soles and ankle parts that are too flexible.

Protect, support, stabilise, absorb

If a shoe is too rigid, it restricts movement. If it is too flexible, it increases the risk of injuries and sprains. A good sports shoe should meet four criteria:

Firstly, it must *provide exterior protection*: resisting knocks from the ball or another player, coping with unevenness in the ground, and keeping the foot warm and dry even when it is freezing cold and raining.

It must *support the foot*, and in particular the ankle joint, to avoid sprains, swelling and other problems, which may even affect the knee.

It must also provide players with good *stability* so that they do not slip on a wet ground or skid on a surface that is too dry.

Finally, it must *absorb shocks*, especially those suffered by volleyball and basketball players who are constantly jumping.

Dry feet

To avoid minor but painful conditions such as blisters or even splits or athlete's foot (fungal infections), the shoe must allow evaporation of perspiration and must prevent outside dampness from getting in. The ideal material for this is leather, which can be water-proofed to prevent the shoe from getting soaked the first time it rains.

Source: Revue ID (16) 1-15 June 1997.

Question 1: RUNNERS

What does the author intend to show in this text?

A   That the quality of many sports shoes has greatly improved.

B   That it is best not to play football if you are under 12 years of age.

C   That young people are suffering more and more injuries due to their poor physical condition.

D   That it is very important for young sports players to wear good sports shoes.

Situation: *Educational*
Text format: *Continuous*
Aspect: *Interpreting texts*
Level: *1*
PISA scale score: *356*

The easiest task in the unit is an interpreting task [R110Q01][1] falling within Level 1 with a PISA scale score of 356. It requires the reader to recognise the article's main idea in a text about a familiar topic.

The author's main message is not stated directly, or synonymously, so the task is classified as interpreting texts rather than retrieving information. There are at least two features that make this task easy. First, the required information is located in the introduction, which is a short section of text. Secondly, there is a good deal of redundancy, the main idea in the introduction being repeated several times throughout the text. Reading tasks tend to be relatively easy when the information they require the reader to use is either near the beginning of the text or repeated. This task meets both of these criteria.

The question is intended to discover whether students can form a broad understanding. Only small percentages of students did not select the correct answer, and they were spread over the three distractors A, B and C. The smallest percentage and least able selected alternative B, "That it is best not to play football if you are under 12 years of age." These students may have been trying to match words from the question with the text, and linked "12" in distractor B with two references to 12-year-olds near the beginning of the article.

Question 2: RUNNERS

According to the article, why should sports shoes not be too rigid?

Situation: *Educational*
Text format: *Continuous*
Aspect: *Retrieving information*
Level: *1*
PISA scale score: *392*

A second task [R110Q04] also falls within Level 1 with a PISA scale score of 392 and is classified as retrieving information in terms of aspect. It requires readers to locate a piece of explicitly stated information that satisfies one single criterion.

The reader can directly match the word "rigid" in the question with the relevant part of the text, making the information easy to find. Although the required information is midway through the text, rather than near the beginning as in the previous task, it is quite prominent because it is near the beginning of one of the three sections marked by sub-headings.

In order to receive full credit, students need to refer to *restriction of movement*. However, this is a relatively easy task as full credit can be gained by quoting directly from the text: "It restricts movement". Many students nonetheless used their own words such as:

"They prevent you from running easily."

or

"So you can move around."

No credit is given if students show *inaccurate comprehension* of the material or gave *implausible or irrelevant* answers. A common error was to give an answer such as:

"Because you need support for your foot."

This is the opposite of the answer required, though it is also an idea located in the text. Students who gave this kind of answer may have overlooked the negative in the question ("… not be too rigid"), or made their own association between the ideas of "rigidity" and "support", leading them to a section of the text that was not relevant to this task. Other than this, there is little competing information to distract the reader.

Graffiti

The stimulus for this unit consists of two letters posted on the Internet, originally from Finland. The tasks simulate typical literacy activities, since as readers we often synthesise, and compare and contrast ideas from two or more different sources.

Because they are published on the Internet, the *Graffiti* letters are classified as public in terms of situation. They are classified as argumentation within the broader classification of continuous texts, as they set forth propositions and attempt to persuade the reader to a point of view.

As with *Runners*, the subject matter of *Graffiti* was expected to be interesting for 15-year-olds: the implied debate between the writers as to whether graffiti makers are artists or vandals would represent a real issue in the minds of the test-takers.

The four tasks from the *Graffiti* unit used to measure reading proficiency in PISA 2000 range in difficulty from Level 2 to Level 4 and address the aspects of interpreting texts and reflection and evaluation.

Three of these tasks are presented here.

I'm simmering with anger as the school wall is cleaned and repainted for the fourth time to get rid of graffiti. Creativity is admirable but people should find ways to express themselves that do not inflict extra costs upon society.

Why do you spoil the reputation of young people by painting graffiti where it's forbidden? Professional artists do not hang their paintings in the streets, do they? Instead they seek funding and gain fame through legal exhibitions.

In my opinion buildings, fences and park benches are works of art in themselves. It's really pathetic to spoil this architecture with graffiti and what's more, the method destroys the ozone layer. Really, I can't understand why these criminal artists bother as their "artistic works" are just removed from sight over and over again.

Helga

Source: Mari Hamkala.

There is no accounting for taste. Society is full of communication and advertising. Company logos, shop names. Large intrusive posters on the streets. Are they acceptable? Yes, mostly. Is graffiti acceptable? Some people say yes, some no.

Who pays the price for graffiti? Who is ultimately paying the price for advertisements? Correct. The consumer.

Have the people who put up billboards asked your permission? No. Should graffiti painters do so then? Isn't it all just a question of communication — your own name, the names of gangs and large works of art in the street?

Think about the striped and chequered clothes that appeared in the stores a few years ago. And ski wear. The patterns and colours were stolen directly from the flowery concrete walls. It's quite amusing that these patterns and colours are accepted and admired but that graffiti in the same style is considered dreadful.

Times are hard for art.

Sophia

Question 3: GRAFFITI

The purpose of each of these letters is to

A   explain what graffiti is.

B   present an opinion about graffiti.

C   demonstrate the popularity of graffiti.

D   tell people how much is spent removing graffiti.

Situation: *Public*
Text format: *Continuous*
Aspect: *Interpreting texts*
Level: *2*
PISA scale score: *421*

This Level 2 interpreting task [R081Q01] with a PISA score of 421 requires students to identify the purpose that two short texts have in common by comparing the main ideas in each of them. The information is not prominent, and low-level inference is required. The intention of the question is to establish whether the student can form a broad understanding and recognise the purpose of the text. The reader needs to follow logical connections, synthesising information from both texts in order to infer the authors' purposes. The need to compare and contrast the two letters makes this task more difficult than, for instance, a task which asks the purpose of a single letter only.

Of those who did not select the correct alternative, B, the largest proportion selected D, "Tell people how much is spent removing graffiti". Although this is not the main idea of even one of the letters, it does relate strongly to the first few lines of the first letter, and thus its choice may reflect the characteristic difficulty of less proficient readers in getting beyond the first part of a text.

Question 4: GRAFFITI

Why does Sophia refer to advertising?

Situation: Public
Text format: Continuous
Aspect: Interpreting texts
Level: 3
PISA scale score: 542

This more difficult Interpreting task based on the *Graffiti* texts [R081Q05] falls within Level 3 with a PISA score of 542. The task requires students to follow an implicit logical link between sentences, in this case a comparison between advertising and graffiti. The relative difficulty of the task can be attributed to the fact that the comparison must be construed from a series of questions and challenges. In order to answer the question correctly, the student must recognise that a *comparison* is being drawn between graffiti and advertising. The answer must be consistent with the idea that advertising is a legal form of graffiti. Or the student must recognise that referring to advertising is a *strategy to defend graffiti.* Typical full-credit answers ranged from those that gave a relatively detailed and specific explanation such as:

"Because there are many billboards and posters that are an eyesore but these are legal."

to those that merely recognised the writer's comparison between graffiti and advertising such as:

"She says advertising is like graffiti."

No credit is given for *insufficient or vague* answers, or if the student shows *inaccurate comprehension* of the material or gave an *implausible or irrelevant answer*.

Question 5: GRAFFITI

We can talk about **what** a letter says (its content).

We can talk about **the way** a letter is written (its style).

Regardless of which letter you agree with, in your opinion, which do you think is the better letter? Explain your answer by referring to **the way** one or both letters are written.

Situation: *Public*
Text format: *Continuous*
Aspect: *Reflection and evaluation*
Level: *4*
PISA scale score: *581*

The most difficult task associated with the *Graffiti* texts [R081Q06B] falls within Level 4 with a PISA score of 581. It requires students to use formal knowledge to evaluate the writer's craft by comparing the two letters. In the five-aspect categorisation, this task is classified as reflection on and evaluation of the form of a text, since to answer it, readers need to draw on their own understanding of what constitutes good writing.

Full credit may be given for many types of answers, including those dealing with one or both writers' tone or argumentative strategies, or with the structure of the piece. Students are expected to explain opinion with *reference to the style or form* of one or both letters. Reference to criteria such as style of writing, structure of argument, cogency of argument, tone, register used and strategies for persuading the reader are given full credit, but terms such as "better arguments" need to be substantiated.

Some typical answers that earned full credit were:

"Helga's letter was effective because of the way she addressed the graffiti artists directly."

"In my opinion, the second letter is better because it has questions that involve you making you feel that you are having a discussion rather than a lecture."

Answers that were not given credit were often vague or could apply equally to either letter, such as:

"Helga's was better because it was more trustworthy."

"Sophia's was written better."

or they related to content rather than style, such as:

"Helga's. I agree with what she said."

"Sophia, because graffiti is a form of art."

or they clearly misunderstood the rhetorical tone of the letters, especially the second:

"Helga's was better, because Sophia didn't show her opinion, she just asked questions."

The relative difficulty of the task, and of other similar tasks in the PISA reading assessment, suggests that many 15-year-olds are not practised in drawing on formal knowledge about structure and style to make critical evaluations of texts.

The gift

The tasks in this unit are classified as personal in the situation dimension, and as continuous in the text format category. The text type is narrative.

This short story from the United States represents the humane, affective and aesthetic qualities of literature that make reading this kind of text an important part of many people's personal lives. A significant reason for its inclusion in the PISA assessment was the literary quality of the piece: its spare, precise use of language and its strong yet subtle rendering of the woman's state of mind and evolving response to the panther.

Another reason for including *The gift* in the PISA assessment was its length. It is a relatively *short* story in comparison with many others that have been published, but it is a long piece compared with the material generally presented to students in assessments of this kind. The international reading expert panel that developed the reading framework and oversaw the test development considered that perseverance in reading longer texts was an important facet in reading proficiency that ought to be addressed in the PISA assessment.

In PISA, the number of tasks attached to each text is roughly proportionate to the amount of reading required. As the longest text, *The gift* supported the greatest number of tasks. Five of the seven tasks are presented here with commentary. The full set of *The gift* tasks covers all three aspects and all five levels of difficulty.

How many days, she wondered, had she sat like this, watching the cold brown water inch up the dissolving bluff. She could just faintly remember the beginning of the rain, driving in across the swamp from the south and beating against the shell of her house. Then the river itself started rising, slowly at first until at last it paused to turn back. From hour to hour it slithered up creeks
5   and ditches and poured over low places. In the night, while she slept, it claimed the road and surrounded her so that she sat alone, her boat gone, the house like a piece of drift lodged on its bluff. Now even against the tarred planks of the supports the waters touched. And still they rose.

As far as she could see, to the treetops where the opposite banks had been, the swamp was an
10   empty sea, awash with sheets of rain, the river lost somewhere in its vastness. Her house with its boat bottom had been built to ride just such a flood, if one ever came, but now it was old. Maybe the boards underneath were partly rotted away. Maybe the cable mooring the house to the great live oak would snap loose and let her go turning downstream, the way her boat had gone.

No one could come now. She could cry out but it would be no use, no one would hear. Down
15   the length and breadth of the swamp others were fighting to save what little they could, maybe even their lives. She had seen a whole house go floating by, so quiet she was reminded of sitting at a funeral. She thought when she saw it she knew whose house it was. It had been bad seeing it drift by, but the owners must have escaped to higher ground. Later, with the rain and darkness pressing in, she had heard a panther scream upriver.

20   Now the house seemed to shudder around her like something alive. She reached out to catch a lamp as it tilted off the table by her bed and put it between her feet to hold it steady. Then creaking and groaning with effort the house struggled up from the clay, floated free, bobbing like a cork and swung out slowly with the pull of the river. She gripped the edge of the bed. Swaying from side to side, the house moved to the length of its mooring. There was a jolt and
25   a complaining of old timbers and then a pause. Slowly the current released it and let it swing back, rasping across its resting place. She caught her breath and sat for a long time feeling the

---

slow pendulous sweeps. The dark sifted down through the incessant rain, and, head on arm, she slept holding on to the bed.

30   Sometime in the night the cry awoke her, a sound so anguished she was on her feet before she was awake. In the dark she stumbled against the bed. It came from out there, from the river. She could hear something moving, something large that made a dredging, sweeping sound. It could be another house. Then it hit, not head on but glancing and sliding down the length of her house. It was a tree. She listened as the branches and leaves cleared themselves and went on downstream, leaving only the rain and the lappings of the flood, sounds so constant now

35   that they seemed a part of the silence. Huddled on the bed, she was almost asleep again when another cry sounded, this time so close it could have been in the room. Staring into the dark, she eased back on the bed until her hand caught the cold shape of the rifle. Then crouched on the pillow, she cradled the gun across her knees. "Who's there?" she called.

        The answer was a repeated cry, but less shrill, tired sounding, then the empty silence closing
40   in. She drew back against the bed. Whatever was there she could hear it moving about on the porch. Planks creaked and she could distinguish the sounds of objects being knocked over. There was a scratching on the wall as if it would tear its way in. She knew now what it was, a big cat, deposited by the uprooted tree that had passed her. It had come with the flood, a gift.

        Unconsciously she pressed her hand against her face and along her tightened throat. The rifle
45   rocked across her knees. She had never seen a panther in her life. She had heard about them from others and heard their cries, like suffering, in the distance. The cat was scratching on the wall again, rattling the window by the door. As long as she guarded the window and kept the cat hemmed in by the wall and water, caged, she would be all right. Outside, the animal paused to rake his claws across the rusted outer screen. Now and then, it whined and growled.

50   When the light filtered down through the rain at last, coming like another kind of dark, she was still sitting on the bed, stiff and cold. Her arms, used to rowing on the river, ached from the stillness of holding the rifle. She had hardly allowed herself to move for fear any sound might give strength to the cat. Rigid, she swayed with the movement of the house. The rain still fell as if it would never stop. Through the grey light, finally, she could see the rain-pitted flood and far

55   away the cloudy shape of drowned treetops. The cat was not moving now. Maybe he had gone away. Laying the gun aside she slipped off the bed and moved without a sound to the window. It was still there, crouched at the edge of the porch, staring up at the live oak, the mooring of her house, as if gauging its chances of leaping to an overhanging branch. It did not seem so frightening now that she could see it, its coarse fur napped into twigs, its sides pinched and ribs

60   showing. It would be easy to shoot it where it sat, its long tail whipping back and forth. She was moving back to get the gun when it turned around. With no warning, no crouch or tensing of muscles, it sprang at the window, shattering a pane of glass. She fell back, stifling a scream, and taking up the rifle, she fired through the window. She could not see the panther now, but she had missed. It began to pace again. She could glimpse its head and the arch of its back as it passed

65   the window.

        Shivering, she pulled back on the bed and lay down. The lulling constant sound of the river and the rain, the penetrating chill, drained away her purpose. She watched the window and kept the

70 gun ready. After waiting a long while she moved again to look. The panther had fallen asleep, its
head on its paws, like a housecat. For the first time since the rains began she wanted to cry, for
herself, for all the people, for everything in the flood. Sliding down on the bed, she pulled the
quilt around her shoulders. She should have got out when she could, while the roads were still
open or before her boat was washed away. As she rocked back and forth with the sway of the
house a deep ache in her stomach reminded her she hadn't eaten. She couldn't remember for
how long. Like the cat, she was starving. Easing into the kitchen, she made a fire with the few
75 remaining sticks of wood. If the flood lasted she would have to burn the chair, maybe even the
table itself. Taking down the remains of a smoked ham from the ceiling, she cut thick slices of
the brownish red meat and placed them in a skillet. The smell of the frying meat made her dizzy.
There were stale biscuits from the last time she had cooked and she could make some coffee.
There was plenty of water.

80 While she was cooking her food, she almost forgot about the cat until it whined. It was hungry
too. "Let me eat," she called to it, "and then I'll see to *you*." And she laughed under her breath. As
she hung the rest of the ham back on its nail the cat growled a deep throaty rumble that made
her hand shake.

After she had eaten, she went to the bed again and took up the rifle. The house had risen so
85 high now it no longer scraped across the bluff when it swung back from the river. The food
had warmed her. She could get rid of the cat while light still hung in the rain. She crept slowly
to the window. It was still there, mewling, beginning to move about the porch. She stared at
it a long time, unafraid. Then without thinking what she was doing, she laid the gun aside and
started around the edge of the bed to the kitchen. Behind her the cat was moving, fretting. She
90 took down what was left of the ham and making her way back across the swaying floor to the
window she shoved it through the broken pane. On the other side there was a hungry snarl and
something like a shock passed from the animal to her. Stunned by what she had done, she drew
back to the bed. She could hear the sounds of the panther tearing at the meat. The house rocked
around her.

95 The next time she awoke she knew at once that everything had changed. The rain had stopped.
She felt for the movement of the house but it no longer swayed on the flood. Drawing her door
open, she saw through the torn screen a different world. The house was resting on the bluff
where it always had. A few feet down, the river still raced on in a torrent, but it no longer
covered the few feet between the house and the live oak. And the cat was gone. Leading from
100 the porch to the live oak and doubtless on into the swamp were tracks, indistinct and already
disappearing into the soft mud. And there on the porch, gnawed to whiteness, was what was left
of the ham.

Source: Louis Dollarhide, "The Gift" in *Mississippi Writers: Reflections of Childhood and Youth*, Volume 1, edited by Dorothy
Abbott, University Press of Mississippi, 1985.

Question 6: GIFT

Here is part of a conversation between two people who read "The gift":

Give evidence from the story to show how each of these speakers could justify their point of view.

Speaker 1 ....

Speaker 2 ....

Situation: Personal
Text format: Continuous
Aspect: Reflection and evaluation
Levels: Level 2 and Level 3
PISA scale scores: 480 and 537

As the easiest among the reflection and evaluation tasks associated with *The gift*, this task [R119Q09] requires students to make comparisons and connections between the text and outside knowledge, drawing on their personal experience and attitudes. In order to gain credit for this task, a connection has to be made between the behaviour of a character in the story and personal values, by drawing on ideas about compassion and cruelty and using evidence from the text.

This task is marked using the full-credit/partial-credit rule, and therefore yields two levels of difficulty. To receive partial credit (Level 2, PISA score of 480), the student needs to find evidence of *either* compassion *or* cruelty in the story. For full credit (Level 3, PISA score of 537), the student needs to find evidence of *both* compassion *and* cruelty. The full-credit score reflects the ability to deal with contrary concepts or ambiguities, a capacity associated with proficiency higher than that typically found at Level 2. No credit is given for insufficient answers or for showing inaccurate comprehension of the material.

The content of the answer does not need to be very elaborate to gain credit. A full-credit answer is typically, for Part A, "Because she was going to shoot the panther" and, for Part B, "Because she fed the panther in the end".

Other tasks, such as the following two, give more credit for more sophisticated readings.

Question 7: GIFT

Do you think that the last sentence of "The gift" is an appropriate ending?

Explain your answer, demonstrating your understanding of how the last sentence relates to the story's meaning.

Situation: *Personal*
Text format: *Continuous*
Aspect: *Reflection and evaluation*
Level: *Level 4 and Level 5*
PISA scale scores: *567 and 652*

This second reflection and evaluation task [R119Q05], like the first discussed here, is marked using the full-credit/partial-credit rule, with the partial-credit score falling within Level 4 with a PISA score of 567 and the full-credit score falling within Level 5 with a PISA score of 652.

For full credit, the reader has to *go beyond a literal interpretation* and is required to evaluate the text critically, drawing on specialised knowledge and a deep understanding of a long and complex text. The reader needs to *comment critically on the appropriateness of the ending* of the narrative by reflecting on how it connects with the general theme or mood of the text. Readers need to draw inferences, making use of ideas activated during reading but not explicitly stated. The reader must implicitly base the response on an internalised sense of what makes an ending "appropriate", and the standards referred to for this level of response are deep or abstract rather than superficial and literal. For example, the full-credit response might comment on the metaphorical significance of the bone, or on the thematic completeness of the ending. These concepts, drawing on formal literary ideas, can be regarded as specialised knowledge for 15-year-olds. The range of interpretations of the story is suggested by the following examples of full-credit answers.

"Yes. I suppose that what was left of the ham by the panther was also a gift, the message being 'live and let live'."

"I think the ending is appropriate because I believe the panther was the gift to stop the flood. Because she fed it instead of shooting it the flood stopped, and almost like a mystery, on the porch lay the remains of the meat almost like a thank you."

"The flood was over and all that was left was the damages and basically that's what the last line says, that the whiteness of the bone was all that was left of the ham."

For partial credit, the task requires students to evaluate the appropriateness of the ending *at a more literal level* by commenting on its consistency with the narrative. Like the full-credit response category, the partial-credit category also requires an evaluation (either positive or negative) based on an idea about what constitutes appropriateness in an ending; but the partial-credit response refers to the *superficial features* of the story, such as consistency of plot. The relative difficulty of this score category (Level 4) reflects the fact that the answer must refer in some way to formal standards of appropriateness and, perhaps more importantly, that it must indicate accurate understanding of a long and complex text. Some examples of partial-credit answers were:

"I think it is a pretty good ending. When she gave it food all was well. The animal left her alone and all had changed."

"Yes, it is finished because the meat is finished and so is the story."

"I think it was a stupid ending, which is perfect to finish off a stupid story! Of course the ham is going to be eaten,

I knew that but I never thought the author – would be ignorant enough to bother mentioning it."

As can be seen from these examples, and as is the case in similar tasks, credit is available for both positive and negative evaluations. The adequacy of the answer is judged according to the quality of insight into the text and the sophistication of critical tools, rather than any idea of a "right" or "wrong" point of view on the reader's part.

Some answers to this task were not given any credit; these included implausible or downright inaccurate readings such as:

"I think it is an appropriate ending. It shows that maybe there never was a panther, and the ham that she threw out of the window is still there to prove this point."

and responses that were considered too vague:

"Yes it is because it tells you what happened in the end."

Like the first two reflection and evaluation tasks, the following interpreting task is marked using the full-credit/partial-credit scoring rule, with the full-credit score falling within Level 5 with a PISA score of 645 and the partial-credit score within Level 3 with a PISA score of 539. The levels of difficulty of these two categories of response are thus more than 100 points apart – over one standard deviation – on the reading literacy scale.

Question 8: GIFT

Here are some of the early references to the panther in the story.

"the cry awoke her, a sound so anguished..." (line 29)

"The answer was a repeated cry, but less shrill, tired sounding..." (line 39)

"She had...heard their cries, like suffering, in the distance." (lines 45-46)

Considering what happens in the rest of the story, why do you think the writer chooses to introduce the panther with these descriptions?

Situation: *Personal*
Text format: *Continuous*
Aspect: *Interpreting texts*
Level: *Level 3 and Level 5*
PISA scale scores: *539 and 645*

For full credit, the task [R119Q07] requires the reader to construe the meaning of language containing nuances while dealing with ideas that are contrary to expectation. The reader needs to negotiate a text whose discourse structure is not clearly marked, in order to discern the relationship of specific parts of the text (indicated in the question) to its implicit theme.

The text deliberately creates ambiguity through ideas that are contrary to expectation. Although the main response of the woman when she realises there is a panther nearby is fear, the carefully chosen descriptions of the panther's cries – "anguished", "tired-sounding" and "suffering" – suggest pathos rather than threat. This hint, near the beginning of the story, is important for a full understanding of the woman's "unexpected" behaviour at the end, and hence to an understanding of the story's implicit theme. Thus, to receive full credit, students must recognise that the *descriptions are intended to evoke pity*.

Partial credit is given for answers that treat the text at a more straightforward level, linking the phrases highlighted in the question with the plot. Students may refer to possible *intentions (or effects) of the quoted descriptions, other than that of evoking pity*. At this level the task is to follow implicit logical links between sentences by inferring that the panther is crying because it is hungry. A second kind of response receiving partial credit brings together different parts of the text so as to identify a main idea. This kind of response identifies the atmosphere of the story at this point. Students may refer to the *literal information given in the quoted descriptions*.

Question 9: GIFT

When the woman says, "and then I'll see to **you**" (line 81) she means that she is

A   sure that the cat won't hurt her.

B   trying to frighten the cat.

C   intending to shoot the cat.

D   planning to feed the cat.

Situation: Personal
Text format: Continuous
Aspect: Interpreting texts
Level: Level 4
PISA scale score: 603

This task [R119Q04] requires a high level of text-based inference in order to construe the meaning of a section of text in context, dealing with ambiguities and ideas that may be contrary to expectation. The reader needs to infer psychological meaning, following thematic links over several paragraphs, in deciding which of the four alternatives is the best answer.

Taken out of context, the sentence that the task focuses on is ambiguous and even in context there are apparently plausible alternative readings. The task is designed specifically to assess proficiency in dealing with this kind of ambiguity. One of the translation notes that was sent to national teams along with the test material (in the source languages of French and English) says of this passage, "'Please ensure that the phrase, "and then I'll see to *you*" allows both of the following interpretations: "and then I'll feed you" and "and then I'll shoot you."'" Nevertheless, only one reading is consistent with the psychological sequence of the story: the woman must be intending to shoot the panther, since just after this moment she takes up the rifle and thinks that "she could get rid of the cat while light still hung in the rain." The woman's eventual compassion towards the panther is powerful distracting information, contrary to the expectations set up elsewhere in the story. The multiple-choice alternative that reflects this reading – "planning to feed the panther" – attracted almost half of the students. These readers were clearly following the storyline at one level, recognising a main theme and construing meaning within a limited part of the text (skills identified with Levels 1 and 2 tasks) but they were not dealing with ambiguities and ideas that were contrary to expectations to the degree demanded by a Level 4 interpreting task.

While the tasks based on this long and relatively subtle text are generally difficult, the unit also contains one Level 1 task:

Question 10: GIFT

"Then creaking and groaning with effort the house struggled up ..." (lines 21-22)

What happened to the house in this part of the story?

  A It fell apart.

  (B) It began to float.

  C It crashed into the oak tree.

  D It sank to the bottom of the river.

Situation: *Personal*
Text format: *Continuous*
Aspect: *Retrieving information*
Level: *Level 1*
PISA scale score: *367*

For this task [R119Q06], the reader needs to locate a piece of explicitly stated information in a short section of text and match it to one of four alternatives stated in the question.

Although the whole text is long, for this task the section of text that the reader needs to refer to is short and is very clearly marked in the question, both by being quoted directly and by reference to line numbers. The correct answer, "It began to float", uses a word directly matching a word closely following the quoted section: "Then creaking and groaning with effort the house struggled up from the clay, floated free ... "

Lake Chad

The tasks related to this stimulus are classified as non-continuous on the text format dimension. The *Lake Chad* unit presents two graphs from an archaeological atlas. Figure A in *Lake Chad* is a line graph, and Figure B is a horizontal histogram. A third non-continuous text type is represented in this unit, by a small map of the lake embedded in Figure A. Two very short passages of prose are also part of the stimulus.

By juxtaposing these pieces of information the author invites the reader to infer a connection between the changing water levels of *Lake Chad* over time, and the periods in which certain species of wildlife inhabited its surroundings.

This is a type of text that might typically be encountered by students in an educational setting. Nevertheless, because the atlas is published for the general reader the text is classified as public in the situation dimension. The full set of five tasks covers all three aspects. The tasks range in difficulty from Level 1 to Level 4.

Four of the tasks from *Lake Chad* are reproduced here.

Figure A shows changing levels of Lake Chad, in Saharan North Africa. Lake Chad disappeared completely in about 20 000 BC, during the last Ice Age. In about 11 000 BC it reappeared. Today, its level is about the same as it was in AD 1000.

Figure A

Lake Chad: changing levels

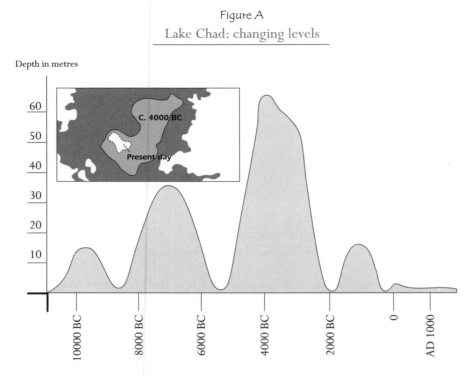

Figure B shows Saharan rock art (ancient drawings or paintings found on the walls of caves) and changing patterns of wildlife.

Figure B

Saharan rock art and changing patterns of wildlife

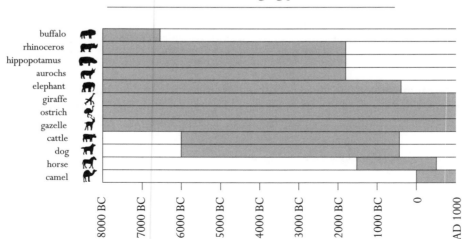

Source: Copyright Bartholomew Ltd. 1988. Extracted from *The Times Atlas of Archaeology* and reproduced by permission of Harper Collins Publishers.

Question 11: LAKE CHAD

What is the depth of Lake Chad today?

A About two metres.

B About fifteen metres.

C About fifty metres.

D It has disappeared completely.

E The information is not provided.

Situation: Public
Text format: Non-continuous
Aspect: Retrieving information
Level: Level 2
PISA scale score: 478

This first task [R040Q02] is a Level 2 retrieving information task with a PISA score of 478 that requires students to locate and combine pieces of information from a line graph and the introduction.

The word "today" in the question can be directly matched in the relevant sentence of the introduction, which refers to the depth of the lake "today" being the same as it was in AD 1000. The reader needs to combine this information with information from Figure A by locating AD 1000 on the graph and then by reading off the depth of the lake at this date. Competing information is present in the form of multiple dates in Figure A, and the repetition of "AD 1000" in Figure B. Nevertheless, the task is relatively easy because key information is supplied explicitly in the prose introduction. Most students who did not select the correct alternative A, "About two metres", selected E, "The information is not provided." This is probably because they looked only at Figure A, rather than combining the relevant part of Figure A with information from the introduction. Level 2 tasks based on non-continuous texts – like this one – may require combining information from different displays, whereas Level 1 non-continuous tasks typically focus on discrete pieces of information, usually within a single display.

Question 12: LAKE CHAD

In about which year does the graph in Figure A start?

Situation: Public
Text format: Non-continuous
Aspect: Retrieving information
Level: Level 3
PISA scale score: 540

This second, more difficult retrieving information task [R040Q03A] is at Level 3 with a PISA score of 540.

For this task students need to locate and recognise the relationship between pieces of information in the line graph and the introduction, and to deal with prominent competing information.

As in the previous task, the reader has to locate relevant information in the introduction ("In about 11000 BC it reappeared") and relate it to the identified part of the graph (the origin). This task might appear to be easier than the previous one, in that students are explicitly directed to look at Figure A. However, the competing information in this task is stronger. The lure of competing information is demonstrated in a common error made in this task, which was to mistake the first date marked on the horizontal axis of Figure A (10000 BC) for the beginning of the line graph representing the depth of Lake Chad, at about 11000 BC.

Although this is classified as a retrieving information task since it primarily requires the locating of information in a text, interpretative strategies must also be drawn upon to infer the correct information from the graph. In addition, readers need to reflect on what they know about dating conventions, drawing on the contextual knowledge that BC dates go "backwards". This suggests that there is considerable overlap between the three aspects of retrieving information, interpreting texts and reflection and evaluation: most tasks make a number of different demands upon readers, and individual readers may approach a task in different ways. As noted in the reading literacy framework (OECD, 1999), the assignment of a task to one of the aspect scales often involves making judgements about what the most salient features of the task are and about the approach that readers are most likely to take when responding to it.

Question 13: LAKE CHAD

Figure B is based on the assumption that

(A) the animals in the rock art were present in the area at the time they were drawn.

B the artists who drew the animals were highly skilled.

C the artists who drew the animals were able to travel widely.

D there was no attempt to domesticate the animals which were depicted in the rock art.

Situation: *Public*
Text format: *Non-continuous*
Aspect: *Interpreting texts*
Level: *Level 1*
PISA scale score: *397*

The easiest task associated with *Lake Chad* [R040Q04], with a PISA scale score of 397, is classified as interpreting texts. This Level 1 task requires students to recognise the main idea of a chart, where the information is not prominent and the focus is on a single display with little explanatory text.

The *Lake Chad* stimulus comprises two figures, but the reader is directed in the question to look at only one of them, Figure B. This figure has few labels (the dates and names of animals) and the symbols are representative rather than abstract; in other words, only fairly low-level processing is needed to interpret the figure. On the other hand the required information in the text is not prominent, since there is no explicit statement that artists painted what they saw – indeed, there is no direct reference to the artists at all. Clearly, however, students did not find it difficult to make this inference.

Question 14: LAKE CHAD

For this question you need to draw together information from Figure A and Figure B.

The disappearance of the rhinoceros, hippopotamus and aurochs from Saharan rock art happened

A   at the beginning of the most recent Ice Age.

B   in the middle of the period when Lake Chad was at its highest level.

C   after the level of Lake Chad had been falling for over a thousand years.

D   at the beginning of an uninterrupted dry period.

Situation: *Public*
Text format: *Non-continuous*
Aspect: *Interpreting texts*
Level: *Level 3*
PISA scale score: *508*

This more difficult interpreting task [R040Q06] (Level 3, PISA score of 508) in the *Lake Chad* unit requires students to draw together several parts of the non-continuous texts in order to understand a relationship. They need to compare information given in two graphs.

The requirement to combine information from two sources contributes to the task's moderate level of difficulty (Level 3). An added feature is that two different types of graph are used (a line graph and a histogram), and the reader needs to have interpreted the structure of both in order to translate the relevant information from one form to the other.

Of those students who did not select the correct answer, the largest proportion chose distractor D, "at the beginning of an uninterrupted dry period." If one disregards the texts, this seems the most plausible of the wrong answers, and its popularity indicates that these students might have been treating the task as if it were a Level 2 reflection and evaluation task, where it would be appropriate to hypothesise about the explanation for a feature of the text, drawing on familiar outside knowledge.

Labour

Tasks in the *Labour* unit are classified as non-continuous in terms of text format. The unit is based on a tree diagram showing the structure and distribution of a national labour force in 1995. The diagram is published in an economics textbook for upper secondary school students, so that the text is classified as educational in terms of situation. The specific information contained in the diagram relates to New Zealand, but the terms and definitions used are those established by the OECD and the stimulus can therefore be regarded as, essentially, international.

This unit does not have the immediate appeal of some of the material presented earlier in this selection. The content is unlikely to excite lively interest among 15-year-olds, and the form of presentation is uncompromisingly academic. Compare, for example, the text of the last unit presented in this selection, which includes some small illustrations to give a more friendly touch to the tabular and numerical information. Nonetheless, the *Labour* unit represents a kind of reading text that adults are likely to encounter and need to be able to interpret in order to participate fully in the economic and political life of a modern society.

The full *Labour* unit comprises five tasks representing all three aspects and spanning Levels 2 to 5. Four of the tasks are reproduced here.

The tree diagram below shows the structure of a country's labour force or "working-age population". The total population of the country in 1995 was about 3.4 million.

The labour force structure, year ended 31 March 1995 (000s)[1]

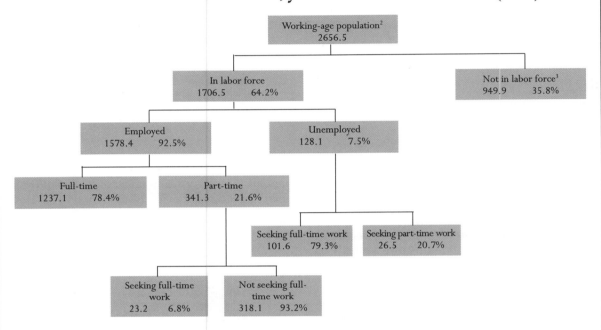

1. Numbers of people are given in thousands (000s).
2. The working-age population is defined as people betwen the ages of 15 and 65.
3. People "Not in the labour force" are those not actively seeking work and/or not available for work.
Source: D. Miller, *Form 6 Economics*, ESA Publications, Box 9453, Newmarker, Auckland, NZ, p. 64.

Question 15: LABOUR

How many people of working age were not in the labour force? (Write the **number** of people, not the percentage.)

Situation: Educational
Text format: Non-continuous
Aspect: Retrieving information
Levels: Level 3 and Level 5
PISA scale scores: 485 and 631

The first task presented here [R088Q03] yields two levels of difficulty, with the partial-credit response category falling within Level 3 with a PISA scale score of 485 and the full-credit category within Level 5 with a PISA scale score of 631. The latter is one of the most difficult retrieving information tasks in the PISA reading assessment.

For full credit (Level 5) students are required to locate and combine a piece of numerical information in the main body of the text (the tree diagram) *with information in a footnote* – that is, outside the main body of the text. In addition, students have to apply this footnoted information in determining the correct number of people fitting into this category. Both of these features contribute to the difficulty of this task.

For partial credit (Level 3) this task merely requires students to locate the number given in the appropriate category of the tree diagram. *They are not required to use the conditional information provided in the footnote* to receive partial credit. Even without this important information the task is still moderately difficult.

Typically, the requirement to use conditional information – that is, information found outside the main body of a text – significantly increases the difficulty of a task. This is clearly demonstrated by the two categories of this task, since the difference between full-credit and partial-credit answers is, substantively, the application or non-application of conditional information to correctly identified numerical information in the body of the text. The difference in difficulty of these two categories of response is more than two proficiency levels.

Question 16: LABOUR

In which part of the tree diagram, if any, would each of the people listed in the table below be included?

Show your answer by placing a cross in the correct box in the table.

The first one has been done for you.

	"In labour force: employed"	"In labour force: unemployed"	"Not in labour force"	Not included in any category
A part-time waiter, aged 35	☒	☐	☐	☐
A business woman, aged 43, who works a sixty-hour week	☒	☐	☐	☐
A full-time student, aged 21	☐	☐	☒	☐
A man, aged 28, who recently sold his shop and is looking for work	☐	☒	☐	☐
A woman, aged 55, who has never worked or wanted to work outside the home	☐	☐	☒	☐
A grandmother, aged 80, who still works a few hours a day at the family's market stall	☐	☐	☐	☒

Situation: Educational
Text format: Non-continuous
Aspect: Interpreting texts
Levels: Level 2 and Level 5
PISA scale scores: 473 and 727

A second task based on the tree diagram [R088Q04] is classified as interpreting texts. It too yields two levels of difficulty, with the partial-credit response category falling within Level 2 with a PISA score of 473 and the full-credit category within Level 5 with a PISA score of 727.

The task requires students to analyse several described cases and to match each case to a category given in the tree diagram. The described cases are designed to determine whether the reader has understood, fully and in detail, the distinctions and definitions provided by the diagram. Again, some of the relevant information is in footnotes that are external to the main display.

For the Level 5 category of response, students need to demonstrate a full and detailed understanding of the text, sometimes referring to information external to the main display. To receive full credit, students need to answer all five parts correctly.

For the Level 2 with a PISA score of 473 or partial-credit category of response, students need to demonstrate some under-standing of the text by correctly matching three or four of the five described cases with the appropriate labour force category. In PISA 2000, students most often chose the correct category of the labour force for the second and fourth cases listed, those for which it is not necessary to deal with the information in Footnotes 2 and 3 (definitions of "working-age population" and "not in labour force"). The cases that are most difficult to categorise correctly are the third, fifth and sixth – those that require assimilation of footnoted information. As in the previous task, conditional information increases the overall difficulty. Another feature contributing to the difficulty of this task is the fact that it requires students to provide several independent answers.

Question 17: LABOUR

Suppose that information about the labour force was presented in a tree diagram like this every year.

Listed below are four features of the tree diagram. Show whether or not you would expect these features to change from year to year, by circling either "Change" or "No change". The first one has been done for you.

Features of Tree Diagram	Answer
The labels in each box (*e.g.* "In labour force")	Change / ~~No change~~
The percentages (*e.g.* "64.2%")	~~Change~~ / No change
The numbers (*e.g.* "2656.5")	~~Change~~ / No change
The footnotes under the tree diagram	Change / ~~No change~~

Situation: Educational
Text format: Non-continuous
Aspect: Reflection and evaluation
Levels: Level 2
PISA scale score: 445

This third task based on Labour is a relatively easy reflection and evaluation task [R088Q05], falling within Level 2 with a PISA score of 445.

This task requires students to recognise features of the text, demonstrating a grasp of the underlying structure of a tree diagram by distinguishing between variables and invariables. Although it is not necessary to know the technical terms "variable" and "invariable", successful completion of this task requires a grasp of the underlying structure of the text. This task is classified as reflection and evaluation, not because it is critically evaluative or because it asks for a personal answer, but because it asks the reader to consider the text as an artefact, in terms of its form and structure. To obtain full credit, students need to answer all three parts correctly. Students with two or fewer parts correct are given no credit.

Question 18: LABOUR

The information about the labour force structure is presented as a tree diagram, but it could have been presented in a number of other ways, such as a written description, a pie chart, a graph or a table.

The tree diagram was probably chosen because it is especially useful for showing

A changes over time.

B the size of the country's total population.

C categories within each group.

D the size of each group.

Situation: *Educational*
Text format: *Non-continuous*
Aspect: *Reflection and evaluation*
Level: *Level 3*
PISA scale score: *486*

This last task [R088Q07] based on the *Labour* diagram requires an evaluation of a feature of the text. The task is to consider the suitability of the tree diagram for particular purposes in comparison with the suitability of other forms of presentation. Formal knowledge of text structures and their advantages and disadvantages is a relatively unfamiliar area of knowledge for 15-year-olds, contributing to the medium level of difficulty (Level 3). Whereas the previous *Labour* question only implicitly requires the reader to demonstrate understanding of the text's structure, this question makes the requirement explicit. To gain credit for this task the student has to recognise the appropriateness of a tree diagram for showing categories within groups. The more explicitly abstract approach of the question may contribute to the comparative difficulty of this task. The second and fourth distractors, which drew significant numbers of students, focus on information that is presented in the diagram, but the structure of the diagram does not particularly emphasise those features. Students who selected these distractors seemed to be treating the question as if it involved retrieving information ("Which of these kinds of information is shown in the diagram?"), rather than evaluating the structure of the presentation.

PLAN International

The third and last non-continuous text presented here is a table containing information about the types of programmes offered by an international aid agency, PLAN International. It is taken from a public report distributed by the agency, and is therefore classified as public in terms of situation.

The table shows the countries in one region of PLAN International's operation, the type of aid programmes it offers (27 categories of aid programme grouped under three main headings) and the amount of work accomplished in each country within each category of aid. There is a great deal of information presented in a rather dense fashion in the table, which might overwhelm the less proficient reader. Confident readers would be most likely to scan the text to gain a broad impression of its structure and content, rather than slavishly reading every detail of the table indiscriminately.

Only one task associated with the *PLAN International* text was used in constructing the PISA scale of reading literacy.

PLAN International Program Results Financial Year 1996

REGION OF EASTERN AND SOUTHERN AFRICA   RESA

Growing up Healthy	Egypt	Ethiopia	Kenya	Malawi	Sudan	Tanzania	Uganda	Zambia	Zimbabwe	Totals
Health posts built with 4 rooms or less	1	0	6	0	7	1	2	0	9	26
Health workers trained for 1 day	1 053	0	719	0	425	1 003	20	80	1 085	4 385
Children given nutrition supplements > 1 week	10 195	0	2 240	2 400	0	0	0	0	251 402	266 237
Children given financial help with health/ dental treatment	984	0	396	0	305	0	581	0	17	2 283

Learning										
Teachers trained for 1 week	0	0	367	0	970	115	565	0	303	2 320
School exercise books bought/donated	667	0	0	41 200	0	69 106	0	150	0	111 123
School textbooks bought/donated	0	0	45 650	9 600	1 182	8 769	7 285	150	58 387	131 023
Uniforms bought/made/donated	8 897	0	5 761	0	2 000	6 040	0	0	434	23 132
Children helped with school fees/a scholarship	12 321	0	1 598	0	154	0	0	0	2 014	16 087
School desks built/bought/donated	3 200	0	3 689	250	1 564	1 725	1 794	0	4 109	16 331
Permanent classrooms built	44	0	50	8	93	31	45	0	82	353
Classrooms repaired	0	0	34	0	0	14	0	0	33	81
Adults receiving training in literacy this financial year	1 160	0	3 000	568	3 617	0	0	0	350	8 695

Habitat										
Latrines or toilets dug/built	50	0	2 403	0	57	162	23	96	4 311	7 102
Houses connected to a new sewage system	143	0	0	0	0	0	0	0	0	143
Wells dug/improved (or springs capped)	0	0	15	0	7	13	0	0	159	194
New positive boreholes drilled	0	0	8	93	14	0	27	0	220	362
Gravity feed drinking water systems built	0	0	28	0	1	0	0	0	0	29
Drinking water systems repaired/improved	0	0	392	0	2	0	0	0	31	425
Houses improved with PLAN project	265	0	520	0	0	0	1	0	2	788
New houses built for beneficiaries	225	0	596	0	0	2	6	0	313	1 142
Community halls built or improved	2	0	2	0	3	0	3	0	2	12
Community leaders trained for 1 day or more	2 214	95	3 522	232	200	3 575	814	20	2 693	13 365
Kilometres of roadway improved	1.2	0	26	0	0	0	0	0	5.34	80.6
Bridges built	0	0	4	2	11	0	0	0	1	18
Families benefited directly from erosion control	0	0	1 092	0	1 500	0	0	0	18 405	20 997
Houses newly served by electrification project	448	0	2	0	0	0	0	0	44	494

Source: Adapted from PLAN International Program Output Chart financial year 1996, appendix to Quarterly Report to the International Board first quarter 1997.

Question 19A: PLAN INTERNATIONAL

What does the table indicate about the level of PLAN International's activity in Ethiopia in 1996, compared with other countries in the region?

A   The level of activity was comparatively high in Ethiopia.

B   The level of activity was comparatively low in Ethiopia.

C   It was about the same as in other countries in the region.

D   It was comparatively high in the Habitat category, and low in the other categories.

Question 19B: PLAN INTERNATIONAL

In 1996 Ethiopia was one of the poorest countries in the world.

Taking this fact and the information in the table into account, what do you think might explain the level of PLAN International's activities in Ethiopia compared with its activities in other countries?

Situation: Public
Text format: Non-continuous
Aspect: Reflection and evaluation
Levels: Level 5
PISA scale scores: 705 and 822

The marking rules for this task [R099Q04B] are somewhat complicated. Although students are asked two questions within this task – one multiple-choice and one constructed-response – only the second of these is counted for scoring purposes. As this task contributes to the reflection and evaluation scale, the multiple-choice component of the task, which predominantly requires retrieval of information, does not earn any credit on its own. However, the multiple-choice question is taken into account in that a correct answer to this question is a necessary condition for earning credit on the second, constructed-response question.

The second question is given either full credit or partial credit, both score categories falling within Level 5 with PISA scale scores of 705 and 822). For this task students must hypothesise about the content of the text, drawing on specialised knowledge, and must deal with a concept contrary to expectations. They also need to identify patterns among the many pieces of information presented in this complex and detailed display.

Specifically, students need to reflect on the amount of aid given to Ethiopia by PLAN International, in comparison with the amount given to other countries in the region. This requires them to form a hypothesis, rather than simply to explain something, given that very few 15-year-olds are likely to know as a matter of fact what might have prompted the aid agency to give the amount of aid it did to Ethiopia. It is specialised knowledge to the extent that thinking about the work of international aid agencies is not familiar territory for most adolescents, although it is a reasonable expectation that 15-year-olds will have some basic knowledge about what aid agencies do. On the other hand, it is not reasonable to assume that students will have specific knowledge about the economic status of a particular country, and for that reason, the information about Ethiopia's poverty is supplied. The task includes reference to a phenomenon that is contrary to expectation: that an aid agency gives a relatively small amount of aid to a very poor country.

In order to gain full credit for this task, students *must have answered 19A correctly* and *then draw on all the information supplied*. They are required to form a hypothesis about why PLAN International gave relatively little aid to Ethiopia, taking into account all the relevant information in the table – both the amount and the type of aid – as well as the information supplied in the question. A number of different hypotheses were offered by students, drawing on all the information given in the table. Among the responses that received full credit were:

"PLAN helped community leaders to try to get them to be self-sufficient. As they are an aid organisation this may seem the best idea."

"The only help to Ethiopia has been with training of community leaders. Ethiopia may not let PLAN International be involved in other aspects of the country."

For partial credit, students also need to have *answered 19A correctly* and must then take into account *some, but not all*, of the relevant information in the table: the amount, but not the type of aid given. In addition, the hypothesis needs to be consistent with broad background knowledge about the work of aid agencies. Some of the more common hypotheses offered, and awarded partial credit, were:

"There may have been floods or something happened in the country to stop them helping."

"PLAN International may have just been introduced to that community and therefore they were low on activities."

"Maybe other aid organisations are already helping in Ethiopia, so they don't need as much from PLAN."

"It's just too hard to help there."

This task is particularly difficult for a number of reasons in addition to those discussed above. First, it requires many pieces of information – both internal and external to the text – to be synthesised. Second, there is minimal direction as to which part of the text needs to be consulted for full credit: specifically, there is no indication that the *type* of aid given in Ethiopia needs to be referred to for the full credit score. This means that the information required is not given any prominence, either in the question or by a marker in the text itself. For a combination of all of these reasons this is probably one of the most difficult tasks in the PISA reading assessment.

Notes

1. In PISA each item has a unique code. The item code is presented in brackets *e.g.,* [R110Q01] in this chapter. This identification code helps users who wish to retrieve student responses to the item from the online database for PISA 2000 (*http://www.pisa.oecd.org/pisa/outcome.htm*).

READERS' GUIDE

Data underlying the figures

The data referred to in Chapters 4 to 8 of this report are presented in Annex B and, with additional detail, on the Web site *www.pisa.oecd.org.* Four symbols are used to denote missing data:

n.a The category does not apply in the country concerned. Data are therefore missing.

m Data are not available. Unless otherwise noted, these data were collected but subsequently removed from the publication for technical or other reasons at the request of the country concerned.

x Data are included in another category or column of the table.

Calculation of international averages

An OECD average was calculated for most indicators presented in this report. In the case of some indicators, a total representing the OECD area as a whole was also calculated.

The **OECD average**, sometimes also referred to as the **country average**, is the mean of the data values for all OECD countries for which data are available or can be estimated. The OECD average can be used to see how a country compares on a given indicator with a typical OECD country. The OECD average does not take into account the absolute size of the student population in each country, *i.e.,* each country contributes equally to the average.

Three OECD countries are excluded from the calculation of averages or other aggregate estimates: the Netherlands, the Slovak Republic (which became a Member of the OECD in 2000) and Turkey. The Netherlands are excluded because low response rates preclude reliable estimates of mean scores. The Slovak Republic and Turkey will join PISA from the 2003 survey cycle onwards.

In the case of other countries, data may not be available for specific indicators, or specific categories may not apply. Readers should, therefore, keep in mind that the terms *OECD average* and *OECD total* refer to the OECD countries included in the respective comparisons.

Index of central tendency

In order to give an overview of the average trend observed among countries, one can use the mean or the median. In some cases, it is better to use the median, in order to avoid to give too much weight to extreme values observed in some countries. The median is the value which cuts the distribution into two equal parts. It is equivalent to the 50th percentile.

In this report, the following rules have been adopted: for descriptive analyses, mean frequencies or means have been used; for bivariate or multivariate analyses (correlations or regression analyses), median values have been used.

Reporting of student data

The report usually uses "15-year-olds" as shorthand for the PISA target population. In practice, this refers to students who were aged between 15 years and 3 (complete) months and 16 years and 2 (complete) months at the beginning of the assessment period and who were enrolled in an educational institution, regardless of the grade level or type of institution, and of whether they were attending full-time or part-time.

Reporting of school data

The principals of the schools in which students were assessed provided information on their school's characteristics by completing a school questionnaire. Where responses from school principals are presented in this publication, they are weighted so that they are proportionate to the number of 15-year-olds enrolled in the school.

Rounding of figures

Because of rounding, some figures in tables may not exactly add up to the totals. Totals, differences and averages are always calculated on the basis of exact numbers and are rounded only after calculation.

Abbreviations used in this report

The following abbreviations are used in this report:

SD   Standard deviation
SE   Standard error

Further documentation

For further information on the PISA assessment instruments and the methods used in PISA, see the *Knowledge and Skills for Life: First Results from PISA 2000* (OECD, 2001*b*), *PISA 2000 Technical Report* (OECD, 2002*b*) and the PISA Web site (*www.pisa.oecd.org*).

THE READING PERFORMANCE
OF 15 –YEAR-OLDS

KEY POINTS

- On a combined reading literacy scale with a mean of 500 points and a standard deviation of 100, the difference in means between the countries with the highest and lowest performances is 150 points, the equivalent of more than two proficiency levels.

- The means of the majority of countries fall within Level 3. On the combined scale and on each of the subscales, Level 3 also accounts for the largest proportion of students in most countries. On average across the OECD countries, a little more than one-quarter of 15-year-olds demonstrate reading proficiency at Level 3 on each of the scales.

- The distribution of students between levels varies considerably from country to country, even when countries have similar mean scores. In particular, proportions of students at the extremes of the scales vary markedly. For example, proportions of students at Level 5 vary between less than 1 per cent and just short of 20 per cent.

- Every country has some students whose reading literacy skills are lower than the most basic level described by the scale, as well as some students at the top level of the scale.

- Large numbers of students in many countries demonstrate limited reading literacy skills. An indication of this is that in over one-third of the countries participating, more than 20 per cent of students fail to achieve Level 2 on the PISA reading scale.

- Correlations between the three aspect subscales and between the two text format subscales are generally high. Nonetheless, there are some noteworthy differences in countries' patterns of performance across the subscales. Some of the countries with the lowest overall performance score better on the reflection and evaluation subscale than on the retrieving information subscale. Countries with low overall performance also score better on the continuous texts subscale than on the non-continuous texts subscale.

- The variation in proficiency on the aspect subscales is narrowest on the interpreting texts subscale and widest on the retrieving information subscale.

- On the text format subscales, variation in performance is considerably greater in the case of tasks based on non-continuous texts, than in that of tasks based on continuous texts. On the combined reading literacy scale the difference in PISA scale scores between the most and least able students (represented by the 90th and 10th percentiles) ranges, within each country, from two and a half to four and a half PISA levels. This indicates that in many countries there is a high and worrying degree of inequality of outcomes in the domain of reading literacy.

Probably the first questions that are provoked by an international study of educational achievement revolve around the topic, "How did we do compared with …?" In this chapter we attempt to answer a series of questions related to this topic. We look not just at the mean performance of countries in reading literacy, but also at how performance is distributed within and between countries, as well as the relative differences in performance in various elements of the reading literacy domain.

We begin by presenting countries' mean scores and score distributions on the combined reading literacy scale. This is followed by a discussion about performance on each of the three aspect subscales (retrieving information, interpreting texts and reflection and evaluation) and the two text format subscales (continuous texts and non-continuous texts). To conclude this chapter we discuss the question of differential access to reading literacy and its consequences for individuals, societies and nations.

Results for the combined reading literacy scale and for the three aspect subscales are published in the initial report of PISA 2000 (OECD, 2001*b*). In terms of international studies of reading, the aspect sub-scales offer a new perspective on reading literacy and this, together with their high relevance for policy-makers, led to the decision to include results on the aspect subscales in the initial report. Analysis of student achievement on the PISA text format subscales, continuous texts and non-continuous texts, is presented in this report for the first time. The division of the reading domain according to text format is a familiar one to those acquainted with previous international studies. For example, the international reading literacy study conducted by the IEA (Elley, 1992; 1994) reported performance by 10- and 14-year-olds in reading comprehension of narrative and expository texts (similar to continuous texts) and documents (similar to non-continuous texts). The International Adult Literacy Survey (see OECD 1995, 1997, 2000) reported separately on prose literacy (similar to continuous texts) and document literacy (similar to non-continuous texts). Reporting on the continuous texts and non-continuous texts subscales in PISA thus provides countries with additional points of comparison with other studies, as well as analyses that in themselves may, like the information on the aspect subscales, have important implications for the curriculum and teaching of reading.

This chapter is mainly descriptive, its intention being to provide basic comparative performance data for countries. The data presented here will inevitably raise questions and hypotheses, some of which are explored later in this report by looking at how reading performance is related to reader profiles and engagement (Chapter 5); how it is related to background characteristics associated with individuals, their families and their learning environments (Chapter 6); and how it is related to combinations of these variables, particularly to the structures of schooling (Chapter 7). While observations about particular countries and groups of countries are made where appropriate, many of the investigations that would answer questions about why particular countries performed in particular ways are beyond the scope of this chapter and indeed this report. It is hoped, however, that the information provided in this chapter will prompt such questions and inspire further investigations, particularly at the country level.

Performance on the combined reading literacy scale

Mean scores

A pool of 141 reading tasks was used as the means of collecting evidence about the abilities of 15-year-olds in participating countries in reading literacy, as defined by the PISA reading literacy framework. Student performance in these items informed the development of the framework-based described proficiency scales for reading. Reading literacy scores were transformed in order to produce a numerical combined reading

Figure 4.1

Multiple comparisons of mean performance on the combined reading literacy scale

Read across the row for a country to compare performance with the countries listed along the top of the chart.

Country (row)	Mean	S.E.	Finland 546 (2.6)	Canada 534 (1.6)	New Zealand 529 (2.8)	Australia 528 (3.5)	Ireland 527 (3.2)	Korea 525 (2.4)	United Kingdom 523 (2.6)	Japan 522 (5.2)	Sweden 516 (2.2)	Austria 507 (2.4)	Belgium 507 (3.6)	Iceland 507 (1.5)	Norway 505 (2.8)	France 505 (2.7)	United States 504 (7.0)	Denmark 497 (2.4)	Switzerland 494 (4.2)	Spain 493 (2.7)	Czech Republic 492 (2.4)	Italy 487 (2.9)	Germany 484 (2.5)	Liechtenstein 483 (4.1)	Hungary 480 (4.0)	Poland 479 (4.5)	Greece 474 (5.0)	Portugal 470 (4.5)	Russian Fed. 462 (4.2)	Latvia 458 (5.3)	Luxembourg 441 (1.6)	Mexico 422 (3.3)	Brazil 396 (3.1)
Finland	546	(2.6)	□	▲	▲	▲	▲	▲	▲	▲	▲	▲	▲	▲	▲	▲	▲	▲	▲	▲	▲	▲	▲	▲	▲	▲	▲	▲	▲	▲	▲	▲	▲
Canada	534	(1.6)	▽	□	○	○	○	▲	▲	○	▲	▲	▲	▲	▲	▲	▲	▲	▲	▲	▲	▲	▲	▲	▲	▲	▲	▲	▲	▲	▲	▲	▲
New Zealand	529	(2.8)	▽	○	□	○	○	○	○	○	▲	▲	▲	▲	▲	▲	▲	▲	▲	▲	▲	▲	▲	▲	▲	▲	▲	▲	▲	▲	▲	▲	▲
Australia	528	(3.5)	▽	○	○	□	○	○	○	○	▲	▲	▲	▲	▲	▲	▲	▲	▲	▲	▲	▲	▲	▲	▲	▲	▲	▲	▲	▲	▲	▲	▲
Ireland	527	(3.2)	▽	○	○	○	□	○	○	○	▲	▲	▲	▲	▲	▲	▲	▲	▲	▲	▲	▲	▲	▲	▲	▲	▲	▲	▲	▲	▲	▲	▲
Korea	525	(2.4)	▽	▽	○	○	○	□	○	○	▲	▲	▲	▲	▲	▲	▲	▲	▲	▲	▲	▲	▲	▲	▲	▲	▲	▲	▲	▲	▲	▲	▲
United Kingdom	523	(2.6)	▽	▽	○	○	○	○	□	○	○	▲	▲	▲	▲	▲	▲	▲	▲	▲	▲	▲	▲	▲	▲	▲	▲	▲	▲	▲	▲	▲	▲
Japan	522	(5.2)	▽	○	○	○	○	○	○	□	○	○	○	○	▲	▲	○	▲	▲	▲	▲	▲	▲	▲	▲	▲	▲	▲	▲	▲	▲	▲	▲
Sweden	516	(2.2)	▽	▽	▽	▽	▽	▽	○	○	□	▲	▲	▲	▲	▲	○	▲	▲	▲	▲	▲	▲	▲	▲	▲	▲	▲	▲	▲	▲	▲	▲
Austria	507	(2.4)	▽	▽	▽	▽	▽	▽	▽	○	▽	□	○	○	○	○	○	▲	▲	▲	▲	▲	▲	▲	▲	▲	▲	▲	▲	▲	▲	▲	▲
Belgium	507	(3.6)	▽	▽	▽	▽	▽	▽	▽	○	▽	○	□	○	○	○	○	○	○	▲	▲	▲	▲	▲	▲	▲	▲	▲	▲	▲	▲	▲	▲
Iceland	507	(1.5)	▽	▽	▽	▽	▽	▽	▽	○	▽	○	○	□	○	○	○	▲	▲	▲	▲	▲	▲	▲	▲	▲	▲	▲	▲	▲	▲	▲	▲
Norway	505	(2.8)	▽	▽	▽	▽	▽	▽	▽	▽	▽	○	○	○	□	○	○	○	○	▲	▲	▲	▲	▲	▲	▲	▲	▲	▲	▲	▲	▲	▲
France	505	(2.7)	▽	▽	▽	▽	▽	▽	▽	▽	▽	○	○	○	○	□	○	○	○	▲	▲	▲	▲	▲	▲	▲	▲	▲	▲	▲	▲	▲	▲
United States	504	(7.0)	▽	▽	▽	▽	▽	▽	▽	○	○	○	○	○	○	○	□	○	○	○	○	○	○	○	▲	▲	▲	▲	▲	▲	▲	▲	▲
Denmark	497	(2.4)	▽	▽	▽	▽	▽	▽	▽	▽	▽	▽	○	▽	○	○	○	□	○	○	○	○	▲	▲	▲	▲	▲	▲	▲	▲	▲	▲	▲
Switzerland	494	(4.2)	▽	▽	▽	▽	▽	▽	▽	▽	▽	▽	○	▽	○	○	○	○	□	○	○	○	○	○	○	○	▲	▲	▲	▲	▲	▲	▲
Spain	493	(2.7)	▽	▽	▽	▽	▽	▽	▽	▽	▽	▽	▽	▽	▽	▽	○	○	○	□	○	○	○	○	○	○	▲	▲	▲	▲	▲	▲	▲
Czech Republic	492	(2.4)	▽	▽	▽	▽	▽	▽	▽	▽	▽	▽	▽	▽	▽	▽	○	○	○	○	□	○	○	○	○	○	▲	▲	▲	▲	▲	▲	▲
Italy	487	(2.9)	▽	▽	▽	▽	▽	▽	▽	▽	▽	▽	▽	▽	▽	▽	○	○	○	○	○	□	○	○	○	○	○	▲	▲	▲	▲	▲	▲
Germany	484	(2.5)	▽	▽	▽	▽	▽	▽	▽	▽	▽	▽	▽	▽	▽	▽	○	▽	○	○	○	○	□	○	○	○	○	▲	▲	▲	▲	▲	▲
Liechtenstein	483	(4.1)	▽	▽	▽	▽	▽	▽	▽	▽	▽	▽	▽	▽	▽	▽	○	▽	○	○	○	○	○	□	○	○	○	○	▲	▲	▲	▲	▲
Hungary	480	(4.0)	▽	▽	▽	▽	▽	▽	▽	▽	▽	▽	▽	▽	▽	▽	▽	▽	○	○	○	○	○	○	□	○	○	○	▲	▲	▲	▲	▲
Poland	479	(4.5)	▽	▽	▽	▽	▽	▽	▽	▽	▽	▽	▽	▽	▽	▽	▽	▽	○	○	○	○	○	○	○	□	○	○	▲	▲	▲	▲	▲
Greece	474	(5.0)	▽	▽	▽	▽	▽	▽	▽	▽	▽	▽	▽	▽	▽	▽	▽	▽	▽	▽	▽	○	○	○	○	○	□	○	○	○	▲	▲	▲
Portugal	470	(4.5)	▽	▽	▽	▽	▽	▽	▽	▽	▽	▽	▽	▽	▽	▽	▽	▽	▽	▽	▽	▽	▽	○	○	○	○	□	○	○	▲	▲	▲
Russian Fed.	462	(4.2)	▽	▽	▽	▽	▽	▽	▽	▽	▽	▽	▽	▽	▽	▽	▽	▽	▽	▽	▽	▽	▽	▽	▽	▽	○	○	□	○	▲	▲	▲
Latvia	458	(5.3)	▽	▽	▽	▽	▽	▽	▽	▽	▽	▽	▽	▽	▽	▽	▽	▽	▽	▽	▽	▽	▽	▽	▽	▽	○	○	○	□	▲	▲	▲
Luxembourg	441	(1.6)	▽	▽	▽	▽	▽	▽	▽	▽	▽	▽	▽	▽	▽	▽	▽	▽	▽	▽	▽	▽	▽	▽	▽	▽	▽	▽	▽	▽	□	▲	▲
Mexico	422	(3.3)	▽	▽	▽	▽	▽	▽	▽	▽	▽	▽	▽	▽	▽	▽	▽	▽	▽	▽	▽	▽	▽	▽	▽	▽	▽	▽	▽	▽	▽	□	▲
Brazil	396	(3.1)	▽	▽	▽	▽	▽	▽	▽	▽	▽	▽	▽	▽	▽	▽	▽	▽	▽	▽	▽	▽	▽	▽	▽	▽	▽	▽	▽	▽	▽	▽	□

Instructions

Read across the row for a country to compare performance with the countries listed along the top of the chart. The symbols indicate whether the mean performance of the country in the row is significantly lower than that of the comparison country, significantly higher than that of the comparison country, or if there is no statistically significant difference between the mean performance of the two countries.

▲ Mean performance statistically significantly higher than in comparison country.
○ No statistically significant difference from comparison country.
▽ Mean performance statistically significantly lower than in comparison country.

Statistically significantly above the OECD average
Not statistically significantly different from the OECD average
Statistically significantly below the OECD average

Source: OECD PISA database, 2001. Table 4.1.

literacy scale that maps on to the described scales. The combined reading literacy scale was constructed to have a mean performance score of 500 and a standard deviation of 100 across OECD countries.

Figure 4.1 shows the mean score and standard error for each country on the combined reading literacy scale.[1] It also compares the performances of countries, and indicates whether the performance of any one country is significantly higher than, lower than, or not different from, the performance of every other participating country.[2]

Box 4.1: Is the difference in scores significant?

When comparing mean scores it is important to take account of the fact that not all differences in scores are statistically significant. There is a degree of error associated with any measurement, and the extent of the error depends on factors such as sample size, sampling methodology and the instrument used. Because of this error, differences in the mean scores achieved by countries may in some cases not represent differences in the mean abilities of the underlying populations. A statistical test is applied to the difference between the means of different countries. If the probability of the difference occurring by chance is less than five per cent, the difference is deemed to be significant.

Countries' mean scores on the combined reading literacy scale range from 396 (Brazil) to 546 (Finland). This range is equivalent to slightly more than two levels on the five-level scale: the average Finnish student performs at the upper end of Level 3, while the average Brazilian student performs at the upper end of Level 1.[3]

The means of 22 countries are within Level 3, eight are within Level 2, and one is within Level 1. The means of five countries (Denmark, France, Norway, Switzerland and the United States) are not significantly different from the OECD average. Fourteen countries (Brazil, the Czech Republic, Germany, Greece, Hungary, Italy, Latvia, Liechtenstein, Luxembourg, Mexico, Poland, Portugal, the Russian Federation and Spain) have means significantly below the OECD average, and 12 (Australia, Austria, Belgium, Canada, Finland, Iceland, Ireland, Japan, Korea, New Zealand, Sweden and the United Kingdom) are significantly above it.

For another picture of the general level of achievement in each country, it is useful to observe where the largest proportion of each population is situated. In the case of 23 countries, this is at Level 3, as Figure 4.2 shows.

In Belgium, Finland and New Zealand, the most common level is Level 4. The most common level for students in Latvia, Luxembourg, Mexico and the Russian Federation is Level 2, and for Brazil it is Level 1.

Figure 4.2

Proficiency level accounting for the highest proportion of students on the combined reading literacy scale

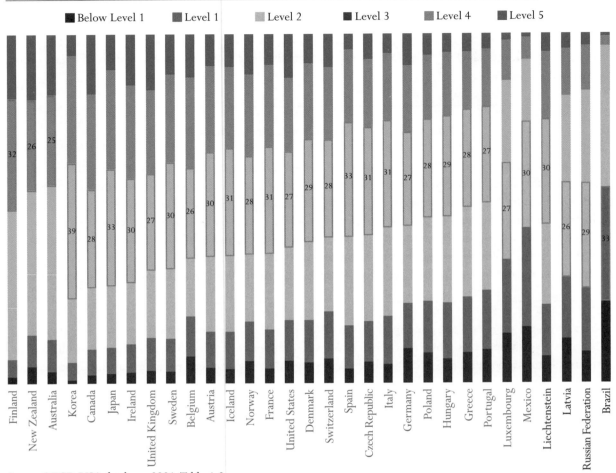

Source: OECD PISA database, 2001. Table 4.2.

Box 4.2: Means and score distributions

Mean scores provide a general indication of the overall performance of each country, but they provide no information about the range and distribution of performances within countries. It is possible for countries to achieve similar means yet to have quite different score patterns.

Consider the graph of three hypothetical countries' performance on the combined reading literacy scale, as shown in Figure 4.3.

Country A has a mean score well above the OECD average, and a narrow distribution of results on the combined reading literacy scale. Country B has a mean below that of Country A, but still above the mean for the OECD average, and a narrow distribution of results. The mean for Country C is identical to that of Country B, but scores are more widely distributed in Country C. This means that

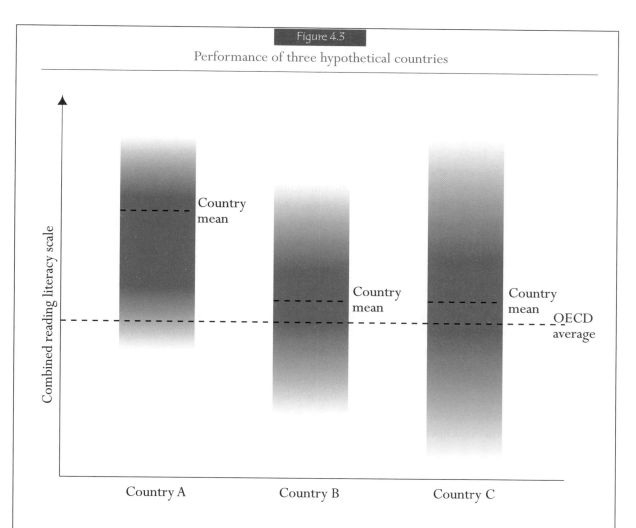

Figure 4.3

Performance of three hypothetical countries

there are more high achievers at the extreme top end of the range, and more low achievers at the extreme bottom end.

There would be little argument that of these three countries, Country A has the most desirable set of results. The students in Country A perform relatively well on average, with the best students achieving excellent results and even the least able students achieving close to the international mean. One could infer that either the population is homogeneous to begin with, or that the education system is succeeding in minimising any inequalities. Whatever the explanation, the high general level of achievement combined with a compact spread of scores indicates that most students have the necessary literacy skills to benefit from and contribute to modern society, and to develop their potential.

Now consider Countries B and C. Which of these countries offers the more desirable distribution of results? In Country B, even the lowest performing students achieve reasonable levels of proficiency, so that almost everyone is able to deal with the normal literacy demands occurring in the daily life of an adult. For example, they will be able to follow current events in a newspaper; to apply for a job; to make sense of the policy statements of a local government candidate; or to read a novel for pleasure. On the other hand, the most proficient readers in this population are not on a par with the best readers worldwide. The country may lack a critical mass of people who are able to compete with the best and brightest internationally, and this may put the country as a whole at a disadvantage. It is also possible that the potential of the most able students is not being fulfilled, although comparatively large resources are being devoted to the least able.

In Country C, the highest performing students are at least as proficient as the best in either of the other countries, and are potentially in a position to lead their country in global contexts. Conversely, it is unlikely that the least proficient students in Country C can meet many of the literacy demands of adult life. This may not matter in a narrow economic sense (even today there are occupations requiring little or no reading), and indeed some would argue that providing high levels of education for everyone leads to shortages of workers for unskilled positions. But individuals are not just economic units: they have families, live in communities and vote for their representatives in government. It is not desirable to have a large proportion of the adult population unable to function in family, cultural and political contexts. In a modern democracy, it is desirable for everyone to be able to fulfil the literacy demands imposed by family life (for example, reading an article about baby care), by community life (for example, reading a notice of a public information evening about a shopping centre development) and by political life.

Clearly, similar mean performances in two different countries may mask very different distributions of ability, but whatever a country's decision about how best to organise its education system and its resources, it is surely a matter of social justice that education systems should aim to equip all students to fulfil their potential.

Score distributions: The spread of scores for different populations

Figure 4.4 shows variation in student performance on the combined reading literacy scale. The dispersion of scores around the mean is summarised in the standard deviation statistic. In interpreting the standard deviation for any country it is useful to bear in mind that 95 per cent of the performances in a normal distribution are accounted for within two standard deviations of the mean, and 68 per cent within one standard deviation. On the PISA reading literacy scale, one standard deviation is the equivalent of 100 points.

Finland's pattern of scores is closest to the distribution represented by Country A in Figure 4.3 above. With a mean score of 546, significantly higher than that of any other country, Finland also shows a relatively small spread of scores. Its standard deviation is 89. Only four OECD countries have smaller standard deviations.

Korea and New Zealand could be regarded as comparable to Country B and Country C, respectively, in Figure 4.3. Both countries have means above the OECD average that are not significantly different from each other; but while the most compact distribution is represented by Korea's standard deviation of 70, New Zealand has the second largest spread of scores of all participating countries.

Two other countries with relatively little dispersion of scores are Brazil and Mexico. For both countries the standard deviation is 86. It should be noted, however, that low school enrolment is likely to play a part

Figure 4.4

Distribution of student performance on the combined reading literacy scale

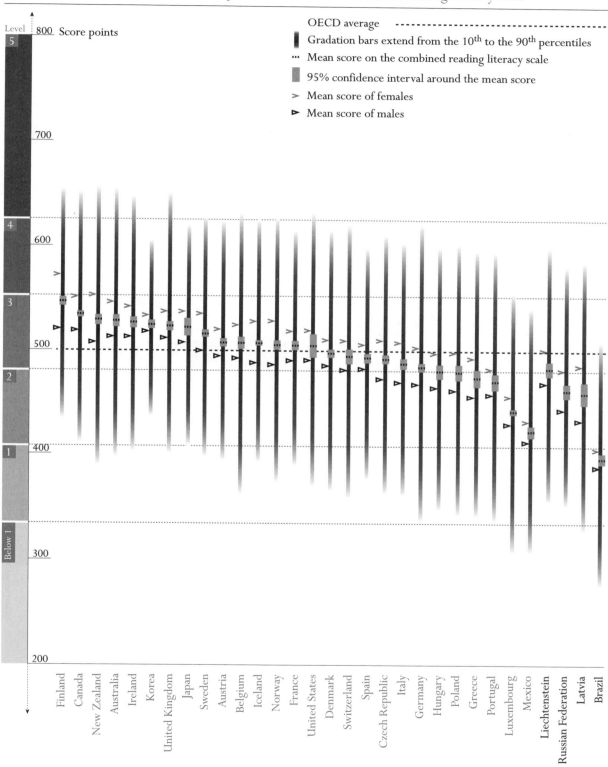

Source: OECD PISA database, 2001. Table 4.16.

in this result. For example, in the case of Brazil only about 53 per cent of the population of 15-year-olds are enrolled in grades 7 to 10, and are covered by the PISA assessment. It is therefore likely that the low standard deviation figures are related to the definition of the target population: a large proportion of the population likely to be at the lowest ability levels is excluded. For details on the population coverage and exclusion rate, see *PISA 2000 Technical Report* (OECD, 2002*b*).

Figure 4.5

Percentage of students performing at each of the proficiency levels
on the combined reading literacy scale

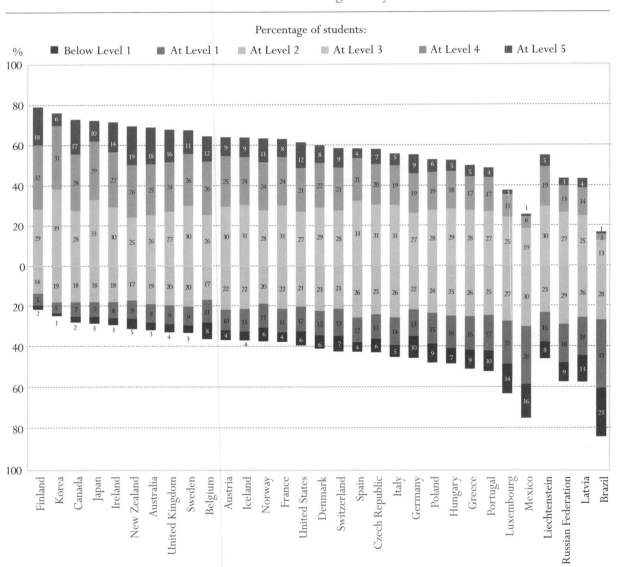

Source: OECD PISA database, 2001. Table 4.2.

It is worth considering the contrast between the standard deviations of Italy and Germany, whose mean scores of 487 and 484 are not significantly different. Italy's standard deviation of 91 is the seventh smallest, whereas Germany's 111 is the largest. This contrast is a reminder that mean scores, although a useful summary of overall performance, do not express differences in distribution.

Another way of looking at distribution is by comparing the percentage of students at each level of proficiency. Figure 4.5 shows the percentage of students at each of Levels 1 to 5, and below Level 1, on the combined reading literacy scale.

Not surprisingly, the picture that emerges from the distribution of students in each country across PISA levels is similar to that which emerges from comparing their mean and standard deviation statistics. About 60 per cent of Finland's students fall within Levels 3 and 4, while only some 7 per cent are below Level 2. New Zealand's standard deviation of 108 is reflected in its smaller proportion within Levels 3 and 4 (about 50 per cent), and larger proportion at the lower end of the scale: 14 per cent below Level 2. In both Finland and New Zealand, however, 19 per cent are at Level 5.

Given its small standard deviation along with its high mean performance, Korea has most of its students – 70 per cent – clustered at levels 3 and 4. On the other hand, only 6 per cent of students are at Level 5, and 6 per cent are below Level 2. This is the smallest proportion below Level 2 in any country.

Japan's distribution also shows a concentration of students at Levels 3 and 4 (62 per cent), but the pattern is less marked than in the case of Korea. Although its mean is lower than Korea's, Japan has a higher proportion at Level 5 (10 per cent).

Spain's standard deviation of 85 reflects a similar spread of scores to Japan's, although the general level of achievement is significantly lower. Thirty-three per cent of Spanish students are at Level 3. Only Japan and Korea have more students at that level. On the other hand, the next largest group of Spanish students is at Level 2 (26 per cent) while the next largest group in both Japan and Korea is at Level 4.

Score distributions: Proportions at the extremes of the scale

Considerable differences in the distribution of reading literacy can be seen in the proportions of countries' populations that can be categorised as either highly literate or having very limited skills in reading literacy. Figure 4.6 shows the percentage of each student population at Level 5, and below Level 2. Level 5 accounts for between 1 per cent and 19 per cent of students in each country. In the OECD countries, the average proportion at this level is 9 per cent. In Australia, Canada, Finland, New Zealand and the United Kingdom, Level 5 accounts for at least 16 per cent of students. As already noted, Korea, whose mean score is not significantly different from the scores of Australia, New Zealand and the United Kingdom, has only 6 per cent at Level 5.

Countries with similar proportions of students achieving Level 5 often have different proportions at other levels, and therefore different mean scores. For example, in Poland, as in Korea, 6 per cent of students are at Level 5, but whereas 47 per cent of Polish students are within Levels 3 and 4, 70 per cent of Korean students are clustered at these levels, resulting in a mean 46 points higher than Poland's. Fourteen per cent of New Zealand's tested population are below Level 2, compared with only 7 per cent in Finland, although both countries have 19 per cent of students at Level 5. In both Austria and Germany the proportion of students at Level 5 is close to the OECD average (8.8 per cent in both cases, compared with 9.5 per cent for the OECD). But Germany's 23 per cent below Level 2 is a considerably higher proportion than the

Figure 4.6

Percentages of students at level 5 and below level 2 on the combined reading literacy scale

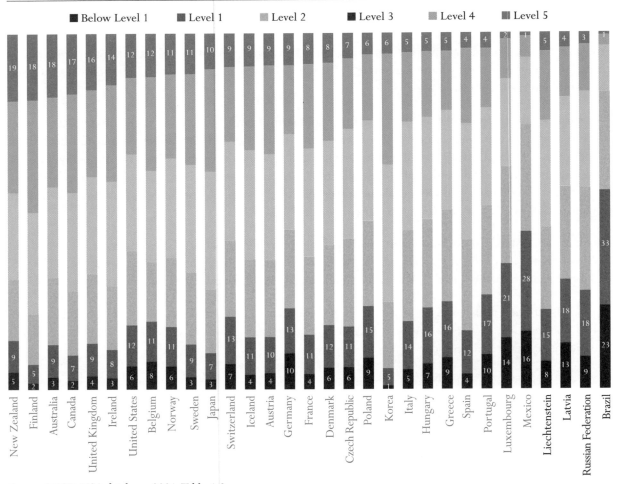

Source: OECD PISA database, 2001. Table 4.2.

average proportion for OECD countries (18 per cent) and contrasts strongly with Austria's 15 per cent. In fact, Germany has the fifth highest percentage of students scoring below Level 1.

Every country has some students whose literacy skills are lower than the most basic level described by the reading literacy scale. The proportion of students in this category varies between 1 per cent (Korea) and 23 per cent (Brazil). The OECD country with the highest proportion below Level 1 is Mexico, with 16 per cent. In 18 countries more than 5 per cent of students fail to achieve Level 1. Students who score below Level 1 are not capable of the most basic type of reading that PISA seeks to measure. Yet this does not suggest that they have no literacy skills. It is likely that most of these students have the technical capacity to read. However, they have serious difficulties in using reading literacy as an effective tool to advance and extend their knowledge and skills in other areas. Thus they may be at risk not only of difficulties in their initial transition from education to work but also of failure to benefit from further education and learning opportunities throughout life.

It is worth noting that the relative proportions of students at the lowest levels may have been influenced to some extent by variation in the decisions made by different countries about which students to exclude from the study. Countries were permitted to exclude from the test students from a number of categories, including those with mental, emotional or physical disabilities that would prevent them performing in the PISA assessment situation, and non-native language speakers with less than one year's instruction in the language of the assessment. All but three countries achieved the required coverage of at least 95 per cent of the desired target population, and half of the countries achieved 98 per cent or more. The ceiling for population exclusion of 5 per cent ensures that potential bias resulting from exclusion is likely to remain within one standard error of sampling. Potential candidates for exclusion are likely to have low reading literacy skills. Overall exclusion rates in PISA 2000 are reported in PISA 2000 Technical Report (2002*b*).

Performance on the aspect subscales of reading literacy

Having discussed performance on the combined reading literacy scale, we now turn to a more detailed view of reading. In OECD PISA, reading literacy is modelled as a complex of interrelated perspectives, strategies or approaches, known as "aspects": retrieving information, interpreting texts and reflection and evaluation. Retrieving information is, as the name suggests, concerned with identifying one or more discrete facts or ideas in the text. Interpreting requires students to demonstrate their skill at making inferences and drawing together parts of the text. In the reflection and evaluation aspect, students must relate the text to their own understanding of the world outside it. All three aspects are essential for meeting the demands of reading in the modern world, and all three can operate at various levels of complexity or difficulty.

Countries' correlations between the aspects are generally high, but not uniform. They are highest between retrieving information and interpreting texts, where the median correlation is 0.95. For individual countries the lowest correlation between these two aspects is 0.90 and the highest is 0.96. Between retrieving information and reflection and evaluation, the correlation coefficients are generally lower, ranging from 0.74 to 0.92, with a median value of 0.88. Between interpreting texts and reflection and evaluation, correlations range from 0.80 to 0.95, with a median of 0.92[4]. Despite the size of these correlations and the general similarity between the results for the aspects and the results for the combined reading literacy scale, there are noteworthy differences in some countries' patterns of performance across the three aspect subscales. Such interactions may indicate different pedagogical emphases between countries, and may suggest potential improvements for policy-makers to consider. For example, at a national level, strong performance on the retrieving information subscale and weak performance on the reflection and evaluation subscale would suggest that future citizens, although highly attuned to factual content, might have limited capacity to form critical judgments about what they read. Policy-makers alerted to such a trend of performance in their country may consider encouraging increased educational emphasis on the skills of critical literacy. Conversely, countries with relatively strong performance in reflecting and weaker performance in retrieving information might consider concentrating teaching efforts on promoting search skills and accuracy in reading.

In this section of the report we discuss the mean performances of countries in each of the aspects, and distributions of performances within each aspect. We then examine differential performances across aspects in individual countries.

Mean scores

Table 4.3 shows each country's mean score and standard deviation for each of the aspects, along with the associated standard errors.

The OECD average score for retrieving information is 498. The mean scores for 12 countries are significantly above the OECD average, 13 are significantly below it, and six countries have scores not significantly different from the OECD average. Countries' mean scores range from 556 (Finland) to 365 (Brazil). Among OECD countries, Mexico has the lowest mean score (402). This range of mean proficiency scores, the equivalent of almost three proficiency levels, is the broadest for any aspect. Table 4.4 compares the performances of countries in the retrieving information aspect, and indicates whether the performance of any one country is significantly higher than, lower than, or not different from, the performance of every other participating country.

On the interpreting texts subscale, country mean scores range from 555 in Finland to 400 in Brazil. Mexico has the lowest mean score among OECD Member countries, 419. Twelve countries have means significantly higher than the OECD average of 501, 14 are significantly below it, and 5 are not significantly different from it. The range of mean scores is equivalent to a little over two proficiency levels. Table 4.5 compares the performances of countries in the interpreting texts aspect, and indicates whether the performance of any one country is significantly higher than, lower than, or not different from, the performance of every other participating country.

In the case of reflection and evaluation, the highest mean score is 542 in Canada, and the lowest is 417 in Brazil. Of the OECD countries, Luxembourg has the lowest mean score, 442. The range of country means is equivalent to somewhat less than two proficiency levels, which is less than for either of the other aspects. Ten countries are significantly above the OECD mean of 502. This figure is smaller than for the other aspects. Table 4.6 compares the performances of countries in the reflection and evaluation aspect, and indicates whether the performance of any one country is significantly higher than, lower than, or not different from, the performance of every other participating country.

In each of the aspects, the mean scores of either 21 or 22 countries fall within Level 3, and the means of between seven and nine countries are within Level 2. Only Finland's mean scores for retrieving information and interpreting texts fall just within Level 4. Mean scores for Brazil and Mexico are within Level 1 in retrieving information, and Brazil's is also within the range of Level 1 in interpreting texts.

Distribution of reading literacy within countries on the aspect subscales

Retrieving information

The OECD average standard deviation for retrieving information is 111, as shown in Table 4.3, indicating that the dispersion of scores is greater in retrieving information than in the other two aspects (100 in interpreting texts and 106 in reflection and evaluation). Standard deviations for individual countries range from 82 (Korea) to 120 (Belgium). The spread of Belgium's scores contrasts with that of Austria (standard deviation 96), although the mean scores of these two countries are not significantly different. Belgium has larger proportions of students than Austria below Level 1 and at Level 5, and smaller proportions at Levels 2 and 3. Belgium's large variance may be associated with differences between its two major language communities (Flemish and French).

Table 4.7 shows the percentage of 15-year-olds in each country performing at each of the PISA levels of proficiency on the retrieving information subscale.

In 22 of the 31 countries reporting, the most common level in retrieving information is Level 3. This proportion, although large, is slightly smaller than in the other aspects.

The reading performance of 15-year-olds **CHAPTER 4**

In retrieving information, there is a large number countries with high proportions of students at the lower end of the scale: in 16 countries at least 20 per cent of students are below Level 2, and in seven of these countries the figure is over 30 per cent. The figures below Level 2 for Brazil and Mexico (68 per cent and 52 per cent respectively) are especially high in retrieving information.

Countries with similar proportions of students below Level 2 often produce very different results further up the scale. For example, although Korea and Finland both have 8 per cent of students below Level 2, 54 per cent of Finnish students are at Levels 4 and 5, compared with 41 per cent of Korea's. Similarly, in both Belgium and Denmark, 19 per cent of students are below Level 2 in retrieving information, but 43 per cent and 32 per cent respectively are at Levels 4 and 5.

Interpreting texts

In interpreting texts, as elsewhere, the largest proportion of students in most countries falls within Level 3. There are 23 countries in this category. The number of countries with 20 per cent or more below Level 2 is smallest in interpreting texts: 11 countries, compared with 16 in retrieving information and 15 in reflection and evaluation.

In several countries, notably Belgium, Germany and New Zealand, the presence of a moderate to high proportion of students unable to achieve more than Level 1 goes hand in hand with a sizeable proportion performing at the upper end of the scale. The high level of dispersion in these countries is reflected in their standard deviation figures, which range from 105 to 111, as shown in Table 4.3. New Zealand's standard deviation (111) is the largest for any country. It contrasts dramatically with the standard deviation for Korea (69), which is the smallest for any country, but is nonetheless associated with mean scores of 525 – only 1 point different from New Zealand's. The international average standard deviation is 100, a lower figure in interpreting texts than in either of the other aspects (111 in retrieving information and 106 in reflection and evaluation).

Table 4.8 shows the percentage of 15-year-olds in each country performing at each of the PISA levels of proficiency on the interpreting texts subscale.

Reflection and evaluation

In reflection and evaluation, as shown in Table 4.9, once again the largest proportion of students in most countries – 24 – are at level 3. In five countries – Canada, Finland, Ireland, Korea and the United Kingdom – more than 90 per cent of the population perform above Level 1. In 15 countries more than 20 per cent of students are below Level 2.

With a standard deviation of 124 (see Table 4.3) Germany's scores are by far the most widely dispersed of any country on the reflection and evaluation subscale – and indeed are more widely dispersed than the scores of any other country on the combined reading literacy scale or any of the other subscales. If Germany's distribution is compared with those of Portugal and Hungary, whose mean scores are not significantly different, it is clear that Germany has markedly more students at Level 5 and below Level 1, and fewer at Levels 2 and 3.

© OECD 2002

89

Comparing performance on the aspect subscales within countries

Mean scores

While the OECD averages on the three aspect subscales are almost identical (498, 501 and 502 score points in retrieving information, interpreting texts and reflection and evaluation respectively), each of the aspects appears to have been easier for some countries, and more difficult for others.

Three countries – Finland, France and Liechtenstein – show relatively strong performance in retrieving information, with a difference of approximately 20 points between mean proficiency in reflection and

Difference in performance between the retrieving information and the reflection and evaluation subscales

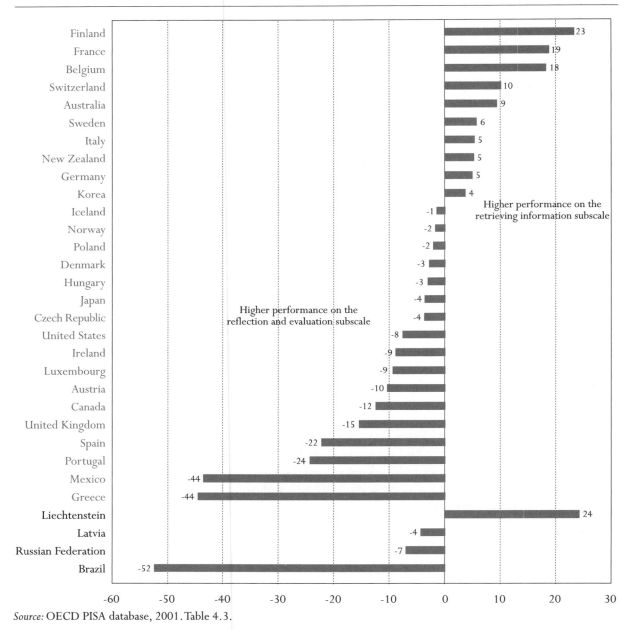

Source: OECD PISA database, 2001. Table 4.3.

Figure 4.7b

Difference in performance between the retrieving information and the interpreting texts subscales

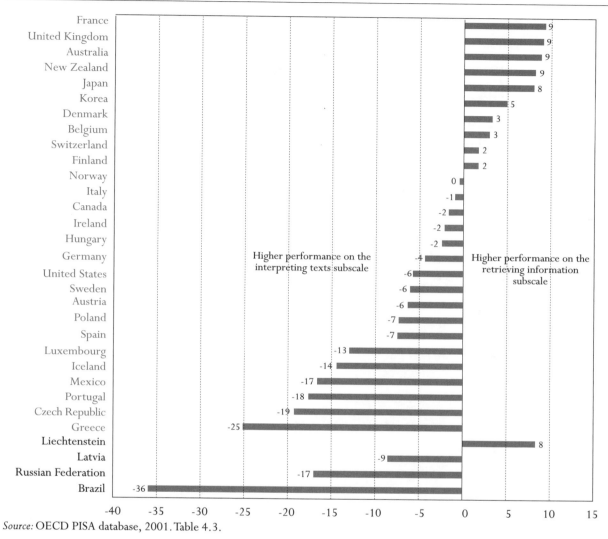

Source: OECD PISA database, 2001. Table 4.3.

evaluation and in retrieving information in favour of the latter (see Figure 4.7a). The Czech Republic, Iceland, Luxembourg and the Russian Federation perform best, relative to other subscales, on the interpreting texts subscale, though by quite small margins in some cases. Mean proficiency is strongest on the reflection and evaluation subscale, and weakest on the retrieving information subscale, to quite a marked degree in the case of Brazil, Greece, Mexico, Portugal and Spain: in these five countries there is a difference of more than 20 PISA score points in the means on the two subscales. It is interesting to note the presence of all four Spanish and Portuguese-speaking countries in this group, which may suggest a linguistic, cultural or pedagogical effect.

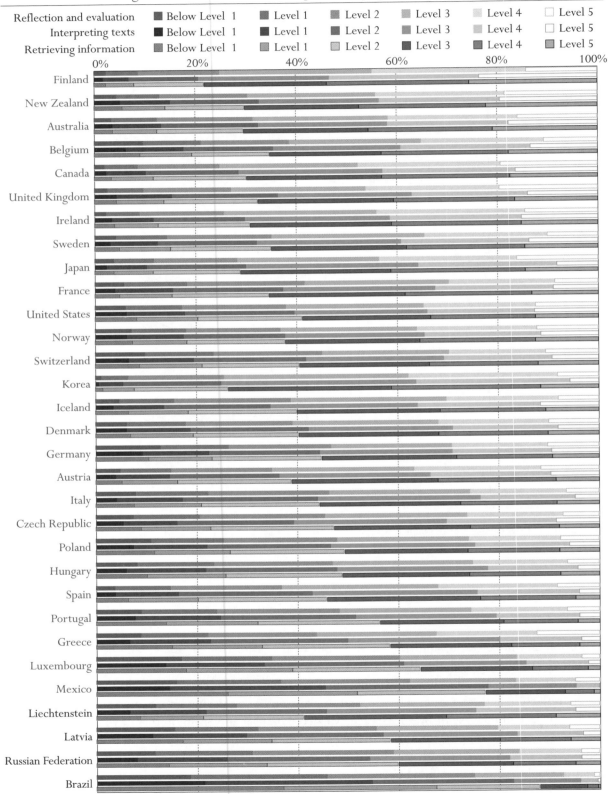

Figure 4.8

Percentage of students at each level of proficiency by reading aspect subscale

Source: OECD PISA database, 2001. Tables 4.7, 4.8 and 4.9.

Box 4.3: Evaluating within-country differences in performance on subscales

Results for retrieving information, interpreting texts and reflection and evaluation are not independent measures, since the levels of difficulty of all the tasks were estimated in the same analysis. The same holds true for the continuous texts and non-continuous texts subscales. Standard tests of significance are therefore not appropriate. The following discussion of within-country profiles of performance on the three aspect subscales, and on the two text format subscales, is based on the observation of patterns in the data, rather than on statistical tests of significance.

There does not appear to be any other obvious pattern within linguistically or culturally linked groups of countries. For example, amongst predominantly English-speaking countries, Canada, Ireland, the United Kingdom and the United States appear to perform more strongly on the reflection and evaluation subscale, while Australia and New Zealand perform more strongly on the retrieving information subscale. Amongst Northern European countries, Finland performs comparatively well in retrieving information and interpreting tasks; Iceland and Sweden perform best on the interpreting texts subscale; and there is virtually no difference in performance across the aspect subscales in Denmark or Norway. In countries with major German-speaking populations, Germany, Liechtenstein and Switzerland perform relatively poorly on the reflection and evaluation subscale, but this is not the case in Austria.

Distribution

Figure 4.8 shows the proportion of the population of each country falling within each of the five proficiency levels, and below the lowest level, on the three aspect subscales.

In the case of Finland, a large difference between the mean scores for retrieving information and reflection and evaluation corresponds to differences in distribution at Levels 3, 4 and 5. The greatest difference is at Level 5, where only 14 per cent of Finnish students are placed in reflection and evaluation, compared with 24 and 26 per cent in interpreting and retrieving information respectively.

Several countries have relatively large proportions within the two highest levels in one aspect: retrieving information in the case of Canada, France, Liechtenstein and the United Kingdom, and reflection and evaluation in the case of Spain. On the other hand, Japan's proportion at Level 5 is markedly lower in interpreting texts than in the other two aspects, and this is balanced by higher proportions at Levels 2 and 3. In the Russian Federation, a relatively large proportion at Level 3 in interpreting texts is balanced by lower numbers at Level 1, not at Level 5, as in the case of Japan.

In Brazil, the major difference between proportions of students in different aspects appears below Level 1, where there are considerably more students on the retrieving information subscale (37 per cent) than on the other aspect subscales (22 per cent in interpreting and 19 per cent in reflection and evaluation).

The pattern for Mexico is similar, although less marked, with 26 per cent of students below Level 1 in retrieving information, compared with 15 and 16 per cent in the other aspects.

Greek students are clustered more heavily below Level 2 in retrieving information than in the other aspects (33 per cent compared with 23 per cent in interpreting texts and 22 per cent in reflection and evaluation), and at Levels 4 and 5 in reflection and evaluation (33 per cent as against 20 per cent in interpreting texts and 18 per cent in retrieving information). The smaller proportions at the ends of the interpreting texts subscale are reflected in Greece's low standard deviation figure of 89 for interpreting texts, compared with 109 for retrieving information and 115 for reflection and evaluation.

Performance on the text format subscales of reading

In this section of the report we consider how countries perform in tasks related to texts with different formats. As discussed in the previous chapter, texts selected for the PISA reading literacy assessment cover a wide variety of text types that are broadly sorted into two categories: continuous texts and non-continuous texts. Continuous texts are in prose, and consist of paragraphs made up of complete sentences. They include narrative, exposition, argument and injunction. Non-continuous texts (sometimes called documents) may include sentences, but are not in paragraph form; they may include graphics of various kinds as well as words, and the layout of the material on the page is generally critical to its meaning. Some examples of non-continuous texts are tables, charts, maps and forms.

Relative strength or weakness in the continuous and non-continuous tasks in PISA reading gives some indications about pedagogical and curriculum practices in countries. Traditionally, reading has been identified mainly with prose: language-of-instruction teachers and systems have concentrated their attention on ensuring that students can read prose literature and exposition. However, in other areas of the curriculum, reading and understanding of non-prose texts is at least as important. For example, students need to be able to read and interpret maps and tables in social studies, and graphs and diagrams in science. Moreover, beyond school, documents make up a large proportion of adults' required reading: tax forms, public transport timetables, graphs of domestic energy consumption and so on. In modern societies, in the workplace, at home and in the community, it is important that citizens should be able to comprehend non-continuous texts. It is of interest therefore, in a study investigating the readiness of young people for the literacy demands of adult life, to assess their proficiency in dealing with non-continuous texts as well as continuous texts. And it follows that evidence of any comparative weakness in dealing with texts in one or the other of these formats might be addressed by devoting formal teaching time to their distinctive structures and purposes.

Mean scores

Table 4.10 presents each country's mean score and standard deviation, and the associated standard errors, for the continuous texts and non-continuous text format subscales.

The OECD average on the continuous texts subscale is 501 score points. Scores on tasks related to continuous texts range from 408 (Brazil) to 544 (Finland). To put this another way, Brazil's average student performs at the boundary between Level 1 and Level 2, while Finland's average student performs near the top of Level 3, a difference of almost two proficiency levels. The mean for most countries falls within Level 3. The exceptions are Brazil, Latvia, Luxembourg, Mexico, Portugal and the Russian Federation, which have means within Level 2.

On the non-continuous texts subscale, the means of countries range from 366 (Brazil) to 554 (Finland), with an OECD average of 500; that is, country means range from within Level 1 (Brazil and Mexico) to within Level 4 (Finland). As with the continuous texts subscale, however, for the majority of countries the mean score is within Level 3. Eight countries – Greece, Hungary, Italy, Latvia, Luxembourg, Poland, Portugal and the Russian Federation – have means falling within Level 2.

Tables 4.11 and 4.12 compare the mean performances of countries on the continuous texts and non-continuous texts subscales respectively, indicating whether the performance of each country is significantly higher than, lower than, or not different from, that of the other countries and the OECD average.

Distribution of reading literacy within countries on the text format subscales

Continuous texts

On the continuous texts subscale, the OECD average of the standard deviation is 101 score points, and ranges from 69 for Korea to 115 for Germany (see Table 4.10). These two figures are at some distance from the second smallest and second largest standard deviations, which are 84 for Spain and 110 for New Zealand respectively. There is no significant difference between the mean scores of Korea, with the smallest standard deviation, and New Zealand, with the second largest.

Elsewhere, countries with mean scores that are not significantly different sometimes show very different degrees of dispersion of results, as measured by standard deviation. For example, consider the contrast between the standard deviations of the following pairs of countries, which have similar means: Germany (mean 484, standard deviation 115) and Hungary (481, 92); Switzerland (494, 104) and Spain (493, 84); Belgium (503, 108) and France (500, 94); and New Zealand (526, 110) and Korea (530, 69). Another perspective on the distribution of literacy within countries is afforded by looking at percentages of students at each proficiency level, as shown in Table 4.13. On the continuous texts subscale, more than 40 per cent of students in Australia, Canada, Finland, Ireland and New Zealand have proficiency levels at or above Level 4. In Finland, this figure is almost 50 per cent. By contrast, in six countries (Brazil, Latvia, Luxembourg, Mexico, Portugal and the Russian Federation) at least 50 per cent of students are at or below Level 2, and in the same group of six countries at least 25 per cent of students perform at or below Level 1.

Non-continuous texts

In the case of non-continuous texts, the standard deviations of countries range from 81 to 114 score points (see Table 4.10). The OECD average standard deviation is 109. All but three countries (Australia, Germany and the United Kingdom) show more variation in proficiency over the non-continuous texts subscale than the continuous texts subscale.

As with the continuous texts subscale, countries with similar means on the non-continuous texts subscale display some differences in their patterns of dispersion, but in this case the phenomenon is less marked. The most notable example of countries with similar means but contrasting distribution on the non-continuous texts subscale concerns the two countries with the highest and lowest standard deviations: Korea (mean 517, standard deviation 81) and Belgium (mean 516, standard deviation 114).

It can be seen in Table 4.14 that the percentages of students at each proficiency level on the non-continuous texts subscale are similar to those on the continuous texts subscale. Countries with more than 40 per cent of students at Levels 4 or 5 on the non-continuous texts subscale are Australia, Belgium, Canada, Finland, Ireland, New Zealand, Sweden and the United Kingdom. In the case of Finland, this figure is over 50 per cent. Eight countries have more than half of their students performing at or below Level 2 on the non-continuous texts subscale: Brazil, Greece, Latvia, Luxembourg, Mexico, Poland, Portugal and the Russian Federation.

Comparing performance on the text format subscales within countries

The assessment instrument was designed so that tasks based on texts in each format covered a range of difficulties, formats (multiple-choice and constructed-response) and aspects, and related to a wide variety of text types. This means that any differences in performance on the two text format subscales can be attributed to the format variable rather than the effects of other variables.

Mean scores

The OECD average performances in continuous and non-continuous tasks are almost identical, the OECD averages for continuous and non-continuous tasks being 501 and 500 respectively (see Table 4.10). The correlation of performance on the two text format subscales ranges from 0.83 to 0.94, with a median of 0.90. Such similarities might lead to the expectation that the performance of a country's students on one of the subscales would be quite close to their performance on the other. There are, in fact, notable differences in many countries in both mean performance and distribution on the two types of tasks as shown in Figure 4.9.

Figure 4.9

Difference in reading literacy performance on the continuous and non-continuous texts subscales

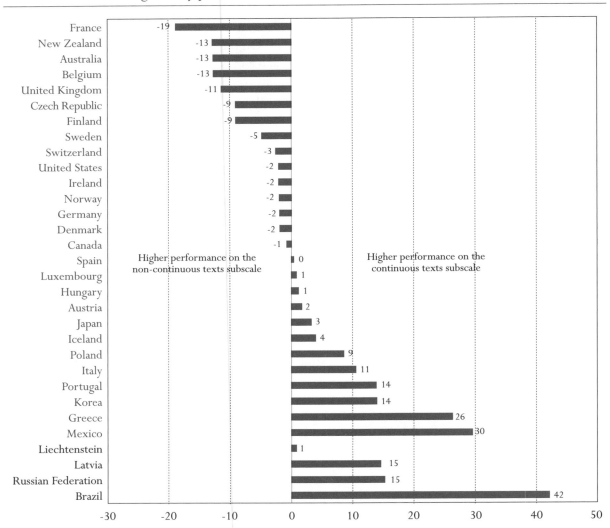

Source: OECD PISA database, 2001. Table 4.10.

In 16 of the participating countries, including all the predominantly English-speaking countries, the Northern European countries (apart from Iceland) and all the countries with French-speaking populations except Luxembourg, students perform at least as well on the non-continuous texts as on the continuous texts subscale. The country with the largest difference (19 PISA scale points) in favour of non-continuous texts is France. Other countries with a difference in means of about 10 points in favour of non-continuous texts are Australia, Belgium, the Czech Republic, Finland, New Zealand and the United Kingdom. In most of these countries, mean scores on the two text format subscales are within the same proficiency level: Level 3. The exception is Finland, whose mean on the continuous texts subscale is within Level 3, and on the non-continuous texts within Level 4.

In eight countries, the average difference between continuous texts and non-continuous texts scores is more than ten points. Included in this group are many of the countries with the lowest mean scores, but also Korea, which is among the most strongly performing countries overall. The means of five countries are within a higher level for continuous than for non-continuous tasks: Greece, Italy and Poland (means within Level 3 for continuous texts and Level 2 for non-continuous texts), and Brazil and Mexico (means within Level 2 for continuous texts and Level 1 for non-continuous texts). As suggested earlier, it may be that more traditional curricula are followed in language subjects in these countries, possibly with stronger emphasis on the development of reading literacy through prose literature and exposition, and less emphasis on non-prose texts found in academic or everyday contexts. This may also account for the relatively weak performance of Japan and Korea in non-continuous texts, or it may be that cultural differences made some non-continuous texts formats unfamiliar, a situation possibly exacerbated by the use of Roman script for the translation of several non-continuous texts.

Distribution

As noted above, the OECD averages on the continuous texts and non-continuous texts subscales are almost identical (501 and 500 score points respectively) but the OECD average standard deviations are somewhat different, 101 and 109. This indicates that, on average, there are wider score ranges on the non-continuous texts subscale than on the continuous texts subscale. Figure 4.10 shows the distribution of students in each participating country over the five proficiency levels on the two text format subscales. The upper bar for each country shows the distribution of performance on the continuous texts subscale, and the lower bar shows the distribution on the non-continuous texts subscale.

In the following countries, the pattern of distribution between levels is similar for each of the two text formats: Australia, Austria, Canada, Denmark, Germany, Iceland, Ireland, Italy, Liechtenstein, Luxembourg, Norway, Poland, Portugal, Switzerland, the United Kingdom and the United States.

In other countries, performance in the two text formats differs. Korea has substantially more students at Level 4 on the continuous texts subscale than on the non-continuous texts subscale, and fewer at Levels 1 and 2. Overall, the distribution of scores for Korea is wider on the non-continuous texts than the continuous texts format subscale, as is the case for most countries. Nonetheless, Korea's standard deviation is lower than that of any other country on both the non-continuous texts and the continuous texts subscale.

The score distributions of Brazil and Mexico are similar to Korea's in that students tend to be grouped higher up the scale in the case of continuous texts than in that of non-continuous texts. However, on both subscales their performance is generally lower than Korea's. In both Brazil and Mexico there are larger percentages of students at Levels 2 and 3 on the continuous texts than on the non-continuous texts

Figure 4.10

Percentage of students at each level of proficiency by text format subscale

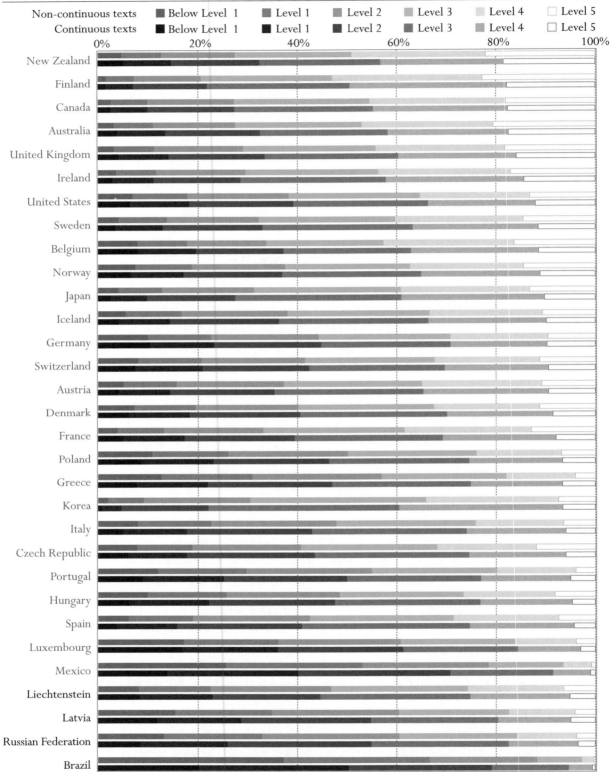

Source: OECD PISA database, 2001. Tables 4.13 and 4.14.

subscale, and many more below Level 1 on the non-continuous texts than on the continuous texts. In the case of the Russian Federation, and in Greece and Latvia, the proportion of students at lower levels is greater on the non-continuous texts than on the continuous texts subscale.

Several other countries show the opposite pattern of distribution. In these countries, there are more students at higher levels of performance in non-continuous than in continuous tasks. Belgium, the Czech Republic, Finland and France have substantially higher percentages of students performing at Level 5 in the non-continuous text items than in the continuous text items, and larger percentages at lower levels on the continuous texts subscale. In the Czech Republic it is particularly at Level 3 that the numbers on the continuous texts subscale are higher than on the non-continuous texts. This concentration of students close to the centre of the distribution is clearly reflected in the Czech Republic's standard deviation for the continuous texts subscale (93), which is markedly lower than that for the non-continuous texts (112). Only four countries have a larger standard deviation on the non-continuous texts subscale, whereas nineteen countries have a wider dispersion than the Czech Republic on the continuous texts format subscale.

The tendency to increased proportions at the extremes of the subscale appears in only one direction: no country has more students at the tails of the distribution for continuous tasks than for non-continuous tasks. Nevertheless, in two countries, students' performances contradict the general trend towards more dispersed scores in non-continuous tasks. On the continuous texts and non-continuous texts subscales respectively, the United Kingdom has standard deviations of 104 and 101, and Germany 115 and 113.

Inequality within and between PISA countries

The question of inequality is relevant to reading literacy because level of literacy has a significant impact on the personal welfare of individuals, on the state of society and on the economic standing of countries in the international arena. The association between level of literacy and life outcomes is dealt with more fully in Chapter 8. Here, by examining the extent of the gap between the most and least able readers, we draw attention to the likely differences between the two groups' access to educational, social and economic opportunities.

One way of measuring inequality is to compare the size of the gap between the least and most able groups within a country. We take as our measure the difference in performance between the 90th percentile and 10th percentile score for a given country. The former is the point in the distribution that is better than 90 per cent of the national sample. The 10th percentile is the point at which performance is better than only 10 per cent of the national sample. The difference between these scores represents the range over which the middle 80 per cent of the country's students are spread. The greater this spread, the greater the difference between the students in the groups at the extremes of the distributions, and the more inequality.

Figure 4.11 shows the differences between the 90th and 10th percentile scores on the combined reading literacy scale. Countries are ranked in the figure according to the magnitude of the difference on the combined reading literacy scale. Tables 4.16 to 4.21 show the standard deviation, and the 10th and 90th percentile figures for the combined reading literacy scale and for the five subscales.

In Korea, the range of scores from the 90th to the 10th percentile on the combined reading scale is around 175 points, just under two and a half proficiency levels. This is by far the smallest difference for any OECD country. Japan and Spain show the next smallest difference, 218 points, or a gap of three proficiency levels.

Figure 4.11

Differences in scores at tenth and ninetieth percentiles on the combined reading literacy scale

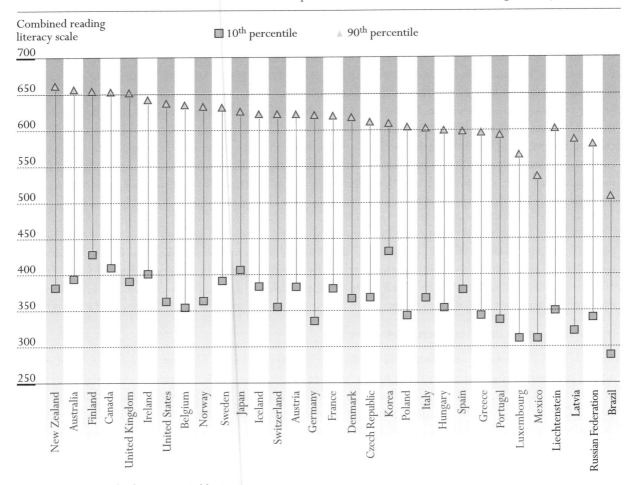

Source: OECD PISA database, 2001. Table 4.16.

At the other extreme, Germany's score difference between the 90th and 10th percentiles is 284, or almost four proficiency levels. In Belgium, New Zealand and the United States, scores for the middle 80 per cent are spread across more than 270 points.

In Finland and Mexico, the difference between the highest and lowest 10 per cent is similar: 225 and 223 points respectively. In contrast with some other countries, no dramatic difference between the most and least able is evident in either Finland or Mexico, but with 44 per cent of Mexico's 15-year-olds below Level 2, a large proportion of the Mexican population would appear to be vulnerable in a changing world. In Finland, all but 7 per cent of the population are ahead of Mexico's lowest 44 per cent.

Of the three aspects, it is in retrieving information that scores are most widely dispersed across the middle 80 per cent of students. In the OECD countries, the average difference between scores at the 90th and 10th percentiles is 284, or four proficiency levels. The spread is greatest in Belgium, where 313 points, or about four and a half proficiency levels, separate students at the top of the range from students at the bottom.

In the case of interpreting, the difference between the 90th and 10th percentiles is less than in the other aspects. The OECD average for the difference between these percentiles is 257, 12 points lower than in reflection and evaluation and 27 points lower than in retrieving information. Korea has a spread of only 176 points. This is 26 score points less than the next smallest spread. The largest difference is New Zealand's 289 points.

In reflection and evaluation, Germany's spread of scores for the middle 80 per cent of students is 316, equal to approximately four and a half proficiency levels, and 20 points greater than Greece's spread, the next largest in reflection and evaluation. No country displays a larger difference between scores at the 10th and 90th percentiles on any subscale.

On the text format subscales, the differences between the 90th and 10th percentiles are greater on the non-continuous texts than the continuous texts subscale in every country except Australia, Germany, Liechtenstein and the United Kingdom. The smallest difference is Korea's 172 on the continuous texts subscale, and the largest is Belgium's 296 on the non-continuous texts.

In both Germany and Belgium, large differences between the 90th and the 10th percentiles can be seen consistently on every subscale. Germany has the largest differences of any country on both the reflection and evaluation and the continuous texts subscale, and Belgium has the largest in retrieving information. These differences are the equivalent of as much as four-and-a-half levels on the defined proficiency scale. Further, on no subscale are there more than five countries with larger differences than either Germany or Belgium.

By contrast, on every subscale, Korea has the smallest gap between the performances of students at the 90th and 10th percentiles.

So far we have pointed out tendencies towards uniformly large or small differences across subscales. Nonetheless, it should not be assumed that wide differences between the extremes on one subscale necessarily mean wide differences on the others. Several countries have very different patterns of spread from one subscale to another. The most dramatic instance is Mexico, which has the second smallest spread of any country in interpreting texts. The middle 80 per cent of students are spread over 202 points, or less than three proficiency levels on this subscale. By contrast, Mexican students are spread over 283 points between these percentiles in the case of reflection and evaluation; that is, almost exactly four proficiency levels. Only seven countries are more dispersed. Other countries with considerable differences between subscales in the spread, either in absolute terms, or relative to other countries, are the Czech Republic, Greece, Hungary, Ireland, Latvia and the United Kingdom.

Some patterns of distribution are observable within different linguistic groups. In interpreting texts, the spread of scores over the middle 80 per cent of students tends to be greater among English-speaking countries than in others. Four English-speaking countries are among the seven countries with the biggest differences in this aspect. In reflection and evaluation, the spread in these four countries is smaller than in interpreting texts in every case. In New Zealand, for example, the spread between the 90th and the 10th percentiles is the largest of any country in interpreting texts, but in reflection and evaluation, ten countries have larger spreads. Among the countries where English is not the language of instruction, a different pattern is evident: the spread over the middle 80 per cent of students is greater in reflection and evaluation than in interpreting texts in every case except Finland, Iceland and Sweden. These patterns of performance may be the result of differences in pedagogy. One hypothesis is that attention to one type of reading at the expense of others may have the effect of enhancing proficiency in that aspect.

This report has repeatedly pointed out the large differences between countries in their performances on both the combined reading literacy scale and the subscales. The gap between the highest and lowest mean scores of any two countries is 150 points on the combined reading literacy scale, or the equivalent of over two proficiency levels. The proportions of students reading at the two highest levels on the scale vary from 4 per cent to over 50 per cent. The consequences of such differences are potentially serious for countries trying to maintain a strong economic and political presence in international contexts. In an era of increasing globalisation, differences in the reading literacy levels on which countries can draw will have a strong impact on their capacity to take their place on the world stage. Countries with low general levels of reading literacy are at risk of falling behind in other ways.

At least as important as differences between countries are differences within countries. Inequality in reading literacy levels within societies is known to be associated with many kinds of social malaise and undesirable outcomes both for the individual and society as a whole. Positive relationships exist between reading literacy and employment opportunities, work satisfaction, income, longevity and health, possibly in part because of enhanced decision-making ability. Literacy is known to have a significant effect not only on gross domestic profit but also on social cohesion and cultural richness (OECD and Statistics Canada, 2000, 80-81). Individuals with higher levels of literacy are the best equipped for self-improvement, particularly through self-directed learning. They are less vulnerable to unemployment resulting from rapid change in the world around them, less likely to be involved in crime, and more likely to participate in civic affairs. The broader society, in short, benefits in many ways from literacy levels that are both high and equitably distributed.

Notes

1. The initial response rate for the Netherlands was only 27 per cent. Mean performance scores for the Netherlands can, therefore, not be compared with those from other countries, and the Netherlands is therefore not included in the analyses in this chapter. The data from the Netherlands is, however, considered sufficiently reliable for some relational analyses. The Netherlands therefore is included in the analyses presented in Chapters 5, 6 and 7. For further details refer to OECD (2001b), p.236.

2. An OECD average was calculated for many of the indicators presented in this chapter. The initial report on PISA 2000 (OECD 2001b) describes the OECD average as: "the mean of the data values for all OECD countries for which data are available or can be estimated. The OECD average can be used to see how a country compares on a given indicator with a typical OECD country. The OECD average does not take into account the absolute size of the student population within each country. ie. each country contributes equally to the average."

3. It will be recalled from Chapter 2 that the reading literacy scale was divided into levels based on both conceptual and statistical criteria. The reader should refer to Chapter 2 for a discussion of these criteria.

4. These, like other correlation coefficients recorded in this chapter, are latent correlation estimations.

Chapter 5

THE READING ENGAGEMENT OF 15-YEAR-OLDS

KEY POINTS

- Several profiles of readers were identified. Some 15-year-olds focus their reading on a limited set of print material; magazines only, or magazines and newspapers. Others, more diversified in their reading interests, choose a broader range of print content. Some choose to read comics in addition to magazines and newspapers while others prefer books, either fiction or non-fiction, to comics.

- Profiles of readers differ perceptibly from one country to another. In some countries, such as Finland and Japan, a high proportion of the students who read a diversity of print content mainly read newspapers, magazines and comics. In other countries, such as Australia, New Zealand and the United Kingdom, students who read a diverse range of materials tend to choose newspapers, magazines and books (fiction and non-fiction).

- Females and males show clearly different profiles of reading. Among the two profiles of students poorly diversified in reading, mainly readers of newspapers and magazines, males and females are more or less equally distributed. The third profile, of readers more oriented towards comics, comprises a majority of males, while the profile oriented towards reading books, especially fiction, comprises a majority of females.

- Not surprisingly, 15-year-olds reading a diversity of print material are more proficient in reading than those reading a limited set of print material. But the gap in reading proficiency between those reading comics and those reading fiction is not huge. Daily engagement in reading magazines, newspapers and comics — a kind of reading that is perhaps less valued by school than fiction books — seems, at least in some cultural contexts, to be a fruitful way of becoming a proficient reader.

- Profiles of reading are weakly linked to students' socio-economic background. By contrast, access to books at home is strongly associated with profiles of reading. Fifteen-year-olds who have access to a limited number of books at home will, on average, be poorly diversified in reading. They mainly read magazines and newspapers. Students who have access to a larger number of books at home are more diversified in their reading and are more interested in reading other material, such as books (fiction and non-fiction) or comics.

- Engagement in reading, as defined in this chapter (time spent reading for pleasure, time spent reading a diversity of material, high motivation and interest in reading), varies widely from country to country. On average, females are more engaged in reading than males.

- Fifteen-year-olds whose parents have the lowest occupational status but who are highly engaged in reading achieve better reading scores than students whose parents have high or medium occupational status but who are poorly engaged in reading.

This chapter first presents "reader profiles" by describing the results of a cluster analysis based on the kinds of materials that 15-year-olds report reading. Each cluster represents a reading profile that is defined by the frequency and diversity of the material read. Then each cluster is related to performance on the combined reading literacy scale and each of the three aspect and two text format subscales. The chapter then looks at the extent to which reader profiles relate to selected background characteristics. Next the chapter focuses on the broader concept of "engagement in reading" by integrating the three variables described above into a single composite index[1]. Countries are compared in terms of their performance on this index both overall and by gender. Finally, this chapter ends with a discussion of the issue: can engagement in reading compensate for the occupational status of parents? The answer to this question is crucial for policy-making in the field of reading instruction.

The analyses undertaken in this chapter are univariate. They do not take into account the fact that several variables may interact in a more complex way. Multivariate analyses will be developed in Chapter 7.

Reading literacy is not only a cognitive issue. It also covers non-cognitive aspects, such as reading attitudes and practices. Most current models of reading achievement or reading acquisition consider both reading practices and reading attitudes or motivation to be key factors related to reading (for a synthesis, see Kamil and al., 2000; McKenna and al., 1995). For Guthrie and Wigfield (2000), motivation is the link between frequent reading and reading achievement. Motivation to read mediates the so-called "Matthew effect" (Stanovich, 1986), which refers to the circular relationship between practice and achievement. Better readers tend to read more because they are motivated to read, which leads to improved vocabulary and better skills. As a result, the gap between good and poor readers grows over time.

The National Assessment of Educational Progress in the United States has reported an interesting study (Campbell, Voelkl and Donahue, 1997) which demonstrates the connection between achievement and engagement in reading. Not surprisingly, the more highly engaged readers showed higher achievement than the less engaged at each of the three ages studied (9, 13 and 17-year-olds). In addition, the 13-year-old students with higher reading engagement demonstrated higher average scores in reading achievement than the 17-year-olds who were less engaged in reading. The same national data indicate that engaged readers from low income/education families have higher achievement than less engaged readers from high income/education backgrounds. According to Guthrie and Wigfield, "As students become engaged readers, they provide themselves with self-generated learning opportunities that are equivalent to several years of education. Engagement in reading may substantially compensate for low family income and educational background" (2000, p. 404).

Empirical studies have also documented the link between reading practices, reading motivation and reading achievement among adults. In the final IALS report (OECD and Statistics Canada, 2000), the amount of reading activity at work and at home is shown to be positively related to the level of reading literacy. Although these variables seem to play a less important role than level of education among an adult population, in some countries (such as Chile and Flemish Belgium), reading practices emerge as one of the four principal factors influencing level of literacy.

Measuring reading engagement in PISA

Reading engagement is measured on the basis of students' responses to questions covering time spent on reading, interest in and attitude towards reading, and diversity and content of reading. This measure is an extension of the index of reading engagement reported in *Knowledge and Skills for Life: First results from*

PISA (OECD, 2001*b*). The index of reading engagement used in this report was constructed to capture a broader and more theory-based construct that would yet be consistent with the earlier measure of reading engagement that focused mainly on students' attitudes towards reading.

In PISA 2000, students were asked several questions aimed at assessing components of reading engagement[2]. In the literature, the concept of engagement covers two different areas: reading practices and reading attitudes. On the one hand, "engaged readers" regularly read different kinds of print; on the other hand, they have developed positive attitudes towards reading, and their interest in reading and motivation to read are strong. They think that reading is a valuable activity, one that provides them with a source of pleasure and knowledge.

Three sets of questions were developed for the PISA student questionnaire to address the concept of engagement:

• *Time spent reading:* Students were asked about how much time they usually spend reading for enjoyment each day. They were asked to respond by indicating which one of five descriptions best represented the time they spent reading. These ranged from "I do not read for enjoyment" to "more than 2 hours a day".

• *Diversity and content of reading:* Students were asked to indicate the kinds of materials they choose to read from a list that included newspapers, magazines, fiction, non-fiction, comics, e-mails and web pages. They were also asked to indicate the frequency with which they read each type of material – from "never" to "several times a week".

• *Reading interest and attitudes:* A reading attitude scale comprising nine statements about reading, either positive or negative, was developed and included in the student questionnaire. Students were asked to indicate their degree of agreement with each statement on a four-point scale ranging from "strongly disagree" to "strongly agree".

Reader profiles

We do know that the time spent on reading is positively correlated with achievement. But, does it make a difference how one spends this time? Is it better to read some materials rather than others? Smith (1996) reports a study addressing this issue using data from the U.S. National Adult Literacy Survey (NALS). Smith constructs patterns of reader practices based on whether they are judged to be high frequency or low frequency readers of each of several types of material[3]. Those adults who are frequent readers of any single type of printed material perform better, on average, than those adults who report not reading any type of material. Literacy proficiency gains diminish with the addition of each print content thereafter but are significant up to a threshold of four types of materials. Two types of material in particular – work documents and books – are strongly associated with a higher level of proficiency. Even after controlling for age and level of education, he finds that reading practices are related to performance on the literacy scales.

In PISA, students were asked to rate how frequently they read different kinds of material. Statistical analyses reveal that the pattern of responses to this question is multidimensional, and that students tend to invest more in some kinds of reading material than in others. In order to try to identify the different patterns or profiles of readers, data were submitted to a cluster analysis[4]. The results reveal four broad clusters of readers.

Figure 5.1

Average percentage of students reading frequently, moderately or not reading each kind of print material by reading profile cluster, all OECD countries

■ no reading ■ moderate reading ■ frequent reading

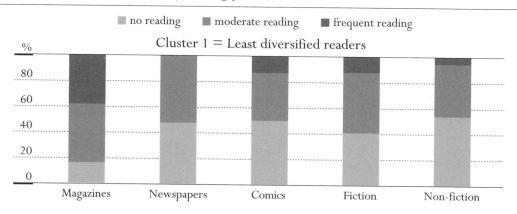

Cluster 1 = Least diversified readers

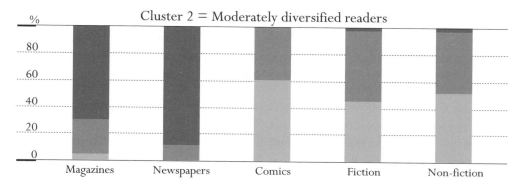

Cluster 2 = Moderately diversified readers

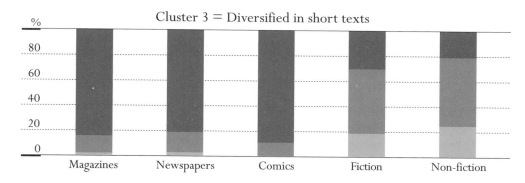

Cluster 3 = Diversified in short texts

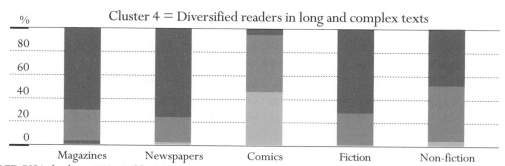

Cluster 4 = Diversified readers in long and complex texts

Source: OECD PISA database, 2001. Table 5.1.

The overall clusters are shown in Figure 5.1 along with the percentages of students reporting frequently, moderately often or never reading each type of material[5]. More detailed figures are presented in Table 5.1.

Cluster 1 contains students who are the least diversified readers[6]. The only type of material they report reading frequently is magazines (38 per cent frequently read magazines). A small percentage frequently read fiction (12 per cent) or comics (13 per cent), and an even smaller percentage report reading non-fiction (6 per cent).

One can hypothesise that these students, on average, do not read for pleasure but may have some limited utilitarian use for printed materials. This may indicate some limited reading of magazines for information (such as TV or film programmes) or limited reading about a specific topic (a hobby, for instance). Twenty-two per cent of the students across OECD countries are estimated to be in this cluster.

In Cluster 2, a majority of students frequently read magazines (70 per cent on average) and newspapers (89 per cent). They report rarely reading any type of book (only 3 per cent report frequently reading fiction or non-fiction books), and almost never read comics (0.5 per cent of the students frequently read comics). Students in this cluster can be considered modestly diversified in their reading choices and probably read for the purpose of obtaining information from newspapers and magazines. Unfortunately, we do not know the types of magazines they read or which sections of the newspapers grab their attention. As shown in Table 5.1 some 27 per cent of the PISA students are found to be in this cluster.

In Cluster 3, the overwhelming majority of students frequently read magazines (85 per cent) and newspapers (81 per cent) – as in Cluster 2 – but they also frequently read comics (89 per cent). They can be considered to be moderate readers of fiction (about 30 per cent of the students frequently read fiction and another 51 per cent sometimes read fiction) or non-fiction (21 per cent frequently read non-fiction and 54 per cent sometimes). By comparison with clusters 1 and 2, these students are more diversified and more involved in reading, but within this group of students, the focus is on quite short and not too demanding texts (materials other than books). Some 28 per cent of the PISA students fall within this cluster.

Cluster 4 contains the students who are also considered to be involved in diversified reading, but the focus here is on more demanding and longer texts (namely books). A majority of these students report frequently reading magazines (70 per cent), newspapers (76 per cent), fiction (72 per cent) and, to a lesser extent, non-fiction books (48 per cent). A relatively small percentage of them report reading comics frequently (6 per cent). The most striking difference between this group of students and those in Cluster 3 is the switch between the frequency with which they report reading books versus newspapers, magazines and comics. Approximately 22 per cent of the PISA students are grouped within this cluster.

Reader profiles by country

Since the four reader profiles identified reveal different patterns of what students report reading, it is interesting to look at their distribution by country. These data are shown in Table 5.2. In general, the countries in Northern Europe appear to have the smallest percentages of students in Cluster 1 (the least diversified readers). For instance, the proportion of students in Cluster 1 ranges from 6.6 per cent in Iceland to 6.9 per cent in Finland, 8.5 per cent in Norway and 11.1 per cent in Sweden. By contrast, there are several countries in which more than 30 per cent of the students are found to be in Cluster 1. These countries are: Belgium (36.3 per cent), France (32.6 per cent), Greece (35.4 per cent), Luxembourg (39.4 per cent), Mexico (37.5 per cent) and Spain (36.2 per cent). Four of these countries have a mean reading score that is

Figure 5.2

Percentage of students in each reading profile cluster and country mean
on the combined reading literacy scale

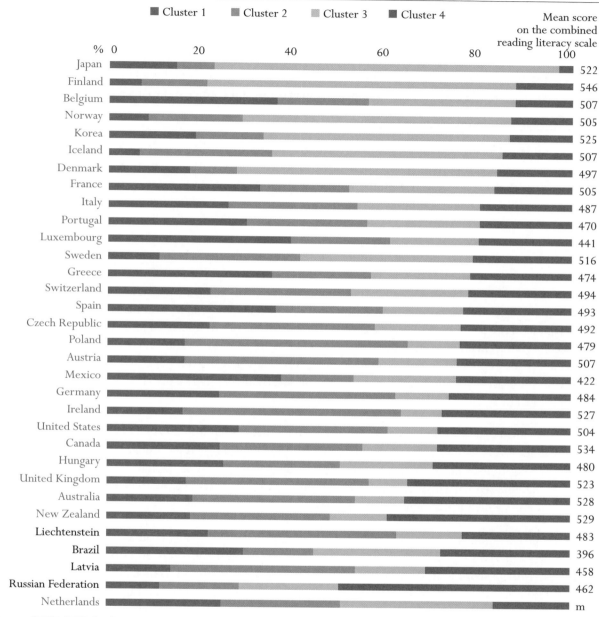

Source: OECD PISA database, 2001. Table 5.2.

significantly below the OECD average of 500. Two countries, Belgium and France, have average scores that are just above the OECD average. Their means are 507 and 505 score points, respectively.

The proportion of students who are highly diversified readers of long texts (Cluster 4) also varies by country (see Table 5.2). The proportion ranges from almost none in Japan (3 per cent), between 10 and

20 per cent of students in countries such as Belgium (12.3 per cent), Denmark (16.2 per cent), Finland (12.3 per cent) and Norway (13.3 per cent), to more than one-third of students in Australia (35.7 per cent), New Zealand (39.4 per cent) and the United Kingdom (35.1 per cent). Clearly, countries that have a high proportion of students who frequently read different kinds of materials including books have mean scores well above the OECD average. The converse, however, is not true. Among the countries with a low proportion of students showing this type of reading profile are Finland and Japan, which have scores that are well above the mean. This is, in part, explained by the fact that both Finland and Japan have two-thirds to three-quarters of their students in Cluster 3, also representing diversified readers but of shorter texts, who report that they frequently read newspapers, magazines and comics and to a lesser extent fiction.

Reader profiles and proficiency by country

Which profiles of readers appear to be more closely related to reading proficiency? Reading literacy is strongly connected across the OECD countries to the frequency with which students report reading a diversity of materials, as indicated by the cluster analysis. Students in Cluster 1, who are judged to be the least diversified readers, have the lowest average score on the combined reading literacy scale (468), one that is significantly below the OECD mean (see Table 5.2). They are followed by students who are moderately diversified readers (Cluster 2) and attain an average score of 498, around the OECD average. Those students judged to be diversified readers of short texts (Cluster 3) have an average combined reading literacy score of 514, which is significantly above the OECD average. Students who are the most involved in diversified reading (Cluster 4), in that they report frequently reading a wide array of materials including more demanding texts (fiction and non-fiction books), have an average of 539 on the reading literacy scale. Their average score is significantly above the OECD average and above those students who are in Cluster 3. The average difference between students who are highly diversified (Cluster 4) and those who are least diversified (Cluster 1) is 71 points or almost a full proficiency level[7]. Even the average difference between those who are least diversified and those who are modestly diversified (Cluster 2) is 30 points, or more than one-third of a proficiency level.

Figure 5.3 shows that, with few exceptions, the pattern that is seen in the OECD average across clusters holds true for every country. In all countries with the exception of Italy, students who are diversified readers of long texts receive the highest average reading literacy scores. In Italy, the average difference between students who are diversified readers of short and long texts (*i.e.*, between Clusters 3 and 4) is only two points, which is not significantly different.

At the other extreme, students who are among the least diversified readers, on average, have the lowest mean scores. The two exceptions here are Ireland and the United Kingdom. In both of these countries, the lowest average score is attained by those students who are considered to be highly diversified readers of short texts (Cluster 3). In Ireland there is no significant difference in the average scores of students in Clusters 1, 2 and 3. However, students who are highly diversified readers of long texts (Cluster 4) attain an average reading score that is higher by almost a full proficiency level than those in the other clusters. It is also worth pointing out that relatively small percentages of students in both of these countries are in Cluster 3 (8.9 per cent in Ireland and 8.4 per cent in the United Kingdom). This could explain why the results are somewhat different in these two countries.

In several English-speaking countries (Ireland, New Zealand, the United Kingdom and the United States), as in several countries in Eastern Europe such as Hungary, Latvia, Poland and the Russian Federation, students in Cluster 2 have better scores on the combined reading scale than students involved in more

Figure 5.3

Performance of students in each reading profile cluster on the combined reading literacy scale

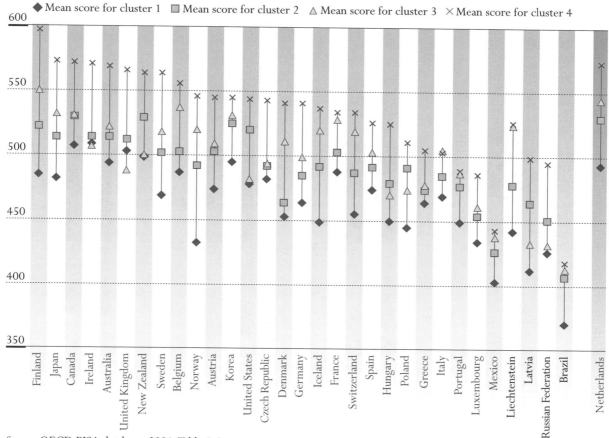

Source: OECD PISA database, 2001. Table 5.2.

diversified reading (Cluster 3). This result is striking and somewhat contrary to expectations: it means that students who report reading a more diverse array of reading materials, especially comics and to a lesser extent books, perform less well than students who report reading only newspapers and magazines. What is most surprising is that this pattern clearly fits with a linguistic or cultural pattern, as it is specifically observed among English-speaking countries and countries in Eastern Europe.

Reader profiles by levels of proficiency and reading subscales

Another way of exploring the link between the diversity and frequency of material read by students and their reading proficiency is to look at the distribution of students located in each cluster across the reading proficiency levels. In Figure 5.4, a few interesting differences are noticeable among students in Cluster 1. The largest percentage of students who read below Level 1 (9.6 per cent) are those who are classified as the least diversified readers (see Table 5.3). Less than half of this percentage of students is found below Level 1 in any of the other clusters. Although there are not large differences between the percentages of students who are below Level 1 in the remaining three clusters, they follow the general pattern of decreasing from Cluster 2 to Cluster 4. The same pattern holds true for students whose reading proficiency is within Level 1.

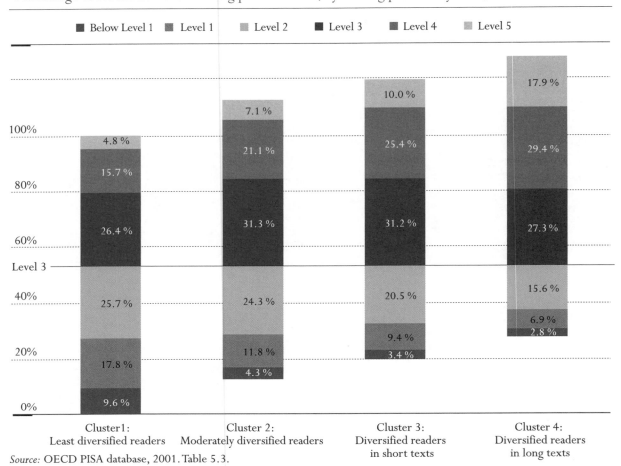

Figure 5.4

Percentage of students in each reading profile cluster, by reading proficiency level, all OECD countries

■ Below Level 1   ■ Level 1   ■ Level 2   ■ Level 3   ■ Level 4   ■ Level 5

Source: OECD PISA database, 2001. Table 5.3.

The largest percentages are those who are the least diversified readers (Cluster 1). The percentages decrease across the clusters as students become more diversified in their reading.

The opposite pattern is discernable at Levels 4 and 5. Here we see that the smallest percentage of students is associated with Cluster 1, the least diversified readers. Increasing percentages of students fall into each of the remaining clusters, indicating higher levels of involvement in diversified reading. It is interesting to note that almost 50 per cent of the students in Levels 4 and 5 on the reading literacy scale are highly diversified readers of demanding texts (Cluster 4), compared with fewer than 20 per cent who are among the least diversified readers (Cluster 1).

As noted in previous chapters, separate subscales of proficiency were constructed for three aspects of reading literacy (retrieving information, interpreting texts and reflection and evaluation) and for two text formats (continuous texts and non-continuous texts). The data were analysed to investigate whether the differences in reading proficiency associated with the profiles of readers were more or less pronounced across the three aspect subscales and the two format subscales. The general pattern seen on the combined reading literacy scale was also found on each of the five subscales, as shown in Figure 5.5. That is, students who are the least diversified readers (Cluster 1) have the lowest average score on each of the subscales, followed by those students in Cluster 2 (modestly diversified), Cluster 3 (diversified readers of short texts) and Cluster 4

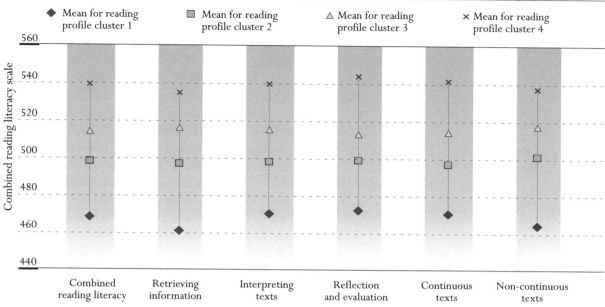

Figure 5.5

Mean scores on the combined reading literacy scale and subscales by reading profile cluster,
all OECD countries

Source: OECD PISA database, 2001. Table 5.4.

(diversified readers of long texts). Across the subscales, the average difference between students who
are the least diversified readers and those who are the most diversified readers of long texts ranges from
69 points on the interpreting texts subscale to 74 points on the retrieving information subscale.
These average differences are more or less equivalent to one full proficiency level or about three-quarters
of a standard deviation (see Table 5.4).

We also see some modest but interesting differences within clusters across the subscales. For example,
there are differences affecting students in Cluster 1, the least diversified readers. Although they have the
lowest average score on each of the reading subscales, their average score on the retrieving information
subscale is lower than on the interpreting texts and reflection and evaluation subscales. Similarly, their
average score on the non-continuous texts subscale is lower than it is on the continuous texts subscale.
There is also a tendency for students who are diversified readers of long texts (Cluster 4) to perform
better on average on the reflection and evaluation and continuous texts subscales. The fact that these
students frequently read more demanding texts such as books could explain this pattern.

Relationship of selected background characteristics to reading profiles

After presenting the distribution of countries in terms of "reader profiles" and discussing the relationship
of this construct to reading proficiency, it is worth considering the association between these profiles of
readers and selected background variables. Only key background variables will be examined here: gender,
socio-economic background, cultural characteristics of the family, and students' access to print (number
of books at home and frequency of borrowing books). Only the results from bivariate analyses will be
reported here. No doubt several of the background variables could be interrelated, such as number of
books and socio-economic background; the more complex interaction between variables will be tackled
in Chapter 7.

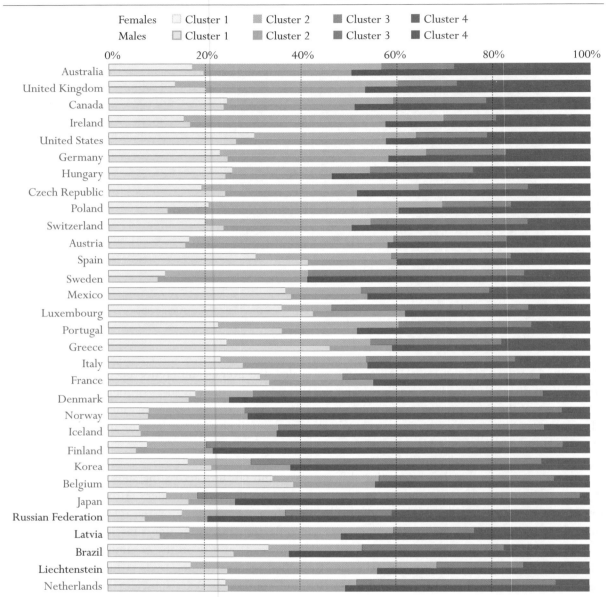

Figure 5.6

Percentage of students in each reading profile cluster by gender

Source: OECD PISA database, 2001. Table 5.5.

Reader profiles by gender

Gender is undoubtedly a crucial variable. Numerous studies in different countries have shown that girls read more than boys; on average, they not only spend more time reading, they also tend to read different types of materials than boys. Figure 5.6 shows the percentage of males and females in each of the four reading clusters.

In Figure 5.6 there is a clear difference in the reading patterns of males and females. Males report more frequently than females that they mainly read newspapers, magazines and comics rather than books (especially fiction). This is evident in Cluster 3 where, across the OECD countries, some 34 per cent of males are found compared with 23 per cent of females (see Table 5.5). Conversely, across all countries, females are more numerous than males in Cluster 4 (29 per cent versus 16 per cent) and identify themselves as reading newspapers, magazines, books (especially fiction), but not comics. It will be recalled that readers in Cluster 3 are considered to be involved in diversified reading (mainly short texts) while those in Cluster 4 are also highly diversified (but mainly read books). The readers more attracted by fiction are clearly females, and this trend is observed in every country participating in PISA.

The distinction between males and females is less pronounced in Clusters 1 and 2, although it is not the same in every country (see Table 5.5). For instance in Cluster 2, which comprises modestly diversified readers who are interested in newspapers and magazines, the OECD average proportion of males is slightly higher than the proportion of females (30 per cent compared with 25 per cent). In several countries such as Mexico, Norway, Poland and Sweden there are no differences in the percentages of males and females while in four countries (Finland, France, Japan and Korea), the proportion of females in Cluster 2 is higher than that of males. In Cluster 1, the differences between males and females are generally small. In one half of the countries, males are more numerous in this cluster; and in the other half, females are more numerous. But among the OECD countries as a whole, females (24 per cent) are a little more numerous than males (21 per cent) in Cluster 1. The fact that the gender pattern is less stable in Clusters 1 and 2 is probably linked to the importance of reading magazines in those two clusters. The category "magazines" covers a wide range of possibilities, is extremely heterogeneous and comprises items typically masculine, items typically feminine and others that are quite neutral.

Reader profiles by socio-economic background

On average, the profiles of readers are weakly related to students' socio-economic background[8]. As can be seen in Table 5.6, average socio-economic background is somewhat higher in the group of students (Cluster 4) who frequently read a diversity of print including books (51.6) and in the group (Cluster 3) who frequently read magazines, newspapers and comics (49.7). It is somewhat lower in the groups where students mainly read magazines and newspapers (48.6) or only magazines (46.0), Clusters 2 and 1 respectively. But the average differences are small in every country. It is reassuring to know that while socio-economic background plays a role, it is not a dominant factor in predicting involvement in diversified reading.

Reader profiles by access to print

By comparison with socio-economic background, there is a stronger link between access to print material at home[9] (number of books at home, access to books of poetry and classical literature at home) and reading profile (see Table 5.7). Students in Cluster 4 who frequently read a diversity of print including books have access to more reading material at home (mean value of the index = 0.36), followed by students in Cluster 3 who frequently read magazines, newspapers and comics (mean = 0.11). Students who mainly read magazines and newspapers (Cluster 2) or only magazines (Cluster 1) have access to fewer reading materials at home (mean value of the index respectively equal to -0.13 and -0.30). Clearly, access to books at home is a strong correlate of reader profiles. Students who have access to a limited number of books at home tend to be least involved or only modestly involved in diversified reading, and they mainly read magazines and/or newspapers. Students who have access to a larger number of books have a tendency to be more interested in reading a broader range of materials. While socio-economic background is weakly related to the profiles of reading, access to books at home seems to play a more important role.

Figure 5.7

Difference in reading engagement between females and males

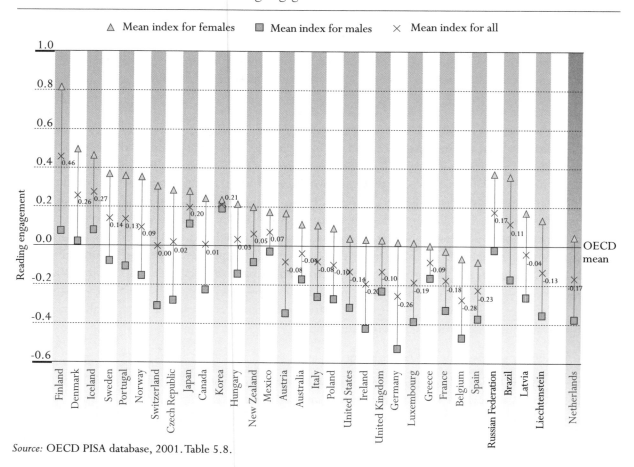

△ Mean index for females   ▢ Mean index for males   ✕ Mean index for all

Source: OECD PISA database, 2001. Table 5.8.

Engagement in reading

Figure 5.7 shows the mean values for countries on the reading engagement index. The mean value of the reading engagement index for the combined OECD student population is set to 0 and the standard deviation to 1. Negative values do not necessarily mean that students responded negatively to the questions. It means that students in a given country as a whole responded less positively than students across OECD countries as a whole. Conversely, a positive value indicates that students in a particular country responded more favourably than did students, on average, across the set of OECD countries.

The country that shows the highest level of engagement in reading (far beyond that of the others) is Finland (0.46). Other countries where the level of engagement in reading is high are Denmark (0.26), Iceland (0.27), Japan (0.20) and Korea (0.21). By comparison, countries where the level of engagement is relatively low are Belgium (-0.28), Germany (-0.26), Ireland (-0.20), Luxembourg (-0.19) and Spain (-0.23).

Engagement in reading by gender

There is a significant difference between males and females in engagement in reading. The average difference between males and females is 0.38 among OECD countries (see Table 5.8). Thus, all the countries have to face more or less the same challenge. Fostering engagement in reading implies actions targeted at males. The reasons why boys are less engaged in reading and the solutions to improve their engagement are widely debated. Some experts assume that boys are discriminated against at school and that if they fail to develop their literacy, this is mainly due to the kind of stereotyped reading material used at school. Others argue that boys' decision not to read is heavily influenced by peers and social norms of masculinity (Young and Brozo, 2001). Not being engaged in reading is only one aspect of a more general attitude towards schoolwork among boys. Jackson (1998) finds that academically successful boys have to manage their academic lives very carefully, avoiding any open commitment to work. Otherwise, they risk being taunted by their peers (Mac An Ghaill, 1994, quoted by Young and Brozo).

The highest engagement in reading is observed among females in Denmark (0.50), Finland (0.82), Iceland (0.46), Norway (0.35), Portugal (0.36) and Sweden (0.37). The lowest engagement in reading is observed among males in Germany (-0.53), Belgium (-0.48), Ireland (-0.43), Luxembourg (-0.39) and Spain (-0.38). In Switzerland and Finland, the gap between males and females is particularly pronounced (0.61 and 0.75 respectively). In a few countries the gap between males and females is relatively low. These include Greece (0.17), Japan (0.17), Korea (0.04) and Mexico (0.20). In no country does the gap favour males.

While females have a higher engagement than males, there are some interesting differences between countries in this respect. Males in some countries are more engaged in reading than females in other countries. For instance, males in Denmark, Finland, Iceland, Japan and Korea report being either as engaged or more engaged in reading than females in Belgium, France and Spain.

Can engagement in reading compensate for the socio-economic background?

There is evidence in the literature that engagement in reading can "compensate" for low family income and educational background (Guthrie and Wigfield, 2000) or other background factors (Campbell, Voelkl and Donahue, 1997). The PISA data were explored to find out whether this evidence, mainly observed in the context of the United States, is also to be found in an international study.

In order to address this question, students were split into nine groups, based on two variables: level of engagement in reading, and occupational status of parents. For each of these two indices, three groups were created: the low group (below the 25th percentile), the middle group (from the 25th to the 75th

Figure 5.8

Expected and observed percentages of students
by level of reading engagement and socio-economic background

	Low reading engagement		Medium reading engagement		High reading engagement	
	Expected (%)	Observed (%)	Expected (%)	Observed (%)	Expected (%)	Observed (%)
Low socio-economic background	6.25	7.60	12.50	12.56	6.25	4.85
Medium socio-economic background	12.25	12.90	25.00	25.14	12.25	11.96
High socio-economic background	6.25	4.50	12.50	12.30	6.25	8.19

percentile) and the high group (above the 75[10] percentile). Using this classification[10], nine categories or groups of students were identified. Figure 5.8 compares the average expected and observed percentages among OECD countries for each of the nine groups.

Among the students whose parents have the lowest occupational status, those who are less engaged readers are somewhat more numerous than would be expected if the two variables were completely independent. It is also the case that highly engaged students are more numerous than expected among the group of students whose parents have the highest occupational status. But it is interesting to acknowledge that engagement is only partially predicted by parents' occupational status: Figure 5.9 shows students from less privileged socio-economic backgrounds who are highly engaged in reading as well as students from more privileged backgrounds who show a low level of engagement in reading. An obvious question is how these groups of students are distributed in terms of their reading literacy proficiency.

Students who have parents with the highest occupational status and who are highly engaged in reading obtain the best average scores on the combined reading literacy scale (583). This is more than one proficiency level or 0.83 of a standard deviation above the OECD average. And students who have parents with the lowest occupational status and who are the least engaged in reading obtain the lowest average score (423). This score is one proficiency level below the OECD average and more than one-and-a-half standard

Figure 5.9

Reading literacy performance and socio-economic background by level of reading engagement

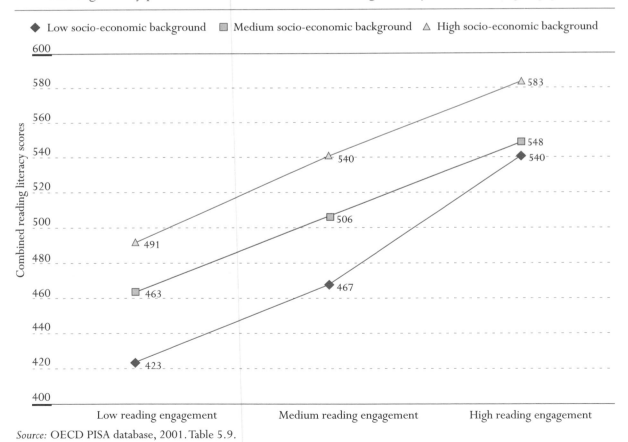

Source: OECD PISA database, 2001. Table 5.9.

deviations below the average of students in the high-engagement, high-status group. More importantly from our perspective, 15-year-old students who are highly engaged readers and whose parents have the lowest occupational status achieve significantly higher average reading scores (540) than students whose parents have the highest occupational status but who are poorly engaged in reading (491). The difference in their average scores is more than half a standard deviation. And these highly engaged students whose parents have low occupational status perform as well on average as those students who are in the middle engagement group but whose parents have high-status occupations.

All the students who are highly engaged in reading achieve reading literacy scores that are significantly above the international mean, whatever their family background. Conversely, students who are poorly engaged in reading achieve scores below the international mean, regardless of their parents' occupational status. Within each occupational status group, students who are among the least engaged readers attain average scores ranging from 85 to 117 points lower than those who are in the highly engaged reading group on the combined reading scale, the largest difference being seen among students from the low occupational status group. These findings are of paramount importance from an educational perspective and may be the most important presented in this report.

Reading practices can play an important role in reducing the gap between the reading proficiency scores of students from different socio-economic backgrounds. They may even have a role to play in reducing the gap seen between males and females. Some teaching practices are well known for their efficiency at fostering students' engagement in reading (Burns, 1998; Ivey, 1999). Guthrie and Davis (2002) have developed a model of engagement through classroom practice aimed at motivating struggling readers in lower secondary education.

Struggling readers need both motivational and cognitive support. Motivational support is increased through real-world interaction, interesting texts, autonomy and collaboration (with peers). However, these qualities of teaching will not guarantee cognitive gains. Cognitive competence is increased by the teaching of reading strategy for substantial amounts of time. There is evidence that cognitive strategy instruction is ineffective in isolation from a rich content domain (Guthrie, Schafer, Vonsecker and Alban, 2000). However, direct strategy instruction is powerful when this is provided, together with motivational support (Guthrie and Davis, 2002).

Cognitive and non-cognitive components of reading engagement clearly go hand in hand. This chapter has shown that they are strongly linked. Cognition and motivation, proficiency and engagement in reading have an entangled relationship. Cause cannot be disentangled from effect. Proficient readers are more engaged in reading and, as a result, acquire more knowledge and skills. Students with poor reading habits often find reading material too difficult (Allington, 1984) and develop a negative attitude towards reading (Oka and Paris, 1986). They find themselves in a vicious circle because by reading less they have fewer opportunities to develop reading comprehension strategies (Brown, Palincsar and Purcell, 1986) and they end up falling further behind in all subjects because reading is a fundamental skill required for all academic areas (Chall, Jacobs and Baldwin, 1990). Contemporary models of reading instruction aimed at fostering reading proficiency acknowledge this and stress that proficiency cannot be improved without taking into consideration the non-cognitive components of reading engagement: motivation and access to interesting and meaningful reading materials. This view accords with the results of the regression analyses developed in the following chapters of this report.

Notes

1. The broader index of engagement in reading correlates 0.88 with the index used in the initial report but has a higher reliability coefficient of 0.83 compared with 0.72 for the earlier measure of reading engagement.

2. Most of the measures presented in this chapter are based on self-reported behaviors and preferences and not on direct observations. Therefore, compliance effects or cultural differences in response behavior could influence responses. Even though the instruments are based on well-established research and were tested extensively before their use in PISA 2000 care should be taken when making comparisons.

3. In Smith's study, the list comprised the following print materials: newspapers, magazines, books, personal documents and work-related documents.

4. E-mail and web pages were not included in the cluster analysis because they seemed to be unrelated to the other materials.

5. For this question, reading one kind of material "several times a month" or "several times a week" has been considered frequent reading, "a few times a year" and "once a month", as moderate reading and "never or hardly ever" as no reading.

6. The distinction into four clusters relies on two dimensions: frequency of reading on the one hand, diversity of reading on the other hand. This twofold dimension is reflected in the expression "involved in diversified reading". For practical and readability reasons, in the following pages, the label for each cluster will be simplified, keeping only the notion of diversity. But the intensity or involvement in reading has always to be kept in mind.

7. A proficiency level equals 72 score points.

8. Socio-economic background of students is measured by an index of socio-economic of occupational status of parents (ISEI). The PISA index is based on either the father's or mother's occupation, whichever is highest. Values on the index range from 0 to 90; low values represent low socio-economic status and high values represent high socio-economic status. The OECD average of the index is 49.

9. Access to print at home is an index grouping the three questions related to access to print material at home has been built: number of books at home, availability of a dictionary and textbooks at home. The seven categories of the question about number of books at home has been recoded into a dichotomous variable. Categories 1 to 4 (from none up to 100 books) have been recoded into 0; categories 5 to 6 (from 100 books to more than 500 books) have been recoded as 1.

10. This cutting up into three groups have been adopted to allow for comparability across countries.

Chapter

6

THE RELATIONSHIP BETWEEN BACKGROUND CHARACTERISTICS AND READING LITERACY

KEY POINTS

- The occupational status of the parents, books in the home, home educational resources and cultural communication are correlated with achievement in reading literacy. The correlations are positive in every PISA country. Interestingly, the correlation between engagement in reading and socio-economic background is only about one-third of the correlation with achievement: 0.12 compared with 0.34. By contrast, engagement in reading has a much higher correlation with books in the home and cultural communication.

- Among student characteristics, engagement in reading has the largest median correlation with achievement in reading literacy. There is no difference in the median correlation between gender and achievement, or between time spent on homework and achievement. Time spent doing homework is also more highly correlated with engagement in reading than is gender. And, time spent doing homework is more highly correlated with engagement than with achievement. Collectively, these and other findings point to the potentially important role that engagement in reading can play in reducing some of the gaps seen in performance between the various subgroups in each country.

- There is an interesting interaction between gender and the reading literacy subscales. In each country the smallest difference between males and females is on the non-continuous texts subscale. In fact the median correlation of 0.19 on the continuous texts subscale is more than double the median correlation of 0.09 on the non-continuous texts subscale.

- While the percentages of 15-year-olds who are non-native students are relatively small in each country, those who are classified as non-native are at a distinct disadvantage in terms of their performance on the reading literacy scale. There seems to be a much smaller and less consistent relationship between non-native status and engagement in reading.

- Students' relationship with their teachers has a positive correlation with engagement in reading. The pattern of relationship is consistent among OECD and non-OECD countries. Disciplinary climate is another classroom environment characteristic that is positively associated with achievement and engagement, whereas sense of belonging and pressure to achieve seem to have a less consistent relationship with both achievement and engagement.

In the two previous chapters, the focus was on reporting the means and distributions of scores achieved by 15-year-olds from participating countries and the extent of their engagement in reading. These are judged to be important outcomes of schooling in that they represent measures of what is expected of students upon leaving secondary education. As Gray and Rogers note, maturity in reading is distinguished by "the attainment of interests, attitudes and skills that enable each person to participate independently and effectively in those reading activities essential to a full, rich and productive life" (Gray and Rogers, 1956, p.56). In this chapter, we examine selected characteristics of students, their families and their learning environments to see how these characteristics relate to both engagement and achievement in reading literacy[1]. While we recognise that these variables do not operate in isolation from one another, it is useful to introduce them in this way so that the reader has a sense of how they relate individually to both reading literacy and engagement in reading. Chapter 7 then goes on to examine the relative "importance" of each variable after adjusting for interdependence.

Students were asked to complete a questionnaire containing a range of questions about their family background, their activities out of school and their perceptions about aspects of their learning environment within the classroom. Their responses to these questions made it possible to examine the relationship of these characteristics to both engagement and achievement. To what extent do girls read better than boys on each of the reading literacy subscales and to what extent are they more engaged readers? How is engagement in reading related to performance on the reading literacy subscales? To what extent is the impact of immigration status and family structure similar across the OECD countries? How are educational resources and the type of communication in the home related to engagement and achievement in reading literacy? Do disciplinary climate and pressure to achieve relate to these two sets of outcomes? These and other questions are explored in this chapter in respect of each of the 28 OECD and four non-OECD countries.

Reading literacy and individual student characteristics

This section focuses on three variables or indices: gender, engagement in reading and time spent on homework. These point to specific student characteristics that are related to student outcomes and can be distinguished from family structure and classroom environment.

Gender

Historically, concern about gender differences has almost universally focused on the underachievement of girls and women. More recently, however, as females have closed some gaps and even surpassed males in various aspects of education, the focus has begun to shift towards the underachievement of males. According to a recent report from the OECD (2001*b*), university graduation rates for women now equal or exceed those for men in 17 of the 25 OECD countries for which comparable data are available. And a report on literacy raises the possibility that the significant gap in reading between school-age females and males in the United States may be a major factor contributing to the widening gap in college attendance and degree attainment rates (Sum, Kirsch and Taggert, 2002).

PISA results show that females outperform males on the combined reading literacy scale in all participating countries. From Figure 6.1 we see that the median correlation between gender and reading literacy is 0.16. The lowest correlation between gender and reading achievement is seen in Korea (0.10). In fact, in 21 of the 28 OECD countries this correlation ranges from 0.10 to 0.19. There is a tendency for this correlation to be somewhat higher in countries in Northern Europe where, with the exception of Denmark (0.13), the correlations all exceed 0.20. The highest correlation between gender and reading achievement is found in Finland (0.29)[2].

Figure 6.1

Relationship between gender and reading engagement and reading literacy performance

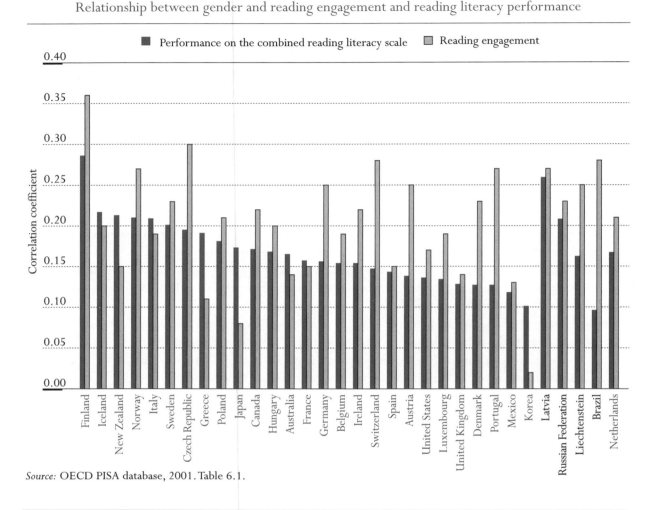

■ Performance on the combined reading literacy scale   ■ Reading engagement

Source: OECD PISA database, 2001. Table 6.1.

Box 6.1: Interpreting the data in this chapter

All of the data reported in this chapter are in the form of correlation coefficients. Regression effects are also provided in the Annex to this report. While each of the variables or indices reported in this chapter is interesting and may have policy implications, the characterisation of their relationship to achievement and engagement is incomplete since they do not operate in isolation from one another. Rather, they interact in complicated ways as they relate to the development of reading literacy skills.

All of the measures discussed in this chapter rely on reports provided by the students themselves and may be influenced by cross-cultural differences in response behaviour or the social desirability of certain responses. Several of the measures in this chapter (*e.g.,* engagement in reading) are presented as indices that summarise student responses to a series of questions. The questions were selected on the basis of theoretical considerations and were confirmed and validated across countries through the use of structural equation modelling.

For this purpose a model was estimated separately for each country and, collectively, for all OECD countries. The indices used in this chapter were constructed so that they have a mean of 0 and a standard deviation of 1. This means that two-thirds of the OECD student population are between the values of 1 and -1. It is important to keep in mind that a negative value on an index does not mean that students responded negatively to the underlying questions. A negative value merely indicates that a group of students responded less positively than all students did, on average, across the OECD countries. Similarly, a positive value means that a group of students responded more favourably, on average, than all students, on average, across the OECD countries. Other measures reported in this chapter are based on either a 2-point scale indicating yes or no, or a 3, 4, 5 or 6-point scale indicating frequency or probability. In the case of social background, this index was created as a continuous measure ranging from 0 to 90 and measures the attributes of occupation that convert a person's education into income. The higher the value on this index, the higher the occupational status of a student's parents.

More interesting perhaps is the fact that gender differences show an interesting pattern or interaction among the reading literacy subscales. In each participating country, the smallest average difference between males and females is on the non-continuous texts scale, one of the two format subscales (see Table 6.2a). In fact, the median correlation among OECD countries is 0.19 on the continuous texts subscale or more than double the median correlation of only 0.09 on the non-continuous texts subscale. This pattern is repeated in every PISA country. The correlation is significantly higher on the continuous texts than on the non-continuous texts reading subscale. If we look at the regression results shown in Table 6.2a, we see that in 17 of the 28 OECD countries, the average difference between females and males on the non-continuous texts scale is less than 20 points or 20 per cent of a standard deviation. This contrasts with the continuous texts scale where only Korea (19 points) has an average difference of less than 20 points.

A similar pattern is apparent (see Table 6.2a) in the three aspect subscales. The smallest median correlation between gender and achievement among OECD countries is shown on the retrieving information subscale (0.12). This correlation increases slightly to 0.15 on the interpreting texts subscale and reaches 0.21 on the reflection and evaluation subscale. In every OECD country, the average difference between males and females on the reflection and evaluation subscale exceeds more than 25 points or a quarter of a standard deviation.

As discussed in the previous chapter on engagement in reading, females, on average, are more engaged readers than males. The median score on the index of reading engagement is 0.19 for females and -0.19 for males. In addition, even among males who are at least moderately diversified readers, there are significant differences in the types of materials that they report reading compared with females. For example, about 34 per cent of males are in Cluster 3 compared with 23 per cent of females. By contrast, only some 15 per cent of males are in Cluster 4 compared with some 29 per cent of females. One of the characteristics that distinguishes Cluster 3 from Cluster 4 is the amount and type of book reading, as well as magazine reading, that is reported. Cluster 3 is characterised by high percentages of students reporting that they read magazines (85) and newspapers (81) frequently, while only 30 per cent report frequently reading fiction and only 21 per cent non-fiction. By contrast, somewhat smaller percentages of students in Cluster 4 report frequently reading newspapers and magazines while more than 70 per cent report reading fiction and some 50 per cent report frequently reading non-fiction books.

The median correlation between gender and engagement in reading is slightly higher (0.20) than between gender and achievement across OECD countries (0.16). Interestingly, however, there is some variation between OECD countries. We see in Table 6.1 that the standard deviation of the correlations of gender with engagement is almost double what we observe in the case of achievement -0.07 compared with 0.04. In six of the 28 OECD countries (Greece, Iceland, Italy, Japan, Korea and New Zealand), the correlation between gender and engagement is lower than it is between gender and achievement while in four countries (France, Mexico, Spain and the United Kingdom) there is only a 0.01 difference in the correlations. In the remaining 18 OECD countries, the correlation between gender and engagement is larger than that found between gender and achievement.

Reading engagement

Motivation to read and amount of time spent reading are important contributors to the gap between good and poor readers. While the relationship is likely to be reciprocal, in that students with better skills are also more likely to be motivated to read and therefore spend more time reading, there are a number of studies that show a connection between engagement and achievement. These findings apply to school-age populations as well as to adults. In fact, the International Adult Literacy Survey (OECD and Statistics Canada, 1995) shows the importance of practice, and of what adults read, in the maintenance of skills in adulthood.

Figure 6.2 also compares countries participating in PISA in terms of the correlation between reading achievement and engagement in reading. Engagement in reading has a moderately strong and meaningful association with reading achievement in every participating country. The median correlation of 0.38 indicates that students who are more engaged in reading achieve, on average, higher scores on the combined reading literacy scale. This correlation ranges from a low of 0.23 in the Russian Federation to a high of 0.48 in Finland. In 12 of the PISA countries the correlation between engagement and reading achievement exceeds 0.40. These countries are: Australia, Austria, the Czech Republic, Denmark, Finland, Germany, Hungary, Iceland, Liechtenstein, Norway, Sweden and Switzerland. The correlations are appreciably lower (*i.e.*, below 0.30) in several other countries including Brazil, Greece, Latvia, Luxembourg, Mexico, Poland and the Russian Federation. These countries attain reading achievement scores well below the OECD average. Indeed they are the countries with the lowest average reading literacy scores.

As in the case of gender, there is a difference in the association between engagement and achievement in reading between the two format subscales (see Table 6.2c). The median correlation across OECD countries is 0.38 for the continuous texts subscale and 0.34 for the non-continuous texts subscale. This difference is relatively consistent across each of the OECD countries. By contrast, while the median correlation between engagement and achievement is somewhat higher on the interpreting texts (0.38) and reflection and evaluation (0.37) subscales than on the retrieving information (0.35) subscale, the pattern across countries tends to be inconsistent and the differences small.

Time spent doing homework

Students were asked to report how much time they spend each week doing homework in their test language as well as in mathematics and science. They could choose from among four categories: "no time", "less than 1 hour", "between 1 and 3 hours" and "more than 3 hours". Figure 6.3 reveals a moderate correlation between time spent doing homework and achievement. The median correlation among OECD countries is 0.18 (see Table 6.1). This table also reveals a correlation between homework and engagement in reading that is 0.28, or almost double that observed for achievement. In 21 of the 28 OECD countries and in

Figure 6.2

Relationship between reading literacy performance and reading engagement

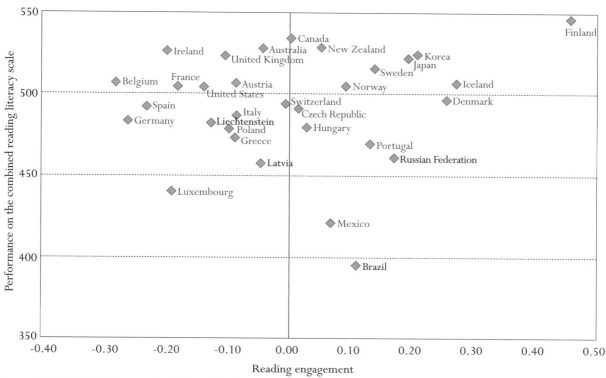

Source: OECD PISA database, 2001. Tables 4.1 and 6.1.

each of the non-OECD countries, the correlation between homework and engagement is higher than the correlation between homework and achievement, while in four of the OECD countries the correlation is lower and in three of the countries the difference is 0.01 or less.

All but one of the 32 PISA countries have a correlation between homework and engagement that is greater than 0.15 (Table 6.2b). The exception is Austria, where the correlation is 0.12. In eight of the countries, the correlation exceeds 0.30 while in an additional 19 the correlation equals or exceeds 0.20. By comparison, some 14 countries have correlations between homework and achievement that are less than 0.15, and only five have correlations that are 0.30 or higher. In the other 13 countries participating in PISA, the correlation between time spent doing homework and achievement ranges from 0.15 to 0.29.

As noted previously, the correlation between homework and engagement tends to be higher in the majority of OECD countries and less variable overall. The average standard deviation in the correlation between engagement and time spent doing homework is 0.06 compared with 0.11 between achievement and homework. Clearly those students who are more engaged in reading tend also to spend more time doing homework and preparing for classes.

Reading literacy and family characteristics

Families are an important source of social capital for students. Together with that of the community and the school, it is the material and social support offered by families that affects students' attitudes towards

Figure 6.3

Relationship between homework and reading engagement
and reading literacy performance

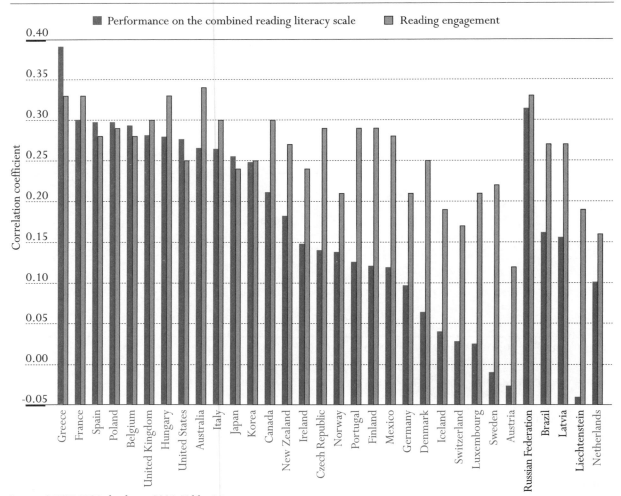

Source: OECD PISA database, 2001. Table 6.1.

education and expectations of achievement. This section examines the connection between reading literacy and a range of characteristics relating to family and home environment, including culture, socio-economic background, family structure and country of origin.

These factors define the early experiences that students receive, their preparation for school, their expectations about school and the value of education, and their familiarity with the kinds of academic language that they will encounter while in school.

Socio-economic background

In PISA, student socio-economic background is measured by the socio-economic index of occupational status of parents (for definitions, see Annex A3). Table 6.4a provides information about the effects of occupational status of parents on reading literacy across both OECD and non-OECD countries.

The median correlation is 0.33 among the OECD countries (see Table 6.4a). This correlation seems to be relatively consistent across each of the five subscales but varies somewhat from country to country; that is, in some countries the correlation is considerably greater than in others. In 24 of the 32 PISA countries the correlation between socio-economic background and reading achievement is equal to or greater than 0.30. All countries have a correlation higher than 0.20. The only exception is Korea where the correlation is 0.19 on the combined reading literacy scale.

The more important finding, which was referred to in Chapter 5, is the relationship between socio-economic background and engagement in reading. Here we see that the median correlation is only 0.15, less than half what is observed for reading achievement. In all OECD countries the correlation with engagement is positive and greater than 0.10, and in all but two additional OECD countries the correlation is 0.20 or lower. These two exceptions are Germany and Switzerland. Here, the correlation between engagement and socio-economic background is 0.23 and 0.22 respectively. As noted in Chapter 5, engagement in reading, as measured by attitude, motivation and practice, has the potential to reduce the gaps between the reading proficiency scores of students from differing backgrounds. The challenge is to find effective ways of increasing engagement.

Number of books in the home

Socio-economic status is seen to provide an advantage to students in terms of the value placed on education and the number of possessions in the home related to education. Students were asked to estimate the number of books in the home, and their responses were coded into seven categories: none; 1 to 10 books; 11 to 50 books, 51 to 100 books; 101 to 250 books, 251 to 500 books and more than 500 books. The median correlation of this variable with reading literacy is 0.35 (see Table 6.3). In eight of the 28 OECD countries, the correlation of books in the home with performance on the combined reading literacy scale is 0.40 or greater. In Hungary the correlation is 0.52. In all other OECD and non-OECD countries the correlation is greater than 0.20.

The number of books in the home has almost the same degree of correlation with engagement as with reading literacy. The median correlation of books in the home with engagement in reading is 0.31, almost as large as the correlation of books in the home with achievement (0.35). With the exception of Mexico, where the correlation is 0.18, the correlation is greater than 0.20 in all OECD countries and 0.30 or higher in 20 of these 28 countries.

There does not seem to be a noticeable interaction between books in the home and the reading subscales (see Table 6.4b).

Home educational resources

To what extent are having a quiet place to study, a calculator and other resources related to education associated with better outcomes as reflected in measures of reading achievement and engagement? This issue is addressed in PISA through a question that asks students about the availability of educational resources in their home: a dictionary, a desk, a quiet place to study, textbooks and calculators. Their responses were combined to form an index with a mean of 0 and a standard deviation of 1.

Among OECD countries, the effect of home educational resources is similar to socio-economic background. The median correlation is 0.26 with achievement and only 0.16 with engagement (Table 6.3). On average, students who live in homes where these resources are present do better than students who do not. In all OECD countries the correlation between home educational resources and achievement is positive and exceeds 0.10 (see Table 6.4c). Mexico has the largest correlation (0.37) between home resources and achievement on the combined reading literacy scale. Other countries having a correlation over 0.30 are Belgium, Hungary, Luxembourg, New Zealand, Norway, Switzerland and the United States. And although access to home educational resources has less of an association with engagement than books in the home, it is positively correlated with engagement in each of the 32 participating countries. Among OECD countries, the correlations range from a low of 0.08 in Luxembourg to a high of 0.24 in the United Kingdom.

Cultural communication in the home

One way in which parents play an important role in the academic success of their children is through their interest and involvement in their children's education. When parents communicate with their children they not only demonstrate an interest in them, they also model language and question-asking behaviours that support the kinds of activities that are common in classrooms. Students were asked to indicate how often their parents discussed social and political issues with them, discussed a book with them, discussed television or films or listened to classical music with them. Their responses were combined to form an index of cultural communication having a mean of 0 and a standard deviation of 1.

This family characteristic correlates with both achievement and engagement. Among OECD countries, the median correlation with achievement is 0.24 (see Table 6.3). The correlation is at least 0.10 in every country except Greece, where it is 0.09. In Belgium, Germany, Mexico, the Netherlands, Spain and the United Kingdom, the correlation is 0.30 or higher (see Table 6.4d). By comparison, the median correlation with engagement is 0.35 or about 50 per cent higher than the correlation of cultural communication with achievement. In every OECD country with the exception of Korea (0.27), the correlation with engagement is greater than 0.30. The standard deviation of the correlations between engagement and cultural communication is 0.03, indicating very little variation among OECD countries. Clearly, the time parents spend communicating with their children about culturally relevant information is associated with both higher achievement and higher engagement in reading.

Family structure

Another family characteristic that may play an important role in the achievement of students is family structure. As we have already noted, parents play an important role in their children's overall success not only in terms of the physical environment and possessions that they provide but also in terms of the support and encouragement that they give to their children. This may be more difficult if students are living in a home with only one parent or guardian as that person is likely to have sole responsibility for work, home and community activities.

Students were asked to indicate who usually lived at home with them. From their responses it was possible to construct a variable and to compare the performance of students from different family structures. A variable was created in which students were coded 1 if they lived with two parents or guardians and 0 if they lived in some other family structure. Table 6.3 shows the relationship between family structure and both achievement and engagement.

In general, students from homes with two parents or guardians do somewhat better in terms of achievement than students from other types of household. The median correlation among OECD countries is 0.10.

Perhaps not surprisingly, there is a considerable range in the size of the effect of this variable among both the OECD and the non-OECD countries.

As shown in Table 6.4e the largest correlation between family structure and achievement is seen in the United States (0.27). Fourteen other OECD countries have correlations that range between 0.10 and 0.15. These countries are Australia, Belgium, Canada, Denmark, Finland, France, Hungary, Ireland, Luxembourg, the Netherlands, New Zealand, Norway, Sweden and the United Kingdom. In the remaining countries the correlation between family structure and achievement is positive but less than 0.10. Again there are no meaningful interactions among the reading literacy subscales. Liechtenstein (0.15) is the only non-OECD country that has a positive correlation greater than 0.10.

It is interesting to note that there is no association between reading engagement and family structure, and there is little variation among OECD countries. The median correlation is 0.04 and the standard deviation of these correlations is 0.03. The correlation between engagement and family structure in all OECD countries is close to zero. In three countries it is negative and ranges between -0.01 and -0.03, while in the remaining 25 countries, the correlation is positive but never exceeds 0.08. Among non-OECD countries, only Liechtenstein (0.15) has a correlation that is positive and greater than 0.10. Thus, despite the importance of families and family structure, there does not appear to be any relationship with student engagement in reading.

Immigration status

Social, political and economic factors have a significant impact on the patterns of movement from one country to another and hence on the environments in which children often have to learn. Students are increasingly finding themselves having to adjust not only to new cultures and customs but also to new languages of instruction. While they may be quite proficient in their native language, many students are recent immigrants and therefore "new" to the language of instruction and testing. Students were asked to indicate whether they themselves and each of their parents were born in the country in which they were living, or in another country. Their responses were coded to reflect the extent to which each student came from a non-native family. That is, their responses were coded 1 if they and both of their parents were born in another country. It should be noted that no information was collected in the questionnaire to indicate how long the student or their family had lived in the country or how similar their first language might be to the language of instruction.

A comparison of the performance between these non-native students and their peers reveals a rather weak correlation between immigration status and achievement (-0.09) and no relationship with engagement (0.00). The overall size and strength of these correlations are somewhat misleading in that they are affected by the relatively small numbers of 15-year-olds who report being non-native students. For those who are, however, there is a strong impact on achievement: the median regression effect across OECD countries is two-thirds of a standard deviation, or 66 points (see Table 6.4f). The negative number shown in Table 6.3 indicates that when compared with their peers, these non-native students perform significantly less well on the combined reading literacy scale. In 15 of the OECD countries, the effect exceeds 65 points and ranges from 66 points in Denmark to 103 points in Switzerland. In Canada, the Czech Republic, New Zealand and Portugal, the effect is between 20 and 25 points.

Australia, Hungary and Ireland provide interesting exceptions to the general pattern observed in the OECD countries. The only country where there is a significant difference in favour of non-native students is Ireland. Here the average effect is 47 points on the combined reading literacy scale in favour of non-native students. Among the other OECD countries, only Australia (-16 points) and Hungary (6 points) have effects that are less than 20 per cent of a standard deviation and are thought not to be meaningful.

The correlation of immigration status with reading engagement appears to be close to zero in every OECD country. Again, the size of the correlation can be misleading due to the relatively small percentages of students who are classified as "non-native." In about 12 of the countries the correlation is negative and ranges from -0.01 to -0.07. In a few of these countries, being a non-native student seems to have a negative impact on reading engagement. As shown in Table 6.7, the effect is about one-quarter of a standard deviation in the Czech Republic, Iceland and Switzerland and almost a full standard deviation in Japan and Poland. In other OECD countries, there appears to be a positive impact on engagement. This is especially true in English-speaking countries. Here we observe that the average effect of regressing reading engagement on immigration status is about one-fifth to one-half of a standard deviation. It ranges from 0.18 and 0.19 in Canada and Australia respectively to 0.23 in New Zealand, 0.32 in the United Kingdom and 0.43 in Ireland. Portugal also demonstrates a similar result, having an average effect of 0.26.

Reading literacy and the classroom environment

While students acquire important characteristics from their parents and the family environment in which they live, the classroom environment is of course also significant. This section takes a look at several characteristics relating to classroom environment that were included in the student questionnaire and might have an impact on student performance. These are student perceptions of achievement pressure, sense of belonging at school, relationship with teachers and disciplinary climate. Perhaps the biggest caution in examining these data relates to the fact that these questions were asked of students at a single point in time. While the questionnaire refers the student to their current "test language" teacher, other teachers are likely to have had a significant influence on their attitudes and achievement.

Pressure to achieve

To what extent do students in various countries perceive that their teachers have high expectations for them to work hard and achieve, and to what extent are these perceptions related to engagement and achievement in reading literacy? Students were asked to respond to questions that dealt with the extent to which teachers want students to work hard and to learn a lot, and how often they display disapproval of poor work and tell them they can do better. These questions were combined into an index with a mean of 0 and a standard deviation of 1. A positive value on this index indicates that students have a more positive perception that their teachers want them to achieve than the OECD average.

Overall, the index measuring pressure to achieve does not have much of a relationship with student reading literacy performance (see Table 6.5). The median correlation with reading achievement among OECD countries is -0.06 and the median regression effect is -6 points. There are no meaningful interactions among the reading literacy subscales (see Table 6.6a). Similarly, there is no relationship between achievement pressure and engagement in reading. Here the median correlation is -0.01.

As one might expect, however, there are some interesting differences between countries in terms of how achievement pressure relates to both achievement and engagement. In 19 of the 28 OECD countries and in two of the four non-OECD countries, the correlation of achievement pressure with reading achievement is negative. In nine of these 19 OECD countries, the negative correlation is greater than -0.10, suggesting that increased pressure to achieve would be expected to have a negative impact on performance. The largest negative effects are observed in Finland, New Zealand and Sweden, each having a correlation of -0.15. In eight of the OECD countries the correlation is positive, while in one country (Mexico) it is zero. In only two countries are the positive correlations greater than 0.10 – Greece, 0.12, and Korea, 0.19.

In terms of reading engagement the pattern is similar, but even fewer countries have correlations, either positive or negative, that exceed 0.10. Finland has the largest negative correlation between achievement pressure and engagement in reading (-0.13). On the positive side there are only two countries that have a positive correlation of at least 0.10. These are Korea (0.12) and the United States (0.10).

Disciplinary climate

Students were also asked to indicate the frequency with which certain behaviours that might affect the learning climate occur in their class. These behaviours concern: the frequency with which students do nothing during the first five minutes of class; students do not begin to work for a long time after the lesson begins; students do not listen to the teacher; students appear unable to work well; there is lots of noise and disorder in the class; and the teacher has to wait a long time for students to settle down. Again, these six variables were combined into a single index with a mean of 0 and standard deviation of 1, positive values on this index indicating an atmosphere more favourable to learning than the OECD average.

As with achievement pressure, there is a small but positive association between classroom disciplinary climate and reading performance, and between disciplinary climate and reading engagement in all OECD countries and in two non-OECD countries. The median correlation is 0.10 in both cases among OECD countries overall (see Table 6.5). The positive correlation of disciplinary climate with achievement reaches or exceeds 0.10 in 17 of the OECD countries and in one of the non-OECD countries. A very similar pattern is seen with engagement in reading. Here the correlation equals or exceeds 0.10 in 17 of the 28 OECD countries and in two of the four non-OECD countries. There does not seem to be a noticeable interaction between disciplinary climate and performance on the subscales of reading literacy (Table 6.6b).

While it appears that being in a classroom that is perceived to be less disruptive has a small association with both achievement and engagement, it is impossible to tease out cause and effect from these data. It may be that students with less skill and motivation are grouped into classes that are less focused and more disruptive. It is also possible that students learn less and become less motivated if they spend more time in disruptive classrooms.

Sense of belonging

To what extent do students feel comfortable being at school and to what degree are these perceptions related to student outcomes in participating countries? Students were asked to respond to five statements: I feel left out of things; I make friends easily; I feel like I belong; I feel awkward and out of place; and Other students seem to like me. An index was formed with a mean of 0 and standard deviation of 1, a positive value on this index indicating a favourable sense of belonging at school. The overall correlation with reading achievement is about zero, 0.07 with reading literacy and 0.04 with engagement in reading. These data are shown in Table 6.5.

As with the other variables in this section there are some interesting differences between countries. With few exceptions, all the correlations between sense of belonging and both achievement and engagement are positive. In three of the OECD countries (Luxembourg, Mexico and Portugal) the correlation with achievement exceeds 0.20. In Brazil, Mexico and Portugal the correlation with engagement in reading is 0.22, 0.21 and 0.19, respectively. There are a few countries where the correlation with either achievement or engagement is negative, and in these cases it does not exceed -0.03. As was the case with disciplinary climate, there seems to be no interaction between sense of belonging and performance on the subscales of reading literacy (Table 6.6c).

Student-teacher relationship

How do students perceive they get along with their teachers and to what extent do students in the various countries feel their teachers are interested in their overall well-being and success? How do these perceptions relate to performance and to engagement in reading? Students were asked the degree to which they agreed with each of five statements related to this issue. These statements were: Students get along with most teachers; Most teachers are interested in students' well-being; Most of my teachers listen to what I really have to say; If I need extra help I will receive it from my teachers; and Most of my teachers treat me fairly. These variables were combined to form an index with a mean of 0 and standard deviation of 1. Positive values on this index indicate a perception about students' relationships with their teachers that is more positive than the OECD average.

As with other variables in this section the correlation between students' reported relationship with their teachers and performance in reading literacy is relatively small. The median correlation shown in Table 6.5 is 0.08 among OECD countries. In 12 of the 28 OECD countries the correlation is both positive and greater than 0.10. While there is a negative correlation in seven OECD countries, only in Hungary does this correlation reach -0.10.

On the other hand, students' relationship with their teachers has a median correlation of 0.17 with engagement in reading, and this correlation is positive in every country. In addition, in all countries the correlation is higher with engagement than with achievement. Not unrelated to this, and perhaps more importantly, there is less variation within both OECD and non-OECD countries. In all 32 participating countries the correlation exceeds 0.10, and in 11 of these 32 countries the correlation is 0.20 or higher. It may also be worth noting that with one exception each of these countries is either English-speaking or located in Northern Europe. The exception is Poland. In this country the correlation between students' relationship with their teachers and achievement is 0.04, while the correlation with engagement is 0.22. There seems to be no noticeable interaction between student-teacher relationship and performance on the subscales of reading literacy.

Notes

1. These background characteristics were selected because they represent important characteristics that are thought to be related to the outcomes of reading engagement and performance and because there is relatively complete data from each country.

2. In this chapter we distinguish between correlation coefficients that are 0.10 or higher from those that are smaller. A correlation of 0.10 or larger indicates that the relationship is accounting for at least 1 per cent of the variance.

THE INTERPLAY BETWEEN INDIVIDUAL BACKGROUND CHARACTERISTICS AND SCHOOL FACTORS

KEY POINTS

- The relationships between reading performance and student and school background characteristics vary from one country to another. Nevertheless, it is possible to identify groups of countries which display some similarities in the way in which student and school context variables interact with reading.

- Countries including Denmark, Finland, Iceland, Norway and Sweden have created educational structures that limit the differences between schools in both student attendance characteristics and achievement. The patterns of relationships in these countries are quite similar: student characteristics seem to have a statistical influence at the student level but no impact at the school level.

- Predominantly English-speaking countries share some similarities with Denmark, Finland, Iceland, Norway and Sweden, but the streaming that takes place in some of these countries modifies the patterns of relationships. Further, where not all schools are free of charge, it appears that social segregation predominates over academic segregation.

- In the remaining European countries, mixed patterns are observed, depending especially on the scale of tracking and streaming processes. In some countries, social segregation predominates over academic segregation; in other countries, the opposite is observed.

- It is very unlikely that education systems will be able to overcome social or other inequities completely. In some countries, inequities are located mainly at the school level, in other countries, inequities seem to be concentrated at the family level, and in the remaining countries, inequities are found at both levels. Trying to reduce the inequities at one level might have the consequence of increasing them at another.

- Nevertheless, some educational structures seem to be associated with fewer inequities. Educational structures do matter.

This chapter seeks to identify and interpret relationships between student achievement in reading literacy and an array of background variables. The aim is to disentangle the complex interactions between factors that may contribute to reading proficiency, including student background characteristics, attitudes to school and learning, and learning environments.

The focus will be on identifying patterns of relationships between the background variables and reading. Although it is undeniable that each country has a unique profile in terms of the relationships between the set of variables used in this report and reading literacy, there are nevertheless clearly identifiable similarities between some countries, as the initial OECD international report on PISA (OECD, 2001) indicates. For instance, countries appear to fall into distinct categories with regard to the relationship between students' achievement in reading and the homogeneity or heterogeneity of the student population within schools. Because this chapter mainly focuses on patterns of relationships, less attention will be given to the profiles of particular countries than to the main tendencies in groups of countries. However, some descriptions of individual countries' results will also be provided in the case of the most important variables.

A multilevel and multifactor model

Chapter 6 presented results showing the linear relationship between a set of background variables and reading literacy as a way of introducing the set of variables to be modelled here. The statistical analyses presented in this chapter differ from those presented in the previous chapter in two ways.

First, whereas the previous chapter analyses the relationship between single background variables and reading, in this chapter, all of the background variables are included in a single model. This type of analysis is useful because, as the different background variables interact with each other, effects may be confounded. For instance, on average girls are more engaged in reading than boys. But when the achievement levels of boys and girls are compared, the performance difference between these two groups is in a sense contaminated by their respective engagement in reading. Controlling the gender difference for engagement in reading is equivalent to answering the question, "What would the gender difference in reading performance be if boys and girls were equally engaged in reading?" By including many background variables in a single model, it is possible to estimate more accurately the effect of each variable while controlling for the effects of the others.

Second, linear regression models, like those described in Chapter 6, are sometimes used to disentangle the complex relationships among a set of variables. This procedure can, however, provide an incomplete or misleading picture of the way education systems function because it ignores the potential effects that may arise from the way in which students are assigned to schools or to classes within schools. In some countries, for instance, the socio-economic background of the student may partly determine the type of school that he or she attends and there may be little variation therefore in the socio-economic background of students within each school. In other countries or systems, it may be that schools by and large draw on students from a wide range of socio-economic backgrounds, but that within the school, the socio-economic background of the student has an impact on the type of class to which he or she is allocated and, therefore, on the within-school variance. A linear regression model that does not take the hierarchical structure of the data into account will not differentiate between these two systems.

The use of multilevel regression models (Bryk and Raudenbush,1992; Goldstein, 1995) offers the possibility of taking into account the fact that students are nested within classes and schools. In this way the relative contribution of class and school can be considered when estimating the contribution of each factor to the outcome measure.

Figure 7.1

Model for the relationship between socio-economic background and student performance at individual and school levels

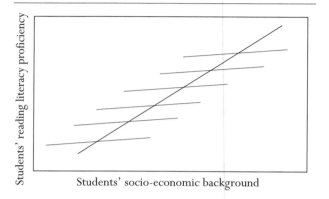

Figure 7.1 shows the distinction between a linear regression and a multilevel linear regression model. Let us suppose that this graph presents the relationship between the student's socio-economic background and his or her reading performance estimate. The black line represents the regression line when the hierarchical structure of the data is not taken into account. It shows that the expected score of a student from a higher socio-economic background is considerably higher than the expected score of a student from a lower socio-economic background.

The red lines represent the relationships between these two variables within particular schools. For each school there is one regression line (a red line in this particular example). The comparison between the two models shows that schools differ in their social intakes (some regression lines are further to the left of the graph than others), and that the effect of the socio-economic background on achievement is less significant within any particular school than it is between schools.

Figure 7.2 presents the three kinds of regression coefficient for students' socio-economic background on the combined reading literacy performance, using three different models. Also included is the regression coefficient for school social intake on reading literacy. Each country has three bars above the horizontal axis and one bar underneath to indicate the effects of students' socio-economic background on reading literacy, based on single regression, multiple regression and hierarchical multilevel model.

The first bar shows the regression coefficients from the simple regression without controlling for other variables. For instance, the regression coefficient for Australia is 31.7, representing in PISA scale points the expected improvement in performance for every standard deviation of student socio-economic background. Socio-economic background is expressed on a scale with an average of about 45 and a standard deviation of about 16. Thus a student with a score of 61 on the socio-economic background scale is expected to have a score 31.7 points higher than a student with a score of 45 on the socio-economic background scale.

The second bar presents the socio-economic background regression coefficient after controlling for other variables. It therefore shows the net statistical effect of socio-economic background, once the statistical effect of other variables has been taken into account. For instance, the regression coefficient for Australia is now 20.0. If two students had the same characteristics, except for their socio-economic background, then the expected difference between these two students would be 20 score points if one standard deviation on the socio-economic background scale separated them.

A comparison between the first and second bars of Figure 7.2 shows that a large proportion of the apparent effect of socio-economic background is due to other variables, such as engagement in reading, cultural communication in the family and so on. It should be noted that on average, the regression coefficient

| Figure 7.2 |

Effects of socio-economic background on reading literacy performance based on three different regression models

Effect of socio-economic background
- ■ as single factor
- ■ on variance among students within schools
- ■ as one of multiple factors
- ■ on variance between schools

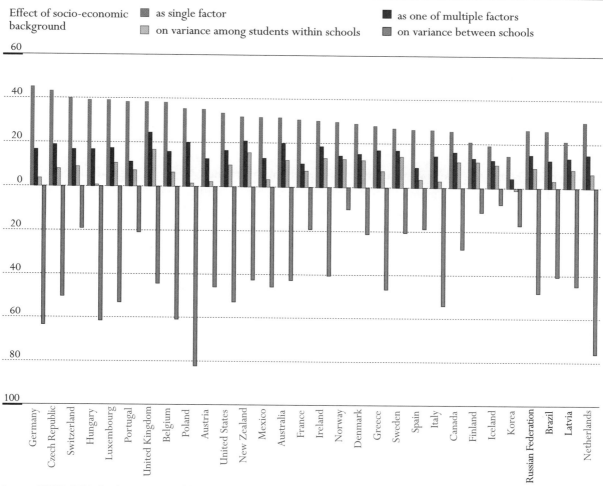

Source: OECD PISA database, 2001. Table 7.1.

for student socio-economic background is reduced by half once other variables are included in the linear regression.

The third column represents the socio-economic background regression coefficient within schools: that is, the red lines in Figure 7.1. For instance, this regression coefficient is 12.2 for Australia. Two students, attending the same school and having the same characteristics except their socio-economic background, will differ, on average, by 12.2 score points on the reading scale if they are separated by one standard deviation on the socio-economic background scale. Using a multilevel regression model again reduces by about half, on average, the regression coefficient for student socio-economic background computed by a multifactor linear regression. This reduction ranges from 10 per cent in the case of Norway to nearly 95 per cent in the case of Hungary.

Finally, the bar underneath the line represents the regression coefficient for the school's socio-economic intake, which indicates the socio-economic make-up of students within a school. School social intake was estimated by averaging the socio-economic background of the participating students of each school. Schools differ in their social intake. Some schools have students from higher socio-economic backgrounds, while others – for instance schools in industrial areas – are mainly attended by students from lower socio-economic backgrounds. The variation in socio-economic background is wider for individual students than for schools. While on average 68 per cent (one standard deviation on either side of the mean) of students have a socio-economic background index between 29 and 61, 68 per cent of schools' social intake are between 37.5 and 52.5. In other words, the standard deviation of the school social intake is about 7.5. The regression coefficient for school social intake is 42.7 in Australia. Two Australian students who had the same profile in terms of socio-economic background, gender, engagement and so on, but attend different schools that vary in social intake by 7.5, would be expected to show a 42.7 difference in reading performance.

As shown in Figure 7.2, the statistical effect of a particular variable can vary a great deal according to the model and the variables included in the model. This chapter will present results from a multilevel multivariate regression analysis that makes it possible to separate the effect at the between-school level and at the within-school level. All the results presented are net effects: that is, the effects after controlling for other variables.

Student and school variables used in the model

In order to explain reading achievement the following groups of variables were included[1]:

- Individual characteristics of the student: Gender, engagement in reading.

- Socio-economic background variables: Family structure, occupational status of parents, number of books at home, cultural communication with parents, home educational resources, immigration status.

- Instruction and learning: Time spent on homework, achievement press, grade.

- Perceptions of school and learning climate: Disciplinary climate, student-teacher relations, sense of belonging to school.

- School characteristics: Mean of parents' occupational status, mean of engagement in reading.

Details about the variables included in the model are provided in Annex A3. Additional variables collected through the school questionnaire were originally included in the analysis, but their effects were very small and usually not significant[2]. Furthermore, including these variables considerably increased the amount of missing data[3]. For these reasons, it was considered appropriate not to include these additional variables in the model.

Socio-economic background and engagement in reading as major effects

Table 7.2 presents the averages of the national regression coefficients for the combined reading literacy scale, the three aspect subscales (retrieving information, interpreting texts and reflection and evaluation) and the two format subscales (continuous texts and non-continuous texts). The first fourteen variables listed in the first column use the within-school multilevel regression model (see the third column in Table 7.1). The last two variables – school engagement and school social intake – use the between-school multilevel regression model (see the last column in Table 7.1).

Combined reading literacy scale

Five variables seem to have an important statistical impact at the within-school level: engagement in reading, immigration status, socio-economic background, grade and gender.

Grade shows the largest effect: 37.3 on average. As previously noted, the target population of PISA is 15-year-olds attending school. In most though not all countries, students in this population are in different grades. Generally, the difference in reading performance of students in two adjacent grades varies between 50 and 80 score points, depending on the two adjacent grades. Nevertheless, these sub-populations cannot be directly compared, as students who have repeated a grade may on average be from a lower socio-economic background, be less engaged in reading and so on[4]. The regression coefficient of 37.3 is a net effect after controlling for the other variables. The regression coefficient of 37.3 represents the difference between two adjacent grades expected in any particular school if students from these two grades have the same characteristics.

The second largest impact is associated with immigration status. When a student and both parents were born in another country, the student's reading performance within a particular school is expected to be lower by 21.8 score points than that of another student who is matched in terms of the other variables.

The third largest impact is associated with engagement in reading. Students with the same characteristics, attending the same school but with a difference of one standard deviation in their engagement in reading, will differ by about 18 score points in their reading performance. This represents about half the grade effect and, more interestingly, twice the impact of socio-economic background. In other words, within any school, student engagement in reading matters more than student socio-economic background in predicting reading proficiency.

Previous chapters have already discussed the large performance difference that exists between boys and girls in reading literacy. Nevertheless, this difference can partly be explained by other differences such as engagement in reading. When such differences are controlled, the gap between boys and girls in any particular school is about 12 score points, approximately one third of the absolute difference.

Finally, the socio-economic background of students has, on average, an impact of 8 score points within any particular school. It would be inappropriate to conclude from this rather small regression coefficient that socio-economic background has a small effect on students' reading performance. This coefficient, like the others discussed in this section, represents the differences associated with reading performance within schools. In many countries, the school attended by a student is at least partly determined by socio-economic background, or by previous academic performance. The regression coefficient for the school social intake reflects how much the school reading performance increases if the average of the students' socio-economic background increases by 7.5 score points (one standard deviation on the socio-economic background index). This regression coefficient is close to an average of 40 score points across all participating countries. In the United States, for instance, the five schools with the lowest social intake have on average a school-level social intake of about 35 and a reading performance average of 387. At the opposite extreme, the five schools with the highest school-level social intake have a social intake average of about 66 and a reading performance average of about 596. A social intake difference of 31 — about four standard deviations of the socio-economic index — is associated with a reading performance difference of about 210 score points: that is, four times the regression coefficient of the school social intake of the United States (52.8).

This reflects the fact that among OECD countries, schools differ according to their social intakes and that these differences are associated with large differences in school reading performance.

As shown by the regression coefficient for school engagement, schools also differ in terms of their students' engagement in reading. Students seem to be more engaged in reading in some schools than in others. These differences are also associated with a reading performance difference of 23. While this is a relatively large coefficient, it appears that at the school level, reading performance differences are associated more strongly with social intake differences than with differences in reading engagement.

The other variables included in the model appear to have a smaller effect. As expected, reading performance is associated with the number of books in the home (5.0). Students whose parents devote time to discussing cultural issues with them tend to perform better in reading (2.9). Educational resources at home are also associated with a small but positive effect (3.0). Not surprisingly, students living in a nuclear family on average perform better than do students living in single-parent or mixed families (2.3).

The five variables that are related to the school are, in decreasing order of their effect: achievement pressure (-3.1), disciplinary climate (1.4), student-teacher relationship (1.0), student's sense of belonging (1.0) and time spent on homework (0.2). In other words, in any particular school, students who perceive higher pressure from their teacher to perform better obtain, on average, lower results in reading. This could be because teachers more often put pressure on, or encourage, students who have academic difficulties. Schools or classes where students perceive greater disciplinary problems are also associated with a small decrease in performance. Not surprisingly, students who have a better relationship with their teachers and who have positive feelings towards being at school on average perform better. Finally, spending more time on homework seems to be associated with a very small difference in reading proficiency.

In summary, the aggregate effects of students' engagement in reading and socio-economic background, including immigration status and number of books in the home, are associated with the greatest differences in the reading literacy score of a given school, and are the likely explanation for these differences. Variables related to students' perception of their school and time spent on homework show, on average, smaller effects.

Reading subscales

The analyses shown here on the combined reading literacy scale were also applied to the three aspect subscales (retrieving information, interpreting texts and reflection and evaluation) as well as to the two format subscales (continuous texts and non-continuous texts). Table 7.2 provides the means of the regression coefficients across countries for each of the five subscales. These coefficients express the "unique" predictive power of each variable, after controlling for all other variables included in the analysis.

With the exception of gender, there are no substantial differences in the regression coefficients across the five subscales of reading literacy. Gender differences do vary markedly from one aspect to another and from one text format to another, once the other variables have been taken into account. On the retrieving information and the non-continuous texts subscales, it appears that the difference between males and females can be explained mostly by the other variables included in the model. On the other hand, substantial differences remain between males and females on the two remaining aspect subscales (interpreting texts and reflection and evaluation) and on the remaining format subscale (continuous texts).

There are a few other meaningful differences across the reading subscales that are worth mentioning, even though these differences are small in absolute value. For instance, in nearly all countries, the effect of cultural communication is smallest on the retrieving information subscale and largest on the reflection and evaluation subscale. It is also smaller for non-continuous texts than for continuous texts.

The disciplinary climate index also shows an interesting pattern across the five subscales. As the disciplinary problems faced by schools increase, their results tend to be lower on the interpreting texts and reflection and evaluation subscales compared with retrieving information. The effect of disciplinary climate is also smaller for in the case of non-continuous texts than in that of continuous texts. Even though these differences are small, they are observable in all or nearly all countries.

Differences between countries in the effects of individual and school factors on reading performance

While small differences are observed from one subscale to another, there are much larger differences in the numerical values of the regression coefficients between countries. Tables 7.3 to 7.8 show, for each country, the regression coefficients for the different variables used in the analyses. A number in bold indicates that the regression coefficient is significantly different from 0 (with an alpha of 0.05).

Table 7.3 shows the regression coefficients within schools for gender and engagement in reading. Within schools, gender differences by country range on average from -0.5 in Poland to 28.6 in New Zealand. In five countries – Brazil, Germany, Ireland, the Netherlands, Poland and Portugal – gender differences within schools are not statistically significant.

The regression coefficients for engagement in reading also show substantial variation. They range from 8.9 in Greece to 31 in Iceland. All regression coefficients for engagement in reading are significantly different from 0.

Table 7.4 shows the within-school association between reading proficiency and three home and family background variables: family structure, occupational status of parents and immigration status.

Living in a nuclear family is commonly assumed to imply better school performance, and this association is confirmed in a number of countries. The largest regression coefficient is for the United States (21.5). On the other hand, living with one parent or with a mixed family is also associated with better performance in some countries, for example Belgium and Mexico. It should be noted that in about half of the countries, the statistical impact of family structure is not significantly different from 0.

The within-school regression coefficients for socio-economic background, determined by means of the socio-economic index of occupational status, range from -1.1 in Korea to 16.7 in the United Kingdom. In four countries – Austria, Hungary, Korea and Poland – these regression coefficients are not significantly different from 0, meaning that students within a particular school but with different socio-economic backgrounds would be expected to have the same performance in reading.

The regression coefficients for the immigration status of students also show great variation between countries. They range from -61.8 in Finland to 8.7 in Ireland. A possible explanation is that the profiles of immigrants differ from country to country. There is little doubt that countries with a positive regression coefficient are characterised by immigrants from middle or high socio-economic backgrounds. The language background of immigrants – whether it is the same as that of the host country or not – is also likely to play an important part in the interaction between immigration status and reading proficiency[5].

Table 7.5 shows regression coefficients at the within-school level for cultural communication with parents, educational resources in the home and the number of books in the home.

The cultural communication between a student and his or her parents – discussing political or social issues; discussing books, films or television programmes; listening to classical music together – is associated with better reading performance in some countries, most markedly Australia (9.2) and Denmark (10.9). In half of the countries, however, the regression coefficient for cultural communication is not significantly different from 0.

Similarly, the availability of educational resources in the home, such as text books, a desk, and a quiet place to study, has a substantial impact in some countries including Norway (10.3) and New Zealand (9.6), but appears to have no impact in quite a large number of countries.

The regression coefficients for the number of books in the home range from 0.6 in Brazil to 9.3 in the United States and are statistically different from 0 in all except three countries: Brazil, Italy and Poland.

PISA 2000 collected information from students about a number of issues related to teaching and learning in schools, and about the learning environment. Regression coefficients for students' perception of pressure to achieve, the amount of time they spend on homework, and their class grade are presented in Table 7.6 , while Table 7.7 shows the regression coefficients for students' perception of their relationship with teachers, their sense of belonging at school and the school's disciplinary climate.

The regression coefficients for grade range from 70.7 in Spain to 10.5 in the United Kingdom, and are significantly different from 0 for every country except Korea and Norway.

Apart from grade, the school variables tend to be associated with small differences in reading achievement, although there is also an indication of some differences between countries. In some countries, school variables do not have significant effects on reading literacy, while in others significant relationships with reading performance, either positive or negative, are observed.

Finally, there are two variables at the school level that are associated with large differences in performance and also show considerable variation between countries (Table 7.8). They are school social intake and school-level engagement in reading.

The school social intake regression coefficients range from 7.5 in Iceland to 82.6 in Poland. In other words, while differences in social intake are not associated with differences in school-level performance in reading in Iceland, a difference of one standard deviation in the school social intake index in Poland is associated with more than 80 PISA scale points in the reading performance.

The regression coefficients for school-level engagement in reading also show great variation. They range from -1 in Brazil to 65 in Greece. In most but not all countries, this regression coefficient is significantly different from 0.

Given that countries show substantial variation in the regression coefficients of student and school factors, it might be thought that each country has a unique profile and that it is not worth trying to identify similarities between countries or between groups of countries. On the other hand, some countries do have similarities in their educational structures and features. For instance, it is well known that in some countries, including Austria, Belgium and Germany, students tend to be grouped according to their academic performance through various mechanisms of the school system: Special Education schools, tracking, streaming, grade retention and competition between schools, to name only the most important. By contrast, to keep the differences between schools as small as possible, countries including Denmark, Finland, Norway and Sweden limit parental choice of school through fixed school catchment areas. Further, in these countries there are no tracks or streams, and automatic promotion regulates the transition from one grade to the next. Such differences in educational structure are likely to be partly reflected in the association of student and school characteristics with reading performance. The next section is concerned with identifying such patterns of relationships.

Similarities and differences between countries

This section focuses on the relationships between the explanatory variables and student performance on the combined reading scale. The purpose here is not to describe each country separately but to try to identify similarities within groups of countries in terms of relationships between the explanatory variables modelled in the previous section and reading literacy. On the basis of the similarities and differences that emerge from this exercise, countries will be grouped into different sets.

There is an issue that makes this attempt problematic. Classifying or grouping countries according to the pattern of relationships between student performance in reading and other variables is not a straight forward process: the analysis of the relationships is based on continuous variables, but in order to construct a classification system, it is necessary to set cut-off points along the continuous variable.

Differences between schools in reading performance

The reading performance of each student can be represented by a test score, or by the difference between his or her score and the country average. In educational research, it is usual to split the difference between the student score and the country average into two parts: *(i)* the distance between the student performance estimate and the corresponding school mean; and *(ii)* the distance between this school mean and the country mean. The first difference is called the within-school variance. It indicates how much student score can vary within any particular school. The second difference — that is, the difference between the school average and the country average — is called the between-school variance. This indicates how much student performance differs from one school to another. It is usual to express the relative sizes of the between-school and within-school variances by an intraclass correlation.

Box 7.1: Intraclass correlation

This coefficient is equal to the between-school variance divided by the sum of the between-school and within-school variances. It is equal to 0 if the school achievement mean estimates are all identical. It increases as school mean achievement estimates differ more widely. A coefficient of 1 means that all schools differ in terms of achievement whereas within schools all the students have exactly the same performance estimate: that is, there is no variation between students within schools, once the difference between schools has been accounted for.

Figure 7.3 presents the intraclass correlation coefficient: that is, the percentage of the total variance in reading literacy achievement accounted for at the school level in each country.

Figure 7.3

Proportion of between-school variance to the total variance in student reading literacy performance

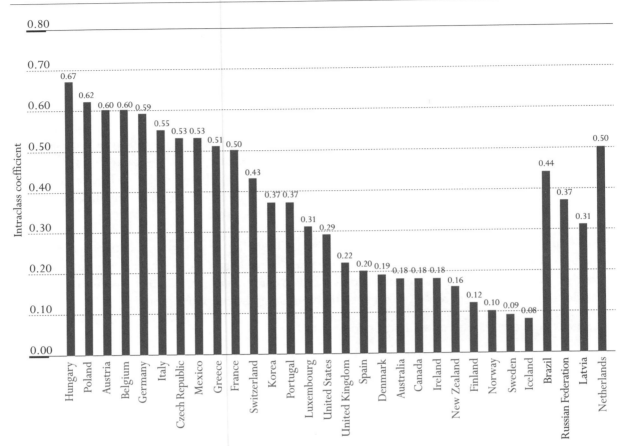

Source: OECD PISA database, 2001. Table 7.9.

Among PISA countries, the intraclass correlations range from 0.08 (meaning that only 8 per cent of the total variance is accounted for by differences between schools) to 0.67 (meaning that more than two thirds of the total variance is accounted for by differences between schools). Some patterns seem to emerge. Excluding Denmark, all Northern European countries (Finland, Iceland, Norway and Sweden) have an intraclass correlation below 0.15, with the coefficients ranging from 0.08 to 0.13. The six predominantly English-speaking countries have intraclass correlations between 0.15 and 0.30. All remaining European countries except Spain have an intraclass correlation above 0.30. As shown by these results, countries that share geographical, political or historical features also appear to share at least some characteristics of educational outcome. It seems likely that these patterns are partly determined by the educational structures.

The influence of student socio-economic background on reading performance

As mentioned earlier, the relationship between students' socio-economic background and academic performance may be mediated through school structures that promote social segregation. For example, in some countries the choice of school depends on the social and economic background of the student: where not all schools are free of charge, some students may have a limited choice because their families cannot afford school fees. Social segregation can also occur through other mechanisms. In particular, in countries where academic and vocational education are provided by different schools, the social intake of the schools may vary greatly because students from lower social and economic backgrounds are more likely to attend a vocational school.

Figure 7.4 plots countries' regression coefficients for student socio-economic background against their regression coefficients for school social intake (or the mean of the student socio-economic background index). The regression coefficients indicate the effect of the explanatory variables on reading performance. In countries appearing at the bottom right of the graph, there is a relatively strong association between reading proficiency and student socio-economic background in comparison with the association between reading proficiency and school-level socio-economic background. Conversely, in countries at the top left of the figure, school social intake has a stronger effect on reading proficiency in comparison with the effect on reading proficiency of individual student socio-economic background.

As shown by Figure 7.4, English-speaking countries and countries in Northern Europe such as Denmark, Finland, Iceland and Norway, are characterised by a relatively large effect of student socio-economic background in comparison with the remaining countries. This effect means that within any particular school, student achievement is associated with the individual student's socio-economic background. When this information is put alongside with the intraclass correlations shown in Figure 7.3, the small effect of

Figure 7.4

Effects of students' socio-economic background and schools' socio-economic background on reading literacy performance

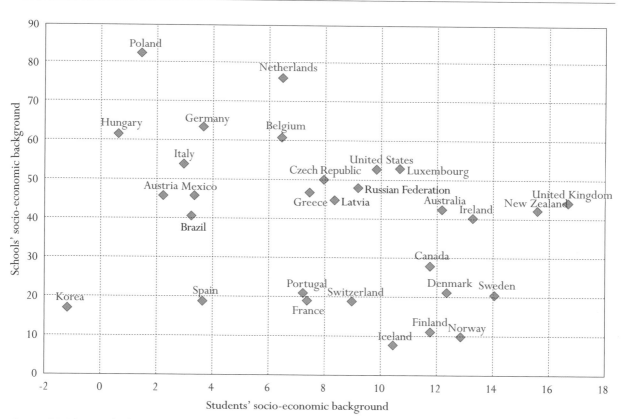

Source: OECD PISA database, 2001. Table 7.8.

school social intake in the countries in Northern Europe shows that this variable does not, however, have a strong effect on the relatively small differences in reading between schools in those countries. The effect of school socio-economic background in English-speaking countries, on the other hand, is larger: that is, in these countries the school which a student attends is determined partly by socio-economic background, and this affects the school mean performance in reading.

Most of the remaining European countries, as well as Brazil, Korea and Mexico, show a smaller effect of student socio-economic background. On the other hand, the school differences in their social intake appear to be strongly related to the performance differences between schools. In countries such as Austria, Belgium, Germany and the Netherlands, the highly tracked system largely contributes to the social segregation effect.

In France, Korea, Portugal, Spain and Switzerland, school social intake does not seem to be associated with difference in school performance.

Figure 7.4 also shows the complexity of the relationship between students' socio-economic background and their academic performance. In countries such as Iceland and Sweden, it does not matter which school the student attends, but the expected performance *within* a particular school is related to the socio-economic background of the student.

By contrast, in Austria, Hungary, Korea and Poland, the expected performance of a student within a particular school is independent of socio-economic background (the regression coefficients for these four countries are not significantly different from 0). The influence of socio-economic background on individual performance is also quite small, though significant, in Brazil, Germany, Italy and Mexico. Yet the influence of the school is crucial, as is shown by the size of the regression coefficients for the school social intake in all of these countries except Korea. In other words, what really matters in this last group of countries would seem not to be the socio-economic background of the individual student but the school that the student attends. Nevertheless, it needs to be remembered that the socio-economic background of the student may also determine the choice of the school.

Figures 7.5 to 7.7 show another way of representing the differences between education systems in terms of the influence of school social intake on the one hand and student socio-economic background on the other. Like Figure 7.1, each line in the figures represents the regression of socio-economic background on reading performance for a particular school. The horizontal axis represents the socio-economic background of the student, and the vertical axis represents reading performance.

Figure 7.5 shows what the school regression lines look like for Iceland. The proximity of the regression lines to each other represents the low between-school variance in reading performance. The slope of the regression lines shows that, within schools, students from different socio-economic backgrounds are expected to have different results.

Figure 7.6 illustrates the case of Greece. The regression lines start and end at different levels on the horizontal axis, showing some differences in school social intake. Also, the lines are now spread further apart on the vertical axis, showing differences in school achievement in reading. On the other hand, the slope of each regression line is now less steep, showing that within schools, individual student socio-economic background has a lower statistical impact on reading.

Figure 7.5

Multilevel regression line of students'
socio-economic background in Iceland

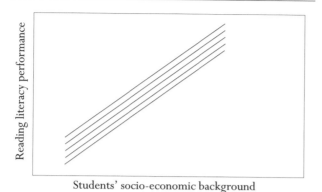

Students' socio-economic background

Figure 7.6

Multilevel regression line of students'
socio-economic background in Greece

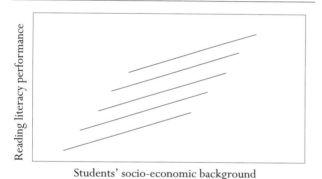

Students' socio-economic background

Figure 7.7

Multilevel regression line of students'
socio-economic background in Poland

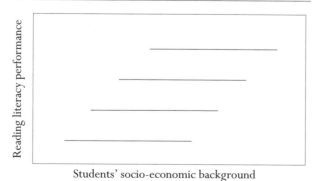

Students' socio-economic background

Finally, Figure 7.7 sketches the regression lines for Poland. The regression lines are parallel to the horizontal axis, indicating that there is no statistical effect of student socio-economic background within schools. On the other hand, the large dispersion of the regression lines on both axes reflects the substantial differences in both school social intake and school performance in reading.

The influence of engagement in reading

The second factor worth attention is student engagement in reading. This is closely correlated with performance in reading and, unlike gender or student socio-economic background, engagement in reading is a characteristic that is amenable to change.

Like socio-economic background, this variable was introduced in the analysis at the student level as well as at the school level, producing a school mean of reading engagement. Engagement in reading is a composite indication of the amount of time students spend reading and of their attitudes towards reading, according to their own reports. At the student level, a high score on this index means that the student reports that he or she reads a lot and enjoys reading. At the school level, this composite reflects how much, on average, students attending the school are engaged in reading, again according to their own reports.

Figure 7.8 shows countries' regression coefficients for student engagement in reading against their regression coefficients for engagement in reading at the school level.

As for the socio-economic background index, countries including Denmark, Finland, Iceland and Norway have a large regression coefficient for engagement at the student level, and English-speaking countries have a medium regression coefficient. In both of these sets of

Figure 7.8

Effects of students' reading engagement and schools' mean reading engagement on reading literacy performance

Source: OECD PISA database, 2001. Tables 7.3 and 7.8.

countries, engagement has a small effect at the school level. All of the other countries are characterised by a small or medium effect at the student level but, on average, the effect at the school level is larger than in Denmark, Finland, Iceland and Norway and English-speaking countries.

Academic versus social segregation

Figure 7.9 plots the regression coefficients of the school means for engagement in reading against the school social intake regression coefficients. This highlights the differences between countries described in the previous section.

In Denmark, Finland, Iceland and Sweden, the two composites appear to have small effects at the school level.

English-speaking countries seem to show a small school effect of engagement in reading but a larger effect of socio-economic background.

Brazil, Luxembourg, Mexico and the Russian Federation share a similar pattern to the English-speaking countries: that is, the regression coefficient for school social intake is larger than the regression coefficient for the school aggregate of student engagement in reading.

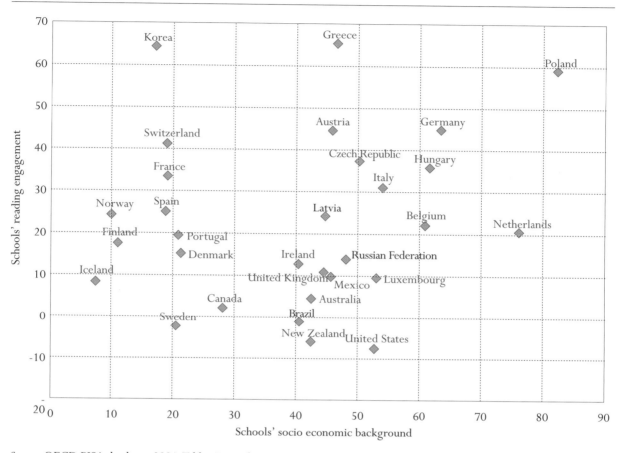

Figure 7.9

Effects of schools' socio-economic background vs schools' reading engagement
on reading literacy performance

Source: OECD PISA database, 2001. Tables 7.4 and 7.8.

In France, Portugal, Spain, Switzerland and, particularly, Korea, the regression coefficient for school social intake is smaller than the regression coefficient for the school aggregate of student engagement in reading.

What are the educational implications of the two regression coefficients at the school level? As mentioned earlier, the regression coefficient for school social intake reflects the importance of social segregation in each country's educational structure. Schools may directly or indirectly recruit students according to their socio-economic background. An example of a direct process is a system in which some schools demand fees and others do not, while not all parents in that country can afford to pay the fees. An example of an indirect process is geographical location, where there is variation in socio-economic background from one area to another and schools draw from the local community. A school located in a wealthy suburb, even if it is not fee-paying, is likely mainly to recruit students from higher socio-economic backgrounds and will therefore generate indirect social segregation.

Unlike social intake, engagement in reading is not the basis on which schools recruit students. No schools accept or refuse a student on the basis of how many books he or she reads per year and how much he or she enjoys reading. Nevertheless, the effect of this school variable is large enough in some countries to be regarded as another segregation effect. How can this be explained? The criterion that immediately comes to mind is the academic performance of the student. Parents of high achievers are likely to enrol their children in a highly demanding school, such as an academic school, while parents of low achievers are more likely to select a less demanding school. Given the high correlation between reading, mathematics and science, and given the correlation between engagement in reading and reading proficiency, it does not appear unreasonable to regard the effect of the school mean for engagement in reading as an indicator of academic selection.

The data presented graphically in Figure 7.9 support this interpretation. In countries such as Australia and the United States, where academic tracking at the school level is unusual, but where a substantial percentage of students attend fee-paying schools, social criteria predominate over academic criteria. A high achiever from a lower socio-economic background has limited opportunity to attend a fee-paying school. On the other hand, parents who can afford to are more likely to send their child to a fee-paying school, regardless of the child's academic performance.

In countries such as Belgium, Germany and Greece, where schools offer different types of programme (academic, technical and vocational), students are primarily grouped according to their academic performance. Since students attending vocational programmes have, on average, a lower socio-economic background than students attending academic programmes, the tracking systems in place in these countries also perpetuate social segregation.

In France, Korea, Portugal, Spain and Switzerland, the differences between schools seem to come mainly from an ability-grouping process.

It should be noted that in France and Greece, where lower secondary and upper secondary education are organised in different schools, academic selection might be overestimated and social segregation underestimated. Finally, it appears that no selection process seems to operate in the countries such as Denmark, Finland, Iceland and Norway. While the effect of low intraclass correlation in these countries appears to be similar to that of the English-speaking countries (though lower), the explanation is different.

Other background variables

The other student characteristic variables included in this model behave according to a similar pattern.

For instance, the average regression coefficient for cultural communication is 4.89 in the countries in Northern Europe and the English-speaking countries while it is 1.71 in the countries with a high intraclass correlation. The influence of family structure, the number of books in the home and student gender also appears to be higher in countries with a low intraclass correlation. In these countries, whether a student lives with one or both parents, and whether the student is a boy or a girl, are factors associated with larger differences in performance, regardless of the school. This does not mean that in the other countries such differences do not exist, but that the effect of these variables is mediated through the school. For example, in tracked education systems, more boys attend vocational or technical schools while more girls are enrolled in academic tracks. Students from higher socio-economic backgrounds, and therefore with more books available at home on average, are more likely to attend an academic school than a technical or vocational school.

School and instructional variables

The within-school effect on reading performance of achievement press, sense of belonging and the student-teacher relationship also differentiates countries with lower intraclass correlation from countries with higher intraclass correlation.

In predominantly English-speaking countries and countries in Northern Europe, as stated earlier, students who perceive that they are encouraged by their teachers to perform better have, on average, a lower reading performance than students who do not perceive such pressure. This perception could be interpreted as resulting from the teachers' efforts to help less proficient students. In the other countries, the within-school relationship between reading performance and pressure to achieve is quite low and even close to zero. On average, at the country level, students perceive slightly more pressure in Denmark, Finland, Iceland, Norway and Sweden and in the predominantly English-speaking countries than in the other countries.

Furthermore, one might expect that in highly tracked education systems, the variation in achievement pressure is not located at the student level but at the school level. It might be expected that students in academic schools are more likely than students in vocational schools to be encouraged by their teachers to perform better. However, the decomposition of the variance of achievement pressure at the school and student levels does not support this hypothesis. In all countries except the Czech Republic, less than 10 per cent of the variance is accounted for by the school. This might be because the perception of pressure to achieve, as reported by students, is relative rather than absolute: students feel more or less pressure in comparison with their classmates, so that school differences are masked. The low effect of pressure to achieve in highly tracked systems might also be a result of within-school streaming, where students who are encouraged to perform better are not necessarily low achievers in the context of the whole cohort.

The regression coefficients for students' sense of belonging to the school also present an interesting pattern. Coefficients range from -4.3 to 6.3 and are only significantly different from 0 in Belgium, Canada, the Czech Republic, Finland, Greece, Hungary, Luxembourg, Mexico, Poland, Portugal, Sweden and Switzerland. Even though the regression coefficients are not significant or are close to 0 in most of the PISA countries, the countries with the lowest regression coefficients form a familiar group: they are, in order of magnitude from the most negative, Finland, Norway, Sweden, Australia, New Zealand, Ireland, Canada, the United Kingdom and Iceland – that is, Northern European and predominantly English-speaking countries. In the other education systems, the regression coefficients are slightly positive, meaning that students who feel that they belong to the school have better results on average than those who do not.

The student-teacher relationship regression coefficients behave in a similar way to the coefficients for students' sense of belonging. The countries with the highest coefficients are, in decreasing order, Norway, Iceland, Finland, Canada, Sweden, New Zealand, Denmark and the United Kingdom. In these countries, students who report having a good relationship with their teachers perform better on average. In the remaining European countries, the regression coefficients are not significant and tend to be negative.

Differences between students within schools in terms of reading performance

With the exception of the aggregation process due to socio-economic background, predominantly English-speaking countries and Denmark, Finland, Iceland, Norway and Sweden seem to share several features in their educational policies. However, the PISA design does not necessarily allow us to identify all the differences. Theoretically, the total variance can be divided into three components: variance between schools; variance between classes within schools; and variance within classes. Since PISA draws simple random samples of students within schools, there is a confounding effect between variance between classes within schools and variance within classes. By contrast, IEA studies usually sample a whole class at random within a school, so that in this case there is confusion between the variance between schools and the variance between classes within schools. By comparing the intraclass correlation available from PISA and from IEA studies, we can gain a rough idea of the size of the variance between classes within schools.

Table 7.10 compares the intraclass correlations for PISA and two IEA studies, the IEA Reading Literacy Study (IEA/RLS, 1991) and the Third International Mathematics and Science Study (TIMSS, 1995).

Denmark, Finland, Iceland, Norway and Sweden participated in the IEA Reading Literacy Study (IEA/RLS) in the early nineties. In these countries the between-class variances, expressed in terms of percentage of total variance, were all below 0.10 (Postlethwaite, 1995, Figure 7.17.). In other words, the school variances reported by PISA for those countries do not differ from the school-plus-class variances reported from the IEA reading literacy data. On the other hand, the class variances for the predominantly English-speaking countries that participated in the IEA reading literacy study differ from the school variances reported by PISA. For instance, the IEA/RLS school-plus-class variance for Ireland, expressed in terms of percentage of total variance, is about 0.48 while the PISA school variance for Ireland is 0.18. The IEA/RLS intraclass correlations for the United States and New Zealand were 0.42 and 0.41 respectively, while in PISA, these coefficients are 0.29 and 0.16. In Australia, Ireland, New Zealand and the United States, some kind of disparity between the PISA intraclass correlation and the TIMSS intraclass correlation can be observed. The intraclass correlation in TIMSS, as in IEA/RLS, was based on whole-class samples. The large difference in the majority of the English-speaking countries reflects an educational policy that consists of grouping students in classes according to their ability or according to other criteria that correlate with academic performance. (In Canada and the United Kingdom, however, the intraclass correlations in mathematics do not suggest any streaming of students, at least for the teaching of mathematics.)

This within-school streaming process in some of the English-speaking countries might explain the differences observed in the regression coefficients for the homework composites. In Denmark, Finland, Iceland, Norway and Sweden, this variable correlates negatively with performance. Students with low results usually spend more time on their homework. Lower achievers may need more time to complete their homework, or teachers may provide more homework for low achievers to help them to reduce the performance gap. On the other hand, in the English-speaking countries, the homework composites correlate positively with student results. It is unlikely that high achievers need more time to complete their homework. Therefore, as students are more often grouped in classes according to their ability, the explanation might be that in English-speaking countries, teachers give more homework to high-achieving classes.

The comparison of the intraclass correlation coefficients between the PISA study and TIMSS and IEA/RLS reminds us that the reference population (a grade or an age population) may affect the pattern of results, particularly in countries where 15-year-olds are enrolled in a wide range of grades. Consequently, results should always be interpreted with reference to the target population.

In the introduction, it was pointed out that although each country has, to some extent, a unique educational profile, countries nevertheless share some characteristics that affect the way in which student background and behaviour interact with school features, jointly affecting students' academic performance.

In this chapter, some similarities in the way in which education systems operate have been identified. The complexity of the patterns of relationships has also been indicated. The time spent at home on homework is a good example. In some countries, more time seems to be associated with a small gain in performance while in other countries, more time is associated with a small decrease in performance. No doubt this opposition reflects differences in countries' homework policies.

Inequities in education have become an important issue in all countries, and several reforms have already been implemented in an attempt to reduce them. Inequities operate differently in different countries, and reforms need to take these differences into account if they are to be effective. For instance, countries interested in reducing gender inequity should consider the way gender and engagement in reading are associated with reading performance at the student level and the school level. In countries with a low intraclass correlation, the question is how to increase boys' engagement in reading, whatever the school. In countries with a high intraclass correlation, the reform is likely to be more effective if it targets particular types of school, such as vocational or technical schools.

It is very unlikely that education systems will be able to overcome social or other inequities completely. In some countries, inequities seem to be located at the within-school level; in other countries, inequities seem to be concentrated at the school level; and in the remaining countries, inequities are found at both levels. Trying to reduce the inequities at one level might have the consequence of increasing them at another.

Nevertheless, some educational structures seem to be associated with fewer inequities. The first-order correlation between socio-economic background and reading performance shows all five countries in the Northern Europe are among those with the smallest association between these two variables, and these countries also show, on average, smaller variation in student performance.

Notes

1. Reading literacy is assumed to be formulated by numerous factors. The Model, however, focused on factors listed below the sake of parsimony and effectiveness. The factors included in the model were selected based on theory and exploratory analysis.

2. Variables such as school physical and educational resources, teacher behaviours, student behaviours, shortage of teachers, teacher morale, and the type of schools or the tracks available in the school were initially included in the model but due to their small impact or to the percentage of missing data, these variables were removed.

3. As regression analyses increase the number of variables included in the model, the number of students excluded from these analyses due to missing data increase. Table A3.1 in the appendix presents the number of students included in the PISA 2000 International data base, and the number of remaining students included in the multilevel regression analyses presented in this chapter, as well as the ratio of these two numbers. On average, about 90 per cent of the students are included. Table A3.1 also clearly shows why Japan was excluded from the analyses in this chapter; only 38 per cent of the students had complete data for the variables used in the analyses. Further, as described in the technical report, the sampling method adopted in Japan precluded the possibility of disentangling the total variance into between-school and within-school components.

4. Students who are in grade lower than modal grade do not necessarily repeat a grade. They might have started schooling late for health or personal reasons.

5. See Annex A3 for note on immigration status.

THE READINESS OF 15-YEAR-OLDS TO MEET THE CHALLENGES OF THE FUTURE

KEY POINTS

- This chapter first discusses the effects of reading literacy skills on social and economic outcomes in adult life drawing on results from the International Adult Literacy Survey. It argues that the relationship between literacy skills and opportunities is significant and growing. Recent literature is cited and information from IALS is presented to show the connections between literacy on the one hand and educational, labour-market and social outcomes on the other. These consequences suggest the importance of knowing how well 15-year-olds are prepared to meet the challenges of the future.

- It then estimates how well PISA students would perform on the IALS prose scale through a statistical analysis of prose literacy tasks embedded in the PISA assessment. By using the prose literacy scale from IALS, it is possible to gain some insight into the degree to which 15-year-old students already possess the knowledge and skills that they will need in adult life.

- The results reveal considerable variation between countries in the percentages of PISA students performing at the various levels of the IALS prose literacy scale. These percentages range at Level 1 from approximately 3 per cent in Korea and Japan to 33 per cent in Luxembourg. At Levels 4 and 5, percentages range from 30 per cent for Finland to only 1.4 per cent in Brazil.

- The data presented in this chapter as well as throughout this report provide an opportunity for countries to consider whether the overall level of skill demonstrated by 15-year-olds is adequate for functioning in increasingly complex societies with their increasing reliance on technology, complex legal systems and expanding formal institutions. They also invite us to ask whether the variation found both between countries and between subgroups within countries should be of concern.

Previous chapters of this report have described the reading literacy skills of 15-year-olds in the principal industrialised nations. For many countries, they revealed a significant minority of 15-year-olds performing at very low levels of proficiency. To what extent do literacy skill gaps at age 15 pose barriers for young adults to succeed in their further education and their transition from school to work? The longitudinal extension of PISA, through which some countries will follow the 15-year-olds that were assessed in PISA over a period of 15 years, can provide conclusive answers to this question.

However, the International Adult Literacy Survey (IALS) that was undertaken by Statistics Canada and the OECD between 1994 and 1999 in more than 20 countries with the aim to obtain a better understanding of the distribution of literacy skills in the adult population provided some first insights into the interrelationships between literacy skills and a variety of social, educational and economic outcomes (OECD and Statistics Canada, 2000). Since OECD Member countries designed PISA such that it would permit comparisons between performance in PISA and performance in IALS, it is possible to make some inferences on the likely social and economic consequences of poor performance in PISA. This is examined more in this chapter.

The literacy data from IALS contribute to an increased understanding of the important role that these skills play in terms of both social and economic outcomes. And, in conjunction with these data, it can be argued that the relationship between skills and opportunities for individuals is strong and growing. Individuals with poor skills do not have much to bargain with; in most countries participating in IALS, these individuals are more likely to earn low wages and to find it difficult to participate fully in increasingly complex societies. In part, it was this growing recognition of the important role of literacy skills that led PISA to want to measure the knowledge and skills that 15-year-old students need both within and outside school. And it was for this reason that the Board of Participating Countries (BPC) overseeing PISA recommended that an effort should be made to place students participating in PISA on the IALS prose literacy scale. This allows us to obtain an indirect estimate of the relationship between literacy performance and social outcomes through a statistical method that enables us to estimate the performance of PISA students on the IALS prose literacy scale.

In IALS, adults between the ages of 16 and 65 were assessed in three types of literacy: prose literacy (similar to the continuous texts subscale in PISA); document literacy (similar to the non-continuous subscale); and quantitative literacy. A subset of the literacy tasks from the IALS prose literacy scale (15 items) was embedded in the PISA assessment. These items allow us to express the performance of 15-year-olds participating in PISA on the IALS prose literacy scale. Extrapolating the relationships between literacy skills and social and economic outcomes to the student population assessed by PISA provides some insights into the possible future consequences of low literacy performance at age 15.

This chapter first presents selected information showing the relationship between literacy and educational, social and labour market outcomes. After briefly summarising what the prose literacy scale in IALS measures, we compare and contrast this with the PISA reading literacy scale. Next, the methodology used to investigate and estimate the IALS prose literacy skills of PISA students is summarised. This is followed by a brief discussion of how PISA students are likely to perform on the IALS prose literacy scale.

The connections between literacy and social outcomes

Literacy was once seen as a set of skills that were acquired mainly in school through formal teaching. Today, however, most people view literacy as a set of knowledge and skills that are acquired throughout life both in and outside formal settings. In addition, many view these skills as necessary for full participation in modern societies with their increasing reliance on technology, and their complex social processes. The data from IALS and other adult surveys clearly demonstrate that literacy plays a significant role in the functioning of labour markets. More specifically, it has a significant impact on access to the labour market, as measured by labour force participation rates and by the ability to secure employment. Literacy is also associated with earnings and access to training.

Box 8.1: Does higher reading literacy improve the prospects for employment?

The International Adult Literacy Survey (IALS) found that people with higher levels of reading literacy are more likely to be employed and to have higher average salaries than those with lower levels (OECD and Statistics Canada, 2000). Is this simply because they have better educational qualifications? If it is, then IALS (and PISA) would, at best, be measuring competencies that help people to gain a better education and, through it, better jobs. In IALS, adults who had completed some form of tertiary education scored, on average, between one and two reading literacy levels higher than those who did not complete secondary education, but there were significant numbers of adults in the 22 participating countries with a high level of reading literacy and a low level of education, or vice versa. Most importantly, reading literacy levels can help to predict how well people will do in the labour market over and above what can be predicted from their educational qualifications alone.

Figure 8.1

Education, literacy and the probability of having a white-collar highly skilled job
Probability of employment in the white-collar highly skilled business sector by level of education and increasing literacy score, all countries combined, IALS prose scale, population aged 26-35, 1994-1998

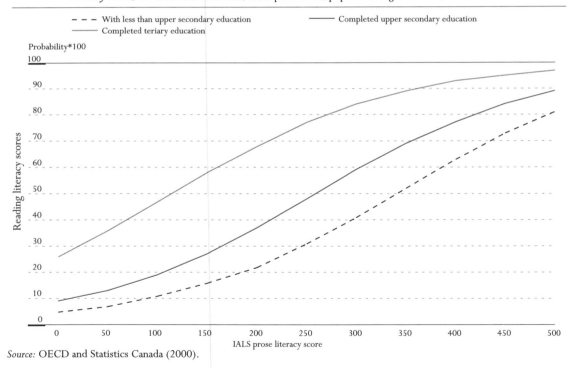

Source: OECD and Statistics Canada (2000).

Figure 8.1 illustrates this by showing the likelihood of young people with different combinations of reading literacy and education having a white-collar, highly skilled job. The gaps between the lines show the effects of increasing levels of education; the slopes of the lines show the effect of higher reading literacy at a given level of education. For a person who is between 26 and 35 years of age and working in the business sector, the probability of working in a white-collar, highly skilled job rises rapidly with an increase in reading literacy skills. The independent effect of reading literacy on labour-market outcomes is comparable to the independent effect of educational qualifications. Someone with medium qualifications (upper secondary only) has a two-in-five chance of being in a high-level job if their reading literacy level is 200 (at the low end of the scale) and a four-in-five chance if it is 400 (a high score). Conversely, someone with a medium level of reading literacy (a score of 300), has a two-in-five chance of getting such as job with a low level of education (lower secondary education only) and more than a four-in-five chance with a high level of education (a tertiary qualification).

Adults between the ages of 25 and 65 who have literacy skills at IALS Levels 3[1] and above are more likely to be in the labour force than adults who perform at IALS Levels 1 and 2 on the prose literacy scale (see Table 8.1). Although the size of the difference varies from country to country, those not in the labour force tend to have lower literacy skills, on average, than those who actively participate in the labour force.

It is perhaps more important to note that, once in the labour force, adults who perform at IALS Levels 1 and 2 on the prose literacy scale face an increased likelihood of being unemployed. Table 8.2 compares the percentages of adults with low literacy skills who reported being unemployed at the time of the IALS survey with those in the three highest literacy levels (Levels 3 to 5). In New Zealand those in the lowest two levels are four times as likely to be unemployed, while in many of the other countries – Australia, Belgium (Flanders), Canada, Denmark, Finland, Germany, Ireland, Slovenia and the United Kingdom – the percentage of adults who reported being unemployed is almost twice as high among those in IALS Levels 1 and 2 as among those in Levels 3, 4 and 5. In a few countries, notably Norway, Switzerland and the United States, the overall level of unemployment during the 1990s was so low that low-skilled adults faced a relatively small risk of unemployment, but even in Norway and the United States the unemployment percentage in Levels 1 and 2 was approximately twice the percentage in the highest three levels.

IALS data also suggest that literacy plays an important role in the wage determination process, explaining up to 33 per cent of the variance in wages in several countries (Osberg, 2000; Green and Riddell, 2001) as well as wage inequality and selection of occupation across countries as a whole (Blau and Kahn, 2001). Table 8.3, for example, illustrates the relationship between literacy proficiency and earnings. The table shows the percentages of adults aged 25 to 65 who are in the top 60 per cent of annual wage earners for each IALS level of prose literacy. The numbers in this table show that the percentage of people who report relatively high annual earnings increases with literacy proficiency. Although not shown here, the data from IALS also indicate that there appears to be a somewhat larger return for quantitative literacy skills in some countries, a finding similar to that of the U.S. National Adult Literacy Survey (Sum, 1999).

The relationship between literacy and earnings is not simple. It is complicated in part by the relationship between literacy and education. Clearly, in every IALS country, adults with more education attain higher average literacy scores, although the size of the average differences varies both between countries and between levels of education within countries.[2]

Although education clearly increases literacy skills, these in turn play a key role in determining educational success. In the United States, for example, literacy plays a part in determining which courses students take in secondary school, whether or not they obtain a secondary diploma or an alternative certificate[3], whether they pursue tertiary education and what types of degrees they obtain (Berlin and Sum, 1988; Sum and Fogg, 1991).

Literacy also influences access to adult education and training systems, having an appreciable impact on the incidence and duration of training and on the likelihood that this training will be provided and supported by employers (OECD and Statistics Canada, 2000; Sum, 1999). Table 8.4 shows the overall participation rates in adult education by countries and also by level of document literacy.

As shown here, participation in adult education programmes during the year preceding the survey varies considerably among the countries participating in IALS. Chile, Hungary, Poland and Portugal report rates below 20 per cent while a few countries – Denmark, Finland and Sweden – report rates exceeding 50 per cent. The majority of countries have participation rates between 20 and 50 per cent.

While participation rates vary among countries, the data within each country also reveal an interesting pattern. Those who are least likely to participate in formal adult education programmes are also those who are most in need of improving their skills. Across the IALS countries the average percentage of adults in IALS Level 1 who reported participating in adult education and training was 14 per cent. The average participation rate almost doubles among those adults performing at Level 2 (29 per cent), is close to 50 per cent (46) for those in Level 3 and approaches 60 per cent (59) for those in Levels 4 and 5. IALS data also indicate that the employer is the most likely provider of this training.

Literacy skills not only influence participation in formal learning systems: there is also some evidence from the IALS data to suggest that this impact extends to informal learning as well (Desjardins, 2002). Participation in activities that are not related to work such as voluntary associations and civic involvement is an important source of social capital that also provides individuals with a source of informal learning, keeping them mentally active. A recent OECD report entitled *The Well Being of Nations* (OECD, 2001a) argues that the development of human capital is correlated with a variety of social benefits including improvements in health, lower crime rates and increased participation in community activities.

Comparing the IALS prose literacy scale with the PISA combined reading literacy scale

Both the IALS and PISA surveys were based on frameworks that guided the development of their respective assessments[4]. In each assessment, a panel of experts developed a working definition of literacy, and this definition was operationalised in terms of three task characteristics. These task characteristics acknowledge that there is a finite set of characteristics that can be manipulated in developing tasks that will provide evidence about the literacy skills of each population.

In both the IALS and PISA surveys, the goal was to develop pools of tasks using each survey's respective framework. In selecting materials from a range of contexts or situations, the objective was to broaden the cultural diversity of the materials along with the vocabulary used in the survey. This would in turn help to ensure that no one group was advantaged or disadvantaged because of the content selected for the assessment. With respect to continuous or prose texts, the focus in IALS was on expository, argumentative and injunctive texts[5] since most of what adults are required to read for work, in their communities and around the house is associated with these types of discourse. PISA provides a balance of texts that is more closely matched to the typical reading of 15-year-olds who are still in school by including a significant set of narrative texts along with the expository, injunctive and argumentative texts. PISA uses the same model for selecting non-continuous texts as IALS, but IALS places an equal emphasis on continuous and non-continuous texts while PISA focuses more heavily on continuous texts.

In terms of processes/strategies, the goal in both studies was to engage respondents in processes that might reasonably be associated with each type of material. That is, the goal was to use the framework to construct questions/directives that are thought to be authentic with regard to the kinds of information that someone might want to understand or use from a particular text. IALS focuses on manipulating and understanding the conditions that affect the overall difficulty of tasks along each of its three literacy scales – prose, document and quantitative. PISA takes a similar approach to item development but focuses primarily on aspects such as retrieving information, interpreting texts and reflection and evaluation. In particular, PISA has broadened the IALS notion of literacy by including a set of tasks that involve reflection on both content and structure of texts.

Box 8.2: Distinctions between PISA and IALS

In IALS, literacy is reported along scales that originally had a mean of 250 and a standard deviation of 50. As in PISA, each literacy scale in IALS is divided into five levels to show the progression of skills and to estimate the percentages of participants demonstrating proficiency in these skills. It should be noted, however, that these levels are not equivalent across the two surveys in terms of what is being measured. While the constructs of reading literacy used in PISA and IALS are similar, each emphasises different parts of the construct, as stated above.

In addition, the IALS and PISA scales and the levels within each scale have different characteristics. IALS, for example, uses five levels but does not try to distinguish the least capable in Level 1. PISA, on the other hand, identifies a group of students who perform "below Level 1". This grouping identifies those students who are estimated not to be proficient in Level 1 PISA tasks.

Different response probabilities are used to characterise proficiency and items along the IALS and PISA scales. Response probability indicates the likelihood that a reader at a specified point on a scale will answer an item correctly at that same point. In PISA the response probability is 0.62, while in IALS it is 0.80. This means that, in PISA, a person who is in the middle of a level is expected to score 62 per cent in a hypothetical test constructed of items from that level while someone at the bottom of a given level is expected to get 50 per cent of the items at this level correct. By contrast, someone in the middle of one of the IALS levels is expected to score 80 per cent on a hypothetical test made up of items from that level while someone at the lower end of a level has an expected score of 60 per cent[6].

Although the IALS prose literacy scale and the PISA combined reading literacy scale correlate highly (0.85) after correcting for attenuation, it would be incorrect to conclude that skills needed to perform tasks successfully at, for example, Level 2 in PISA are identical to those needed to perform tasks successfully in Level 2 in IALS. Nevertheless, the methodological procedures applied to the IALS prose items embedded in the PISA assessment allow us to estimate how well PISA students do on the IALS prose literacy scale.

In IALS, all the tasks are open-ended and require the reader to select, underline, transfer or produce a response. In PISA, about half of the reading literacy tasks are open-ended, among them many requiring extended responses, and the remaining half are multiple choice.

Placing PISA students on the IALS prose literacy scale

The parameters for the cognitive items used in IALS were originally estimated in 1994 using over 25,000 adults and then validated, first in 1996 during the second round of IALS, and then again in 1998 during the third cycle of testing. In order to place PISA students on the IALS prose literacy scale, it is necessary to determine how well the item parameters estimated in IALS fit the pattern of responses obtained in PISA. Several analytic procedures were applied to evaluate the extent to which the original parameters held. Yamamoto (2002) provides a complete technical report describing what was done[7]. A brief overview and summary is given here.

First, a simple comparison was made between the average percentage of correct responses to the 15 prose literacy IALS items used in the PISA reading literacy instrument, and the average percentage of correct responses to the complete set of PISA items for each country. This simple calculation made it possible to determine whether there were any factors operating which might negatively affect comparability between countries. For example, one or more countries could have translated the assessment items differently, or systematically applied one or more marking guides differently. This was not apparent, however, in these data. The correlation between the two sets of average percentages of correct responses across the 32 countries participating in PISA was 0.89. This is shown in Figure 8.2.

Next, IRT analyses were applied and several statistics calculated to verify the fit of each item for every country. These included a statistic that evaluated the overall model fit using a chi square statistic as well as the weighted mean deviation and square root of the weighted mean squared deviation. These two statistics based on deviations compare the model-based expected proportion correct with the observed proportion correct at 31 points along the ability distribution.

Figure 8.2

Relationship between the average percentage correct on the PISA reading literacy items and the average percentage correct on the IALS prose literacy items

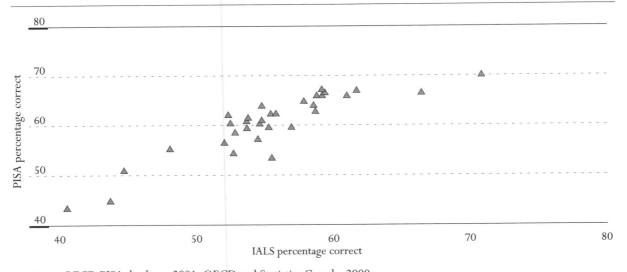

Source: OECD PISA database, 2001; OECD and Statistics Canada, 2000.

Ideally, each of the parameters estimated on the 15 IALS tasks would fit for each of the 32 PISA countries. This rarely happens in studies of this nature, however, which leaves the challenge of how best to accommodate the misfit of item parameters across the participating countries. One approach is to ignore the misfit, but doing this adds error and bias to the overall estimation. Another approach is to drop the deviant items from the analysis. A major drawback of this option is that it results in a smaller number of items being used to estimate ability. A third approach, and the one used in this study, is to estimate new parameters for those items that do not fit for a particular country. In the case of a few items, the misfit of item parameters was very similar across countries in terms of both direction and magnitude. For these items and countries, a set of item parameters was estimated for that set of countries. This reduced the overall number of new item parameters that needed to be estimated and improved the overall model fit significantly.

According to Yamamoto (2002), the overall model fit was quite good for the 15 IALS items used in PISA. On average, only 4.4 items per country had absolute weighted mean squared deviations greater than 0.10, which required new parameters to be estimated. For the majority of the items, 11 out of 15, either no or one additional pair of item parameters needed to be estimated in addition to the original IALS item parameters. The fact that only one set of item parameters had to be estimated for these tasks indicates that the deviation was similar in both direction and magnitude for those countries in which a deviation occurred. For the remaining four items, two additional sets of item parameters had to be estimated.

Once it was determined that the model fit was good, meaning that IALS items used in PISA could be linked at the item level, the next step involved estimating proficiency values and matching them to the existing IALS prose literacy scale. This was accomplished using plausible values methodology (Mislevy, 1991; Rubin, 1987), the application of which to placing PISA students on the IALS prose literacy scale is described in Yamamoto (2002). It should be remembered that the PISA reading literacy items were created using a framework that was related to but different from the one used in IALS. We would, therefore, expect to see this difference reflected in the statistical relationship between scores on PISA reading literacy and those on IALS prose literacy. The correlation between the reading literacy scale for PISA and the IALS prose literacy scale is 0.85 after correcting for attenuation and is 0.73 without applying the correction. This correlation was estimated from the entire PISA sample that received both the IALS and PISA reading literacy items and is very similar to the correlation between the IALS prose and document literacy scales (0.89) after correcting for attenuation.

Performance of PISA students on the IALS prose literacy scale

Given the relationships seen in the IALS data between literacy and social, educational and labour-market outcomes, the IALS report concluded that those adults who do not perform at Level 3 or higher on the IALS prose literacy scale are at some risk in terms of future opportunities (OECD and Statistics Canada, 1995). While those who performed at IALS Levels 1 and 2 were seen as capable of performing a wide range of literacy tasks, they were also seen to face a changing environment in which information and technology are playing an increasingly important role, and knowledge and skills have a significant influence on individual opportunities. Although it is always challenging to select a single point, Level 3 was seen in IALS as a target goal for policy-makers in determining the levels of literacy that are needed by citizens for full participation in society.

Box 8.3: Description of the IALS prose literacy levels

Level 1
0-225

Most tasks require the reader to locate information in texts that is identical to or synonymous with information given in the question. Distracting information, if present, tends not to be near the correct answer.

Level 2
226-275

Many tasks at this level ask the reader to locate one or more pieces of information in the text when distracting information may be present, or make low-level inferences. Some tasks may also require the reader to begin to integrate pieces of information or make simple comparisons.

Level 3
276-325

Tasks at this level tend to require the reader to search texts in order to match information that meet specified conditions or make low-level inferences. Some tasks at this level also require the reader to integrate information or compare and contrast information from different parts or sections of texts.

Level 4
326-375

At this level, tasks often require the reader to make higher-order inferences. Some tasks require readers to perform multiple-feature matches or provide multiple responses where the information that is requested must be identified through text-based inferences. Typically texts associated with tasks at this level contain more distracting and abstract information.

Level 5
376-500

Tasks at this highest level require readers to search through dense texts containing multiple distractors, make high-level inferences, process conditional information, or use specialised knowledge.

Source: Literacy, Economy and Society, OECD and Statistics Canada, 1995.

Figure 8.3 provides the overall mean score for each PISA country on the IALS prose literacy scale as well as the estimated percentage of 15-year-olds at IALS Levels 1, 2, 3 and 4/5[8]. What is most apparent from these data is that, regardless of their overall mean score, there is considerable variation in the percentages of 15-year-olds who are estimated to be at Levels 1 and 2 on the IALS prose literacy scale. There is also considerable variation between countries in the percentages that are estimated to be in Levels 4 and 5.

Figure 8.3

Mean performance and percentage of PISA students at each level of the IALS prose literacy scale

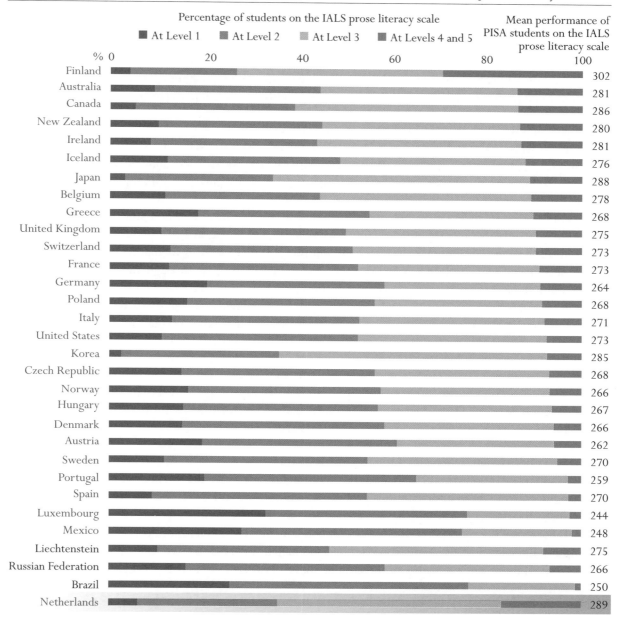

Source: OECD PISA database, 2001 and International Adult Literacy Survey 1994-1998. Table 8.5.

Tables 8.5 to 8.8 show that the percentages of 15-year-olds in IALS Level 1 range from a low of about 3 per cent in Korea and Japan to about 33 per cent in Luxembourg. Across all participating countries, approximately 15 per cent of 15-year-olds are estimated to be performing at Level 1 on the IALS prose literacy scale. Some 42 per cent are estimated to be at Level 2, and 36 per cent at Level 3. Only some 7 per cent of 15-year-olds across all PISA countries are estimated to be performing at the highest literacy levels (4 and 5). Again, there is considerable variation among PISA countries. The average percentages of

15-year-olds estimated to be performing at Levels 4 and 5 ranges from a little over 1 per cent in Brazil to almost 30 per cent in Finland.

The picture is better for females than for males in that females have an average IALS prose literacy score of 275 compared with 261 for males, the difference being about one-third of a standard deviation (see Tables 8.6 to 8.7). Across all PISA countries, 11 per cent of females are estimated to be performing at Level 1 compared with 19 per cent of males. Additionally, 9 per cent of females across participating countries are estimated to be performing at Levels 4 and 5 compared with less than 5 per cent of males.

Figure 8.4 shows the difference in average scores between females and males by country. The largest difference between males and females is seen in Finland where the mean score difference is 26 points, or 66 per cent of a standard deviation. The smallest average difference between males and females is seen in Korea. Here the average difference is 5 points or 12 per cent of the overall standard deviation (see Table 8.8).

The results represent only a snapshot of performance at a point in time when students in most of the participating countries are completing compulsory schooling. It is reasonable to expect that literacy skills will continue to develop, on average, through continued participation in formal learning systems such as post-secondary education and/or work-related training, as well as through more informal means. The data in Table 8.9 compare the average prose literacy scores of PISA 15-year-olds and IALS 16 to 25-year-olds by gender and country. These data reveal a pattern in which the mean score for females are higher than that for males but in which males have larger gains than females between the ages of 16 and 25[9].

These data provide an initial projection of the literacy proficiency of 15-year-old students when they become young adults. It is important, therefore, that they should not be interpreted out of context. Rather, the projection should be viewed as a preliminary attempt to get an estimate of how PISA can be related to adult literacy. Data from the longitudinal component of PISA will provide a more complete answer to the question of how prepared PISA students are for adult life.

Fifteen-year-olds cannot be expected to have learned everything they will need to know and do as adults, but they should have a solid foundation of literacy skills in order to continue learning and to participate fully in a changing world where information is growing at a rapid rate and where the ability to access, manage and evaluate this information will be increasingly important. Economists point out that technological change is currently the most powerful driver of income inequalities. According to a recent study from the Institute for International Economics, technological change was perhaps five times more powerful than trade in widening income inequality in the United States between 1973 and 1993 (Cline, 1997).

To what extent do 15-year-olds have the literacy skills needed for adult life? The answer to this question will vary from country to country. The data presented in this chapter and in this report compel us to ask whether the overall level of skills demonstrated by students in participating countries is adequate. They also raises the question as to whether the variation seen between countries and between subgroups within countries should be of concern. As a recent OECD (2001a) report argues, the development of human capital is correlated not only with educational and labour-market outcomes, but also with better health, lower crime, and political and community participation. Thus the economic impact of acquiring literacy skills may be matched in importance by the social impact, for individuals, communities and countries.

Figure 8.4

Difference in mean scores between females and males on the IALS prose literacy scale

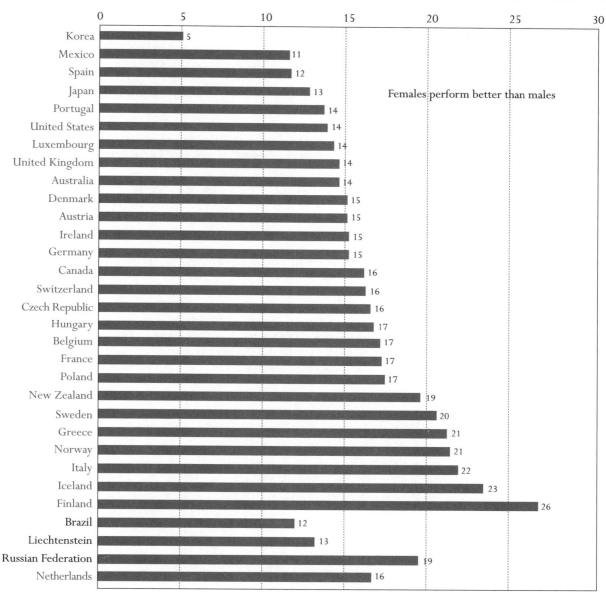

Difference between females and males

Source: International Adult Literacy Survey 1994-1998. Table 8.7.

Notes

1. It is important to note that IALS levels are not the same as PISA levels. For details, see Box 8.1.

2. The largest average differences observed in IALS are between those who completed upper secondary education and those who did not. According to IALS, the range of mean scores for adults in participating countries with the lowest level of formal education "is about 1.5 times the range of mean scores for those with the highest level of education." (OECD and Statistics Canada, 2000, p. 25).

3. In the United States an alternative secondary school certificate is awarded to individuals who take and pass the GED or General Educational Development Test.

4. The framework for PISA is summarised in Chapter 2 of this report. For the IALS framework the reader is referred to Kirsch, I. The Framework Used in Developing and Interpreting the International Adult Literacy Survey. *European Journal of Psychology of Education*, Vol XVI (3), pp. 335-362.

5. These are discussed in the framework documents for PISA and IALS. Exposition is a type of text in which information is presented as composite concepts or mental constructs. Argumentative texts take a point of view and present propositions as to the relationships between concepts, or other propositions. Injunctive texts typically provide directions or instructions.

6 . The two surveys also apply different item response theory (IRT) models, resulting in the underlying metric having different origins and unit size or logit before any transformations.

7. The report can be found on the PISA website *www.oecd.pisa.org*.

8 . A decision was made in IALS to collapse the percentages of adults in these two levels because of the relatively small numbers of respondents from several participating countries. This was done to provide accurate estimates of the standard errors for this cell. If the percentages in the two cells were simply added together, it would be difficult to estimate the correct standard error.

9. It is difficult to estimate the overall size of this effect from these data because they were obtained with two different types of samples covering different age cohorts. PISA is an in-school sample while IALS samples from households and thus is likely to include a wider range of the ability distribution in each country.

REFERENCES

Allington, R.L. (1984), Content, coverage, and contextual reading in reading groups. *Journal of Reading Behavior, 16*, 85-96.

Anderson, R.C., Wilson, P.T. and Fielding, L.G. (1988), Growth in reading and how children spend their time outside school. *Reading Research Quarterly, 23*, 285-303.

Au, K.H. and Raphael, T.E. (2000), Equity and literacy in the next millennium. *Reading Research Quarterly, 35, 1,* 170-188.

Bellorado, D. (1986), *Making Literacy Programs Work: A Practical Guide for Correctional* U.S. Department of Justice, National Institute of Corrections, Accession no. NIC-006253.

Berlin, G. and Sum, A. (1988), *Toward A More Perfect Union: Basic Skills, Poor Families and Our Economic Future*, Ford Foundation, New York.

Birkerts, S. (1998), *Readings*. St. Paul, Minn: Greywolf Press.

Birkerts, S. (1994), *The Gutenberg Elegies: The Fate of Reading in an Electronic Age*. Boston/London: Faber and Faber.

Blau, F.D. and Kahn, L.M. (2001), *Do cognitive test scores explain higher US wage inequality?* NBER Working Paper 8210, National Bureau of Economic Research, Cambridge, MA.

Brown, A.L., Palincsar, A.S. and Purcell, L. (1986), Poor readers: Teach, don't label. In: U. Neisser (Ed.), *The school achievement of minority children: New perspectives* (pp. 105-43). Hillsdale, NJ: Lawrence Erlbaum Associates, Publishers.

Bryk, A.S. and Raudenbush, S.W. (1992), *Hierarchical Linear Models in Social and Behavioral Research: Applications and Data Analysis Methods*. Beverly Hills: Sage Publications.

Burns, B. (1998), Changing the classroom climate with literature circles. *Journal of Adolescent and Adult Literacy, 42/2,* 124-129.

Campbell, J.R., Kelly, D.L., Mullis, I.V.S., Martin, M.O. and Sainsbury, M. (2001), *Progress International Reading Literacy Study (PIRLS)*. International Association for the Evaluation of Educational Achievement (IEA), Second Edition. Chestnut Hill, MA, USA: PIRLS International Study Center.

Campbell, J.R., Voelkl, K.E. and Donahue, P.L. (1997), *NAEP 1996 trends in academic progress* (NCES Publication n°97-985. Washington, D.C. : U.S. Department of Education.

Central Intelligence Agency (2001), *The World Factbook 2001 www.cia.gov/cia/publications/factbook*.

Chall, J., Jacobs, V. and Baldwin, L. (1990), *The reading crisis: Why poor children fall behind*. Cambridge, MA: Harvard University Press.

Cline, W. (1997), *Trade and income distribution*. Washington, DC. Institute for International Economics.

Cornoldi, C. (1990), Metacognitive control processes and memory deficits in poor comprehenders. *Learning Disability Quarterly, 13*, 245-255.

Council of Europe (2001), *Common European Framework of Reference for Languages: Learning, teaching, assessment*. Cambridge: Cambridge University Press.

Cunningham, A.E. and Stanovich, K.E. (1998), Early reading acquisition and its relation to reading experience and ability 10 years later. *Developmental Psychology, 33*, 934-945.

Dechant, E. (1991), *Understanding and teaching reading: An interactive model*. Hillsdale, NJ: Lawrence Erlbaum.

Desjardins, R. (in press), The effect of learning on economic and social well-being: A comparative analysis, *Peabody Journal of Education*, Vol. 75, No. 3/4.

Elley, W.B. (1992), *How in the World Do Students Read?* The Hague: The International Association for the Evaluation of Educational Assessment.

Elley, W.B. (Ed.), (1994), *The IEA study of reading literacy: achievement and instruction in thirty-two school systems,* Oxford: Pergamon.

Elwert, G. (2001), Societal literacy: Writing Culture and Development. In: D. Olson and N. Torrance (Eds.) *The making of literate societies.* Oxford: Blackwell: 54-67.

European Commission (2001), *European report on the quality of school education: Sixteen quality indicators.* Luxembourg: Office for Official Publications of the European Communities.

Freire, P. and Macedo, D. (1987), *Literacy: Reading the Word and the World.* Bergin and Garvey: Mass, USA.

Gambrell, L.B. (1996), Creating classroom cultures that foster reading motivation. *The Reading Teacher, 50,* 14-25.

Ganzeboom, H.B.G., de Graaf, P.M. and Treiman, D.J. (1992), A standard international socio-economic index of occupational status. *Social Science Research*, 21, 1-56.

Goldstein, H. (1995), *Multilevel Statistical Models.* London: Arnold.

Graesser, A.C., Millis, K.K. and Zwaan, R.A. (1997), Discourse comprehension. *Annual Review of Psychology, 48*, 163 - 189.

Gray, W.S. and Rogers, B. (1956), *Maturity in reading.* Chicago: University of Chicago Press.

Green, D.A. and Riddell, W.C. (2001), *Literacy, Numeracy and Labour Market Outcomes in Canada*, Statistics Canada, Ottawa.

Guthrie, J. and Davis, M.H. (in press), Motivating struggling readers in middle school through an engagement model of classroom practice. *Reading and Writing Quarterly.*

Guthrie, J.T., Schafer, W.D., Von Secker, C. and Alban, T. (2000), Contribution of reading instruction and text resources to achievement and engagement in a statewide school improvement program. *Journal of Educational Research,* 93, 211-226.

Guthrie, J. and Wigfield, A. (2000), Engagement and motivation in reading. In M. L. Kamil, P. B. Mosenthal, P. D. Pearson and R. Barr (Eds.), *Handbook of reading research. Vol III.* LEA, 403-425.

Halpern, D.F. (1989), *Thought and knowledge: An introduction to critical thinking.* Hillsdale, NJ: Lawrence Erlbaum Associates.

Ivey, G. (1999), Reflections on teaching struggling middle school readers. *Journal of Adolescent and Adult Literacy, 42/5,* 372-381.

Jackson, D. (1998), Breaking out of the binary trap : boy's underachievement, schooling and gender relations. In D. Epstein, J. Elwood, V. Hey and J. Maw (Eds.), *Failing boys ? Issues in gender and achievement.* Philadelphia : Open University Press, 77-95.

Kamil, M.L., Mosenthal, P.B., Pearson, P. D. and Barr, R. (Eds.) (2000), *Handbook of reading research. Vol III.* Lawrence Erlbaum Associates.

Kintsch, W. and van Dijk, T. (1978), Toward a Model of Text Comprehension and Production. *Psychological Review*, 85: 363-394.

Kirsch, I. (2001), *The International Adult Literacy Survey: Understanding What Was Measured.* Princeton, NJ: Educational Testing Service, RR-01-25.

Kirsch, I.S. and Mosenthal, P.B. (1990), Exploring document literacy: Variables underlying the performance of young adults. *Reading Research Quarterly 25, 1*, 5-30.

Kirsch, I. S. and Mosenthal, P.B. (1989-1991), Understanding documents. A monthly column appearing in the *Journal of Reading*. Newark, DE: International Reading Association.

Kirsch, I.S., Jungeblut, A., Jenkins, L. and Kolstad, A. (1993), *Adult literacy in America: A first look at the results of the National Adult Literacy Survey.* Washington, DC: U.S. Department of Education.

LaFontaine, D. (1999), From Comprehension to Literacy: Thirty Years of Reading Assessment. Unpublished paper presented at the INES General Assembly.

Langer, J. (1995), *Envisioning literature.* Newark, DE: International Reading Association.

Lewis, B. (2002), Guide Picks - Top 5 Professional Books about Reading *http://k-6educators.about.com/library/products/ aatp111201.htm?PM=ss03_k-6educators*, About, Inc.

Littell, R.C., Milliken, G.A., Stroup, W.W. and Wolfinger, R.D. (1996), *SAS System for Mixed Models*. Cary (NC): SAS publications.

Mac An Ghaill, M. (1994), *The making of men : masculinities, sexualities and schooling.* Philadelphia : Open University Press.

McCormick, Th. W. (1988), *Theories of reading in dialogue: An interdisciplinary study.* New York: University Press of America.

McKenna, M., Kear, D.J., and Ellsworth, R.A. (1995), Children's attitudes toward reading: a national survey. *Reading Research Quarterly, 30/4* 934-956.

Messick, S. (1989), Validity. In R. Linn (Ed.), *Educational measurement* (3rd ed.) (pp. 13-103), New York: Macmillan.

Mislevy, R.J. (1991). Randomization-based inference about latent variables from complex samples. *Psychometrika, 56*, 177-1.

Moffett, J. and Wagner, B.J. (1983), *Student-Centered Language Arts and Reading K-13: A Handbook for Teachers.* Boston: Houghton Mifflin.

Mokhtari, K. and Sheory, P. (2001), Differences in the meta-cognitive awareness of reading strategies among native and non-native readers. *System, 29, 4,* 431-450.

Neuman, S.B. and Celano, D. (2001), Access to print in low-income and middle-income communities: An ecological study of four neighborhoods. *Reading Research Quarterly*, 36 (1), 8-26.

Oka, E.. and Paris, S. (1986), Patterns of motivation and reading skills in underachieving children. In S. Ceci (Ed.), *Handbook of cognitive, social, and neuropsychological aspects of learning disabilities (Vol 2),* Hillsdale, NJ: Erlbaum.

Olson, D.R. (1977b), The language of instruction: The literate bias of schooling. In R. Anderson, R. Spiro, and W. Montague (Eds.), *Schooling and the acquisition of knowledge*, Hillsdale, NJ: Erlbaum, pp. 65-89.

Olson, D.R. (1977a), From Utterance to Text: The Bias of Language in Speech and Writing. *Harvard Educational Review* 47: 257-81.

Olson, D.R. (1994), *The World on Paper.* Cambridge: Cambridge University Press.

Organisation for Economic Co-operation and Development (OECD) and Statistics Canada (STATCAN) (2000), *Literacy in the Information Age: Final Report of the International Adult Literacy Survey*, Paris and Ottawa: Author.

Organisation for Economic Co-operation and Development (OECD) and Statistics Canada (STATCAN) (1997*), Literacy Skills for the Knowledge Society: Further Results from the International Adult Literacy Study.* Paris and Ottawa: Author.

Organisation for Economic Co-operation and Development (OECD) and Statistics Canada (STATCAN) (1995*), Literacy Economy and Society: Results of the First International Adult Literacy Survey.* Paris and Ottawa: Author.

Organisation for Economic Co-operation and Development (OECD) (2002*a*), *Sample Tasks from the PISA 2000 Assessment — Reading, Mathematical, and Scientific Literacy.* Paris: Author.

Organisation for Economic Co-operation and Development (OECD) (2002*b*), *PISA 2000 Technical Report.* Paris: Author.

Organisation for Economic Co-operation and Development (OECD) (2001*a*), *The Well Being of Nations.* Paris: Author.

Organisation for Economic Co-operation and Development (OECD) (2001*b*), *Knowledge and Skills for Life: First Results from PISA 2000.* Paris: Author.

Organisation for Economic Co-operation and Development (OECD) (2000), *Measuring Student Knowledge and Skills: The PISA 2000 Assessment of Reading, Mathematical and Scientific Literacy*. Paris: Author.

Organisation for Economic Co-operation and Development (OECD) (1999), *Measuring Student Knowledge and Skills: A New Framework for Assessment*. Paris.

Organisation for Economic Co-operation and Development (OECD) (1992), *Adult Illiteracy and Economic Performance*, Paris: Author.

Osberg, L. (2000), *Schooling, Literacy and Individual Earnings*, Statistics Canada, Ottawa and Human Resource Development Canada.

Paris, S.G. and Winograd, P. (1990), How metacognition can promote academic learning and instruction. In B.F. Jones, and L. Idol (Eds.), *Dimensions of thinking and cognitive instruction* (pp. 15-52), Hillsdale, NJ: Erlbaum.

Postlethwaite, T.N. (1995), Calculation and Interpretation of Between-School and Within-School Variation in Achievement (rho). In OECD: *Measuring what students learn*. Paris: OECD, CERI.

Rubin, D.B. (1987), *Multiple imputation for nonresponse in surveys.* New York: John Wiley and Sons.

Rumelhart, D.E. (1985), Toward an interactive model of reading. In: Singer, H., and R. B. Ruddell (Eds.) *Theoretical models and the processes of reading.* 3rd edition. Newark, DE: International.

Secretary's Commission on Achieving Necessary (1991), *What Work Requires of Schools: A SCANS Report for America 2000.* US Department of Labor.

Shetzer, H., and Warschauer, M. (2000), An electronic literacy approach to network-based language teaching. In M. Warschauer and R. Kern (Eds.), *Network-based language teaching: Concepts and practice* (pp. 171-185), New York: Cambridge University Press.

Smith, C.M. (1996), Differences in adults' reading practices and literacy proficiencies. *Reading Research Quarterly, 31/2,* 196-219.

Smith, M.C., Mikulecky, L., Kibby, M.W. and Dreher, M.J. (2000), What will be the demands of literacy in the workplace in the next millennium? *Reading Research Quarterly,* 35 (3), 378-383.

Stanovich, K. (1986). Matthew effects in reading: some consequences of individual differences in the acquisition of literacy. *Reading Research Quarterly, 21,* 360-407.

Sticht, T.G. (Ed.) (1975), *Reading for working: A functional literacy anthology.* Alexandria, VA: Human Resources Research Organization.

Sticht, T.G. (1977), Comprehending reading at work. In: M. Just and P. Carpenter (Eds.), *Cognitive Processes in Comprehension.* Hillsdale, NJ: Erlbaum. Reading Association.

Stiggins, R.J. (1982), An analysis of the dimensions of job-related reading. *Reading World, 82,* 237-247.

Sum, A. and Fogg, W.N. (1991), The Adolescent Poor and the Transition to Early Adulthood, in Edelman, P.B. and Ladner, J. (Eds.) (1991), *Adolescence and Poverty: Challenge for the 1990s*, Center for National Policy Press, Washington, D.C.

Sum, A. (1999), *Literacy in the Labor Force*, National Center for Education Statistics, Washington, D.C.

Sum, A., Kirsch, I. and Taggert, R. (February, 2002), *The Twin Challenges of Mediocrity and Inequality: Literacy in the United States from an International Perspective.* A Policy Information Center Report. Princeton, NJ: Educational Testing Service.

UNDP. (2002), Human Development Report 2002: Deepening democracy in a fragmented world. New York, Oxford: Oxford University Press.

Van Dijk, T.A. and Kintsch, W. (1983), *Strategies of Discourse Comprehension*. Orlando: Academic Press.

Walker, D.A., Anderson, C.A. and Wolf, R.M. (1976), *IEA Six Subject Survey; An Empirical Study of Education in Twenty-one Countries*. New York: John Wiley and Sons Ltd.

Warschauer, M. (1999), *Electronic Literacies: Language Culture and Power in Online Education*. Mahwah, NJ, USA: Lawrence Erlbaum Associates.

Warschauer, M. (in press), *Technology and social inclusion: Rethinking the digital divide* Cambridge: MIT Press.

Werlich, E. (1976), *A text grammar of English*. Heidelberg: Quelle and Meyer.

Winn, J.A. (1994), Promises and challenges of scaffolded instruction. *Learning Disability Quarterly, 17,* 89-104.

Yamamoto, K. (2002), *Estimating PISA Students on the IALS Prose Literacy Scale*. Princeton, NJ: Educational Testing Service.

Young, P.J. and Brozo, W.G. (2001), Boys will be boys, or will they? Literacy and masculinities. *Reading Research Quarterly, 36/3,* 316-325.

ANNEX

TECHNICAL BACKGROUND

Annex A1: Quantitative indices for the cultural balance of PISA 2000 assessment items

In the item development stage, PISA asked the participating countries to contribute items to make PISA cover a wide range of cultures and languages. Twenty countries contributed items (see Table A1.1). PISA also adopted items from the International Adult Literacy Survey (IALS) in an attempt to link assessment results to these assessments.

Table A1.1
Countries and international organisations contributing items for PISA 2000

Domain/Country	Reading	Mathematics	Science	Total
ACER	123	3	29	155
Australia			4	4
Austria	7	5		12
Belgium	13			13
CITO group	51	34	20	130
Czech Republic		2		2
Denmark	4			4
Finland	21			21
France	14	7	11	32
Germany		2		2
Greece	6	3		9
IALS	48			48
Ireland	7			7
Italy	8			8
Japan	8			8
Korea	6		8	14
New Zealand	13			13
Norway	7		6	13
Sweden	8	6	6	20
Switzerland	6			6
Russian Federation			4	4
TIMSS		5	5	10
United Kingdom	6			6
United States	20	10	15	45
Total	*376*	*77*	*108*	*586*

PISA asked each country to rate the appropriateness of the items and stimuli in terms of students' exposure to the content of the item, item difficulty, cultural concerns, other bias concerns, translation problems, and their overall appropriateness for inclusion in PISA. The results of the national ratings are summarised in Table A1.2. The ratings were made on a scale ranging from 1 (not appropriate) to 4 (fully appropriate). The ratings together with the qualitative comments from the national experts served a basis upon which to select and revise items for the PISA 2000.

Table A1.2
National ratings of the appropriateness of the PISA 2000 assessment items

Item identification	Unit title	Number of countries providing ratings	Number of countries rated below:				Item appropriateness based on average rates
			1	2	3	4	
R040Q02	Chad Animals	25	0	3	12	6	2.64
R040Q03A	Chad Animals	25	2	4	7	9	2.68
R040Q03B	Chad Animals	25	2	6	6	8	2.56
R040Q04	Chad Animals	25	2	5	7	8	2.60
R040Q06	Chad Animals	25		4	9	8	2.68
R055Q01	Drugged Spiders	26	1	2	8	11	2.92
R055Q02	Drugged Spiders	26		4	7	10	2.76
R055Q03	Drugged Spiders	26	2	1	10	9	2.80
R055Q05	Drugged Spiders	26		3	7	12	3.00
R061Q01	Macondo	25	3	3	9	7	2.56

Item identification	Unit title	Number of countries providing ratings	Number of countries rated below:				Item appropriateness based on average rates
			1	2	3	4	
R061Q03	Macondo	25	2	4	9	7	2.60
R061Q04	Macondo	25	3	4	9	6	2.48
R061Q05	Macondo	25	6	6	6	3	1.92
R067Q01	Aesop	25	1	3	5	12	2.80
R067Q04	Aesop	25	2	7	5	8	2.52
R067Q05	Aesop	25	3	6	6	7	2.44
R070Q02	Beach	25	1	6	9	5	2.40
R070Q03	Beach	25	2	6	7	6	2.36
R070Q04	Beach	25	4	11	5	2	1.96
R070Q07	Beach	25	3	5	7	5	2.16
R076Q03	FlightTimetable	26	5	3	8	6	2.36
R076Q04	FlightTimetable	26	5	3	10	4	2.28
R076Q05	FlightTimetable	26	6	1	10	5	2.32
R076Q06	FlightTimetable	26	3	3	10	6	2.52
R077Q02	Flu Immunisation	25		3	12	6	2.64
R077Q03	Flu Immunisation	25	4	6	8	3	2.08
R077Q04	Flu Immunisation	25	1	5	9	5	2.32
R077Q05	Flu Immunisation	25	4	6	9	2	2.04
R077Q06	Flu Immunisation	25	1	4	13	2	2.24
R081Q01	Graffiti	25	2	6	5	8	2.44
R081Q02	Graffiti	25	4	6	8	4	2.24
R081Q05	Graffiti	25	3	6	6	7	2.44
R081Q06A	Graffiti	25	6	6	5	5	2.12
R081Q06B	Graffiti	25	4	10	3	4	1.96
R083Q01	House Age	25	5	4	7	6	2.32
R083Q02	House Age	25	3	4	11	3	2.24
R083Q03	House Age	25	3	6	9	3	2.16
R083Q04	House Age	25	4	5	9	4	2.28
R083Q06	House Age	25	5	6	7	3	2.00
R086Q04	If	25	4	7	4	6	2.16
R086Q05	If	25	3	5	5	9	2.56
R086Q07	If	25	5	6	2	8	2.20
R088Q01	Labour	26	1	7	7	6	2.40
R088Q03	Labour	26	2	3	12	6	2.72
R088Q04	Labour	26	1	6	11	5	2.64
R088Q05	Labour	26	3	4	11	4	2.40
R088Q07	Labour	26	4	4	9	5	2.36
R091Q05	Moreland	25	4	2	7	9	2.60
R091Q06	Moreland	25	2	6	5	8	2.44
R091Q07	Moreland	25	4	6	2	10	2.48
R093Q03	Newsagency	25	4	7	7	2	1.88
R093Q04	Newsagency	25	4	8	5	4	2.04
R099Q02	Planint	25	1	4	8	9	2.76
R099Q03	Planint	25	3	4	7	8	2.56
R099Q04A	Planint	25		5	9	7	2.60
R099Q04B	Planint	25	4	3	7	7	2.36
R100Q04	Police	28	1	5	8	9	2.84
R100Q05	Police	28	1	3	8	10	2.84
R100Q06	Police	28	3	3	8	8	2.60
R100Q07	Police	28	1	4	8	10	2.92
R101Q01	Rhinoceros	28	3	3	7	10	2.80
R101Q02	Rhinoceros	27	3	6	5	6	2.16
R101Q03	Rhinoceros	25	1	3	6	10	2.60

Item identification	Unit title	Number of countries providing ratings	Number of countries rated below:				Item appropriateness based on average rates
			1	2	3	4	
R101Q04	Rhinoceros	25	1	3	7	9	2.56
R101Q05	Rhinoceros	28	3	4	7	8	2.56
R101Q08	Rhinoceros	28	3	5	6	9	2.68
R102Q01	Shirt	28	3	6	6	7	2.44
R102Q04A	Shirt	28	5	9	7	2	2.08
R102Q05	Shirt	28	4	3	10	5	2.40
R102Q06	Shirt	28	8	6	6	2	1.84
R102Q07	Shirt	28	2	8	8	4	2.32
R104Q01	Telephone	25	2	4	11	3	2.20
R104Q02	Telephone	25	2	3	10	5	2.32
R104Q05	Telephone	25	2	3	10	5	2.32
R104Q06	Telephone	25	3	2	10	5	2.28
R110Q01	Runners	25	1	5	9	7	2.64
R110Q04	Runners	25		6	10	5	2.48
R110Q05	Runners	25	1	4	11	6	2.64
R110Q06	Runners	25	1	6	7	7	2.48
R111Q01	Exchange	25	2	4	7	8	2.52
R111Q02B	Exchange	12	1	5	2	4	1.32
R111Q04	Exchange	25	1	5	5	10	2.64
R111Q06A	Exchange	25		5	9	7	2.60
R111Q06B	Exchange	25	1	6	7	8	2.64
R119Q01	Gift	26	2	5	5	10	2.68
R119Q04	Gift	26	5	4	6	7	2.36
R119Q05	Gift	26	6	9	4	4	2.08
R119Q06	Gift	25	1	7	5	8	2.48
R119Q07	Gift	25	4	6	6	6	2.32
R119Q08	Gift	25		8	7	7	2.60
R119Q09	Gift	25	4	6	5	6	2.20
R120Q01	Argument	28	1	4	5	12	2.88
R120Q03	Argument	28	1	6	7	8	2.64
R120Q06	Argument	28	6	1	9	6	2.36
R120Q07	Argument	28	1	5	8	9	2.84
R122Q01	Justart	25	4	8	5	4	2.04
R122Q02	Justart	25	6	7	6	2	1.84
R122Q03	Justart	25	4	11	4	2	1.84
R216Q01	Anouihl	26	2	5	11	4	2.44
R216Q02	Anouihl	26	2	6	9	5	2.44
R216Q03	Anouihl	26	3	5	8	6	2.44
R216Q04	Anouihl	26	4	8	6	5	2.32
R216Q06	Anouihl	26	3	5	8	6	2.44
R219Q01	Employment	26	4	6	3	9	2.44
R219Q02	Employment	26	5	7	5	5	2.16
R220Q01	Polesud	26		6	11	5	2.60
R220Q02B	Polesud	26		3	13	6	2.76
R220Q04	Polesud	26	1	4	8	10	2.92
R220Q05	Polesud	26	3	3	8	8	2.60
R220Q06	Polesud	26	1	3	8	11	3.00
R225Q01	Nuclear	25		8	7	5	2.28
R225Q02	Nuclear	25		8	7	5	2.28
R225Q03	Nuclear	25		4	12	4	2.40
R225Q04	Nuclear	25	1	5	8	6	2.36
R227Q01	Optician	25	2	10	7	3	2.20
R227Q02	Optician	25	4	6	8	2	1.92

Item identification	Unit title	Number of countries providing ratings	Number of countries rated below: 1	2	3	4	Item appropriateness based on average rates
R227Q03	Optician	25	4	8	6	3	2.00
R227Q04	Optician	25	1	8	8	5	2.44
R227Q06	Optician	25	1	9	5	6	2.32
R228Q01	Guide	26	2	3	7	10	2.76
R228Q02	Guide	26	1	4	7	10	2.80
R228Q04	Guide	25	3	3	5	10	2.56
R234Q01	personnel	25	5	9	3	4	1.92
R234Q02	personnel	25	6	7	4	3	1.76
R236Q01	newrules	25	7	5	6	3	1.88
R236Q02	newrules	25	4	8	5	4	2.04
R237Q01	jobinterview	25		6	10	6	2.64
R237Q03	jobinterview	25	1	7	7	6	2.40
R238Q01	BicycleIALS	25	1	11	6	4	2.28
R238Q02	BicycleIALS	25	3	8	6	5	2.28
R239Q01	Allergies	25	4	9	6	1	1.76
R239Q02	Allergies	25	4	9	5	3	1.96
R241Q01	Warrantyhotpoint	25	6	9	4	1	1.60
R241Q02	Warrantyhotpoint	25	5	7	6	3	1.96
R245Q01	moviesummaries	25	3	7	6	5	2.20
R245Q02	moviesummaries	25	2	9	6	3	2.00
R246Q01	Contactemployer	25	4	4	7	5	2.12
R246Q02	Contactemployer	25	2	5	9	5	2.36
Total							**2.38**

An international cultural review panel was established to scrutinise the possible cultural and linguistic bias in the PISA field trial items and stimuli. This international panel met in October 1999 to review and discuss the set of reading literacy items used in the field trial along with the marking guides. The feedback from the panel was used to revise and select the final set of tasks used in the assessment. Table A1.3 contains the geographic and cultural coverage of the international cultural review panel.

Table A1.3
Cultural and geographical composition of cultural review panel

Country	Number of participants	Country	Number of participants
Austria	1	Netherlands	3
Belgium	1	New Zealand	1
France	1	Switzerland	1
Germany	1	Spain	1
Ireland	1	Sweden	1
Italy	2	United Kingdom	2
Korea	1	United States	2
Luxembourg	1		
Total			**20**

A statistical index called *differential item functioning* was used to detect items that worked differently in some countries. These items were suspected of cultural bias and reviewed in consultation with national experts. As a result, some items were excluded from scaling as if they had not been administered in that particular country. Table A1.4 lists the items that are excluded from the national scaling for each country.

Table A1.4
Items excluded from scaling for suspected cultural bias

Country	Item identification	Country	Item identification
Austria	M155Q03	Korea	R237Q03
Austria	R055Q03	Korea	R246Q02
Austria	S133Q04T	Mexico	R040Q02
Belgium Dutch Version	R076Q05	Netherlands	R076Q05
Belgium Dutch version	R100Q05	Netherlands	R100Q05
Brazil	M033Q01	Netherlands	S268Q02T
Canada French version	R101Q08	Poland	R099Q04B
England	R076Q03	Russian Federation	R091Q05
England	R076Q04	Spain	R227Q01
Germany	R055Q03	Sweden	R091Q07B
Germany	S133Q04T	Switzerland, German version	M155Q01
Greece	R040Q02	Switzerland, German version	M155Q03
Hungary	R119Q04	Switzerland, German version	M155Q04
Iceland	R236Q01	Switzerland, German version	R055Q03
Iceland	S268Q02T	Switzerland, German version	R076Q03
Italy	R040Q06	Switzerland, German version	R091Q05
Italy	R219Q01T	Switzerland, German version	R111Q06B
Japan	M155Q01	Switzerland, German version	R239Q02
Korea	R102Q04A	Switzerland, German version	S133Q04T
Korea	R216Q02	Switzerland, Italian version	S268Q06

Source: PISA 2000 Technical Report (OECD, 2002b).

Annex A2: Index of reading engagement

Extension of initial reading engagement index

For the initial PISA report, an index of reading engagement had been constructed that was solely based on the students' attitudes toward reading (OECD, 2001*b*).

Subsequent research suggested, however, that reading engagement subsumes multiple aspects including reading practice as well as attitudes to and interests in reading. For this report, an attempt was therefore made to extend the initial index of reading engagement by combining the two aspects of engagement in reading.

The new index of reading engagement is built on three components - frequency of reading, diversity of reading and the interest in reading. The first two components represent reading practice and the latter taps into attitudinal aspects of reading engagement.

The index has been constructed in such a way that around two-thirds of the OECD student population are between values of -1 and 1, with an average score of zero (*i.e.,* the mean for the combined student population from participating OECD countries is set to zero and the standard deviation is set to one). It is important to note that negative values on the index do not necessarily imply that students responded negatively to the underlying questions. A negative value merely indicates that a group of students (or all students, collectively, in a single country) responded less positively than students did, on average, in OECD countries. Likewise, a positive value on an index indicates that a group of students responded more favourably, or more positively, than all students did, on average, in OECD countries.

A structural equation model was used to confirm the theoretical dimensions of the index and to validate its comparability across countries. The new index of reading engagement index has a reliability of 0.83. With the extension of reading engagement concept into reading frequency and diversity, the reliability has increased to from 0.72 to 0.83. The new index of reading engagement also has a high correlation (0.88) with the initial reading engagement index based on the reading attitudes.

Relationship with gender difference and the reading literacy performance

Table A2.1 compares the two reading engagement indices in terms of country means, gender differences and their effects on reading literacy performance. The mean reading engagement scores have consistent relative standing to the OECD average. In other words, countries that are above the OECD average on the initial reading engagement index also show higher mean scores than the OECD average on the new index. Two exceptions are Norway and Sweden. These two countries have mean scores that are above the OECD average on the initial index but below the OECD average on the new index. It is assumed that the students of these two countries reported relatively lower frequency and diversity of reading than students in other OECD countries. It should be noted that despite of the discrepancy in the mean reading engagement between the initial and new index of reading engagement, the gender difference in reading engagement shows a consistent pattern and the relative standing of the gender disparity remain stable.

Table A2.1 also shows that the new reading engagement index tends to have larger effects on the reading literacy performance than the initial index. On the other hand, Ireland, Latvia, New Zealand, Poland and the Russian Federation displayed substantially smaller effects associated with new index.

Table A2.1
Comparison of country means based on the two PISA reading engagement indices

		Country mean				Gender difference				Effects on reading literacy per-formance[2]	
		New index	S.E.	Initial index	S.E.	New index	Rank[1]	Initial index	Rank[1]	New index	Initial index
OECD COUNTRIES	Australia	-0.04	(0.03)	-0.07	(0.03)	0.28	26	0.45	22	42.52	41.8
	Austria	-0.08	(0.03)	-0.04	(0.03)	0.52	6	0.82	4	36.76	29.3
	Belgium	-0.28	(0.02)	-0.25	(0.02)	0.41	15	0.56	15	35.83	30.8
	Canada	0.01	(0.01)	0.00	(0.01)	0.47	10	0.61	11	35.14	36.2
	Czech Republic	0.02	(0.02)	0.17	(0.02)	0.57	3	0.78	5	41.23	33.8
	Denmark	0.26	(0.02)	0.00	(0.02)	0.48	9	0.63	10	40.99	40.0
	Finland	0.46	(0.02)	0.20	(0.02)	0.74	1	0.92	1	42.48	40.0
	France	-0.18	(0.02)	-0.06	(0.02)	0.30	23	0.53	16	31.18	27.5
	Germany	-0.26	(0.02)	-0.08	(0.03)	0.55	4	0.82	3	37.57	33.3
	Greece	-0.09	(0.02)	-0.01	(0.02)	0.17	30	0.41	26	33.31	35.7
	Hungary	0.03	(0.02)	0.07	(0.02)	0.36	21	0.44	24	43.71	43.0
	Iceland	0.27	(0.01)	0.02	(0.02)	0.39	18	0.51	17	42.11	43.7
	Ireland	-0.20	(0.02)	-0.07	(0.02)	0.46	12	0.57	14	35.18	40.1
	Italy	-0.08	(0.02)	0.00	(0.03)	0.37	19	0.57	13	28.54	28.0
	Japan	0.20	(0.03)	0.09	(0.03)	0.17	29	0.31	30	26.87	23.8
	Korea	0.21	(0.02)	0.02	(0.02)	0.04	31	0.22	31	24.96	25.9
	Luxembourg	-0.19	(0.02)	-0.10	(0.02)	0.40	16	0.66	8	22.02	19.4
	Mexico	0.07	(0.01)	0.29	(0.02)	0.20	28	0.34	28	26.93	14.6
	New Zealand	0.05	(0.02)	0.01	(0.02)	0.29	25	0.43	25	39.75	43.7
	Norway	0.09	(0.02)	-0.22	(0.02)	0.51	7	0.66	7	47.25	42.5
	Poland	-0.10	(0.02)	-0.01	(0.03)	0.36	20	0.45	21	30.84	34.1
	Portugal	0.13	(0.02)	0.31	(0.02)	0.47	11	0.65	9	35.14	33.5
	Spain	-0.23	(0.02)	-0.04	(0.02)	0.29	24	0.50	19	32.38	31.3
	Sweden	0.14	(0.02)	-0.06	(0.02)	0.45	13	0.59	12	41.53	39.5
	Switzerland	0.00	(0.01)	0.06	(0.03)	0.62	2	0.90	2	38.10	34.8
	United Kingdom	-0.10	(0.02)	-0.10	(0.02)	0.26	27	0.44	23	37.95	40.4
	United States	-0.14	(0.03)	-0.13	(0.03)	0.36	22	0.40	27	29.32	33.0
	OECD average	*0.00*	*(0.00)*	*0.00*	*(0.00)*	*0.38*		*0.56*			
NON-OECD COUNTRIES	Brazil	0.11	(0.02)	0.15	(0.02)	0.53	5	0.50	18	23.76	20.6
	Latvia	-0.04	(0.02)	-0.04	(0.02)	0.44	14	0.48	20	36.19	42.3
	Liechtenstein	-0.13	(0.05)	-0.08	(0.06)	0.49	8	0.77	6	43.81	35.7
	Russian Federation	0.17	(0.02)	0.05	(0.01)	0.39	17	0.34	29	24.82	34.9

1. Ranks are made in the order of magnitude in the difference between female and male students.
2. Change in the combined reading literacy score per unit of the reading engagement index.

Mean index statistically significantly above the OECD average ▪ Mean index not statistically significantly different from the OECD average ▪ Mean index statistically significantly below the OECD average

Annex A3: Technical notes on the multilevel multivariate analyses

Description of variables used in the multilevel multivariate analyses

Individual characteristics of the student

• **Gender:** Females were recoded to 1, males to 0.

• **Engagement in reading:** This is an index of how much the student engages in reading and is composed of the amount of time spent on reading in general, on different sources (magazines, comic books, fictions, non-fiction books, newspapers), and nine items measuring the student's attitude toward reading. This variable is an indicator of the student's engagement and interest in reading and motivation to read.

Home and family background variables

• **Family structure:** Students living with two parents/guardians were coded to 1. Other students have a 0 on this variable. It indicates whether the student lives in a nuclear family.

• **Socio-economic background:** In PISA 2000, students' socio-economic background was measured by the occupational status of parents. Students were asked to report their mothers' and fathers' occupations, and to state whether each parent was: in full-time paid work; part time paid work; not working but looking for a paid job; or "other". The open-ended responses were then coded in accordance with the International Standard Classification of Occupations (ISCO 1988). The PISA International Socio-economic Index of Occupation Status (ISEI) was derived from students' responses on parental occupation. The index captures the attributes of occupations that convert parents' education into income. The index was derived by the optimal scaling of occupation groups to maximise the indirect effect of education on income through occupation and to minimise the direct effect of education on income, net of occupation (both effects being net of age). For more information on the methodology, see Ganzeboom, Draaf, and Treiman (1992). The PISA international Socio-economic Index of Occupational Status is based on either the father's or the mother's occupations, whichever is the higher.

• **Number of books in the home:** This is an indicator of literacy resources at home and reflects also the educational and socio-economic background of the family. This variable has been used as an indicator for students' socio-economic and educational background in most international studies on educational achievement (TIMSS, IEA Civic Education Study, IEA Reading Literacy Study).

• **Cultural communication with parents:** This is an index of students' reports on how often parents discuss political or social issues, discuss books, films or television programmes or listen to classical music with the student. It indicates how often parents spend time in communicating with the student on socio-cultural issues.

• **Home educational resources:** This index is derived from students' reports on the availability and number of resources at home that may have a favourable impact on the student's learning (quiet place to study, desk for study, text books, number of calculators.).

• **Immigration status:** Students' reports on where they and their parents were born were recoded so that 1 indicates that a student and both of his or her parents were born in another country (0 for all other students). This variable indicates whether a student comes from a 'first-generation' immigrant family. Preliminary analyses showed that the language spoken at home has a strong effect in many countries, typically those with a higher proportion of immigrants. That is, students who, most of the time, speak a language at home different from the test language on average have lower reading scores. But as this question was not included in two countries' questionnaires and as in a considerable number of countries this variable had a high percentage of non-responses it was decided not to include this variable in the final model.

Instruction and learning

- **Achievement press**: This index is derived from students' reports on the frequency with which, in their <class of the language of assessment>: the teacher wants them to work hard; the teacher tells students that they can do better; the teacher does not like it when students deliver <careless> work; and, students have to learn a lot.

- **Time spent on homework**: This index was derived from the students' reports on how much time in a week he or she spends on homework in the test language, mathematics and science.

- **Grade**: This variable contains the grade the student attends. It was recoded to reflect the difference between the student's level and the modal level for 15-year-old students in the country. It was included mainly for the purpose of controlling for different levels of instruction. Without controlling for grade level some (school-related) predictors may appear to be have an effect, which is only due to grade differences.

Perceptions of school and learning climate

- **Sense of belonging to school**: This is an index measuring students' feelings about being at school. Positive values indicating a favourable perception of the school.

- **Disciplinary climate**: This index summarises students' reports on the frequency with which, in their <class of the language of assessment>: the teacher has to wait a long time for students to <quiet down>; students cannot work well; students don't listen to what the teacher says; students don't start working for a long time after the lesson begins; there is noise and disorder; and at the start of the class, more than five minutes are spent doing nothing. The index was inverted so that low values indicate a poor disciplinary climate.

- **Student-teacher relations**: This index is derived from students' reports on their level of agreement with the following statements: I get along well with most teachers; most teachers are interested in students' well-being; most of my teachers really listen to what I have to say; if I need extra help, I will receive it from my teachers; and most of my teachers treat me fairly.

School characteristics

- **Mean of parents' occupational status for school:** This variable indicates the average of the occupational status of parents within a school. It is an indicator for the 'intake' of a school: that is, whether its students on average come from families with a higher or a lower socio-economic status.

- **Mean of engagement in reading for school:** This variable reflects the average of the students' engagement in reading for each school.

Technical notes on the statistical model

With multilevel linear regression models, student explanatory variables can be considered as:

• fixed, if the regression lines (red lines) are identical for all schools (the red lines need to be parallel); or

• random, if the effect of social background on achievement can differ from one school to another (the red lines do not need to be parallel).

For the analyses presented in this chapter, the explanatory variables at the student level were considered fixed. Identifying school variables that might reinforce or weaken the relationship between, for example, student social background and reading performance in a particular country is of interest; but would be quite difficult accomplish this at the international level without a deep knowledge of the local context.

For estimating the regression models, the SAS procedure for mixed models (see Littell, Milliken, Stroup and Wolfinger, 1996) was used which gives researchers flexibility in handling a large number of student data sets and facilitates the estimation of correct standard errors using replication methods. In PISA, the Fay's method was used to compute the standard errors.

Typically, regression coefficients in multilevel analyses are not standardised; that is, they show to what extent the dependent variable increases or decreases with each unit in the explanatory variable. To make effect sizes comparable across countries, all continuous variables were standardised to have a national (within-country) mean of 0 and a standard deviation of 1. Aggregates of student variables at the school level were not standardised.

Table 7.11 presents the percentage of variance explained at the school level and at the student level. On average, 23 percent of the variance is explained at the student level and 72 per cent at the school level.

The number of students in the multilevel multivariate model presented in chapter 7 is different from the number of students in the PISA international database because of the missing data on some of the variables used in the analysis. Table A3.1 presents the number of students in the international database, number of students included in the analysis and the ratio of these two numbers.

Table A3.1
**Number of students in the PISA 2000 International data base, number of students included
in the analysis and ratio of students included in multilevel model analyses.**

	No of students included in the analysis (1)	No of students in the PISA database(2)	Ratio of students (1) to (2)
Australia	4795	5176	0.93
Austria	4181	4745	0.88
Belgium	5968	6670	0.90
Canada	26859	29687	0.91
Czech Republic	5007	5365	0.93
Denmark	3667	4235	0.87
Finland	4570	4864	0.94
France	4087	4673	0.88
Germany	4675	5073	0.92
Greece	4170	4672	0.89
Hungary	4523	4887	0.93
Iceland	3157	3372	0.94
Ireland	3642	3854	0.95
Italy	4622	4984	0.93
Japan	1992	5256	0.38
Korea	4528	4982	0.91
Luxembourg	2874	3528	0.82
Mexico	3848	4600	0.84
New Zealand	3353	3667	0.91
Norway	3779	4147	0.91
Poland	3165	3654	0.87
Portugal	4172	4585	0.91
Spain	5473	6214	0.88
Sweden	4186	4416	0.95
Switzerland	5516	6100	0.90
United Kingdom	8524	9340	0.91
United States	2990	3846	0.78
Brazil	4065	4893	0.83
Latvia	3562	3893	0.92
Russian Federation	6072	6701	0.91
Netherlands[1]	2346	2503	0.94

OECD COUNTRIES / NON-OECD COUNTRIES

1. Response rate is too low to ensure comparability.

Annex A4: Standard errors, significance tests and multiple comparisons

The statistics in this report represent *estimates* of national performance based on samples of students rather than values that could be calculated if every student in every country had answered every question. Consequently, it is important to have measures of the degree of uncertainty of the estimates. In PISA 2000, each estimate has an associated degree of uncertainty, which is expressed through a *standard error*. The use of *confidence intervals* provides a way to make inferences about the population means and proportions in a manner that reflects the uncertainty associated with the sample estimates. From an observed sample statistic it can, under the assumption of a normal distribution, be inferred that the corresponding population result would lie within the confidence interval in 95 out of 100 replications of the measurement on different samples drawn from the same population.

In many cases, readers are primarily interested in whether a given value in a particular country is different from a second value in the same or another country, *e.g.*, whether females in a country perform better than males in the same country. In the tables and charts used in this report, differences are labelled as *statistically significant* when a difference of that size, or larger, would be observed less than 5 per cent of the time, if there was actually no difference in corresponding population values. Similarly, the risk of reporting as significant if there is, in fact, no correlation between to measures is contained at 5 per cent.

Although the probability that a particular difference will falsely be declared to be statistically significant is low (5 per cent) in each single comparison, the probability of making such an error increases when several comparisons are made simultaneously.

It is possible to make an adjustment for this which reduces to 5 per cent the maximum probability that differences will be falsely declared as statistically significant at least once among all the comparisons that are made. Such an adjustment, based on the Bonferroni method, has been incorporated into the multiple comparison charts in Chapters 2 and 3 since the likely interest of readers in those contexts is to compare a country's performance with that of all other countries.

For all other tables and charts readers should note that, if there were no real differences on a given measure, then the *multiple comparison* in conjunction with a 5 per cent significance level, would erroneously identify differences on 0.05 times the number of comparisons made, occasions. For example, even though the significance tests applied in PISA for identifying gender differences ensure that, for each country, the likelihood of identifying a gender difference erroneously is less than 5 per cent, a comparison showing differences for 27 countries would, on average, identify 1.4 cases (0.05 times 27) with significant gender differences, even if there were no real gender difference in any of the countries. The same applies for other statistics for which significance tests have been undertaken in this publication, such as correlations and regression coefficients.

DATA TABLES

Table 4.1
Mean and standard deviation in student performance on the combined reading literacy scale

		Mean score	S.E.	Standard deviation	S.E.
OECD COUNTRIES	Australia	528	(3.5)	102	(1.6)
	Austria	507	(2.4)	93	(1.6)
	Belgium	507	(3.6)	107	(2.4)
	Canada	534	(1.6)	95	(1.1)
	Czech Republic	492	(2.4)	96	(1.9)
	Denmark	497	(2.4)	98	(1.8)
	Finland	546	(2.6)	89	(2.6)
	France	505	(2.7)	92	(1.7)
	Germany	484	(2.5)	111	(1.9)
	Greece	474	(5.0)	97	(2.7)
	Hungary	480	(4.0)	94	(2.1)
	Iceland	507	(1.5)	92	(1.4)
	Ireland	527	(3.2)	94	(1.7)
	Italy	487	(2.9)	91	(2.7)
	Japan	522	(5.2)	86	(3.0)
	Korea	525	(2.4)	70	(1.6)
	Luxembourg	441	(1.6)	100	(1.5)
	Mexico	422	(3.3)	86	(2.1)
	New Zealand	529	(2.8)	108	(2.0)
	Norway	505	(2.8)	104	(1.7)
	Poland	479	(4.5)	100	(3.1)
	Portugal	470	(4.5)	97	(1.8)
	Spain	493	(2.7)	85	(1.2)
	Sweden	516	(2.2)	92	(1.2)
	Switzerland	494	(4.3)	102	(2.0)
	United Kingdom	523	(2.6)	100	(1.5)
	United States	504	(7.0)	105	(2.7)
	OECD average	*500*	*(0.6)*	*100*	*(0.4)*
NON-OECD COUNTRIES	Brazil	396	(3.1)	86	(1.9)
	Latvia	458	(5.3)	102	(2.3)
	Liechtenstein	483	(4.1)	96	(3.9)
	Russian Federation	462	(4.2)	92	(1.8)

Table 4.2
Percentage of students at each level of proficiency on the combined reading literacy scale

		Proficiency levels										
		Below Level 1 (less than 335 score points)		Level 1 (from 335 to 407 score points)		Level 2 (from 408 to 480 score points)		Level 3 (from 481 to 552 score points)		Level 4 (from 553 to 625 score points)		Level 5 (above 625 score points)	
		%	S.E.	%	S.E.	%	S.E.	%	S.E.	%	S.E.	%	S.E.
OECD COUNTRIES	Australia	3.3	(0.5)	9.1	(0.8)	19.0	(1.1)	25.7	(1.1)	25.3	(0.9)	17.6	(1.2)
	Austria	4.4	(0.4)	10.2	(0.6)	21.7	(0.9)	29.9	(1.2)	24.9	(1.0)	8.8	(0.8)
	Belgium	7.7	(1.0)	11.3	(0.7)	16.8	(0.7)	25.8	(0.9)	26.3	(0.9)	12.0	(0.7)
	Canada	2.4	(0.3)	7.2	(0.3)	18.0	(0.4)	28.0	(0.5)	27.7	(0.6)	16.8	(0.5)
	Czech Republic	6.1	(0.6)	11.4	(0.7)	24.8	(1.2)	30.9	(1.1)	19.8	(0.8)	7.0	(0.6)
	Denmark	5.9	(0.6)	12.0	(0.7)	22.5	(0.9)	29.5	(1.0)	22.0	(0.9)	8.1	(0.5)
	Finland	1.7	(0.5)	5.2	(0.4)	14.3	(0.7)	28.7	(0.8)	31.6	(0.9)	18.5	(0.9)
	France	4.2	(0.6)	11.0	(0.8)	22.0	(0.8)	30.6	(1.0)	23.7	(0.9)	8.5	(0.6)
	Germany	9.9	(0.7)	12.7	(0.6)	22.3	(0.8)	26.8	(1.0)	19.4	(1.0)	8.8	(0.5)
	Greece	8.7	(1.2)	15.7	(1.4)	25.9	(1.4)	28.1	(1.7)	16.7	(1.4)	5.0	(0.7)
	Hungary	6.9	(0.7)	15.8	(1.2)	25.0	(1.1)	28.8	(1.3)	18.5	(1.1)	5.1	(0.8)
	Iceland	4.0	(0.3)	10.5	(0.6)	22.0	(0.8)	30.8	(0.9)	23.6	(1.1)	9.1	(0.7)
	Ireland	3.1	(0.5)	7.9	(0.8)	17.9	(0.9)	29.7	(1.1)	27.1	(1.1)	14.2	(0.8)
	Italy	5.4	(0.9)	13.5	(0.9)	25.6	(1.0)	30.6	(1.0)	19.5	(1.1)	5.3	(0.5)
	Japan	2.7	(0.6)	7.3	(1.1)	18.0	(1.3)	33.3	(1.3)	28.8	(1.7)	9.9	(1.1)
	Korea	0.9	(0.2)	4.8	(0.6)	18.6	(0.9)	38.8	(1.1)	31.1	(1.2)	5.7	(0.6)
	Luxembourg	14.2	(0.7)	20.9	(0.8)	27.5	(1.3)	24.6	(1.1)	11.2	(0.5)	1.7	(0.3)
	Mexico	16.1	(1.2)	28.1	(1.4)	30.3	(1.1)	18.8	(1.2)	6.0	(0.7)	0.9	(0.2)
	New Zealand	4.8	(0.5)	8.9	(0.5)	17.2	(0.9)	24.6	(1.1)	25.8	(1.1)	18.7	(1.0)
	Norway	6.3	(0.6)	11.2	(0.8)	19.5	(0.8)	28.1	(0.8)	23.7	(0.9)	11.2	(0.7)
	Poland	8.7	(1.0)	14.6	(1.0)	24.1	(1.4)	28.2	(1.3)	18.6	(1.3)	5.9	(1.0)
	Portugal	9.6	(1.0)	16.7	(1.2)	25.3	(1.0)	27.5	(1.2)	16.8	(1.1)	4.2	(0.5)
	Spain	4.1	(0.5)	12.2	(0.9)	25.7	(0.7)	32.8	(1.0)	21.1	(0.9)	4.2	(0.5)
	Sweden	3.3	(0.4)	9.3	(0.6)	20.3	(0.7)	30.4	(1.0)	25.6	(1.0)	11.2	(0.7)
	Switzerland	7.0	(0.7)	13.3	(0.9)	21.4	(1.0)	28.0	(1.0)	21.0	(1.0)	9.2	(1.0)
	United Kingdom	3.6	(0.4)	9.2	(0.5)	19.6	(0.7)	27.5	(0.9)	24.4	(0.9)	15.6	(1.0)
	United States	6.4	(1.2)	11.5	(1.2)	21.0	(1.2)	27.4	(1.3)	21.5	(1.4)	12.2	(1.4)
	OECD average	*6.0*	*(0.1)*	*11.9*	*(0.2)*	*21.7*	*(0.2)*	*28.7*	*(0.2)*	*22.3*	*(0.2)*	*9.5*	*(0.1)*
NON-OECD COUNTRIES	Brazil	23.3	(1.4)	32.5	(1.2)	27.7	(1.3)	12.9	(1.1)	3.1	(0.5)	0.6	(0.2)
	Latvia	12.7	(1.3)	17.9	(1.3)	26.3	(1.1)	25.2	(1.3)	13.8	(1.1)	4.1	(0.6)
	Liechtenstein	7.6	(1.5)	14.5	(2.1)	23.2	(2.9)	30.1	(3.4)	19.5	(2.2)	5.1	(1.6)
	Russian Federation	9.0	(1.0)	18.5	(1.1)	29.2	(0.8)	26.9	(1.1)	13.3	(1.0)	3.2	(0.5)

Table 4.3
Mean scores for the aspect subscales by country

		Retrieving information				Interpreting texts				Reflection and evaluation			
		Mean score	S.E.	S.D.	S.E.	Mean score	S.E.	S.D.	S.E.	Mean score	S.E.	S.D.	S.E.
OECD COUNTRIES	Australia	536	(3.7)	108	(1.6)	527	(3.5)	104	(1.5)	526	(3.5)	100	(1.5)
	Austria	502	(2.3)	96	(1.5)	508	(2.4)	93	(1.6)	512	(2.7)	100	(1.8)
	Belgium	515	(3.9)	120	(2.7)	512	(3.2)	105	(2.0)	497	(4.3)	114	(4.1)
	Canada	530	(1.7)	102	(1.2)	532	(1.6)	95	(1.0)	542	(1.6)	96	(1.0)
	Czech Republic	481	(2.7)	107	(1.9)	500	(2.4)	96	(1.6)	485	(2.6)	103	(1.8)
	Denmark	498	(2.8)	105	(1.9)	494	(2.4)	99	(1.7)	500	(2.6)	102	(2.1)
	Finland	556	(2.8)	102	(2.1)	555	(2.9)	97	(3.3)	533	(2.7)	91	(3.9)
	France	515	(3.0)	101	(2.1)	506	(2.7)	92	(1.7)	496	(2.9)	98	(1.8)
	Germany	483	(2.4)	114	(2.0)	488	(2.5)	109	(1.8)	478	(2.9)	124	(1.8)
	Greece	450	(5.4)	109	(3.0)	475	(4.5)	89	(2.4)	495	(5.6)	115	(3.1)
	Hungary	478	(4.4)	107	(2.2)	480	(3.8)	90	(1.9)	481	(4.3)	100	(2.2)
	Iceland	500	(1.6)	103	(1.3)	514	(1.4)	95	(1.4)	501	(1.3)	93	(1.3)
	Ireland	524	(3.3)	100	(1.7)	526	(3.3)	97	(1.7)	533	(3.1)	90	(1.7)
	Italy	488	(3.1)	104	(3.0)	489	(2.6)	86	(2.4)	483	(3.1)	101	(2.9)
	Japan	526	(5.5)	97	(3.1)	518	(5.0)	83	(2.9)	530	(5.5)	100	(3.3)
	Korea	530	(2.5)	82	(1.6)	525	(2.3)	69	(1.5)	526	(2.6)	76	(1.7)
	Luxembourg	433	(1.6)	109	(1.4)	446	(1.6)	101	(1.3)	442	(1.9)	115	(1.8)
	Mexico	402	(3.9)	101	(2.2)	419	(2.9)	78	(1.7)	446	(3.7)	109	(2.2)
	New Zealand	535	(2.8)	116	(2.1)	526	(2.7)	111	(2.0)	529	(2.9)	107	(1.8)
	Norway	505	(2.9)	110	(1.9)	505	(2.8)	104	(1.6)	506	(3.0)	108	(1.8)
	Poland	475	(5.0)	112	(3.3)	482	(4.3)	97	(2.7)	477	(4.7)	110	(3.2)
	Portugal	455	(4.9)	107	(2.2)	473	(4.3)	93	(1.6)	480	(4.5)	101	(1.7)
	Spain	483	(3.0)	92	(1.2)	491	(2.6)	84	(1.1)	506	(2.8)	91	(1.2)
	Sweden	516	(2.4)	104	(1.5)	522	(2.1)	96	(1.3)	510	(2.3)	95	(1.2)
	Switzerland	498	(4.4)	113	(2.1)	496	(4.2)	101	(2.0)	488	(4.8)	113	(2.2)
	United Kingdom	523	(2.5)	105	(1.5)	514	(2.5)	102	(1.4)	539	(2.5)	99	(1.6)
	United States	499	(7.4)	112	(2.7)	505	(7.1)	106	(2.6)	507	(7.1)	105	(2.7)
	OECD average	*498*	*(0.7)*	*111*	*(0.4)*	*501*	*(0.6)*	*100*	*(0.4)*	*502*	*(0.7)*	*106*	*(0.4)*
NON-OECD COUNTRIES	Brazil	365	(3.4)	97	(2.1)	400	(3.0)	84	(1.8)	417	(3.3)	93	(2.2)
	Latvia	451	(5.7)	117	(2.4)	459	(4.9)	95	(2.0)	458	(5.9)	113	(2.3)
	Liechtenstein	492	(4.9)	106	(4.7)	484	(4.5)	94	(3.6)	468	(5.7)	108	(4.3)
	Russian Federation	451	(4.9)	108	(2.1)	468	(4.0)	92	(1.8)	455	(4.0)	98	(1.7)

■ Mean performance statistically significantly above the OECD average   ■ Mean performance not statistically significantly different from the OECD average   ■ Mean performance statistically significantly below the OECD average

Table 4.4

Multiple comparisons of mean performance on the retrieving information subscale

Read across the row for a country to compare performance with the countries listed along the top of the chart. Key to symbols: ▲ = significantly higher, ○ = no significant difference, ▽ = significantly lower.

Country	Mean	S.E.	Finland (556, 2.8)	Australia (536, 3.7)	New Zealand (535, 2.8)	Canada (530, 1.7)	Korea (530, 2.5)	Japan (526, 5.5)	Ireland (524, 3.3)	United Kingdom (523, 2.5)	Sweden (516, 2.4)	France (515, 3.0)	Belgium (515, 3.9)	Norway (505, 2.9)	Austria (502, 2.3)	Iceland (500, 1.6)	United States (499, 7.4)	Switzerland (498, 4.4)	Denmark (498, 2.8)	Liechtenstein (492, 4.9)	Italy (488, 3.1)	Spain (483, 3.0)	Germany (483, 2.4)	Czech Republic (481, 2.7)	Hungary (478, 4.4)	Poland (475, 5.0)	Portugal (455, 4.9)	Russian Fed. (451, 4.9)	Latvia (451, 5.7)	Greece (450, 5.4)	Luxembourg (433, 1.6)	Mexico (402, 3.9)	Brazil (365, 3.4)
Finland	556	(2.8)	□	▲	▲	▲	▲	▲	▲	▲	▲	▲	▲	▲	▲	▲	▲	▲	▲	▲	▲	▲	▲	▲	▲	▲	▲	▲	▲	▲	▲	▲	▲
Australia	536	(3.7)	▽	□	○	○	○	○	▲	▲	▲	▲	▲	▲	▲	▲	▲	▲	▲	▲	▲	▲	▲	▲	▲	▲	▲	▲	▲	▲	▲	▲	▲
New Zealand	535	(2.8)	▽	○	□	○	○	○	▲	▲	▲	▲	▲	▲	▲	▲	▲	▲	▲	▲	▲	▲	▲	▲	▲	▲	▲	▲	▲	▲	▲	▲	▲
Canada	530	(1.7)	▽	○	○	□	○	○	○	▲	▲	▲	▲	▲	▲	▲	▲	▲	▲	▲	▲	▲	▲	▲	▲	▲	▲	▲	▲	▲	▲	▲	▲
Korea	530	(2.5)	▽	○	○	○	□	○	○	▲	▲	▲	▲	▲	▲	▲	▲	▲	▲	▲	▲	▲	▲	▲	▲	▲	▲	▲	▲	▲	▲	▲	▲
Japan	526	(5.5)	▽	○	○	○	○	□	○	○	○	○	○	▲	▲	▲	▲	▲	▲	▲	▲	▲	▲	▲	▲	▲	▲	▲	▲	▲	▲	▲	▲
Ireland	524	(3.3)	▽	▽	▽	○	○	○	□	○	○	▲	○	▲	▲	▲	▲	▲	▲	▲	▲	▲	▲	▲	▲	▲	▲	▲	▲	▲	▲	▲	▲
United Kingdom	523	(2.5)	▽	▽	▽	▽	▽	○	○	□	▲	▲	○	▲	▲	▲	▲	▲	▲	▲	▲	▲	▲	▲	▲	▲	▲	▲	▲	▲	▲	▲	▲
Sweden	516	(2.4)	▽	▽	▽	▽	▽	○	○	▽	□	○	○	▲	▲	▲	▲	▲	▲	▲	▲	▲	▲	▲	▲	▲	▲	▲	▲	▲	▲	▲	▲
France	515	(3.0)	▽	▽	▽	▽	▽	○	▽	▽	○	□	○	▲	▲	▲	▲	▲	▲	▲	▲	▲	▲	▲	▲	▲	▲	▲	▲	▲	▲	▲	▲
Belgium	515	(3.9)	▽	▽	▽	▽	▽	○	○	○	○	○	□	▲	▲	▲	▲	▲	▲	▲	▲	▲	▲	▲	▲	▲	▲	▲	▲	▲	▲	▲	▲
Norway	505	(2.9)	▽	▽	▽	▽	▽	▽	▽	▽	▽	▽	▽	□	○	○	○	○	○	▲	▲	▲	▲	▲	▲	▲	▲	▲	▲	▲	▲	▲	▲
Austria	502	(2.3)	▽	▽	▽	▽	▽	▽	▽	▽	▽	▽	▽	○	□	○	○	○	○	○	▲	▲	▲	▲	▲	▲	▲	▲	▲	▲	▲	▲	▲
Iceland	500	(1.6)	▽	▽	▽	▽	▽	▽	▽	▽	▽	▽	▽	○	○	□	○	○	○	○	▲	▲	▲	▲	▲	▲	▲	▲	▲	▲	▲	▲	▲
United States	499	(7.4)	▽	▽	▽	▽	▽	▽	▽	▽	▽	▽	○	○	○	○	□	○	○	○	○	▲	▲	▲	▲	▲	▲	▲	▲	▲	▲	▲	▲
Switzerland	498	(4.4)	▽	▽	▽	▽	▽	▽	▽	▽	▽	▽	▽	○	○	○	○	□	○	○	○	▲	▲	▲	▲	▲	▲	▲	▲	▲	▲	▲	▲
Denmark	498	(2.8)	▽	▽	▽	▽	▽	▽	▽	▽	▽	▽	▽	○	○	○	○	○	□	○	▲	▲	▲	▲	▲	▲	▲	▲	▲	▲	▲	▲	▲
Liechtenstein	492	(4.9)	▽	▽	▽	▽	▽	▽	▽	▽	▽	▽	▽	▽	○	○	○	○	○	□	○	○	○	▲	▲	▲	▲	▲	▲	▲	▲	▲	▲
Italy	488	(3.1)	▽	▽	▽	▽	▽	▽	▽	▽	▽	▽	▽	▽	▽	▽	○	○	▽	○	□	○	○	○	○	▲	▲	▲	▲	▲	▲	▲	▲
Spain	483	(3.0)	▽	▽	▽	▽	▽	▽	▽	▽	▽	▽	▽	▽	▽	▽	▽	▽	▽	○	○	□	○	○	○	○	▲	▲	▲	▲	▲	▲	▲
Germany	483	(2.4)	▽	▽	▽	▽	▽	▽	▽	▽	▽	▽	▽	▽	▽	▽	▽	▽	▽	○	○	○	□	○	○	○	▲	▲	▲	▲	▲	▲	▲
Czech Republic	481	(2.7)	▽	▽	▽	▽	▽	▽	▽	▽	▽	▽	▽	▽	▽	▽	▽	▽	▽	▽	○	○	○	□	○	○	▲	▲	▲	▲	▲	▲	▲
Hungary	478	(4.4)	▽	▽	▽	▽	▽	▽	▽	▽	▽	▽	▽	▽	▽	▽	▽	▽	▽	▽	○	○	○	○	□	○	▲	▲	▲	▲	▲	▲	▲
Poland	475	(5.0)	▽	▽	▽	▽	▽	▽	▽	▽	▽	▽	▽	▽	▽	▽	▽	▽	▽	▽	▽	○	○	○	○	□	▲	▲	▲	▲	▲	▲	▲
Portugal	455	(4.9)	▽	▽	▽	▽	▽	▽	▽	▽	▽	▽	▽	▽	▽	▽	▽	▽	▽	▽	▽	▽	▽	▽	▽	▽	□	○	○	○	▲	▲	▲
Russian Fed.	451	(4.9)	▽	▽	▽	▽	▽	▽	▽	▽	▽	▽	▽	▽	▽	▽	▽	▽	▽	▽	▽	▽	▽	▽	▽	▽	○	□	○	○	▲	▲	▲
Latvia	451	(5.7)	▽	▽	▽	▽	▽	▽	▽	▽	▽	▽	▽	▽	▽	▽	▽	▽	▽	▽	▽	▽	▽	▽	▽	▽	○	○	□	○	▲	▲	▲
Greece	450	(5.4)	▽	▽	▽	▽	▽	▽	▽	▽	▽	▽	▽	▽	▽	▽	▽	▽	▽	▽	▽	▽	▽	▽	▽	▽	○	○	○	□	▲	▲	▲
Luxembourg	433	(1.6)	▽	▽	▽	▽	▽	▽	▽	▽	▽	▽	▽	▽	▽	▽	▽	▽	▽	▽	▽	▽	▽	▽	▽	▽	▽	▽	▽	▽	□	▲	▲
Mexico	402	(3.9)	▽	▽	▽	▽	▽	▽	▽	▽	▽	▽	▽	▽	▽	▽	▽	▽	▽	▽	▽	▽	▽	▽	▽	▽	▽	▽	▽	▽	▽	□	▲
Brazil	365	(3.4)	▽	▽	▽	▽	▽	▽	▽	▽	▽	▽	▽	▽	▽	▽	▽	▽	▽	▽	▽	▽	▽	▽	▽	▽	▽	▽	▽	▽	▽	▽	□

Instructions

Read across the row for a country to compare performance with the countries listed along the top of the chart. The symbols indicate whether the mean performance of the country in the row is significantly lower than that of the comparison country, significantly higher than that of the comparison country, or if there is no statistically significant difference between the mean performance of the two countries.

▲ Mean performance statistically significantly higher than in comparison country.
○ No statistically significant difference from comparison country.
▽ Mean performance statistically significantly lower than in comparison country.

Statistically significantly above the OECD average
Not statistically significantly different from the OECD average
Statistically significantly below the OECD average

Table 4.5

Multiple comparisons of mean performance on the interpreting texts subscale

Country	Mean	S.E.	Finland 555 (2.9)	Canada 532 (1.6)	Australia 527 (3.5)	Ireland 526 (3.3)	New Zealand 526 (2.7)	Korea 525 (2.3)	Sweden 522 (2.1)	Japan 518 (5.0)	Iceland 514 (1.4)	United Kingdom 514 (2.5)	Belgium 512 (3.2)	Austria 508 (2.4)	France 506 (2.7)	Norway 505 (2.8)	United States 505 (7.1)	Czech Republic 500 (2.4)	Switzerland 496 (4.2)	Denmark 494 (2.4)	Spain 491 (2.6)	Italy 489 (2.6)	Germany 488 (2.5)	Liechtenstein 484 (4.5)	Poland 482 (4.3)	Hungary 480 (3.8)	Greece 475 (4.5)	Portugal 473 (4.3)	Russian Fed. 468 (4.0)	Latvia 459 (4.9)	Luxembourg 446 (1.6)	Mexico 419 (2.9)	Brazil 400 (3.0)
Finland	555	(2.9)	□	▲	▲	▲	▲	▲	▲	▲	▲	▲	▲	▲	▲	▲	▲	▲	▲	▲	▲	▲	▲	▲	▲	▲	▲	▲	▲	▲	▲	▲	▲
Canada	532	(1.6)	▽	□	○	○	○	○	○	▲	○	▲	▲	▲	▲	▲	▲	▲	▲	▲	▲	▲	▲	▲	▲	▲	▲	▲	▲	▲	▲	▲	▲
Australia	527	(3.5)	▽	○	□	○	○	○	○	○	○	▲	○	▲	▲	▲	▲	○	▲	▲	▲	▲	▲	▲	▲	▲	▲	▲	▲	▲	▲	▲	▲
Ireland	526	(3.3)	▽	○	○	□	○	○	○	○	○	▲	▲	▲	▲	▲	○	▲	▲	▲	▲	▲	▲	▲	▲	▲	▲	▲	▲	▲	▲	▲	▲
New Zealand	526	(2.7)	▽	○	○	○	□	○	○	○	○	○	▲	▲	▲	▲	○	▲	▲	▲	▲	▲	▲	▲	▲	▲	▲	▲	▲	▲	▲	▲	▲
Korea	525	(2.3)	▽	○	○	○	○	□	○	○	○	○	▲	○	▲	▲	○	▲	▲	▲	▲	▲	▲	▲	▲	▲	▲	▲	▲	▲	▲	▲	▲
Sweden	522	(2.1)	▽	▽	○	○	○	○	□	○	○	○	○	○	▲	▲	○	▲	▲	▲	▲	▲	▲	▲	▲	▲	▲	▲	▲	▲	▲	▲	▲
Japan	518	(5.0)	▽	○	○	○	○	○	○	□	○	○	○	○	○	○	○	▲	▲	▲	▲	▲	▲	▲	▲	▲	▲	▲	▲	▲	▲	▲	▲
Iceland	514	(1.4)	▽	▽	▽	▽	▽	▽	○	○	□	○	○	○	○	○	○	▲	▲	▲	▲	▲	▲	▲	▲	▲	▲	▲	▲	▲	▲	▲	▲
United Kingdom	514	(2.5)	▽	▽	○	▽	○	○	○	○	○	□	○	○	○	○	○	▲	▲	▲	▲	▲	▲	▲	▲	▲	▲	▲	▲	▲	▲	▲	▲
Belgium	512	(3.2)	▽	▽	▽	▽	▽	▽	○	○	○	○	□	○	○	○	○	○	▲	▲	▲	▲	▲	▲	▲	▲	▲	▲	▲	▲	▲	▲	▲
Austria	508	(2.4)	▽	▽	▽	▽	▽	▽	▽	○	○	○	○	□	○	○	○	○	▲	▲	▲	▲	▲	▲	▲	▲	▲	▲	▲	▲	▲	▲	▲
France	506	(2.7)	▽	▽	▽	▽	▽	▽	▽	○	○	○	○	○	□	○	○	○	○	▲	▲	▲	▲	▲	▲	▲	▲	▲	▲	▲	▲	▲	▲
Norway	505	(2.8)	▽	▽	▽	▽	▽	▽	▽	○	○	○	○	○	○	□	○	○	○	▲	▲	▲	▲	▲	▲	▲	▲	▲	▲	▲	▲	▲	▲
United States	505	(7.1)	▽	▽	○	○	○	○	○	○	○	○	○	○	○	○	□	○	○	○	○	▲	▲	▲	▲	▲	▲	▲	▲	▲	▲	▲	▲
Czech Republic	500	(2.4)	▽	▽	▽	▽	▽	▽	▽	▽	▽	▽	○	○	○	○	○	□	○	○	○	▲	▲	▲	▲	▲	▲	▲	▲	▲	▲	▲	▲
Switzerland	496	(4.2)	▽	▽	▽	▽	▽	▽	▽	▽	▽	▽	▽	○	○	○	○	○	□	○	○	○	○	▲	▲	▲	▲	▲	▲	▲	▲	▲	▲
Denmark	494	(2.4)	▽	▽	▽	▽	▽	▽	▽	▽	▽	▽	▽	▽	○	○	○	○	○	□	○	○	○	▲	▲	▲	▲	▲	▲	▲	▲	▲	▲
Spain	491	(2.6)	▽	▽	▽	▽	▽	▽	▽	▽	▽	▽	▽	▽	▽	▽	○	○	○	○	□	○	○	○	○	▲	▲	▲	▲	▲	▲	▲	▲
Italy	489	(2.6)	▽	▽	▽	▽	▽	▽	▽	▽	▽	▽	▽	▽	▽	▽	○	▽	○	○	○	□	○	○	○	○	▲	▲	▲	▲	▲	▲	▲
Germany	488	(2.5)	▽	▽	▽	▽	▽	▽	▽	▽	▽	▽	▽	▽	▽	▽	○	▽	○	○	○	○	□	○	○	○	▲	▲	▲	▲	▲	▲	▲
Liechtenstein	484	(4.5)	▽	▽	▽	▽	▽	▽	▽	▽	▽	▽	▽	▽	▽	▽	○	▽	○	○	○	○	○	□	○	○	○	○	▲	▲	▲	▲	▲
Poland	482	(4.3)	▽	▽	▽	▽	▽	▽	▽	▽	▽	▽	▽	▽	▽	▽	○	▽	○	○	○	○	○	○	□	○	○	○	▲	▲	▲	▲	▲
Hungary	480	(3.8)	▽	▽	▽	▽	▽	▽	▽	▽	▽	▽	▽	▽	▽	▽	○	▽	○	▽	○	○	○	○	○	□	○	○	▲	▲	▲	▲	▲
Greece	475	(4.5)	▽	▽	▽	▽	▽	▽	▽	▽	▽	▽	▽	▽	▽	▽	▽	▽	○	▽	▽	▽	▽	○	○	○	□	○	○	○	▲	▲	▲
Portugal	473	(4.3)	▽	▽	▽	▽	▽	▽	▽	▽	▽	▽	▽	▽	▽	▽	▽	▽	○	▽	▽	▽	▽	○	○	○	○	□	○	○	▲	▲	▲
Russian Fed.	468	(4.0)	▽	▽	▽	▽	▽	▽	▽	▽	▽	▽	▽	▽	▽	▽	▽	▽	▽	▽	○	○	○	○	○	▽	○	○	□	○	▲	▲	▲
Latvia	459	(4.9)	▽	▽	▽	▽	▽	▽	▽	▽	▽	▽	▽	▽	▽	▽	▽	▽	▽	▽	▽	▽	▽	▽	▽	▽	○	○	○	□	▲	▲	▲
Luxembourg	446	(1.6)	▽	▽	▽	▽	▽	▽	▽	▽	▽	▽	▽	▽	▽	▽	▽	▽	▽	▽	▽	▽	▽	▽	▽	▽	▽	▽	▽	▽	□	▲	▲
Mexico	419	(2.9)	▽	▽	▽	▽	▽	▽	▽	▽	▽	▽	▽	▽	▽	▽	▽	▽	▽	▽	▽	▽	▽	▽	▽	▽	▽	▽	▽	▽	▽	□	▲
Brazil	400	(3.0)	▽	▽	▽	▽	▽	▽	▽	▽	▽	▽	▽	▽	▽	▽	▽	▽	▽	▽	▽	▽	▽	▽	▽	▽	▽	▽	▽	▽	▽	▽	□

Instructions

Read across the row for a country to compare performance with the countries listed along the top of the chart. The symbols indicate whether the mean performance of the country in the row is significantly lower than that of the comparison country, significantly higher than that of the comparison country, or if there is no statistically significant difference between the mean performance of the two countries.

▲ Mean performance statistically significantly higher than in comparison country.

○ No statistically significant difference from comparison country.

▽ Mean performance statistically significantly lower than in comparison country.

Statistically significantly above the OECD average
Not statistically significantly different from the OECD average
Statistically significantly below the OECD average

Table 4.6
Multiple comparisons of mean performance on the reflection and evaluation subscale

Country	Mean	S.E.	Canada	United Kingdom	Ireland	Finland	Japan	New Zealand	Australia	Korea	Austria	Sweden	United States	Norway	Spain	Iceland	Denmark	Belgium	France	Greece	Switzerland	Czech Republic	Italy	Hungary	Portugal	Germany	Poland	Liechtenstein	Latvia	Russian Fed.	Mexico	Luxembourg	Brazil
(Mean)			542	539	533	533	530	529	526	526	512	510	507	506	506	501	500	497	496	495	488	485	483	481	480	478	477	468	458	455	446	442	417
(S.E.)			(1.6)	(2.5)	(3.1)	(2.7)	(5.4)	(2.9)	(3.4)	(2.6)	(2.7)	(2.3)	(7.1)	(3.0)	(2.8)	(1.3)	(2.6)	(4.3)	(2.9)	(5.6)	(4.8)	(2.6)	(3.1)	(4.3)	(4.5)	(2.9)	(4.7)	(5.7)	(5.9)	(4.0)	(3.7)	(1.9)	(3.3)
Canada	542	(1.6)		○	○	○	○	▲	▲	▲	▲	▲	▲	▲	▲	▲	▲	▲	▲	▲	▲	▲	▲	▲	▲	▲	▲	▲	▲	▲	▲	▲	▲
United Kingdom	539	(2.5)	○		○	○	○	○	○	▲	▲	▲	▲	▲	▲	▲	▲	▲	▲	▲	▲	▲	▲	▲	▲	▲	▲	▲	▲	▲	▲	▲	▲
Ireland	533	(3.1)	○	○		○	○	○	○	○	▲	▲	▲	▲	▲	▲	▲	▲	▲	▲	▲	▲	▲	▲	▲	▲	▲	▲	▲	▲	▲	▲	▲
Finland	533	(2.7)	○	○	○		○	○	○	○	▲	▲	▲	▲	▲	▲	▲	▲	▲	▲	▲	▲	▲	▲	▲	▲	▲	▲	▲	▲	▲	▲	▲
Japan	530	(5.4)	○	○	○	○		○	○	○	○	▲	○	▲	▲	▲	▲	▲	▲	▲	▲	▲	▲	▲	▲	▲	▲	▲	▲	▲	▲	▲	▲
New Zealand	529	(2.9)	▽	○	○	○	○		○	○	▲	▲	○	▲	▲	▲	▲	▲	▲	▲	▲	▲	▲	▲	▲	▲	▲	▲	▲	▲	▲	▲	▲
Australia	526	(3.4)	▽	○	○	○	○	○		○	▲	▲	○	▲	▲	▲	▲	▲	▲	▲	▲	▲	▲	▲	▲	▲	▲	▲	▲	▲	▲	▲	▲
Korea	526	(2.6)	▽	▽	○	○	○	○	○		▲	▲	▲	▲	▲	▲	▲	▲	▲	▲	▲	▲	▲	▲	▲	▲	▲	▲	▲	▲	▲	▲	▲
Austria	512	(2.7)	▽	▽	▽	▽	○	▽	▽	▽		○	○	○	○	▲	○	○	▲	○	▲	▲	▲	▲	▲	▲	▲	▲	▲	▲	▲	▲	▲
Sweden	510	(2.3)	▽	▽	▽	▽	▽	▽	▽	▽	○		○	○	○	○	○	○	▲	○	▲	▲	▲	▲	▲	▲	▲	▲	▲	▲	▲	▲	▲
United States	507	(7.1)	▽	▽	▽	▽	○	○	○	▽	○	○		○	○	○	○	○	○	○	○	○	○	○	○	○	○	▲	▲	▲	▲	▲	▲
Norway	506	(3.0)	▽	▽	▽	▽	▽	▽	▽	▽	○	○	○		○	○	○	○	○	○	○	○	○	○	○	○	○	▲	▲	▲	▲	▲	▲
Spain	506	(2.8)	▽	▽	▽	▽	▽	▽	▽	▽	○	○	○	○		○	○	○	○	○	○	○	○	○	○	○	○	▲	▲	▲	▲	▲	▲
Iceland	501	(1.3)	▽	▽	▽	▽	▽	▽	▽	▽	▽	○	○	○	○		○	○	○	○	○	○	○	○	○	○	○	▲	▲	▲	▲	▲	▲
Denmark	500	(2.6)	▽	▽	▽	▽	▽	▽	▽	▽	○	○	○	○	○	○		○	○	○	○	○	○	○	○	○	○	▲	▲	▲	▲	▲	▲
Belgium	497	(4.3)	▽	▽	▽	▽	▽	▽	▽	▽	○	○	○	○	○	○	○		○	○	○	○	○	○	○	○	○	▲	▲	▲	▲	▲	▲
France	496	(2.9)	▽	▽	▽	▽	▽	▽	▽	▽	▽	▽	○	○	○	○	○	○		○	○	○	○	○	○	○	○	▲	▲	▲	▲	▲	▲
Greece	495	(5.6)	▽	▽	▽	▽	▽	▽	▽	▽	○	○	○	○	○	○	○	○	○		○	○	○	○	○	○	○	▲	▲	▲	▲	▲	▲
Switzerland	488	(4.8)	▽	▽	▽	▽	▽	▽	▽	▽	▽	▽	○	○	○	○	○	○	○	○		○	○	○	○	○	○	○	▲	▲	▲	▲	▲
Czech Republic	485	(2.6)	▽	▽	▽	▽	▽	▽	▽	▽	▽	▽	○	○	○	○	○	○	○	○	○		○	○	○	○	○	○	▲	▲	▲	▲	▲
Italy	483	(3.1)	▽	▽	▽	▽	▽	▽	▽	▽	▽	▽	○	○	○	○	○	○	○	○	○	○		○	○	○	○	○	▲	▲	▲	▲	▲
Hungary	481	(4.3)	▽	▽	▽	▽	▽	▽	▽	▽	▽	▽	○	○	○	○	○	○	○	○	○	○	○		○	○	○	○	▲	▲	▲	▲	▲
Portugal	480	(4.5)	▽	▽	▽	▽	▽	▽	▽	▽	▽	▽	○	○	○	○	○	○	○	○	○	○	○	○		○	○	○	▲	▲	▲	▲	▲
Germany	478	(2.9)	▽	▽	▽	▽	▽	▽	▽	▽	▽	▽	○	○	○	○	○	○	○	○	○	○	○	○	○		○	○	▲	▲	▲	▲	▲
Poland	477	(4.7)	▽	▽	▽	▽	▽	▽	▽	▽	▽	▽	○	○	○	○	○	○	○	○	○	○	○	○	○	○		○	▲	▲	▲	▲	▲
Liechtenstein	468	(5.7)	▽	▽	▽	▽	▽	▽	▽	▽	▽	▽	▽	▽	▽	▽	▽	▽	▽	▽	○	○	○	○	○	○	○		○	○	▲	▲	▲
Latvia	458	(5.9)	▽	▽	▽	▽	▽	▽	▽	▽	▽	▽	▽	▽	▽	▽	▽	▽	▽	▽	▽	▽	▽	▽	▽	▽	▽	○		○	○	○	▲
Russian Fed.	455	(4.0)	▽	▽	▽	▽	▽	▽	▽	▽	▽	▽	▽	▽	▽	▽	▽	▽	▽	▽	▽	▽	▽	▽	▽	▽	▽	○	○		○	○	▲
Mexico	446	(3.7)	▽	▽	▽	▽	▽	▽	▽	▽	▽	▽	▽	▽	▽	▽	▽	▽	▽	▽	▽	▽	▽	▽	▽	▽	▽	▽	○	○		○	▲
Luxembourg	442	(1.9)	▽	▽	▽	▽	▽	▽	▽	▽	▽	▽	▽	▽	▽	▽	▽	▽	▽	▽	▽	▽	▽	▽	▽	▽	▽	▽	○	○	○		▲
Brazil	417	(3.3)	▽	▽	▽	▽	▽	▽	▽	▽	▽	▽	▽	▽	▽	▽	▽	▽	▽	▽	▽	▽	▽	▽	▽	▽	▽	▽	▽	▽	▽	▽	

Instructions

Read across the row for a country to compare performance with the countries listed along the top of the chart. The symbols indicate whether the mean performance of the country in the row is significantly lower than that of the comparison country, significantly higher than that of the comparison country, or if there is no statistically significant difference between the mean performance of the two countries.

▲ Mean performance statistically significantly higher than in comparison country.

○ No statistically significant difference from comparison country.

▽ Mean performance statistically significantly lower than in comparison country.

Statistically significantly above the OECD average
Not statistically significantly different from the OECD average
Statistically significantly below the OECD average

Table 4.7
Percentage of students at each level of proficiency on the retrieving information subscale

		Proficiency levels										
		Below Level 1 (less than 335 score points)		Level 1 (from 335 to 407 score points)		Level 2 (from 408 to 480 score points)		Level 3 (from 481 to 552 score points)		Level 4 (from 553 to 625 score points)		Level 5 (above 625 score points)	
		%	S.E.	%	S.E.	%	S.E.	%	S.E.	%	S.E.	%	S.E.
OECD COUNTRIES	Australia	3.7	(0.4)	8.8	(0.8)	17.2	(1.0)	24.7	(1.0)	24.7	(1.0)	20.9	(1.2)
	Austria	5.2	(0.5)	11.1	(0.7)	22.6	(0.9)	29.1	(1.0)	23.5	(0.9)	8.6	(0.7)
	Belgium	9.1	(1.0)	10.3	(0.6)	15.4	(0.7)	22.2	(0.8)	25.2	(0.9)	17.8	(0.7)
	Canada	3.4	(0.3)	8.4	(0.3)	18.5	(0.5)	26.8	(0.6)	25.5	(0.6)	17.4	(0.6)
	Czech Republic	9.0	(0.7)	13.8	(0.8)	24.5	(0.8)	27.1	(0.8)	17.6	(1.0)	8.0	(0.6)
	Denmark	6.9	(0.7)	12.4	(0.6)	21.0	(0.8)	27.8	(0.8)	21.7	(0.8)	10.2	(0.7)
	Finland	2.3	(0.5)	5.6	(0.4)	13.9	(0.9)	24.3	(1.2)	28.3	(0.8)	25.5	(0.9)
	France	4.9	(0.6)	10.5	(0.9)	19.2	(0.8)	27.0	(0.9)	25.2	(1.1)	13.2	(1.0)
	Germany	10.5	(0.8)	12.6	(0.7)	21.8	(0.9)	26.8	(1.1)	19.0	(1.0)	9.3	(0.5)
	Greece	15.1	(1.6)	17.9	(1.1)	25.3	(1.2)	24.1	(1.2)	13.5	(1.0)	4.1	(0.6)
	Hungary	10.2	(0.9)	15.7	(1.1)	23.0	(0.9)	25.3	(1.2)	18.1	(1.2)	7.8	(0.9)
	Iceland	6.5	(0.4)	12.0	(0.6)	21.6	(0.9)	28.4	(1.2)	21.0	(0.9)	10.6	(0.6)
	Ireland	4.0	(0.5)	8.7	(0.7)	18.2	(0.9)	28.1	(1.0)	25.8	(0.9)	15.2	(0.8)
	Italy	7.6	(0.8)	13.4	(0.8)	23.4	(0.9)	28.1	(0.9)	19.2	(0.9)	8.4	(0.6)
	Japan	3.8	(0.8)	7.8	(1.0)	17.3	(1.1)	29.8	(1.1)	26.7	(1.3)	14.5	(1.2)
	Korea	1.5	(0.3)	6.3	(0.6)	18.6	(0.9)	32.4	(1.0)	29.7	(1.0)	11.6	(0.8)
	Luxembourg	17.9	(0.7)	21.1	(0.9)	25.4	(0.8)	22.2	(0.9)	11.1	(0.8)	2.4	(0.4)
	Mexico	26.1	(1.4)	25.6	(1.3)	25.5	(1.0)	15.8	(1.1)	5.8	(0.8)	1.2	(0.3)
	New Zealand	5.6	(0.5)	8.6	(0.6)	15.7	(0.7)	22.7	(1.2)	25.2	(1.1)	22.2	(1.0)
	Norway	7.4	(0.6)	10.8	(0.6)	19.5	(0.9)	26.7	(1.3)	23.0	(1.2)	12.6	(0.8)
	Poland	11.5	(1.1)	15.1	(1.0)	22.7	(1.2)	24.5	(1.1)	18.2	(1.3)	8.0	(1.2)
	Portugal	13.9	(0.9)	18.2	(1.1)	24.3	(1.0)	24.5	(1.2)	14.8	(1.0)	4.4	(0.5)
	Spain	6.4	(0.6)	13.9	(1.0)	25.6	(0.8)	30.5	(1.0)	19.0	(0.9)	4.8	(0.4)
	Sweden	4.9	(0.4)	10.2	(0.8)	19.9	(0.9)	26.8	(0.9)	23.5	(0.9)	14.6	(0.8)
	Switzerland	8.8	(0.8)	12.5	(0.8)	19.3	(0.9)	25.9	(1.1)	21.6	(0.9)	12.1	(1.1)
	United Kingdom	4.4	(0.4)	9.4	(0.6)	18.6	(0.7)	26.9	(0.9)	24.1	(0.9)	16.5	(0.9)
	United States	8.3	(1.4)	12.2	(1.1)	20.7	(1.0)	25.6	(1.2)	20.8	(1.4)	12.6	(1.4)
	OECD average	*8.1*	*(0.2)*	*12.3*	*(0.2)*	*20.7*	*(0.2)*	*26.1*	*(0.2)*	*21.2*	*(0.2)*	*11.6*	*(0.2)*
NON-OECD COUNTRIES	Brazil	37.1	(1.6)	30.4	(1.3)	20.5	(1.2)	9.4	(0.6)	2.2	(0.5)	0.4	(0.2)
	Latvia	17.1	(1.6)	17.7	(1.2)	23.6	(1.1)	21.6	(1.0)	14.1	(1.1)	5.9	(0.7)
	Liechtenstein	8.6	(1.6)	12.6	(2.1)	19.9	(2.5)	28.3	(3.6)	21.8	(3.6)	8.8	(1.6)
	Russian Federation	14.4	(1.3)	19.4	(0.8)	26.0	(0.8)	22.9	(1.0)	12.4	(0.9)	4.9	(0.6)

Table 4.8
Percentage of students at each level of proficiency on the interpreting texts subscale

		Proficiency levels										
		Below Level 1 *(less than 335 score points)*		**Level 1** *(from 335 to 407 score points)*		**Level 2** *(from 408 to 480 score points)*		**Level 3** *(from 481 to 552 score points)*		**Level 4** *(from 553 to 625 score points)*		**Level 5** *(above 625 score points)*	
		%	S.E.	%	S.E.	%	S.E.	%	S.E.	%	S.E.	%	S.E.
OECD COUNTRIES	Australia	3.7	(0.4)	9.7	(0.7)	19.3	(1.0)	25.6	(1.1)	24.0	(1.2)	17.7	(1.3)
	Austria	4.0	(0.4)	10.7	(0.6)	21.8	(1.0)	30.0	(1.1)	23.8	(1.0)	9.7	(0.8)
	Belgium	6.3	(0.7)	11.5	(0.8)	17.8	(0.7)	25.3	(0.9)	25.7	(0.9)	13.4	(0.7)
	Canada	2.4	(0.2)	7.8	(0.4)	18.4	(0.4)	28.6	(0.6)	26.4	(0.5)	16.4	(0.5)
	Czech Republic	5.4	(0.6)	10.7	(0.6)	23.2	(0.9)	30.3	(0.7)	21.7	(0.9)	8.7	(0.7)
	Denmark	6.2	(0.6)	12.6	(0.8)	23.5	(0.8)	28.7	(0.9)	20.8	(1.0)	8.2	(0.7)
	Finland	1.9	(0.5)	5.1	(0.4)	13.8	(0.8)	26.0	(0.9)	29.7	(0.9)	23.6	(0.9)
	France	4.0	(0.5)	11.5	(0.8)	21.8	(0.9)	30.3	(1.0)	23.4	(1.1)	9.0	(0.7)
	Germany	9.3	(0.8)	13.2	(0.9)	22.0	(1.0)	26.4	(1.0)	19.7	(0.7)	9.5	(0.5)
	Greece	6.6	(1.1)	16.0	(1.4)	27.3	(1.2)	30.1	(1.5)	16.2	(1.2)	3.7	(0.6)
	Hungary	6.0	(0.7)	15.9	(1.3)	26.0	(1.1)	29.9	(1.3)	17.9	(1.1)	4.3	(0.6)
	Iceland	3.6	(0.4)	10.1	(0.6)	21.1	(0.7)	29.2	(1.1)	24.4	(1.0)	11.7	(0.6)
	Ireland	3.5	(0.5)	8.3	(0.7)	18.2	(0.9)	28.8	(1.1)	26.1	(1.1)	15.2	(1.0)
	Italy	4.1	(0.7)	13.1	(0.8)	26.9	(1.2)	32.3	(1.3)	18.8	(0.9)	4.8	(0.4)
	Japan	2.4	(0.7)	7.9	(1.1)	19.7	(1.4)	34.2	(1.5)	27.5	(1.6)	8.3	(1.0)
	Korea	0.7	(0.2)	4.8	(0.6)	19.5	(1.0)	38.7	(1.4)	30.5	(1.2)	5.8	(0.6)
	Luxembourg	13.8	(0.6)	19.5	(0.9)	27.7	(1.0)	24.3	(0.9)	12.3	(0.6)	2.3	(0.4)
	Mexico	14.5	(0.9)	31.0	(1.5)	32.3	(1.3)	17.6	(1.2)	4.4	(0.6)	0.3	(0.1)
	New Zealand	5.2	(0.5)	9.9	(0.7)	17.7	(0.7)	23.9	(1.1)	23.9	(0.9)	19.5	(0.9)
	Norway	6.3	(0.5)	11.3	(0.8)	20.2	(0.7)	27.7	(0.8)	23.0	(0.9)	11.5	(0.7)
	Poland	7.5	(0.9)	14.6	(0.9)	24.5	(1.4)	28.7	(1.3)	18.7	(1.3)	6.0	(0.9)
	Portugal	7.8	(0.9)	16.9	(1.3)	26.9	(1.1)	27.9	(1.2)	16.6	(1.1)	4.0	(0.5)
	Spain	3.8	(0.5)	12.6	(0.9)	26.5	(0.8)	32.8	(1.1)	20.1	(0.8)	4.1	(0.4)
	Sweden	3.1	(0.3)	9.5	(0.6)	19.7	(0.8)	28.6	(1.0)	25.4	(1.0)	13.7	(0.8)
	Switzerland	6.7	(0.6)	12.9	(0.9)	22.3	(0.9)	27.4	(1.1)	21.4	(1.0)	9.3	(1.1)
	United Kingdom	4.4	(0.5)	11.0	(0.6)	21.1	(0.7)	26.6	(0.7)	22.9	(0.9)	14.0	(0.9)
	United States	6.3	(1.2)	11.6	(1.1)	21.7	(1.2)	26.5	(1.2)	21.2	(1.5)	12.7	(1.3)
	OECD average	*5.5*	*(0.1)*	*12.2*	*(0.2)*	*22.3*	*(0.2)*	*28.4*	*(0.3)*	*21.7*	*(0.2)*	*9.9*	*(0.1)*
NON-OECD COUNTRIES	Brazil	21.5	(1.3)	33.2	(1.4)	28.1	(1.5)	13.4	(1.0)	3.3	(0.5)	0.6	(0.2)
	Latvia	11.1	(1.2)	18.6	(1.4)	27.2	(1.3)	26.6	(1.2)	13.1	(1.2)	3.4	(0.6)
	Liechtenstein	6.6	(1.7)	15.2	(2.7)	23.9	(3.3)	29.7	(3.0)	19.8	(2.3)	4.9	(1.2)
	Russian Federation	8.0	(0.9)	18.0	(0.8)	28.3	(0.9)	27.8	(1.1)	14.2	(1.1)	3.8	(0.6)

Table 4.9
Percentage of students at each level of proficiency on the reflection and evaluation subscale

| | Proficiency levels | | | | | | | | | | | |
| | Below Level 1 (less than 335 score points) | | Level 1 (from 335 to 407 score points) | | Level 2 (from 408 to 480 score points) | | Level 3 (from 481 to 552 score points) | | Level 4 (from 553 to 625 score points) | | Level 5 (above 625 score points) | |
	%	S.E.	%	S.E.	%	S.E.	%	S.E.	%	S.E.	%	S.E.
Australia	3.4	(0.4)	9.1	(0.7)	19.0	(0.9)	26.9	(1.2)	25.6	(1.2)	15.9	(1.2)
Austria	5.0	(0.5)	10.1	(0.5)	20.0	(0.9)	28.2	(1.1)	25.2	(1.3)	11.6	(1.0)
Belgium	9.8	(1.2)	11.5	(0.8)	17.5	(0.7)	26.2	(1.0)	24.3	(0.8)	10.7	(0.6)
Canada	2.1	(0.2)	6.6	(0.4)	16.2	(0.4)	27.5	(0.5)	28.3	(0.5)	19.4	(0.5)
Czech Republic	7.5	(0.7)	13.2	(0.9)	24.9	(0.9)	28.3	(0.8)	19.0	(1.0)	7.2	(0.7)
Denmark	6.2	(0.6)	11.7	(0.7)	21.3	(0.8)	29.0	(1.0)	21.9	(0.8)	9.9	(0.8)
Finland	2.4	(0.5)	6.4	(0.5)	16.2	(0.7)	30.3	(0.9)	30.6	(0.9)	14.1	(0.7)
France	5.9	(0.7)	12.5	(0.8)	23.4	(0.8)	28.7	(1.1)	21.0	(1.0)	8.6	(0.6)
Germany	13.0	(0.8)	13.5	(0.7)	20.4	(1.1)	24.0	(0.9)	18.9	(0.8)	10.2	(0.6)
Greece	8.9	(1.1)	13.3	(1.1)	21.6	(1.1)	23.8	(1.1)	19.8	(1.2)	12.5	(1.1)
Hungary	8.2	(0.8)	15.2	(1.3)	23.6	(1.3)	27.9	(1.1)	18.8	(1.2)	6.3	(0.8)
Iceland	4.8	(0.5)	11.0	(0.6)	23.1	(0.8)	30.9	(0.9)	22.1	(0.8)	8.1	(0.5)
Ireland	2.4	(0.4)	6.6	(0.8)	16.8	(1.0)	30.3	(1.0)	29.5	(1.0)	14.5	(0.9)
Italy	8.0	(0.9)	14.3	(1.1)	24.1	(1.3)	28.0	(1.0)	19.1	(0.8)	6.5	(0.6)
Japan	3.9	(0.8)	7.9	(0.9)	16.6	(1.1)	28.2	(1.1)	27.3	(1.2)	16.2	(1.4)
Korea	1.2	(0.3)	5.4	(0.5)	19.0	(1.0)	36.7	(1.2)	29.5	(1.2)	8.2	(0.7)
Luxembourg	17.0	(0.7)	17.9	(0.8)	25.4	(1.1)	23.3	(0.8)	12.9	(0.5)	3.6	(0.4)
Mexico	16.0	(0.9)	20.7	(1.0)	25.6	(0.9)	21.1	(0.8)	11.8	(0.9)	4.8	(0.6)
New Zealand	4.5	(0.5)	8.5	(0.6)	17.5	(0.9)	25.4	(1.2)	25.6	(1.0)	18.5	(1.2)
Norway	7.3	(0.7)	10.8	(0.7)	18.8	(0.8)	27.1	(0.9)	23.8	(1.0)	12.2	(0.8)
Poland	11.0	(1.1)	14.4	(1.2)	22.6	(1.8)	26.2	(1.4)	18.1	(1.3)	7.7	(1.1)
Portugal	9.1	(0.9)	15.0	(1.2)	24.4	(1.2)	26.2	(1.1)	19.0	(1.1)	6.4	(0.7)
Spain	3.9	(0.4)	11.0	(0.7)	22.1	(1.2)	31.1	(1.2)	23.6	(0.6)	8.4	(0.6)
Sweden	4.3	(0.4)	10.2	(0.6)	20.7	(0.7)	30.4	(0.8)	24.3	(0.9)	10.1	(0.7)
Switzerland	9.9	(0.9)	13.6	(0.9)	21.6	(1.1)	25.2	(1.0)	19.1	(0.9)	10.5	(1.1)
United Kingdom	2.6	(0.3)	7.2	(0.6)	17.4	(0.7)	26.7	(0.7)	26.5	(0.9)	19.6	(1.0)
United States	6.2	(1.1)	11.2	(1.2)	20.6	(1.1)	27.3	(1.1)	22.2	(1.7)	12.5	(1.3)
OECD average	*6.8*	*(0.1)*	*11.4*	*(0.2)*	*20.7*	*(0.2)*	*27.6*	*(0.2)*	*22.5*	*(0.2)*	*10.9*	*(0.2)*
Brazil	18.7	(1.2)	27.2	(1.1)	29.3	(1.1)	17.7	(1.0)	6.0	(0.7)	1.2	(0.2)
Latvia	15.6	(1.5)	16.6	(1.1)	23.4	(1.6)	24.1	(1.6)	14.2	(1.2)	6.0	(0.9)
Liechtenstein	11.9	(2.0)	16.1	(3.1)	24.4	(3.3)	24.8	(2.8)	17.0	(2.9)	5.8	(1.3)
Russian Federation	11.7	(1.1)	19.3	(1.0)	28.1	(1.1)	24.9	(0.9)	12.3	(0.8)	3.7	(0.5)

OECD COUNTRIES

NON-OECD COUNTRIES

Table 4.10
Mean scores for text format subscales

		Continuous texts				Non-continuous texts			
		Mean score	S.E.	S.D.	S.E.	Mean score	S.E.	S.D.	S.E.
OECD COUNTRIES	Australia	526	(3.5)	104	(1.6)	539	3.3	104	(1.6)
	Austria	509	(2.5)	94	(1.5)	507	2.4	99	(1.5)
	Belgium	503	(4.0)	108	(3.5)	516	3.5	114	(2.4)
	Canada	536	(1.6)	98	(1.1)	536	1.6	99	(1.1)
	Czech Republic	489	(2.3)	93	(1.8)	498	2.9	112	(2.3)
	Denmark	497	(2.4)	99	(1.9)	499	2.6	109	(1.8)
	Finland	544	(2.7)	90	(2.8)	554	2.7	95	(2.0)
	France	500	(2.8)	94	(1.8)	518	2.7	97	(1.8)
	Germany	484	(2.6)	115	(1.9)	486	2.4	113	(2.2)
	Greece	483	(5.0)	99	(2.8)	456	4.9	103	(2.5)
	Hungary	481	(3.9)	92	(1.9)	479	4.4	108	(2.1)
	Iceland	509	(1.4)	93	(1.2)	505	1.5	100	(1.4)
	Ireland	528	(3.2)	94	(1.7)	530	3.3	100	(1.8)
	Italy	491	(2.8)	91	(1.5)	480	3.0	100	(2.8)
	Japan	524	(5.1)	85	(2.9)	521	5.6	98	(3.2)
	Korea	530	(2.4)	69	(1.8)	517	2.5	81	(1.7)
	Luxembourg	442	(1.7)	108	(1.3)	441	1.6	113	(1.5)
	Mexico	431	(3.2)	86	(1.8)	401	3.7	97	(2.4)
	New Zealand	526	(2.9)	110	(1.7)	539	2.9	110	(1.9)
	Norway	506	(2.8)	103	(1.6)	508	2.8	114	(1.7)
	Poland	482	(4.4)	101	(2.9)	471	4.8	107	(3.2)
	Portugal	474	(4.5)	98	(1.8)	460	4.5	102	(1.8)
	Spain	493	(2.6)	84	(1.1)	493	3.0	96	(1.3)
	Sweden	516	(2.2)	93	(1.2)	521	2.4	100	(1.3)
	Switzerland	494	(4.3)	104	(2.0)	496	4.4	109	(2.0)
	United Kingdom	521	(2.5)	104	(1.5)	533	2.4	101	(1.5)
	United States	504	(7.1)	105	(2.5)	506	7.2	109	(2.8)
	OECD average	*501*	*(0.6)*	*101*	*(0.4)*	*500*	*0.7*	*109*	*(0.4)*
NON-OECD COUNTRIES	Brazil	408	(3.1)	88	(1.8)	366	3.4	97	(1.9)
	Latvia	462	(5.2)	104	(2.3)	447	5.3	109	(2.5)
	Liechtenstein	483	(4.5)	97	(4.0)	482	4.3	99	(3.9)
	Russian Federation	465	(4.1)	92	(1.8)	450	4.5	102	(2.0)

Statistically significantly above the OECD average · Not statistically significantly different from the OECD average · Statistically significantly below the OECD average

Table 4.11
Multiple comparisons of mean performance on the continuous texts subscale

Comparison columns (in order, with Mean and SE):

Country	Mean	SE
Finland	544	(2.7)
Canada	536	(1.6)
Korea	530	(2.4)
Ireland	528	(3.2)
New Zealand	526	(2.9)
Australia	526	(3.6)
Japan	524	(5.1)
United Kingdom	521	(2.5)
Sweden	516	(2.2)
Austria	509	(2.5)
Iceland	509	(1.4)
Norway	506	(2.8)
United States	504	(7.1)
Belgium	503	(4.0)
France	500	(2.8)
Denmark	497	(2.4)
Switzerland	494	(4.3)
Spain	493	(2.6)
Italy	491	(2.8)
Czech Republic	489	(2.3)
Germany	484	(2.6)
Liechtenstein	483	(4.5)
Greece	483	(5.0)
Poland	482	(4.4)
Hungary	481	(3.9)
Portugal	474	(4.5)
Russian Federation	465	(4.1)
Latvia	462	(5.2)
Luxembourg	442	(1.7)
Mexico	431	(3.2)
Brazil	408	(3.1)

Comparison matrix (read across the row; ▲ = row country significantly higher, ○ = no significant difference, ▽ = row country significantly lower). Column order is the same as the country order above (Finland … Brazil):

Row country	Mean	SE	FIN	CAN	KOR	IRL	NZL	AUS	JPN	GBR	SWE	AUT	ISL	NOR	USA	BEL	FRA	DNK	CHE	ESP	ITA	CZE	DEU	LIE	GRC	POL	HUN	PRT	RUS	LVA	LUX	MEX	BRA
Finland	544	(2.7)	■	○	▲	▲	▲	▲	▲	▲	▲	▲	▲	▲	▲	▲	▲	▲	▲	▲	▲	▲	▲	▲	▲	▲	▲	▲	▲	▲	▲	▲	▲
Canada	536	(1.6)	○	■	○	○	○	○	○	▲	▲	▲	▲	▲	▲	▲	▲	▲	▲	▲	▲	▲	▲	▲	▲	▲	▲	▲	▲	▲	▲	▲	▲
Korea	530	(2.4)	▽	○	■	○	○	○	○	○	▲	▲	▲	▲	▲	▲	▲	▲	▲	▲	▲	▲	▲	▲	▲	▲	▲	▲	▲	▲	▲	▲	▲
Ireland	528	(3.2)	▽	○	○	■	○	○	○	○	○	▲	▲	▲	○	▲	▲	▲	▲	▲	▲	▲	▲	▲	▲	▲	▲	▲	▲	▲	▲	▲	▲
New Zealand	526	(2.9)	▽	○	○	○	■	○	○	○	○	▲	▲	▲	○	▲	▲	▲	▲	▲	▲	▲	▲	▲	▲	▲	▲	▲	▲	▲	▲	▲	▲
Australia	526	(3.6)	▽	○	○	○	○	■	○	○	○	▲	▲	▲	○	▲	▲	▲	▲	▲	▲	▲	▲	▲	▲	▲	▲	▲	▲	▲	▲	▲	▲
Japan	524	(5.1)	▽	○	○	○	○	○	■	○	○	○	○	○	○	○	▲	▲	▲	▲	▲	▲	▲	▲	▲	▲	▲	▲	▲	▲	▲	▲	▲
United Kingdom	521	(2.5)	▽	▽	○	○	○	○	○	■	○	○	○	○	○	▲	▲	▲	▲	▲	▲	▲	▲	▲	▲	▲	▲	▲	▲	▲	▲	▲	▲
Sweden	516	(2.2)	▽	▽	▽	○	○	○	○	○	■	○	○	○	○	○	▲	▲	▲	▲	▲	▲	▲	▲	▲	▲	▲	▲	▲	▲	▲	▲	▲
Austria	509	(2.5)	▽	▽	▽	▽	▽	▽	○	▽	○	■	○	○	○	○	○	▲	○	▲	▲	▲	▲	▲	▲	▲	▲	▲	▲	▲	▲	▲	▲
Iceland	509	(1.4)	▽	▽	▽	▽	▽	▽	○	▽	○	○	■	○	○	○	○	▲	▲	▲	▲	▲	▲	▲	▲	▲	▲	▲	▲	▲	▲	▲	▲
Norway	506	(2.8)	▽	▽	▽	▽	▽	▽	○	▽	○	○	○	■	○	○	○	○	▲	▲	▲	▲	▲	▲	▲	▲	▲	▲	▲	▲	▲	▲	▲
United States	504	(7.1)	▽	▽	○	○	○	○	○	○	○	○	○	○	■	○	○	○	○	○	○	○	○	○	○	○	○	▲	▲	▲	▲	▲	▲
Belgium	503	(4.0)	▽	▽	▽	▽	▽	▽	○	▽	○	○	○	○	○	■	○	○	○	▲	▲	▲	▲	▲	▲	▲	▲	▲	▲	▲	▲	▲	▲
France	500	(2.8)	▽	▽	▽	▽	▽	▽	▽	▽	▽	○	○	○	○	○	■	○	○	▲	▲	○	▲	▲	▲	▲	▲	▲	▲	▲	▲	▲	▲
Denmark	497	(2.4)	▽	▽	▽	▽	▽	▽	▽	▽	▽	○	○	○	○	○	○	■	○	○	○	○	▲	○	○	○	▲	▲	▲	▲	▲	▲	▲
Switzerland	494	(4.3)	▽	▽	▽	▽	▽	▽	▽	▽	▽	○	○	○	○	○	○	○	■	○	○	○	○	○	○	○	○	○	▲	▲	▲	▲	▲
Spain	493	(2.6)	▽	▽	▽	▽	▽	▽	▽	▽	▽	▽	▽	▽	○	▽	▽	○	○	■	○	○	○	○	○	○	○	○	▲	▲	▲	▲	▲
Italy	491	(2.8)	▽	▽	▽	▽	▽	▽	▽	▽	▽	▽	▽	▽	○	▽	▽	○	○	○	■	○	○	○	○	○	○	○	▲	▲	▲	▲	▲
Czech Republic	489	(2.3)	▽	▽	▽	▽	▽	▽	▽	▽	▽	▽	▽	▽	○	▽	○	○	○	○	○	■	○	○	○	○	○	○	▲	▲	▲	▲	▲
Germany	484	(2.6)	▽	▽	▽	▽	▽	▽	▽	▽	▽	▽	▽	▽	○	▽	▽	▽	○	○	○	○	■	○	○	○	○	○	○	○	▲	▲	▲
Liechtenstein	483	(4.5)	▽	▽	▽	▽	▽	▽	▽	▽	▽	▽	▽	▽	○	▽	▽	○	○	○	○	○	○	■	○	○	○	○	○	○	▲	▲	▲
Greece	483	(5.0)	▽	▽	▽	▽	▽	▽	▽	▽	▽	▽	▽	▽	○	○	▽	○	○	○	○	○	○	○	■	○	○	○	○	○	▲	▲	▲
Poland	482	(4.4)	▽	▽	▽	▽	▽	▽	▽	▽	▽	▽	▽	▽	○	▽	▽	○	○	○	○	○	○	○	○	■	○	○	○	○	▲	▲	▲
Hungary	481	(3.9)	▽	▽	▽	▽	▽	▽	▽	▽	▽	▽	▽	▽	○	▽	▽	▽	○	○	○	○	○	○	○	○	■	○	○	○	▲	▲	▲
Portugal	474	(4.5)	▽	▽	▽	▽	▽	▽	▽	▽	▽	▽	▽	▽	▽	▽	▽	▽	○	○	○	○	○	○	○	○	○	■	○	○	▲	▲	▲
Russian Federation	465	(4.1)	▽	▽	▽	▽	▽	▽	▽	▽	▽	▽	▽	▽	▽	▽	▽	▽	○	▽	▽	▽	○	○	○	○	○	○	■	○	▲	▲	▲
Latvia	462	(5.2)	▽	▽	▽	▽	▽	▽	▽	▽	▽	▽	▽	▽	▽	▽	▽	▽	○	▽	▽	▽	○	○	○	○	○	○	○	■	▲	▲	▲
Luxembourg	442	(1.7)	▽	▽	▽	▽	▽	▽	▽	▽	▽	▽	▽	▽	▽	▽	▽	▽	▽	▽	▽	▽	▽	▽	▽	▽	▽	▽	▽	▽	■	▲	▲
Mexico	431	(3.2)	▽	▽	▽	▽	▽	▽	▽	▽	▽	▽	▽	▽	▽	▽	▽	▽	▽	▽	▽	▽	▽	▽	▽	▽	▽	▽	▽	▽	▽	■	▲
Brazil	408	(3.1)	▽	▽	▽	▽	▽	▽	▽	▽	▽	▽	▽	▽	▽	▽	▽	▽	▽	▽	▽	▽	▽	▽	▽	▽	▽	▽	▽	▽	▽	▽	■

Instructions

Read across the row for a country to compare performance with the countries listed along the top of the chart. The symbols indicate whether the mean performance of the country in the row is significantly lower than that of the comparison country, significantly higher than that of the comparison country, or if there is no statistically significant difference between the mean performance of the two countries.

▲ Mean performance statistically significantly higher than in comparison country.

○ No statistically significant difference from comparison country.

▽ Mean performance statistically significantly lower than in comparison country.

Statistically significantly above the OECD average

Not statistically significantly different from the OECD average

Statistically significantly below the OECD average

Table 4.12
Multiple comparisons of mean performance on the non-continuous texts subscale

			Finland	New Zealand	Australia	Canada	United Kingdom	Ireland	Sweden	Japan	France	Korea	Belgium	Norway	Austria	United States	Iceland	Denmark	Czech Republic	Switzerland	Spain	Germany	Liechtenstein	Italy	Hungary	Poland	Portugal	Greece	Russian Federation	Latvia	Luxembourg	Mexico	Brazil
	Mean		554	539	539	536	533	530	521	521	518	517	516	508	507	506	505	499	498	496	493	486	482	480	479	473	460	456	450	447	441	401	366
		SE	(2.7)	(2.9)	(3.3)	(1.6)	(2.4)	(3.3)	(2.4)	(5.6)	(2.7)	(2.5)	(3.5)	(2.8)	(2.4)	(7.2)	(1.5)	(2.6)	(2.9)	(4.4)	(3.0)	(2.4)	(4.3)	(3.0)	(4.4)	(4.8)	(4.5)	(4.9)	(4.5)	(5.3)	(1.6)	(3.7)	(3.4)
Finland	554	(2.7)		▲	▲	▲	▲	▲	▲	▲	▲	▲	▲	▲	▲	▲	▲	▲	▲	▲	▲	▲	▲	▲	▲	▲	▲	▲	▲	▲	▲	▲	▲
New Zealand	539	(2.9)	▽		O	O	O	O	▲	O	▲	▲	▲	▲	▲	▲	▲	▲	▲	▲	▲	▲	▲	▲	▲	▲	▲	▲	▲	▲	▲	▲	▲
Australia	539	(3.3)	▽	O		O	O	O	▲	O	▲	▲	▲	▲	▲	▲	▲	▲	▲	▲	▲	▲	▲	▲	▲	▲	▲	▲	▲	▲	▲	▲	▲
Canada	536	(1.6)	▽	O	O		O	O	▲	O	▲	▲	▲	▲	▲	▲	▲	▲	▲	▲	▲	▲	▲	▲	▲	▲	▲	▲	▲	▲	▲	▲	▲
United Kingdom	533	(2.4)	▽	O	O	O		O	▲	O	▲	▲	▲	▲	▲	▲	▲	▲	▲	▲	▲	▲	▲	▲	▲	▲	▲	▲	▲	▲	▲	▲	▲
Ireland	530	(3.3)	▽	O	O	O	O		O	O	O	▲	O	▲	▲	O	▲	▲	▲	▲	▲	▲	▲	▲	▲	▲	▲	▲	▲	▲	▲	▲	▲
Sweden	521	(2.4)	▽	▽	▽	▽	▽	O		O	O	O	O	▲	▲	O	▲	▲	▲	▲	▲	▲	▲	▲	▲	▲	▲	▲	▲	▲	▲	▲	▲
Japan	521	(5.6)	▽	O	O	O	O	O	O		O	O	O	O	O	O	O	▲	▲	▲	▲	▲	▲	▲	▲	▲	▲	▲	▲	▲	▲	▲	▲
France	518	(2.7)	▽	▽	▽	▽	▽	O	O	O		O	O	O	O	O	▲	▲	▲	▲	▲	▲	▲	▲	▲	▲	▲	▲	▲	▲	▲	▲	▲
Korea	517	(2.5)	▽	▽	▽	▽	▽	▽	O	O	O		O	O	O	O	▲	▲	▲	▲	▲	▲	▲	▲	▲	▲	▲	▲	▲	▲	▲	▲	▲
Belgium	516	(3.5)	▽	▽	▽	▽	▽	O	O	O	O	O		O	O	O	O	▲	▲	▲	▲	▲	▲	▲	▲	▲	▲	▲	▲	▲	▲	▲	▲
Norway	508	(2.8)	▽	▽	▽	▽	▽	▽	▽	O	O	O	O		O	O	O	O	O	O	▲	▲	▲	▲	▲	▲	▲	▲	▲	▲	▲	▲	▲
Austria	507	(2.4)	▽	▽	▽	▽	▽	▽	▽	O	O	O	O	O		O	O	O	O	O	▲	▲	▲	▲	▲	▲	▲	▲	▲	▲	▲	▲	▲
United States	506	(7.2)	▽	▽	▽	▽	▽	O	O	O	O	O	O	O	O		O	O	O	O	O	O	O	▲	▲	▲	▲	▲	▲	▲	▲	▲	▲
Iceland	505	(1.5)	▽	▽	▽	▽	▽	▽	▽	O	▽	▽	O	O	O	O		O	O	O	▲	▲	▲	▲	▲	▲	▲	▲	▲	▲	▲	▲	▲
Denmark	499	(2.6)	▽	▽	▽	▽	▽	▽	▽	▽	▽	▽	▽	O	O	O	O		O	O	O	▲	▲	▲	▲	▲	▲	▲	▲	▲	▲	▲	▲
Czech Republic	498	(2.9)	▽	▽	▽	▽	▽	▽	▽	▽	▽	▽	▽	O	O	O	O	O		O	O	O	O	▲	▲	▲	▲	▲	▲	▲	▲	▲	▲
Switzerland	496	(4.4)	▽	▽	▽	▽	▽	▽	▽	▽	▽	▽	▽	O	O	O	O	O	O		O	O	O	O	O	▲	▲	▲	▲	▲	▲	▲	▲
Spain	493	(3.0)	▽	▽	▽	▽	▽	▽	▽	▽	▽	▽	▽	▽	▽	O	▽	O	O	O		O	O	O	O	▲	▲	▲	▲	▲	▲	▲	▲
Germany	486	(2.4)	▽	▽	▽	▽	▽	▽	▽	▽	▽	▽	▽	▽	▽	O	▽	▽	O	O	O		O	O	O	O	▲	▲	▲	▲	▲	▲	▲
Liechtenstein	482	(4.3)	▽	▽	▽	▽	▽	▽	▽	▽	▽	▽	▽	▽	▽	O	▽	▽	O	O	O	O		O	O	O	▲	▲	▲	▲	▲	▲	▲
Italy	480	(3.0)	▽	▽	▽	▽	▽	▽	▽	▽	▽	▽	▽	▽	▽	▽	▽	▽	▽	O	O	O	O		O	O	▲	▲	▲	▲	▲	▲	▲
Hungary	479	(4.4)	▽	▽	▽	▽	▽	▽	▽	▽	▽	▽	▽	▽	▽	▽	▽	▽	▽	O	O	O	O	O		O	O	▲	▲	▲	▲	▲	▲
Poland	473	(4.8)	▽	▽	▽	▽	▽	▽	▽	▽	▽	▽	▽	▽	▽	▽	▽	▽	▽	▽	▽	O	O	O	O		O	O	▲	▲	▲	▲	▲
Portugal	460	(4.5)	▽	▽	▽	▽	▽	▽	▽	▽	▽	▽	▽	▽	▽	▽	▽	▽	▽	▽	▽	▽	▽	▽	O	O		O	O	O	▲	▲	▲
Greece	456	(4.9)	▽	▽	▽	▽	▽	▽	▽	▽	▽	▽	▽	▽	▽	▽	▽	▽	▽	▽	▽	▽	▽	▽	▽	O	O		O	O	O	▲	▲
Russian Federation	450	(4.5)	▽	▽	▽	▽	▽	▽	▽	▽	▽	▽	▽	▽	▽	▽	▽	▽	▽	▽	▽	▽	▽	▽	▽	▽	O	O		O	O	▲	▲
Latvia	447	(5.3)	▽	▽	▽	▽	▽	▽	▽	▽	▽	▽	▽	▽	▽	▽	▽	▽	▽	▽	▽	▽	▽	▽	▽	▽	O	O	O		O	▲	▲
Luxembourg	441	(1.6)	▽	▽	▽	▽	▽	▽	▽	▽	▽	▽	▽	▽	▽	▽	▽	▽	▽	▽	▽	▽	▽	▽	▽	▽	▽	O	O	O		▲	▲
Mexico	401	(3.7)	▽	▽	▽	▽	▽	▽	▽	▽	▽	▽	▽	▽	▽	▽	▽	▽	▽	▽	▽	▽	▽	▽	▽	▽	▽	▽	▽	▽	▽		▲
Brazil	366	(3.4)	▽	▽	▽	▽	▽	▽	▽	▽	▽	▽	▽	▽	▽	▽	▽	▽	▽	▽	▽	▽	▽	▽	▽	▽	▽	▽	▽	▽	▽	▽	

Instructions

Read across the row for a country to compare performance with the countries listed along the top of the chart. The symbols indicate whether the mean performance of the country in the row is significantly lower than that of the comparison country, significantly higher than that of the comparison country, or if there is no statistically significant difference between the mean performance of the two countries.

▲ Mean performance statistically significantly higher than in comparison country.

O No statistically significant difference from comparison country.

▽ Mean performance statistically significantly lower than in comparison country.

Statistically significantly above the OECD average

Not statistically significantly different from the OECD average

Statistically significantly below the OECD average

Table 4.13
Percentage of students at each level of proficiency on the continuous texts subscale

	Below Level 1 (less than 335 score points)		Level 1 (from 335 to 407 score points)		Level 2 (from 408 to 480 score points)		Level 3 (from 481 to 552 score points)		Level 4 (from 553 to 626 score points)		Level 5 (above 626 score points)	
	%	S.E.	%	S.E.	%	S.E.	%	S.E.	%	S.E.	%	S.E.
Australia	3.8	(0.4)	9.8	0.8	19.0	1.1	25.7	1.0	24.2	0.9	17.5	1.1
Austria	4.2	(0.4)	10.3	0.7	21.0	0.9	29.9	0.9	25.1	1.0	9.5	0.8
Belgium	8.1	(1.1)	11.6	0.8	17.6	0.9	25.6	1.0	25.6	0.9	11.5	0.6
Canada	2.5	(0.2)	7.5	0.3	17.4	0.4	27.9	0.6	27.0	0.5	17.6	0.5
Czech Republic	6.1	(0.6)	11.8	0.8	25.7	1.0	31.0	1.0	19.4	1.0	6.0	0.5
Denmark	6.2	(0.6)	12.2	0.7	22.3	1.0	29.6	1.1	21.2	1.0	8.6	0.6
Finland	1.7	(0.5)	5.4	0.5	14.8	0.7	28.7	0.9	31.5	0.9	17.8	0.9
France	5.0	(0.7)	12.4	0.8	22.1	0.9	29.8	1.2	22.7	1.0	8.0	0.6
Germany	10.5	(0.8)	12.9	0.7	21.5	1.0	26.0	1.1	19.3	0.9	9.8	0.6
Greece	7.8	(1.2)	14.3	1.4	25.0	1.4	27.9	1.4	18.4	1.2	6.7	0.8
Hungary	6.3	(0.8)	16.0	1.2	25.3	1.1	29.3	1.4	18.4	1.1	4.7	0.7
Iceland	4.2	(0.4)	10.3	0.6	21.9	0.8	30.1	1.0	23.7	0.9	9.9	0.6
Ireland	3.0	(0.5)	8.2	0.8	17.5	0.8	29.2	0.9	27.7	1.0	14.4	0.9
Italy	5.0	(0.8)	12.8	0.8	25.2	1.2	31.1	1.1	19.9	0.8	6.0	0.5
Japan	2.6	(0.6)	7.2	1.1	17.8	1.3	33.4	1.3	28.7	1.6	10.3	1.3
Korea	0.7	(0.2)	4.0	0.5	17.5	0.9	38.4	1.5	32.9	1.4	6.6	0.7
Luxembourg	17.0	(0.7)	19.2	0.8	25.2	0.9	23.1	0.9	12.6	0.6	3.0	0.3
Mexico	13.9	(0.9)	26.4	1.2	30.6	1.3	20.6	1.2	7.5	0.8	1.0	0.3
New Zealand	5.1	(0.5)	9.6	0.6	17.9	1.0	24.3	1.0	24.7	0.9	18.5	1.0
Norway	6.5	(0.6)	10.7	0.7	19.9	0.8	27.9	0.8	23.9	1.1	11.2	0.9
Poland	8.7	(1.1)	14.5	1.1	23.3	1.2	28.2	1.3	18.7	1.3	6.7	1.0
Portugal	9.0	(1.0)	16.3	1.2	24.8	1.0	27.0	1.0	18.0	1.1	5.0	0.6
Spain	3.7	(0.4)	12.1	0.8	25.2	0.8	33.7	0.8	20.9	0.9	4.3	0.4
Sweden	3.5	(0.4)	9.5	0.6	20.1	0.9	30.1	1.0	25.2	1.0	11.5	0.7
Switzerland	7.4	(0.7)	13.6	1.0	21.5	1.2	27.3	1.2	20.8	1.0	9.5	1.1
United Kingdom	4.2	(0.4)	10.0	0.6	19.4	0.7	26.9	0.9	23.7	0.8	15.9	0.8
United States	6.4	(1.2)	11.9	1.2	21.0	1.0	27.1	1.2	21.5	1.6	12.1	1.4
OECD average	*6.0*	*(0.1)*	*11.9*	*0.2*	*21.5*	*0.2*	*28.5*	*0.2*	*22.3*	*0.0*	*9.8*	*0.1*
Brazil	20.3	(1.3)	30.1	1.1	28.8	1.1	15.5	1.0	4.7	0.7	0.6	0.2
Latvia	11.9	(1.3)	16.9	1.3	26.1	1.0	25.6	1.0	14.5	1.1	5.0	0.8
Liechtenstein	8.2	(1.6)	14.8	2.2	21.7	3.1	30.2	3.1	19.9	2.1	5.2	1.3
Russian Federation	8.5	(0.9)	17.6	0.9	29.0	1.0	27.7	1.0	13.9	1.0	3.5	0.5

OECD COUNTRIES / NON-OECD COUNTRIES

Table 4.14
Percentage of students at each level of proficiency on the non-continuous texts subscale

		Below Level 1 (less than 335 score points)		Level 1 (from 335 to 407 score points)		Level 2 (from 408 to 480 score points)		Level 3 (from 481 to 552 score points)		Level 4 (from 553 to 626 score points)		Level 5 (above 626 score points)	
		%	S.E.	%	S.E.	%	S.E.	%	S.E.	%	S.E.	%	S.E.
OECD COUNTRIES	Australia	3.2	0.4	7.9	0.7	16.5	0.9	25.5	1.0	26.3	1.0	20.6	1.1
	Austria	5.1	0.5	10.7	0.7	21.6	1.2	27.8	1.4	24.0	1.1	10.9	0.8
	Belgium	7.9	0.8	10.0	0.7	15.9	0.7	23.7	0.9	26.1	1.0	16.4	0.8
	Canada	2.6	0.3	7.4	0.3	17.4	0.4	27.3	0.5	27.2	0.5	18.1	0.5
	Czech Republic	7.8	0.6	11.1	0.6	21.9	0.9	27.4	1.0	19.8	0.8	12.0	0.8
	Denmark	7.3	0.6	12.3	0.6	20.7	0.9	27.3	0.8	21.1	1.0	11.3	0.8
	Finland	1.7	0.4	5.5	0.4	13.5	0.6	26.4	0.7	30.0	0.9	22.8	1.0
	France	3.9	0.5	9.3	0.7	20.0	0.9	28.5	1.2	25.4	1.0	13.0	0.9
	Germany	10.0	0.7	12.6	0.7	21.7	0.9	26.6	0.9	19.5	0.8	9.6	0.5
	Greece	12.7	1.4	18.3	1.3	26.0	1.1	25.1	1.3	13.8	1.0	4.1	0.6
	Hungary	9.9	1.0	15.9	1.2	22.7	1.1	25.0	1.2	18.3	1.2	8.2	0.8
	Iceland	5.5	0.5	11.3	0.6	21.3	1.3	28.6	1.3	22.6	1.0	10.7	0.6
	Ireland	3.6	0.5	8.1	0.8	18.0	1.2	26.8	1.1	26.5	1.0	17.1	0.9
	Italy	8.0	0.8	14.7	1.0	25.2	1.1	28.1	1.0	17.6	0.8	6.5	0.6
	Japan	4.0	0.8	8.9	1.2	18.4	1.0	29.6	1.1	25.8	1.3	13.3	1.2
	Korea	2.0	0.3	7.2	0.6	21.4	0.9	35.4	1.0	26.6	1.1	7.5	0.7
	Luxembourg	17.2	0.7	18.9	0.8	24.6	1.1	23.1	1.0	12.2	0.6	3.9	0.3
	Mexico	25.7	1.3	27.5	1.2	25.4	0.9	15.1	1.1	5.5	0.8	0.9	0.2
	New Zealand	4.7	0.5	8.0	0.6	14.8	0.7	23.5	0.9	26.8	1.2	22.1	1.1
	Norway	7.5	0.6	11.3	0.8	18.8	0.8	25.2	0.8	22.7	0.9	14.5	0.8
	Poland	10.9	1.2	15.3	1.2	24.0	1.3	25.9	1.1	17.0	1.4	6.9	1.1
	Portugal	12.1	1.1	17.8	1.0	25.2	1.0	25.3	1.1	15.7	1.0	4.0	0.5
	Spain	6.1	0.6	12.9	0.7	23.5	1.0	29.0	1.0	20.9	0.9	7.5	0.5
	Sweden	4.1	0.4	9.7	0.7	18.5	0.7	27.5	0.8	25.6	0.9	14.6	0.7
	Switzerland	8.1	0.8	12.7	0.8	20.8	1.1	26.2	1.2	21.0	0.9	11.3	1.1
	United Kingdom	3.1	0.3	8.2	0.5	17.9	0.8	26.8	0.8	25.9	0.9	18.2	0.9
	United States	6.9	1.2	11.1	1.1	20.4	1.0	26.4	1.3	22.0	1.3	13.3	1.5
	OECD average	*7.5*	*0.1*	*12.0*	*0.2*	*20.6*	*0.2*	*26.4*	*0.2*	*21.7*	*0.2*	*11.8*	*0.2*
NON-OECD COUNTRIES	Brazil	37.3	1.6	29.3	1.1	21.7	1.3	9.1	0.8	2.2	0.4	0.4	0.2
	Latvia	15.5	1.5	19.3	1.1	25.6	1.1	22.2	1.1	13.1	1.2	4.2	0.7
	Liechtenstein	8.2	1.6	14.4	2.4	24.3	2.8	27.6	3.0	19.2	2.3	6.5	1.4
	Russian Federation	13.3	1.2	19.7	0.9	27.6	0.8	23.8	1.1	11.9	0.8	3.8	0.5

Table 4.15
Score differences between the 10th and 90th percentiles on the combined reading literacy scale and subscales

		Combined reading literacy	Retrieving information	Interpreting texts	Reflection and evaluation	Continuous texts	Non-continuous texts
OECD COUNTRIES	Australia	261	278	270	257	272	267
	Austria	238	245	240	254	239	253
	Belgium	279	313	275	292	283	296
	Canada	242	260	245	245	249	250
	Czech Republic	242	272	245	257	238	281
	Denmark	250	267	254	260	255	276
	Finland	225	259	242	225	225	243
	France	238	262	240	253	246	249
	Germany	284	291	283	316	294	289
	Greece	252	278	232	296	256	267
	Hungary	244	279	235	259	239	280
	Iceland	238	266	246	237	241	258
	Ireland	240	256	250	228	242	256
	Italy	234	265	222	258	232	257
	Japan	218	247	212	254	218	249
	Korea	175	210	176	191	172	202
	Luxembourg	253	277	257	288	281	292
	Mexico	223	263	202	283	226	252
	New Zealand	279	300	289	275	283	290
	Norway	268	281	269	278	267	283
	Poland	260	291	254	285	263	278
	Portugal	255	278	243	265	257	267
	Spain	218	236	215	236	216	250
	Sweden	239	267	248	244	241	258
	Switzerland	265	292	264	293	271	282
	United Kingdom	260	271	264	255	267	259
	United States	273	290	276	271	274	280
	OECD average	*257*	*284*	*257*	*269*	*259*	*279*
NON-OECD COUNTRIES	Brazil	219	250	216	238	225	248
	Latvia	264	304	248	294	252	284
	Liechtenstein	252	275	241	280	269	251
	Russian Federation	239	278	240	254	238	262

Table 4.16
Variation in student performance on the combined reading literacy scale

| | | Standard deviation | | Percentiles | | | |
| | | | | 10th | | 90th | |
		S.D.	S.E.	Score	S.E.	Score	S.E.
OECD COUNTRIES	Australia	102	(1.6)	394	(4.4)	656	(4.2)
	Austria	93	(1.6)	383	(4.2)	621	(3.2)
	Belgium	107	(2.4)	354	(8.9)	634	(2.5)
	Canada	95	(1.1)	410	(2.4)	652	(1.9)
	Czech Republic	96	(1.9)	368	(4.9)	610	(3.2)
	Denmark	98	(1.8)	367	(5.0)	617	(2.9)
	Finland	89	(2.6)	429	(5.1)	654	(2.8)
	France	92	(1.7)	381	(5.2)	619	(2.9)
	Germany	111	(1.9)	335	(6.3)	619	(2.8)
	Greece	97	(2.7)	342	(8.4)	595	(5.1)
	Hungary	94	(2.1)	354	(5.5)	598	(4.4)
	Iceland	92	(1.4)	383	(3.6)	621	(3.5)
	Ireland	94	(1.7)	401	(6.4)	641	(4.0)
	Italy	91	(2.7)	368	(5.8)	601	(2.7)
	Japan	86	(3.0)	407	(9.8)	625	(4.6)
	Korea	70	(1.6)	433	(4.4)	608	(2.9)
	Luxembourg	100	(1.5)	311	(4.4)	564	(2.8)
	Mexico	86	(2.1)	311	(3.4)	535	(5.5)
	New Zealand	108	(2.0)	382	(5.2)	661	(4.4)
	Norway	104	(1.7)	364	(5.5)	631	(3.1)
	Poland	100	(3.1)	343	(6.8)	603	(6.6)
	Portugal	97	(1.8)	337	(6.2)	592	(4.2)
	Spain	85	(1.2)	379	(5.0)	597	(2.6)
	Sweden	92	(1.2)	392	(4.0)	630	(2.9)
	Switzerland	102	(2.0)	355	(5.8)	621	(5.5)
	United Kingdom	100	(1.5)	391	(4.1)	651	(4.3)
	United States	105	(2.7)	363	(11.4)	636	(6.5)
	OECD average	100	(0.4)	366	(1.1)	623	(0.8)
NON-OECD COUNTRIES	Brazil	86	(1.9)	288	(4.5)	507	(4.2)
	Latvia	102	(2.3)	322	(8.2)	586	(5.8)
	Liechtenstein	96	(3.9)	350	(11.8)	601	(7.1)
	Russian Federation	92	(1.8)	340	(5.4)	579	(4.4)

Table 4.17
Variation in student performance on the retrieving information subscale

		Standard deviation		Percentiles			
				10th		90th	
		S.D.	S.E.	Score	S.E.	Score	S.E.
OECD COUNTRIES	Australia	108	(1.6)	393	(4.7)	671	(5.0)
	Austria	96	(1.5)	374	(4.6)	619	(3.1)
	Belgium	120	(2.7)	343	(8.5)	656	(2.6)
	Canada	102	(1.2)	397	(2.9)	657	(2.4)
	Czech Republic	107	(1.9)	343	(5.6)	614	(3.9)
	Denmark	105	(1.9)	359	(5.9)	626	(3.3)
	Finland	102	(2.1)	423	(4.7)	682	(3.2)
	France	101	(2.1)	376	(6.4)	638	(4.0)
	Germany	114	(2.0)	331	(6.2)	621	(3.1)
	Greece	109	(3.0)	306	(9.2)	585	(5.0)
	Hungary	107	(2.2)	333	(6.2)	613	(4.9)
	Iceland	103	(1.3)	362	(4.2)	628	(2.9)
	Ireland	100	(1.7)	392	(6.5)	647	(3.3)
	Italy	104	(3.0)	352	(5.8)	617	(4.0)
	Japan	97	(3.1)	397	(10.2)	644	(4.7)
	Korea	82	(1.6)	421	(4.3)	631	(3.4)
	Luxembourg	109	(1.4)	290	(4.3)	567	(2.6)
	Mexico	101	(2.2)	270	(4.5)	533	(6.0)
	New Zealand	116	(2.1)	377	(6.3)	677	(3.9)
	Norway	110	(1.9)	356	(6.5)	637	(3.3)
	Poland	112	(3.3)	324	(8.6)	615	(7.1)
	Portugal	107	(2.2)	311	(7.9)	588	(4.3)
	Spain	92	(1.2)	361	(4.9)	597	(2.8)
	Sweden	104	(1.5)	378	(4.3)	645	(2.7)
	Switzerland	113	(2.1)	344	(6.4)	636	(5.2)
	United Kingdom	105	(1.5)	384	(4.5)	656	(4.3)
	United States	112	(2.7)	348	(12.0)	638	(6.0)
	OECD average	*111*	*(0.4)*	*349*	*(1.3)*	*634*	*(0.9)*
NON-OECD COUNTRIES	Brazil	97	(2.1)	239	(5.2)	489	(3.5)
	Latvia	117	(2.4)	296	(8.5)	599	(5.7)
	Liechtenstein	106	(4.7)	345	(13.9)	620	(7.7)
	Russian Federation	108	(2.1)	309	(7.1)	587	(5.6)

Table 4.18
Variation in student performance on the interpreting texts subscale

| | | Standard deviation | | Percentiles | | | |
| | | | | 10th | | 90th | |
		S.D.	S.E.	Score	S.E.	Score	S.E.
OECD COUNTRIES	Australia	104	(1.5)	389	(4.9)	659	(4.8)
	Austria	93	(1.6)	384	(3.6)	624	(3.9)
	Belgium	105	(2.0)	363	(6.2)	638	(2.6)
	Canada	95	(1.0)	406	(2.8)	651	(2.1)
	Czech Republic	96	(1.6)	374	(4.9)	619	(3.3)
	Denmark	99	(1.7)	362	(4.5)	617	(3.7)
	Finland	97	(3.3)	429	(4.4)	671	(2.8)
	France	92	(1.7)	381	(5.0)	621	(3.3)
	Germany	109	(1.8)	340	(6.0)	623	(2.3)
	Greece	89	(2.4)	356	(7.3)	588	(4.3)
	Hungary	90	(1.9)	359	(4.6)	594	(4.5)
	Iceland	95	(1.4)	387	(3.8)	633	(3.1)
	Ireland	97	(1.7)	396	(5.8)	646	(3.3)
	Italy	86	(2.4)	376	(5.3)	598	(2.9)
	Japan	83	(2.9)	406	(9.4)	618	(4.6)
	Korea	69	(1.5)	434	(3.8)	609	(2.7)
	Luxembourg	101	(1.3)	314	(3.6)	571	(2.6)
	Mexico	78	(1.7)	319	(3.3)	521	(4.9)
	New Zealand	111	(2.0)	376	(4.3)	665	(4.4)
	Norway	104	(1.6)	364	(5.0)	633	(2.8)
	Poland	97	(2.7)	350	(6.4)	604	(6.2)
	Portugal	93	(1.6)	348	(5.9)	591	(4.4)
	Spain	84	(1.1)	380	(3.6)	595	(2.2)
	Sweden	96	(1.3)	393	(3.8)	641	(2.7)
	Switzerland	101	(2.0)	359	(5.9)	622	(5.5)
	United Kingdom	102	(1.4)	380	(4.0)	644	(4.1)
	United States	106	(2.6)	363	(10.5)	640	(6.6)
	OECD average	*100*	*(0.4)*	*368*	*(1.1)*	*625*	*(0.7)*
NON-OECD COUNTRIES	Brazil	84	(1.8)	295	(4.4)	511	(4.9)
	Latvia	95	(2.0)	332	(7.6)	580	(5.3)
	Liechtenstein	94	(3.6)	356	(12.1)	597	(8.8)
	Russian Federation	92	(1.8)	346	(5.6)	586	(4.4)

Table 4.19
Variation in student performance on the reflection and evaluation subscale

| | | Standard deviation | | Percentiles | | | |
| | | | | 10th | | 90th | |
		S.D.	S.E.	Score	S.E.	Score	S.E.
OECD COUNTRIES	Australia	100	(1.5)	393	(5.3)	651	(4.7)
	Austria	100	(1.8)	379	(5.0)	633	(4.6)
	Belgium	114	(4.1)	336	(9.4)	629	(2.4)
	Canada	96	(1.0)	416	(3.1)	661	(1.8)
	Czech Republic	103	(1.8)	354	(5.0)	611	(3.9)
	Denmark	102	(2.1)	365	(5.5)	625	(4.0)
	Finland	91	(3.9)	415	(5.0)	640	(2.5)
	France	98	(1.8)	365	(6.1)	618	(3.5)
	Germany	124	(1.8)	311	(7.4)	627	(3.1)
	Greece	115	(3.1)	343	(9.3)	638	(5.8)
	Hungary	100	(2.2)	347	(5.6)	606	(4.5)
	Iceland	93	(1.3)	378	(3.8)	616	(2.5)
	Ireland	90	(1.7)	414	(6.3)	642	(3.3)
	Italy	101	(2.9)	348	(6.3)	607	(3.1)
	Japan	100	(3.3)	397	(9.1)	651	(4.7)
	Korea	76	(1.7)	428	(4.5)	619	(3.0)
	Luxembourg	115	(1.8)	293	(4.9)	581	(3.6)
	Mexico	109	(2.2)	303	(4.4)	586	(6.5)
	New Zealand	107	(1.8)	387	(5.1)	662	(4.7)
	Norway	108	(1.8)	357	(5.2)	636	(3.1)
	Poland	110	(3.2)	328	(8.0)	613	(6.4)
	Portugal	101	(1.7)	342	(6.8)	607	(3.8)
	Spain	91	(1.2)	383	(4.3)	618	(2.7)
	Sweden	95	(1.2)	382	(4.1)	626	(4.0)
	Switzerland	113	(2.2)	336	(6.5)	629	(6.0)
	United Kingdom	99	(1.6)	408	(4.5)	664	(3.5)
	United States	105	(2.7)	367	(11.9)	638	(6.3)
	OECD average	*106*	*(0.4)*	*361*	*(1.4)*	*630*	*(0.9)*
NON-OECD COUNTRIES	Brazil	93	(2.2)	298	(5.2)	536	(5.6)
	Latvia	113	(2.3)	305	(7.3)	598	(7.1)
	Liechtenstein	108	(4.3)	323	(12.9)	603	(9.6)
	Russian Federation	98	(1.7)	326	(6.2)	580	(4.2)

Table 4.20
Variation in student performance on the continuous texts subscale

| | | Standard deviation | | Percentiles | | | |
| | | | | 10th | | 90th | |
		S.D.	S.E.	Score	S.E.	Score	S.E.
OECD COUNTRIES	Australia	104	(1.6)	386	(4.5)	658	(4.8)
	Austria	94	(1.5)	384	(4.5)	623	(3.8)
	Belgium	108	(3.5)	349	(8.3)	632	(2.5)
	Canada	98	(1.1)	407	(3.2)	656	(2.0)
	Czech Republic	93	(1.8)	366	(5.4)	604	(3.2)
	Denmark	99	(1.9)	364	(5.1)	619	(3.5)
	Finland	90	(2.8)	427	(4.6)	653	(2.7)
	France	94	(1.8)	370	(5.0)	616	(3.3)
	Germany	115	(1.9)	331	(6.8)	624	(3.2)
	Greece	99	(2.8)	351	(9.1)	607	(5.0)
	Hungary	92	(1.9)	357	(5.3)	596	(4.7)
	Iceland	93	(1.2)	384	(3.4)	625	(2.8)
	Ireland	94	(1.7)	401	(5.3)	643	(3.5)
	Italy	91	(2.7)	371	(6.0)	604	(3.2)
	Japan	85	(2.9)	408	(9.8)	627	(4.7)
	Korea	69	(1.8)	441	(4.2)	613	(2.8)
	Luxembourg	108	(1.3)	298	(4.1)	578	(2.7)
	Mexico	86	(1.8)	319	(3.8)	545	(5.0)
	New Zealand	110	(1.7)	378	(5.8)	661	(3.7)
	Norway	103	(1.6)	364	(5.6)	631	(3.6)
	Poland	101	(2.9)	343	(6.6)	606	(6.6)
	Portugal	98	(1.8)	341	(6.4)	597	(3.8)
	Spain	84	(1.1)	381	(3.7)	596	(2.2)
	Sweden	93	(1.2)	390	(4.0)	632	(3.0)
	Switzerland	104	(2.0)	352	(6.0)	623	(4.9)
	United Kingdom	104	(1.5)	384	(3.5)	651	(3.7)
	United States	105	(2.5)	363	(11.2)	637	(6.7)
	OECD average	*101*	*(0.4)*	*366*	*(1.2)*	*624*	*(0.7)*
NON-OECD COUNTRIES	Brazil	88	(1.8)	297	(5.2)	522	(4.2)
	Latvia	104	(2.3)	323	(7.5)	592	(6.2)
	Liechtenstein	97	(4.0)	348	(12.5)	600	(8.6)
	Russian Federation	92	(1.8)	344	(5.8)	582	(4.6)

Table 4.21
Variation in student performance on the non–continuous subscale

		Standard deviation		Percentiles			
				10th		90th	
		S.D.	S.E.	Score	S.E.	Score	S.E.
OECD COUNTRIES	Australia	104	(1.6)	401	(5.2)	667	(3.8)
	Austria	99	(1.5)	376	(3.8)	629	(3.7)
	Belgium	114	(2.4)	354	(7.2)	650	(2.7)
	Canada	99	(1.1)	407	(3.0)	657	(2.0)
	Czech Republic	112	(2.3)	354	(4.7)	635	(4.0)
	Denmark	109	(1.8)	356	(4.9)	631	(4.0)
	Finland	95	(2.0)	427	(4.8)	670	(3.4)
	France	97	(1.8)	389	(5.2)	638	(3.0)
	Germany	113	(2.2)	334	(5.5)	623	(3.2)
	Greece	103	(2.5)	319	(8.5)	586	(5.0)
	Hungary	108	(2.1)	335	(5.7)	615	(5.4)
	Iceland	100	(1.4)	372	(3.7)	629	(3.3)
	Ireland	100	(1.8)	397	(6.2)	653	(3.5)
	Italy	100	(2.8)	348	(5.4)	604	(3.9)
	Japan	98	(3.2)	391	(9.5)	639	(5.2)
	Korea	81	(1.7)	412	(4.2)	614	(2.9)
	Luxembourg	113	(1.5)	289	(4.6)	580	(2.5)
	Mexico	97	(2.4)	275	(5.0)	527	(7.2)
	New Zealand	110	(1.9)	389	(5.6)	672	(5.7)
	Norway	114	(1.7)	356	(5.1)	646	(3.9)
	Poland	107	(3.2)	329	(8.2)	607	(6.3)
	Portugal	102	(1.8)	322	(6.3)	589	(4.2)
	Spain	96	(1.3)	363	(5.5)	613	(3.1)
	Sweden	100	(1.3)	386	(4.3)	644	(3.2)
	Switzerland	109	(2.0)	350	(6.4)	632	(5.5)
	United Kingdom	101	(1.5)	400	(3.9)	659	(4.0)
	United States	109	(2.8)	362	(12.2)	641	(7.2)
	OECD average	*109*	*(0.4)*	*355*	*(1.2)*	*634*	*(0.8)*
NON-OECD COUNTRIES	Brazil	97	(1.9)	241	(4.9)	489	(4.5)
	Latvia	109	(2.5)	303	(7.6)	587	(5.8)
	Liechtenstein	99	(3.9)	351	(15.8)	602	(14.6)
	Russian Federation	102	(2.0)	316	(6.3)	579	(5.2)

Table 5.1
Percentage of students reading each kind of print content within each reading profile cluster

	No reading (%)	Moderate reading (%)	Frequent reading (%)
Least diversified readers			
Magazines	15.6	46.0	38.4
Comics	49.6	37.4	12.9
Fiction	40.6	47.1	12.3
Non-fiction	53.7	40.7	5.7
Newspapers	47.6	52.2	0.2
Moderately diversified readers			
Magazines	4.6	25.4	69.9
Comics	60.7	38.9	0.4
Fiction	45.3	51.9	2.7
Non-fiction	51.7	45.3	3.1
Newspapers	-	11.4	88.6
Diversified readers in short texts			
Magazines	1.8	13.5	84.7
Comics	-	10.6	89.4
Fiction	18.2	51.3	30.5
Non-fiction	24.5	54.4	21.0
Newspapers	2.4	16.1	81.4
Diversified readers in long texts			
Magazines	3.2	26.3	70.5
Comics	46.0	48.4	5.6
Fiction	0.7	27.4	71.9
Non-fiction	4.3	47.5	48.3
Newspapers	2.2	21.7	76.1

Table 5.2
Performance on the combined reading literacy scale and percentage of students by reading profile cluster

	Least diversified readers				Moderately diversified readers				Diversified readers in short texts				Diversified readers in long texts			
	Mean score	S.E.	%	S.E.	Mean score	S.E.	%	S.E.	Mean score	S.E.	%	S.E.	Mean score	S.E.	%	S.E.
Australia	494	(4.9)	18.5	(0.9)	514	(3.7)	35.0	(1.1)	522	(6.3)	10.8	(0.6)	569	(4.4)	35.7	(1.2)
Austria	474	(4.6)	16.6	(0.7)	503	(2.4)	41.9	(0.9)	509	(3.5)	17.0	(0.5)	545	(3.6)	24.6	(0.8)
Belgium	487	(4.4)	36.3	(0.6)	503	(5.4)	19.6	(0.6)	537	(3.4)	31.8	(0.7)	556	(5.5)	12.3	(0.5)
Canada	507	(2.3)	24.3	(0.4)	528	(1.7)	30.8	(0.5)	531	(2.5)	16.2	(0.3)	572	(1.9)	28.7	(0.5)
Czech Republic	482	(3.5)	22.0	(0.7)	492	(2.8)	35.6	(0.9)	494	(3.4)	18.7	(0.6)	543	(2.9)	23.8	(0.7)
Denmark	453	(5.0)	17.5	(0.8)	464	(6.0)	10.1	(0.6)	511	(2.3)	56.2	(1.0)	541	(5.2)	16.2	(0.6)
Finland	485	(14.6)	6.9	(0.5)	522	(4.4)	14.2	(0.6)	550	(2.2)	66.6	(0.9)	597	(3.5)	12.3	(0.5)
France	488	(4.1)	32.6	(0.9)	503	(3.4)	19.2	(0.7)	528	(2.9)	31.3	(0.9)	534	(4.1)	16.8	(0.7)
Germany	464	(4.2)	24.1	(0.8)	485	(2.8)	38.0	(0.8)	499	(5.9)	11.6	(0.6)	541	(3.1)	26.3	(0.7)
Greece	464	(5.3)	35.4	(0.9)	474	(6.6)	21.3	(0.8)	478	(5.8)	21.5	(0.7)	505	(5.2)	21.8	(0.9)
Hungary	450	(4.8)	25.1	(1.0)	479	(4.3)	25.1	(0.8)	470	(4.7)	20.1	(0.7)	525	(4.7)	29.6	(1.0)
Iceland	449	(6.5)	6.6	(0.5)	492	(2.6)	28.6	(0.7)	520	(2.1)	49.7	(0.8)	537	(4.3)	15.1	(0.6)
Ireland	510	(5.9)	16.3	(0.7)	515	(3.3)	47.0	(0.8)	507	(5.9)	8.9	(0.6)	571	(3.6)	27.8	(1.0)
Italy	469	(4.7)	25.8	(0.9)	485	(3.3)	27.9	(0.7)	505	(3.3)	26.5	(0.8)	503	(4.1)	19.8	(0.7)
Japan	482	(8.2)	14.5	(0.9)	514	(7.2)	8.1	(0.5)	532	(4.6)	74.4	(0.9)	573	(7.7)	3.0	(0.3)
Korea	495	(3.9)	18.8	(0.6)	525	(3.7)	14.6	(0.6)	531	(2.4)	53.1	(1.1)	545	(3.8)	13.6	(0.7)
Luxembourg	434	(2.5)	39.4	(0.8)	454	(4.3)	21.3	(0.6)	461	(4.0)	19.2	(0.7)	486	(3.8)	20.0	(0.6)
Mexico	403	(3.6)	37.5	(1.3)	426	(5.9)	15.6	(0.8)	438	(4.3)	22.2	(5.9)	443	(4.9)	24.7	(0.7)
New Zealand	499	(4.8)	18.0	(0.7)	529	(3.1)	30.1	(0.9)	500	(6.4)	12.4	(0.6)	564	(3.7)	39.4	(1.0)
Norway	433	(7.1)	8.5	(0.6)	492	(4.2)	20.2	(0.7)	520	(2.7)	58.0	(0.9)	546	(4.3)	13.3	(0.5)
Poland	445	(7.0)	16.7	(0.9)	491	(4.2)	48.0	(1.1)	474	(6.6)	11.4	(0.7)	511	(6.3)	24.0	(1.1)
Portugal	449	(5.8)	29.8	(0.9)	477	(4.1)	25.9	(0.7)	487	(5.8)	24.4	(0.6)	489	(5.9)	19.8	(0.6)
Spain	474	(3.4)	36.2	(1.1)	492	(3.6)	23.0	(0.7)	503	(3.4)	17.5	(0.7)	526	(2.9)	23.3	(0.7)
Sweden	469	(4.8)	11.1	(0.5)	502	(2.8)	30.3	(0.8)	518	(2.8)	37.3	(0.8)	564	(3.6)	21.3	(0.7)
Switzerland	455	(4.6)	22.1	(0.9)	487	(4.3)	30.3	(0.8)	519	(5.1)	25.4	(0.8)	534	(5.2)	22.2	(0.8)
United Kingdom	503	(4.3)	17.1	(0.6)	512	(2.7)	39.4	(0.9)	488	(5.3)	8.4	(0.5)	566	(3.7)	35.1	(1.0)
United States	478	(7.6)	28.4	(1.3)	520	(5.8)	32.1	(1.5)	482	(10.9)	10.8	(1.1)	544	(6.0)	28.7	(1.5)
OECD average	*468*	*(1.0)*	*22.4*	*(0.2)*	*498*	*(0.7)*	*27.1*	*(0.1)*	*514*	*(0.9)*	*28.3*	*(0.2)*	*539*	*(0.9)*	*22.2*	*(0.2)*
Brazil	370	(4.4)	29.5	(1.1)	407	(5.1)	15.1	(0.8)	413	(4.3)	27.5	(1.0)	418	(3.6)	27.9	(1.1)
Latvia	412	(8.2)	13.8	(0.8)	464	(5.3)	39.9	(1.3)	433	(8.7)	15.2	(0.9)	499	(5.3)	31.1	(1.4)
Liechtenstein	442	(11.0)	21.9	(2.1)	478	(8.0)	40.7	(2.5)	524	(12.6)	14.3	(2.1)	526	(11.7)	23.2	(2.5)
Russian Federation	426	(6.3)	11.5	(0.5)	451	(5.1)	17.1	(0.6)	432	(4.8)	21.6	(1.2)	495	(3.9)	49.7	(1.1)
Netherlands[1]	494	(5.4)	24.7	(1.3)	530	(4.5)	25.8	(1.0)	544	(4.0)	33.1	(1.2)	573	(4.9)	16.5	(0.9)

OECD COUNTRIES / NON-OECD COUNTRIES

1. Response rate is too low to ensure comparability.

Table 5.3
Percentage of students in each reading profile cluster by proficiency level of the combined reading literacy scale

	Below Level 1 (%)	Level 1 (%)	Level 2 (%)	Level 3 (%)	Level 4 (%)	Level 5 (%)
Least diversified readers	9.6	17.8	25.7	26.4	15.7	4.8
Moderately diversified readers	4.3	11.8	24.3	31.3	21.1	7.1
Diversified readers in short texts	3.4	9.4	20.5	31.2	25.4	10.0
Diversified readers in long texts	2.8	6.9	15.6	27.3	29.4	17.9

Table 5.4
Mean scores on the combined literacy reading scale and subscales by reading profile cluster

	Combined reading literacy		Retrieving information		Interpreting texts		Reflection and evaluation		Continuous texts		Non-continuous texts	
	Mean score	S.E.	Mean score	S.E.	Mean score	S.E.	Mean score	S.E.	Mean score	S.E.	Mean score	S.E.
Least diversified readers	468	(1.01)	461	(1.10)	470	(0.99)	472	(1.05)	470	(1.00)	464	(1.08)
Moderately diversified readers	498	(0.72)	497	(0.78)	498	(0.69)	499	(0.81)	497	(0.72)	501	(0.79)
Diversified readers in short texts	514	(0.85)	516	(0.92)	515	(0.84)	513	(0.93)	514	(0.85)	517	(0.95)
Diversified readers in long texts	539	(0.88)	535	(0.96)	539	(0.88)	544	(0.88)	541	(0.94)	537	(0.98)

Table 5.5
Percentage of students in each reading profile cluster by gender

		Least diversified readers		Moderately diversified readers		Diversified readers in short texts		Diversified readers in long texts	
		Males (%)	Females (%)	Males (%)	Females (%)	Males (%)	Females (%)	Males (%)	Females (%)
OECD COUNTRIES	Australia	17.4	19.7	39.0	30.7	15.5	5.7	28.2	43.9
	Austria	16.9	16.0	42.1	42.0	23.6	10.9	17.4	31.2
	Belgium	34.2	38.5	22.1	16.9	36.3	26.9	7.4	17.6
	Canada	24.7	23.9	34.3	27.2	19.4	13.1	21.6	35.8
	Czech Republic	19.4	24.3	44.8	27.3	22.9	14.9	12.9	33.5
	Denmark	18.2	16.8	11.7	8.4	60.3	52.1	9.7	22.8
	Finland	8.1	5.8	12.2	15.9	74.1	59.7	5.6	18.6
	France	31.7	33.5	16.7	21.6	41.2	22.2	10.4	22.8
	Germany	23.3	24.8	42.6	33.3	16.7	6.7	17.4	35.2
	Greece	24.7	46.0	29.6	12.9	27.4	15.7	18.3	25.3
	Hungary	25.8	24.3	28.3	22.0	21.6	18.7	24.3	35.0
	Iceland	6.5	6.8	29.0	28.2	55.2	44.3	9.4	20.7
	Ireland	15.7	16.9	53.7	40.6	11.2	6.7	19.5	35.8
	Italy	23.4	28.0	30.0	25.9	31.0	21.9	15.5	24.3
	Japan	12.2	16.7	6.4	9.7	79.5	69.5	1.9	4.0
	Korea	16.6	21.5	13.1	16.4	60.3	44.1	10.0	18.1
	Luxembourg	36.2	42.5	23.6	19.1	27.4	11.3	12.8	27.1
	Mexico	36.9	38.0	15.4	15.8	26.8	17.7	20.9	28.5
	New Zealand	18.2	17.9	33.9	26.5	17.6	7.2	30.4	48.4
	Norway	8.6	8.3	19.6	20.7	66.0	49.9	5.8	21.0
	Poland	21.0	12.3	48.1	48.0	14.6	8.2	16.3	31.6
	Portugal	22.9	36.0	37.2	15.7	27.8	21.4	12.1	26.9
	Spain	30.7	41.5	27.9	18.4	25.1	10.4	16.4	29.8
	Sweden	11.9	10.2	29.5	31.1	45.0	29.5	13.6	29.2
	Switzerland	20.2	23.9	34.2	26.5	32.7	18.2	13.0	31.3
	United Kingdom	13.9	20.2	46.0	33.1	12.5	4.4	27.6	42.3
	United States	30.4	26.5	33.2	31.1	15.0	7.0	21.4	35.4
	OECD average	*20.9*	*23.6*	*29.8*	*24.7*	*33.8*	*22.9*	*15.5*	*28.8*
NON-OECD COUNTRIES	Brazil	33.4	26.2	19.5	11.4	29.4	25.9	17.7	36.5
	Latvia	17.0	10.8	42.3	37.5	16.7	13.8	23.9	37.8
	Liechtenstein	17.3	24.8	51.1	31.1	17.9	10.9	13.7	33.2
	Russian Federation	15.4	7.7	21.4	13.0	22.1	21.3	41.0	58.1
	Netherlands[1]	24.5	25.0	27.2	24.3	41.4	24.3	6.9	26.3

1. Response rate is too low to ensure comparability.

Table 5.6
Socio–economic background[1] by reading profile cluster

	Least diversified readers		Moderately diversified readers		Diversified readers in short texts		Diversified readers in long texts	
	Mean index	S.E.	Mean index	S.E.	Mean index	S.E.	Mean index	S.E.
Australia	50.7	(0.7)	50.3	(0.6)	51.8	(1.0)	55.3	(0.7)
Austria	47.7	(0.5)	48.6	(0.3)	50.3	(0.6)	52.8	(0.5)
Belgium	47.6	(0.5)	47.4	(0.6)	51.4	(0.5)	51.0	(0.8)
Canada	50.8	(0.3)	52.6	(0.3)	53.0	(0.4)	54.8	(0.4)
Czech Republic	47.3	(0.4)	48.5	(0.4)	48.1	(0.5)	51.2	(0.5)
Denmark	47.3	(0.8)	47.4	(0.9)	50.0	(0.5)	53.2	(0.9)
Finland	48.1	(1.2)	48.7	(0.7)	49.9	(0.4)	53.1	(0.9)
France	47.3	(0.5)	45.9	(0.8)	51.0	(0.6)	47.3	(0.5)
Germany	45.7	(0.6)	48.9	(0.4)	50.4	(0.7)	53.2	(0.6)
Greece	45.1	(0.7)	47.1	(0.9)	49.9	(0.9)	50.8	(0.8)
Hungary	47.3	(0.6)	49.4	(0.6)	47.7	(0.6)	53.2	(0.8)
Iceland	49.5	(1.2)	52.2	(0.6)	53.1	(0.4)	53.8	(0.7)
Ireland	50.1	(0.9)	46.8	(0.5)	46.2	(0.9)	51.3	(0.6)
Italy	45.2	(0.5)	46.1	(0.5)	49.6	(0.6)	47.8	(0.6)
Japan[2]	m	m	m	m	m	m	m	m
Korea	38.2	(0.7)	43.6	(0.7)	43.8	(0.5)	44.7	(0.8)
Luxembourg	42.9	(0.5)	45.6	(0.7)	46.9	(0.7)	48.0	(0.7)
Mexico	39.1	(0.6)	44.5	(1.2)	45.2	(0.9)	44.5	(0.9)
New Zealand	51.5	(0.7)	51.5	(0.4)	51.7	(0.9)	53.8	(0.6)
Norway	50.9	(0.9)	52.7	(0.7)	54.3	(0.4)	55.9	(0.8)
Poland	44.1	(1.0)	46.2	(0.6)	46.7	(0.9)	47.9	(0.8)
Portugal	41.2	(0.7)	44.6	(0.8)	45.6	(0.8)	45.7	(0.8)
Spain	42.5	(0.7)	46.1	(0.9)	46.3	(0.9)	47.0	(0.8)
Sweden	48.4	(0.9)	49.7	(0.5)	50.1	(0.5)	54.0	(0.6)
Switzerland	46.1	(0.6)	47.8	(0.6)	51.6	(0.9)	52.0	(0.7)
United Kingdom	51.0	(0.5)	50.1	(0.4)	48.5	(0.8)	53.8	(0.6)
United States	49.4	(1.0)	54.7	(1.0)	50.8	(1.4)	54.0	(0.9)
OECD average	*46.0*	*(0.1)*	*48.6*	*(0.1)*	*49.7*	*(0.1)*	*51.6*	*(0.2)*
Brazil	41.1	(0.7)	45.6	(1.0)	45.5	(0.9)	45.5	(0.7)
Latvia	47.9	(1.1)	51.3	(0.8)	47.1	(1.1)	51.8	(0.7)
Liechtenstein	47.2	(1.9)	46.2	(1.3)	47.9	(3.2)	51.0	(1.9)
Russian Federation	46.9	(0.9)	48.2	(0.7)	45.5	(0.6)	52.4	(0.5)
Netherlands[3]	47.7	(1.0)	50.2	(0.8)	52.5	(0.6)	53.3	(0.9)

(Left margin labels: OECD COUNTRIES; NON-OECD COUNTRIES)

1. Socio-economic background is measured by the socio-economic index of occupational status of parents. See Annex A3 for definition.
2. Japan is excluded from the comparison because of a high proportion of missing data.
3. Response rate is too low to ensure comparability.

Table 5.7
Access to print[1] by reading profile cluster

		Least diversified readers		Moderately diversified readers		Diversified readers in short texts		Diversified readers in long texts	
		Mean index	S.E.	Mean index	S.E.	Mean index	S.E.	Mean index	S.E.
OECD COUNTRIES	Australia	-0.39	(0.04)	-0.30	(0.04)	-0.03	(0.05)	0.31	(0.03)
	Austria	-0.28	(0.05)	-0.20	(0.03)	0.05	(0.04)	0.43	(0.04)
	Belgium	-0.57	(0.02)	-0.64	(0.03)	-0.22	(0.03)	0.01	(0.04)
	Canada	-0.45	(0.02)	-0.31	(0.02)	-0.06	(0.02)	0.25	(0.02)
	Czech Republic	0.12	(0.03)	0.26	(0.03)	0.43	(0.03)	0.67	(0.02)
	Denmark	-0.54	(0.04)	-0.53	(0.06)	-0.09	(0.03)	0.14	(0.05)
	Finland	-0.45	(0.06)	-0.42	(0.04)	-0.02	(0.03)	-0.45	(0.06)
	France	-0.31	(0.03)	-0.28	(0.04)	0.16	(0.03)	0.29	(0.04)
	Germany	-0.36	(0.03)	-0.18	(0.03)	0.18	(0.04)	0.48	(0.03)
	Greece	-0.10	(0.03)	-0.04	(0.04)	0.11	(0.05)	0.34	(0.03)
	Hungary	0.26	(0.04)	0.45	(0.03)	0.54	(0.04)	0.86	(0.03)
	Iceland	0.23	(0.06)	0.42	(0.03)	0.64	(0.02)	0.70	(0.03)
	Ireland	-0.23	(0.05)	-0.30	(0.03)	-0.02	(0.07)	0.34	(0.03)
	Italy	0.02	(0.03)	0.09	(0.03)	0.41	(0.03)	0.49	(0.03)
	Japan	-0.59	(0.05)	-0.41	(0.06)	-0.13	(0.02)	0.40	(0.07)
	Korea	-0.10	(0.03)	0.32	(0.04)	0.40	(0.02)	0.64	(0.03)
	Luxembourg	-0.37	(0.03)	-0.18	(0.04)	0.06	(0.04)	0.32	(0.04)
	Mexico	-0.77	(0.03)	-0.64	(0.06)	-0.44	(0.05)	-0.32	(0.05)
	New Zealand	-0.51	(0.04)	-0.39	(0.03)	-0.19	(0.06)	0.03	(0.03)
	Norway	-0.33	(0.06)	-0.14	(0.04)	0.19	(0.03)	0.36	(0.04)
	Poland	-0.02	(0.05)	0.26	(0.02)	0.37	(0.06)	0.60	(0.04)
	Portugal	-0.35	(0.04)	-0.16	(0.04)	0.16	(0.04)	0.26	(0.04)
	Spain	-0.01	(0.04)	0.19	(0.04)	0.47	(0.03)	0.61	(0.03)
	Sweden	-0.36	(0.04)	-0.19	(0.03)	0.04	(0.03)	0.39	(0.03)
	Switzerland	-0.43	(0.03)	-0.35	(0.04)	0.10	(0.04)	0.28	(0.03)
	United Kingdom	-0.26	(0.04)	-0.32	(0.03)	-0.09	(0.04)	0.40	(0.03)
	United States	-0.48	(0.05)	-0.23	(0.05)	-0.18	(0.09)	0.27	(0.04)
	OECD average	*-0.30*	*(0.01)*	*-0.13*	*(0.01)*	*0.11*	*(0.01)*	*0.36*	*(0.01)*
NON-OECD COUNTRIES	Brazil	-0.78	(0.02)	-0.62	(0.05)	-0.33	(0.04)	-0.22	(0.04)
	Latvia	0.37	(0.06)	0.66	(0.03)	0.46	(0.05)	0.89	(0.03)
	Liechtenstein	-0.22	(0.11)	-0.37	(0.09)	-0.02	(0.13)	0.32	(0.10)
	Russian Federation	0.38	(0.05)	0.45	(0.04)	0.50	(0.04)	0.76	(0.03)
	Netherlands[2]	-0.76	(0.03)	-0.62	(0.05)	-0.41	(0.04)	-0.16	(0.06)

1. For definition, see note 9 in chapter 5.
2. Response rate is too low to ensure comparability.

Table 5.8
Difference in reading engagement between females and males

	All students	S.E.	Females	Males	Difference between females and males
Australia	-0.04	(0.03)	0.11	-0.18	0.28
Austria	-0.08	(0.03)	0.17	-0.35	0.52
Belgium	-0.28	(0.02)	-0.07	-0.48	0.41
Canada	0.01	(0.01)	0.24	-0.23	0.47
Czech Republic	0.02	(0.02)	0.29	-0.29	0.57
Denmark	0.26	(0.02)	0.50	0.02	0.48
Finland	0.46	(0.02)	0.82	0.08	0.74
France	-0.18	(0.02)	-0.03	-0.33	0.30
Germany	-0.26	(0.02)	0.01	-0.53	0.55
Greece	-0.09	(0.02)	0.00	-0.17	0.17
Hungary	0.03	(0.02)	0.21	-0.15	0.36
Iceland	0.27	(0.01)	0.46	0.08	0.39
Ireland	-0.20	(0.02)	0.03	-0.43	0.46
Italy	-0.08	(0.02)	0.10	-0.27	0.37
Japan	0.20	(0.03)	0.28	0.11	0.17
Korea	0.21	(0.02)	0.23	0.19	0.04
Luxembourg	-0.19	(0.02)	0.01	-0.39	0.40
Mexico	0.07	(0.01)	0.17	-0.03	0.20
New Zealand	0.05	(0.02)	0.20	-0.09	0.29
Norway	0.09	(0.02)	0.35	-0.16	0.51
Poland	-0.10	(0.02)	0.09	-0.28	0.36
Portugal	0.13	(0.02)	0.36	-0.11	0.47
Spain	-0.23	(0.02)	-0.09	-0.38	0.29
Sweden	0.14	(0.02)	0.37	-0.08	0.45
Switzerland	0.00	(0.01)	0.31	-0.31	0.62
United Kingdom	-0.10	(0.02)	0.03	-0.24	0.26
United States	-0.14	(0.03)	0.04	-0.32	0.36
OECD average	*0.00*	*~*	*0.19*	*-0.19*	*0.38*
Brazil	0.11	(0.02)	0.36	-0.17	0.53
Latvia	-0.04	(0.02)	0.17	-0.27	0.44
Liechtenstein	-0.13	(0.05)	0.13	-0.36	0.49
Russian Federation	0.17	(0.02)	0.37	-0.02	0.39
Netherlands[1]	-0.17	(0.04)	0.04	-0.38	0.42

OECD COUNTRIES / NON-OECD COUNTRIES

1. Response rate is too low to ensure comparability.

Table 5.9
Performance on the combined reading literacy scale by level of reading engagement and socio–economic background[1]

	Low reading engagement	Medium reading engagement	High reading engagement
Low socio-economic background	423	467	540
Medium socio-economic background	463	506	548
High socio-economic background	491	540	583

1. See Annex A3 for definition.

Table 6.1
Correlation between individual student background characteristics and performance on the combined reading literacy scale

		Gender				Time spent on homework				Reading engagement	
		Performance	S.E.	Reading engagement	S.E.	Performance	S.E.	Reading engagement	S.E.	Performance	S.E.
OECD COUNTRIES	Australia	0.17	(0.03)	0.14	(0.02)	0.27	(0.02)	0.34	(0.02)	0.42	(0.02)
	Austria	0.14	(0.03)	0.25	(0.02)	-0.03	(0.02)	0.12	(0.02)	0.41	(0.02)
	Belgium	0.15	(0.03)	0.19	(0.02)	0.29	(0.01)	0.28	(0.01)	0.36	(0.02)
	Canada	0.17	(0.01)	0.22	(0.01)	0.21	(0.01)	0.30	(0.01)	0.40	(0.01)
	Czech Republic	0.20	(0.02)	0.23	(0.02)	0.14	(0.02)	0.29	(0.02)	0.42	(0.01)
	Denmark	0.13	(0.02)	0.23	(0.02)	0.06	(0.03)	0.25	(0.02)	0.43	(0.02)
	Finland	0.29	(0.02)	0.36	(0.01)	0.12	(0.02)	0.29	(0.01)	0.48	(0.01)
	France	0.16	(0.02)	0.15	(0.02)	0.30	(0.02)	0.33	(0.01)	0.35	(0.01)
	Germany	0.16	(0.02)	0.25	(0.01)	0.10	(0.02)	0.21	(0.01)	0.41	(0.02)
	Greece	0.19	(0.02)	0.11	(0.02)	0.39	(0.02)	0.33	(0.02)	0.25	(0.02)
	Hungary	0.17	(0.03)	0.20	(0.02)	0.28	(0.03)	0.33	(0.02)	0.41	(0.02)
	Iceland	0.22	(0.02)	0.20	(0.01)	0.04	(0.02)	0.19	(0.02)	0.45	(0.02)
	Ireland	0.15	(0.02)	0.22	(0.02)	0.15	(0.02)	0.24	(0.02)	0.39	(0.02)
	Italy	0.21	(0.04)	0.19	(0.02)	0.26	(0.03)	0.30	(0.02)	0.30	(0.02)
	Japan	0.17	(0.04)	0.08	(0.02)	0.26	(0.03)	0.24	(0.02)	0.32	(0.01)
	Korea	0.10	(0.04)	0.02	(0.02)	0.25	(0.02)	0.25	(0.02)	0.35	(0.01)
	Luxembourg	0.13	(0.02)	0.19	(0.02)	0.03	(0.02)	0.21	(0.02)	0.25	(0.02)
	Mexico	0.12	(0.03)	0.13	(0.02)	0.12	(0.02)	0.28	(0.02)	0.24	(0.02)
	New Zealand	0.21	(0.03)	0.15	(0.02)	0.18	(0.02)	0.27	(0.01)	0.35	(0.02)
	Norway	0.21	(0.02)	0.27	(0.02)	0.14	(0.02)	0.21	(0.02)	0.45	(0.02)
	Poland	0.18	(0.03)	0.21	(0.02)	0.30	(0.02)	0.29	(0.02)	0.28	(0.02)
	Portugal	0.13	(0.02)	0.27	(0.02)	0.13	(0.02)	0.29	(0.02)	0.32	(0.02)
	Spain	0.14	(0.02)	0.15	(0.02)	0.30	(0.02)	0.28	(0.02)	0.38	(0.01)
	Sweden	0.20	(0.02)	0.23	(0.02)	-0.01	(0.02)	0.22	(0.02)	0.45	(0.02)
	Switzerland	0.15	(0.02)	0.28	(0.02)	0.03	(0.02)	0.17	(0.02)	0.46	(0.02)
	United Kingdom	0.13	(0.02)	0.14	(0.01)	0.28	(0.02)	0.30	(0.01)	0.37	(0.02)
	United States	0.14	(0.02)	0.17	(0.02)	0.28	(0.02)	0.25	(0.02)	0.31	(0.02)
	OECD median	*0.16*	*~*	*0.20*	*~*	*0.18*	*~*	*0.28*	*~*	*0.38*	*~*
	SD of correlation	*0.04*	*~*	*0.07*	*~*	*0.11*	*~*	*0.05*	*~*	*0.07*	*~*
NON-OECD COUNTRIES	Brazil	0.10	(0.02)	0.28	(0.01)	0.16	(0.02)	0.27	(0.03)	0.26	(0.02)
	Latvia	0.26	(0.02)	0.27	(0.03)	0.16	(0.02)	0.27	(0.02)	0.29	(0.03)
	Liechtenstein	0.16	(0.06)	0.25	(0.06)	-0.04	(0.08)	0.19	(0.06)	0.45	(0.04)
	Russian Federation	0.21	(0.02)	0.23	(0.01)	0.31	(0.02)	0.33	(0.01)	0.23	(0.02)
	Netherlands[1]	0.17	(0.03)	0.21	(0.02)	0.10	(0.03)	0.16	(0.03)	-	(0.02)

1. Response rate is too low to ensure comparability.

Table 6.2a
Correlation between gender and reading literacy performance

	Combined reading literacy	Retrieving information	Interpreting texts	Reflection and evaluation	Continuous texts	Non-continuous texts
Australia	0.17	0.13	0.16	0.21	0.19	0.10
Austria	0.14	0.08	0.12	0.20	0.18	0.04
Belgium	0.15	0.11	0.15	0.20	0.19	0.09
Canada	0.17	0.12	0.15	0.24	0.20	0.09
Czech Republic	0.20	0.13	0.18	0.26	0.24	0.11
Denmark	0.13	0.07	0.11	0.21	0.16	0.04
Finland	0.29	0.22	0.26	0.35	0.33	0.18
France	0.16	0.11	0.15	0.20	0.19	0.07
Germany	0.16	0.11	0.15	0.19	0.19	0.07
Greece	0.19	0.15	0.18	0.23	0.23	0.10
Hungary	0.17	0.12	0.16	0.22	0.20	0.09
Iceland	0.22	0.16	0.20	0.29	0.24	0.14
Ireland	0.15	0.11	0.14	0.21	0.18	0.08
Italy	0.21	0.15	0.23	0.24	0.24	0.10
Japan	0.17	0.14	0.15	0.21	0.20	0.10
Korea	0.10	0.04	0.06	0.18	0.13	0.03
Luxembourg	0.13	0.09	0.13	0.18	0.18	0.06
Mexico	0.12	0.06	0.11	0.16	0.15	0.05
New Zealand	0.21	0.17	0.20	0.27	0.24	0.16
Norway	0.21	0.15	0.20	0.28	0.26	0.10
Poland	0.18	0.13	0.18	0.24	0.23	0.07
Portugal	0.13	0.08	0.13	0.18	0.16	0.06
Spain	0.14	0.09	0.13	0.21	0.18	0.06
Sweden	0.20	0.15	0.18	0.27	0.24	0.10
Switzerland	0.15	0.10	0.13	0.20	0.19	0.04
United Kingdom	0.13	0.09	0.12	0.18	0.15	0.06
United States	0.14	0.12	0.13	0.17	0.16	0.10
OECD median	*0.16*	*0.12*	*0.15*	*0.21*	*0.19*	*0.09*
Brazil	0.10	0.05	0.08	0.13	0.12	0.03
Latvia	0.26	0.20	0.27	0.31	0.29	0.20
Liechtenstein	0.16	0.10	0.12	0.21	0.19	0.04
Russian Federation	0.21	0.16	0.19	0.25	0.24	0.13
Netherlands[1]	0.17	0.11	0.17	0.21	0.20	0.07

Regression of gender on reading literacy performance[2]

	Combined reading literacy	Retrieving information	Interpreting texts	Reflection and evaluation	Continuous texts	Non-continuous texts
Australia	33.61	28.47	33.61	41.66	39.56	21.20
Austria	25.63	15.90	22.77	39.30	33.24	6.84
Belgium	32.81	25.12	31.01	46.52	40.28	19.81
Canada	32.21	24.67	28.84	44.89	39.10	17.55
Czech Republic	37.44	27.37	34.37	53.98	44.10	23.44
Denmark	24.84	14.41	21.08	43.02	32.16	8.24
Finland	51.25	44.22	50.78	62.84	59.46	33.89
France	28.76	23.22	26.99	38.87	35.62	13.64
Germany	34.65	25.57	33.00	47.95	43.54	15.04
Greece	37.04	31.95	32.79	53.91	45.68	20.86
Hungary	31.62	25.48	28.02	43.23	37.41	19.49
Iceland	39.68	31.88	37.90	53.72	44.97	28.07
Ireland	28.68	22.33	27.18	37.23	33.64	16.85
Italy	38.17	30.53	38.68	47.34	44.17	20.07
Japan	29.66	26.88	25.18	42.39	34.15	20.18
Korea	14.21	5.97	8.79	27.11	18.56	4.97
Luxembourg	26.88	20.36	26.83	40.42	38.89	14.24
Mexico	20.27	11.86	17.10	34.98	25.85	9.07
New Zealand	45.83	38.83	43.10	56.99	51.92	34.57
Norway	43.20	32.49	40.48	59.96	52.64	22.74
Poland	36.13	27.98	34.55	52.54	46.46	15.45
Portugal	24.67	16.38	23.91	35.70	31.18	11.48
Spain	24.14	15.91	21.36	38.79	30.34	10.72
Sweden	36.96	30.04	34.43	50.68	44.10	19.16
Switzerland	29.97	22.44	26.24	46.08	39.15	8.82
United Kingdom	25.63	19.44	23.54	35.08	31.17	11.39
United States	28.57	26.05	27.08	36.09	33.37	20.71
OECD median	*31.62*	*25.48*	*28.02*	*43.23*	*39.10*	*17.55*
Brazil	16.67	9.82	14.20	24.58	21.42	5.50
Latvia	52.79	45.90	50.67	70.67	59.52	43.92
Liechtenstein	31.17	20.37	23.16	44.72	36.10	7.11
Russian Federation	38.18	34.41	35.63	48.94	43.89	25.88
Netherlands[1]	29.57	21.79	32.47	34.85	36.09	12.53

1. Response rate is too low to ensure comparability.
2. The numbers in the table represent difference in mean performance between females and males on the combined reading literacy scale.

Table 6.2b
Correlation between time spent on homework and reading literacy performance

		Combined reading literacy	Retrieving information	Interpreting texts	Reflection and evaluation	Continuous texts	Non-continuous texts
OECD COUNTRIES	Australia	0.27	0.26	0.26	0.28	0.26	0.27
	Austria	-0.03	-0.04	-0.04	0.00	-0.02	-0.03
	Belgium	0.29	0.28	0.28	0.32	0.30	0.28
	Canada	0.21	0.19	0.19	0.24	0.21	0.19
	Czech Republic	0.14	0.10	0.13	0.16	0.15	0.11
	Denmark	0.06	0.06	0.05	0.08	0.07	0.06
	Finland	0.12	0.09	0.10	0.15	0.13	0.10
	France	0.30	0.29	0.29	0.29	0.30	0.28
	Germany	0.10	0.08	0.09	0.11	0.10	0.07
	Greece	0.39	0.36	0.39	0.38	0.39	0.36
	Hungary	0.28	0.26	0.27	0.30	0.28	0.25
	Iceland	0.04	0.02	0.03	0.08	0.05	0.01
	Ireland	0.15	0.14	0.14	0.18	0.15	0.14
	Italy	0.26	0.25	0.26	0.28	0.27	0.23
	Japan	0.26	0.23	0.24	0.25	0.25	0.23
	Korea	0.25	0.24	0.25	0.23	0.24	0.25
	Luxembourg	0.03	-0.01	0.03	0.03	0.05	0.02
	Mexico	0.12	0.11	0.12	0.10	0.12	0.10
	New Zealand	0.18	0.18	0.16	0.19	0.17	0.19
	Norway	0.14	0.12	0.11	0.17	0.15	0.12
	Poland	0.30	0.25	0.29	0.33	0.31	0.25
	Portugal	0.13	0.13	0.11	0.16	0.13	0.12
	Spain	0.30	0.30	0.27	0.30	0.29	0.29
	Sweden	-0.01	-0.03	-0.03	0.04	0.00	-0.03
	Switzerland	0.03	0.02	0.03	0.04	0.04	0.01
	United Kingdom	0.28	0.28	0.26	0.31	0.28	0.27
	United States	0.28	0.26	0.27	0.30	0.28	0.25
	OECD median	*0.18*	*0.18*	*0.16*	*0.19*	*0.17*	*0.19*
NON-OECD COUNTRIES	Brazil	0.16	0.13	0.15	0.18	0.16	0.13
	Latvia	0.16	0.15	0.17	0.15	0.16	0.14
	Liechtenstein	-0.04	-0.05	-0.02	0.00	-0.02	-0.03
	Russian Federation	0.31	0.30	0.31	0.30	0.31	0.29
	Netherlands[1]	0.10	0.11	0.08	0.10	0.10	0.08

Regression of reading literacy performance on time spent on homework[2]

		Combined reading literacy	Retrieving information	Interpreting texts	Reflection and evaluation	Continuous texts	Non-continuous texts
OECD COUNTRIES	Australia	27.31	27.82	26.96	28.19	27.42	27.99
	Austria	-2.85	-4.15	-4.19	-0.32	-2.43	-3.62
	Belgium	32.94	35.04	30.63	37.93	34.16	33.06
	Canada	18.99	18.45	17.56	22.15	19.48	17.54
	Czech Republic	12.58	10.13	11.96	15.42	13.33	11.24
	Denmark	7.55	8.05	5.65	9.44	7.90	7.18
	Finland	12.97	11.24	11.68	15.91	13.47	11.23
	France	31.58	33.26	30.82	32.75	32.13	30.80
	Germany	11.57	9.75	10.39	14.80	12.74	8.85
	Greece	34.28	35.52	31.30	39.23	35.09	33.37
	Hungary	32.67	34.55	30.02	36.82	32.28	33.77
	Iceland	4.17	2.33	2.98	8.83	5.46	1.27
	Ireland	13.05	13.44	12.80	14.74	12.96	12.92
	Italy	26.61	28.21	24.69	30.63	26.57	25.79
	Japan	17.70	18.18	16.14	20.05	17.27	18.51
	Korea	13.24	14.86	13.12	13.24	12.73	15.51
	Luxembourg	2.58	-1.12	3.05	3.97	5.87	2.77
	Mexico	11.27	11.65	10.27	12.29	11.51	10.46
	New Zealand	20.07	20.64	18.48	20.50	18.49	21.46
	Norway	15.05	13.86	12.22	19.73	15.92	14.64
	Poland	30.28	28.64	29.04	36.82	32.32	27.64
	Portugal	12.28	13.44	10.07	15.66	13.04	11.97
	Spain	24.65	26.62	22.18	26.70	23.31	27.58
	Sweden	-1.01	-2.98	-3.15	3.88	-0.35	-3.34
	Switzerland	3.38	2.05	3.15	4.89	4.59	0.75
	United Kingdom	31.92	32.91	30.61	34.96	33.22	30.44
	United States	26.53	26.46	26.49	28.96	26.99	24.96
	OECD median	*15.05*	*14.86*	*13.12*	*19.73*	*15.92*	*15.51*
NON-OECD COUNTRIES	Brazil	14.13	12.28	12.48	17.08	14.53	12.80
	Latvia	16.91	18.42	17.07	18.22	17.69	16.17
	Liechtenstein	-4.94	-6.73	-2.06	0.36	-2.15	-3.28
	Russian Federation	25.93	28.55	25.44	26.16	25.45	26.63
	Netherlands[1]	10.38	13.36	8.99	9.29	10.92	8.70

1. Response rate is too low to ensure comparability.

2. The numbers in the table represent change in the reading literacy performance per unit of changes in the index of time spent on homework.

Table 6.2c
Correlation of reading engagement and reading literacy performance

		Combined reading literacy	Retrieving information	Interpreting texts	Reflection and evaluation	Continuous texts	Non-continuous texts
OECD COUNTRIES	Australia	0.42	0.40	0.42	0.42	0.43	0.38
	Austria	0.41	0.39	0.40	0.40	0.42	0.35
	Belgium	0.36	0.34	0.38	0.35	0.38	0.33
	Canada	0.40	0.36	0.40	0.40	0.40	0.34
	Czech Republic	0.42	0.36	0.40	0.44	0.43	0.36
	Denmark	0.43	0.41	0.42	0.44	0.44	0.37
	Finland	0.48	0.44	0.48	0.48	0.50	0.43
	France	0.35	0.30	0.34	0.35	0.36	0.28
	Germany	0.41	0.38	0.42	0.41	0.43	0.35
	Greece	0.25	0.24	0.25	0.26	0.26	0.23
	Hungary	0.41	0.39	0.41	0.41	0.42	0.37
	Iceland	0.45	0.43	0.45	0.44	0.46	0.40
	Ireland	0.39	0.36	0.38	0.39	0.39	0.35
	Italy	0.30	0.27	0.31	0.31	0.31	0.26
	Japan	0.32	0.29	0.33	0.28	0.33	0.28
	Korea	0.35	0.32	0.36	0.32	0.35	0.32
	Luxembourg	0.25	0.23	0.26	0.26	0.30	0.26
	Mexico	0.24	0.20	0.25	0.23	0.25	0.19
	New Zealand	0.35	0.34	0.36	0.34	0.36	0.33
	Norway	0.45	0.41	0.45	0.44	0.46	0.40
	Poland	0.28	0.24	0.28	0.29	0.29	0.24
	Portugal	0.32	0.29	0.31	0.34	0.33	0.28
	Spain	0.38	0.35	0.38	0.37	0.38	0.34
	Sweden	0.45	0.43	0.44	0.44	0.47	0.39
	Switzerland	0.46	0.42	0.46	0.44	0.47	0.40
	United Kingdom	0.37	0.35	0.36	0.37	0.38	0.33
	United States	0.31	0.27	0.32	0.31	0.33	0.26
	OECD median	*0.38*	*0.35*	*0.38*	*0.37*	*0.38*	*0.34*
NON-OECD COUNTRIES	Brazil	0.26	0.20	0.26	0.27	0.27	0.20
	Latvia	0.29	0.24	0.30	0.28	0.30	0.23
	Liechtenstein	0.45	0.41	0.46	0.43	0.46	0.41
	Russian Federation	0.23	0.20	0.23	0.23	0.24	0.18
	Netherlands[1]	0.38	0.34	0.39	0.37	0.40	0.31

Regression of reading literacy performance on engagement in reading[2]

		Combined reading literacy	Retrieving information	Interpreting texts	Reflection and evaluation	Continuous texts	Non-continuous texts
OECD COUNTRIES	Australia	42.52	42.76	43.65	41.72	44.73	39.59
	Austria	36.76	36.23	36.44	38.51	38.45	33.64
	Belgium	35.83	37.06	37.36	36.75	37.58	34.26
	Canada	35.14	34.36	35.85	35.40	36.86	31.65
	Czech Republic	38.10	37.18	37.36	42.89	38.48	37.99
	Denmark	40.99	41.64	40.66	43.91	42.27	39.09
	Finland	42.48	43.60	45.51	43.07	43.67	40.62
	France	31.18	30.27	31.14	33.18	32.85	26.96
	Germany	37.57	35.91	38.56	41.41	40.41	33.13
	Greece	33.31	34.62	29.86	40.26	34.63	32.35
	Hungary	43.71	46.79	41.12	46.44	43.20	45.45
	Iceland	42.11	44.52	43.06	41.08	43.70	39.75
	Ireland	35.18	34.83	36.12	33.29	35.67	33.36
	Italy	28.54	29.18	27.39	32.10	29.17	27.12
	Japan	26.87	27.33	27.00	27.65	27.75	26.73
	Korea	24.96	26.80	25.19	24.64	24.32	25.87
	Luxembourg	22.02	21.98	22.67	25.90	28.86	26.57
	Mexico	26.93	26.77	25.00	32.36	28.48	23.57
	New Zealand	39.75	40.24	41.15	37.61	40.81	37.20
	Norway	47.25	46.32	48.06	48.20	48.56	46.41
	Poland	30.84	29.78	30.97	35.39	33.06	28.44
	Portugal	35.14	35.82	32.90	38.92	36.59	32.59
	Spain	32.38	32.82	31.95	34.09	32.16	32.78
	Sweden	41.53	44.59	42.30	41.70	43.74	38.70
	Switzerland	41.23	41.78	41.61	44.34	43.23	38.66
	United Kingdom	37.95	36.67	37.88	37.55	39.89	33.57
	United States	29.32	27.43	30.87	29.52	31.43	25.77
	OECD median	*35.83*	*35.91*	*36.44*	*37.61*	*37.58*	*33.36*
NON-OECD COUNTRIES	Brazil	23.76	20.44	23.05	26.43	24.95	20.08
	Latvia	36.19	34.85	35.60	38.90	38.89	31.40
	Liechtenstein	43.81	44.59	43.84	47.42	45.40	41.01
	Russian Federation	24.82	24.83	25.06	26.39	26.20	21.30
	Netherlands[1]	34.09	34.85	36.75	31.61	36.34	28.43

1. Response rate is too low to ensure comparability.

2. The numbers in the table represent change in the reading literacy performance per unit of change in the reading engagement index.

© OECD 2002

Table 6.3
Correlation between student home background and reading engagement and performance on the combined reading literacy scale

	Socio-economic background				Books in the home				Home educational resources			
	Performance	S.E.	Reading engagement	S.E.	Performance	S.E.	Reading engagement	S.E.	Performance	S.E.	Reading engagement	S.E.
OECD COUNTRIES												
Australia	0.32	(0.02)	0.17	(0.02)	0.29	(0.02)	0.30	(0.02)	0.23	(0.02)	0.23	(0.02)
Austria	0.33	(0.02)	0.18	(0.02)	0.40	(0.02)	0.34	(0.02)	0.20	(0.02)	0.14	(0.02)
Belgium	0.37	(0.02)	0.18	(0.01)	0.34	(0.02)	0.33	(0.02)	0.33	(0.03)	0.16	(0.01)
Canada	0.27	(0.01)	0.13	(0.01)	0.28	(0.01)	0.30	(0.01)	0.18	(0.01)	0.17	(0.01)
Czech Republic	0.39	(0.02)	0.18	(0.01)	0.42	(0.02)	0.32	(0.02)	0.31	(0.02)	0.18	(0.01)
Denmark	0.31	(0.02)	0.15	(0.02)	0.35	(0.02)	0.31	(0.02)	0.22	(0.02)	0.19	(0.01)
Finland	0.24	(0.02)	0.11	(0.01)	0.26	(0.02)	0.30	(0.02)	0.14	(0.02)	0.16	(0.02)
France	0.36	(0.02)	0.16	(0.02)	0.40	(0.02)	0.36	(0.01)	0.28	(0.02)	0.16	(0.02)
Germany	0.40	(0.02)	0.22	(0.02)	0.46	(0.02)	0.38	(0.01)	0.28	(0.05)	0.12	(0.02)
Greece	0.32	(0.03)	0.14	(0.02)	0.30	(0.03)	0.25	(0.02)	0.26	(0.02)	0.16	(0.02)
Hungary	0.41	(0.02)	0.18	(0.02)	0.52	(0.02)	0.35	(0.02)	0.31	(0.03)	0.19	(0.02)
Iceland	0.22	(0.02)	0.11	(0.02)	0.27	(0.02)	0.29	(0.02)	0.11	(0.02)	0.15	(0.02)
Ireland	0.31	(0.02)	0.13	(0.02)	0.33	(0.02)	0.32	(0.01)	0.26	(0.02)	0.20	(0.01)
Italy	0.28	(0.02)	0.15	(0.01)	0.29	(0.02)	0.28	(0.01)	0.17	(0.03)	0.13	(0.01)
Japan[1]	m	m	m	m	0.23	(0.02)	0.33	(0.01)	0.20	(0.03)	0.09	(0.02)
Korea	0.19	(0.03)	0.17	(0.02)	0.33	(0.02)	0.31	(0.02)	0.18	(0.02)	0.20	(0.02)
Luxembourg	0.40	(0.02)	0.11	(0.02)	0.43	(0.02)	0.27	(0.02)	0.34	(0.02)	0.08	(0.02)
Mexico	0.39	(0.03)	0.12	(0.02)	0.37	(0.03)	0.18	(0.02)	0.37	(0.02)	0.18	(0.02)
New Zealand	0.31	(0.02)	0.13	(0.02)	0.36	(0.02)	0.29	(0.02)	0.31	(0.02)	0.20	(0.02)
Norway	0.28	(0.02)	0.14	(0.02)	0.32	(0.02)	0.31	(0.02)	0.31	(0.01)	0.23	(0.01)
Poland	0.35	(0.02)	0.12	(0.02)	0.34	(0.02)	0.25	(0.02)	0.29	(0.02)	0.14	(0.02)
Portugal	0.39	(0.02)	0.16	(0.02)	0.39	(0.02)	0.28	(0.02)	0.28	(0.02)	0.19	(0.02)
Spain	0.32	(0.02)	0.18	(0.02)	0.39	(0.02)	0.31	(0.02)	0.21	(0.02)	0.16	(0.02)
Sweden	0.30	(0.02)	0.13	(0.02)	0.35	(0.02)	0.33	(0.01)	0.15	(0.02)	0.14	(0.02)
Switzerland	0.40	(0.02)	0.23	(0.02)	0.43	(0.02)	0.39	(0.02)	0.24	(0.02)	0.16	(0.02)
United Kingdom	0.38	(0.01)	0.14	(0.02)	0.39	(0.01)	0.35	(0.01)	0.25	(0.02)	0.24	(0.02)
United States	0.34	(0.02)	0.12	(0.02)	0.42	(0.02)	0.33	(0.02)	0.33	(0.03)	0.18	(0.02)
OECD median	*0.33*	*~*	*0.15*	*~*	*0.35*	*~*	*0.31*	*~*	*0.26*	*~*	*0.16*	*(0.02)*
SD of correlation	*0.08*	*~*	*0.04*	*~*	*0.07*	*~*	*0.04*	*~*	*0.07*	*~*	*0.04*	*(0.00)*
NON-OECD COUNTRIES												
Brazil	0.32	(0.02)	0.10	(0.02)	0.26	(0.02)	0.23	(0.02)	0.33	(0.02)	0.22	(0.02)
Latvia	0.24	(0.02)	0.07	(0.02)	0.29	(0.02)	0.16	(0.04)	0.19	(0.03)	0.07	(0.02)
Liechtenstein	0.33	(0.05)	0.20	(0.05)	0.33	(0.06)	0.30	(0.05)	0.27	(0.05)	0.26	(0.04)
Russian Federation	0.30	(0.02)	0.08	(0.02)	0.34	(0.02)	0.17	(0.02)	0.24	(0.02)	0.12	(0.02)
Netherlands[2]	0.34	(0.03)	0.19	(0.02)	0.36	(0.03)	0.34	(0.03)	0.29	(0.03)	0.17	(0.03)

	Cultural communication				Family structure				Immigration status			
	Performance	S.E.	Reading engagement	S.E.	Performance	S.E.	Reading engagement	S.E.	Performance	S.E.	Reading engagement	S.E.
OECD COUNTRIES												
Australia	0.27	(0.02)	0.38	(0.01)	0.10	(0.02)	0.05	(0.02)	-0.05	(0.03)	0.07	(0.02)
Austria	0.26	(0.02)	0.35	(0.01)	0.06	(0.02)	0.03	(0.02)	-0.23	(0.02)	-0.01	(0.01)
Belgium	0.34	(0.02)	0.32	(0.02)	0.13	(0.02)	0.07	(0.01)	-0.13	(0.02)	-0.02	(0.01)
Canada	0.26	(0.01)	0.33	(0.01)	0.10	(0.01)	0.03	(0.01)	-0.08	(0.02)	0.05	(0.01)
Czech Republic	0.27	(0.02)	0.35	(0.01)	0.04	(0.02)	0.03	(0.01)	-0.02	(0.01)	-0.01	(0.01)
Denmark	0.23	(0.02)	0.38	(0.02)	0.10	(0.02)	0.04	(0.02)	-0.13	(0.02)	0.03	(0.02)
Finland	0.17	(0.02)	0.32	(0.01)	0.13	(0.03)	0.07	(0.02)	-0.09	(0.02)	0.00	(0.02)
France	0.27	(0.02)	0.33	(0.01)	0.10	(0.02)	0.05	(0.01)	-0.11	(0.02)	0.02	(0.02)
Germany	0.30	(0.02)	0.37	(0.01)	0.08	(0.02)	0.09	(0.01)	-0.19	(0.02)	-0.06	(0.02)
Greece	0.09	(0.03)	0.33	(0.01)	0.04	(0.02)	0.03	(0.02)	-0.15	(0.04)	0.01	(0.03)
Hungary	0.26	(0.02)	0.36	(0.02)	0.10	(0.02)	0.06	(0.02)	0.01	(0.02)	0.00	(0.01)
Iceland	0.23	(0.02)	0.30	(0.02)	0.05	(0.02)	0.01	(0.02)	-0.05	(0.02)	-0.03	(0.02)
Ireland	0.16	(0.02)	0.35	(0.02)	0.11	(0.02)	0.02	(0.02)	0.06	(0.01)	0.05	(0.02)
Italy	0.20	(0.02)	0.36	(0.02)	0.07	(0.02)	0.03	(0.02)	-0.04	(0.02)	0.01	(0.02)
Japan	0.20	(0.02)	0.30	(0.02)	0.07	(0.02)	-0.01	(0.02)	-0.02	(0.02)	-0.01	(0.02)
Korea[3]	0.11	(0.02)	0.27	(0.02)	0.09	(0.02)	0.04	(0.02)	m	m	m	m
Luxembourg	0.24	(0.02)	0.33	(0.02)	0.10	(0.02)	0.06	(0.02)	-0.31	(0.02)	0.00	(0.02)
Mexico	0.31	(0.03)	0.31	(0.01)	0.05	(0.02)	-0.03	(0.02)	-0.17	(0.02)	-0.03	(0.01)
New Zealand	0.14	(0.02)	0.36	(0.02)	0.14	(0.02)	0.08	(0.02)	-0.08	(0.02)	0.08	(0.02)
Norway	0.19	(0.02)	0.36	(0.01)	0.13	(0.02)	0.04	(0.02)	-0.10	(0.02)	0.00	(0.02)
Poland	0.23	(0.03)	0.35	(0.02)	0.03	(0.02)	-0.01	(0.02)	-0.04	(0.02)	-0.04	(0.02)
Portugal	0.23	(0.03)	0.35	(0.02)	0.03	(0.02)	0.00	(0.02)	-0.02	(0.02)	0.02	(0.03)
Spain	0.32	(0.02)	0.35	(0.01)	0.08	(0.02)	0.05	(0.02)	-0.05	(0.03)	-0.01	(0.01)
Sweden	0.16	(0.02)	0.34	(0.02)	0.12	(0.02)	0.07	(0.02)	-0.18	(0.02)	-0.04	(0.01)
Switzerland	0.24	(0.03)	0.36	(0.02)	0.05	(0.02)	0.02	(0.02)	-0.32	(0.02)	-0.07	(0.01)
United Kingdom	0.30	(0.02)	0.37	(0.01)	0.14	(0.02)	0.06	(0.02)	-0.10	(0.03)	0.04	(0.01)
United States	0.27	(0.03)	0.37	(0.01)	0.27	(0.02)	0.06	(0.02)	-0.09	(0.02)	0.02	(0.02)
OECD median	*0.24*	*~*	*0.35*	*~*	*0.10*	*~*	*0.04*	*~*	*-0.09*	*~*	*0.00*	*~*
SD of correlation	*0.06*	*~*	*0.03*	*~*	*0.05*	*~*	*0.03*	*~*	*0.09*	*~*	*0.04*	*~*
NON-OECD COUNTRIES												
Brazil	0.24	(0.02)	0.35	(0.02)	0.04	(0.02)	0.00	(0.02)	-0.03	(0.02)	-0.01	(0.02)
Latvia	0.13	(0.03)	0.28	(0.02)	0.07	(0.03)	0.02	(0.02)	-0.01	(0.03)	0.08	(0.02)
Liechtenstein	0.27	(0.06)	0.26	(0.06)	0.15	(0.06)	0.15	(0.06)	-0.29	(0.07)	-0.05	(0.07)
Russian Federation	0.19	(0.02)	0.35	(0.01)	0.04	(0.02)	0.03	(0.01)	-0.01	(0.02)	0.01	(0.02)
Netherlands[2]	0.32	(0.02)	0.33	(0.02)	0.13	(0.03)	0.06	(0.02)	-0.19	(0.04)	-0.01	(0.02)

1. Japan is excluded from the comparison because of a high proportion of missing data.

2. Response rate is too low to ensure comparability.

3. Korea did not collect information on immigration status.

Table 6.4a
Correlation between socio-economic background and reading literacy performance

		Combined reading literacy	Retrieving information	Interpreting texts	Reflection and evaluation	Continuous texts	Non-continuous texts
OECD COUNTRIES	Australia	0.32	0.31	0.32	0.32	0.32	0.31
	Austria	0.33	0.30	0.33	0.34	0.33	0.31
	Belgium	0.37	0.36	0.37	0.36	0.37	0.36
	Canada	0.27	0.26	0.27	0.26	0.26	0.27
	Czech Republic	0.39	0.38	0.38	0.37	0.38	0.38
	Denmark	0.31	0.29	0.29	0.29	0.29	0.29
	Finland	0.24	0.23	0.23	0.23	0.21	0.26
	France	0.36	0.34	0.35	0.33	0.35	0.33
	Germany	0.40	0.39	0.39	0.39	0.39	0.37
	Greece	0.32	0.31	0.32	0.29	0.31	0.32
	Hungary	0.41	0.39	0.40	0.38	0.40	0.38
	Iceland	0.22	0.21	0.21	0.21	0.21	0.21
	Ireland	0.31	0.29	0.32	0.31	0.31	0.30
	Italy	0.28	0.28	0.28	0.27	0.28	0.26
	Japan[1]	m	m	m	m	m	m
	Korea	0.19	0.19	0.21	0.15	0.19	0.18
	Luxembourg	0.40	0.39	0.40	0.38	0.40	0.37
	Mexico	0.39	0.39	0.39	0.31	0.36	0.38
	New Zealand	0.31	0.30	0.30	0.31	0.30	0.32
	Norway	0.28	0.25	0.28	0.28	0.28	0.27
	Poland	0.35	0.34	0.36	0.32	0.35	0.34
	Portugal	0.39	0.37	0.40	0.38	0.38	0.38
	Spain	0.32	0.31	0.32	0.30	0.32	0.31
	Sweden	0.30	0.29	0.28	0.28	0.29	0.29
	Switzerland	0.40	0.38	0.39	0.38	0.39	0.39
	United Kingdom	0.38	0.37	0.38	0.38	0.38	0.38
	United States	0.34	0.33	0.34	0.30	0.33	0.34
	OECD median	*0.33*	*0.31*	*0.33*	*0.31*	*0.32*	*0.32*
NON-OECD COUNTRIES	Brazil	0.32	0.31	0.32	0.29	0.31	0.32
	Latvia	0.24	0.24	0.24	0.24	0.24	0.24
	Liechtenstein	0.33	0.32	0.33	0.32	0.32	0.31
	Russian Federation	0.30	0.28	0.30	0.27	0.30	0.28
	Netherlands[2]	0.34	0.29	0.34	0.34	0.34	0.32

Regression of reading literacy performance on socio-economic background[3]

		Combined reading literacy	Retrieving information	Interpreting texts	Reflection and evaluation	Continuous texts	Non-continuous texts
OECD COUNTRIES	Australia	32.66	33.30	33.34	32.45	33.32	31.99
	Austria	36.28	34.05	36.13	39.80	36.31	36.19
	Belgium	39.39	42.42	38.96	40.43	39.36	40.53
	Canada	26.53	27.23	26.75	25.85	26.04	27.30
	Czech Republic	44.56	49.38	43.20	46.08	42.92	50.48
	Denmark	29.96	30.99	29.15	29.58	29.29	31.33
	Finland	21.48	23.99	22.26	21.27	19.61	25.07
	France	31.72	33.40	31.37	31.58	32.03	31.03
	Germany	46.69	46.39	45.52	50.68	47.77	43.98
	Greece	28.98	31.53	26.94	30.81	28.29	30.45
	Hungary	40.41	44.41	38.32	40.40	38.61	43.38
	Iceland	19.90	21.87	19.80	19.08	19.75	20.69
	Ireland	31.23	31.05	32.95	29.91	31.14	31.66
	Italy	27.19	29.74	24.83	28.88	26.97	27.60
	Japan[1]	m	m	m	m	m	m
	Korea	15.05	17.95	16.52	13.09	14.79	16.62
	Luxembourg	40.39	42.20	40.77	43.38	42.71	41.85
	Mexico	32.74	38.48	29.76	33.63	31.05	36.58
	New Zealand	32.89	33.75	32.99	32.46	31.79	34.17
	Norway	30.66	29.95	31.12	31.91	30.54	32.64
	Poland	36.55	39.78	36.40	36.49	36.83	38.50
	Portugal	39.63	41.48	38.49	39.93	39.00	40.41
	Spain	27.31	29.07	26.64	27.86	26.85	30.44
	Sweden	27.92	31.20	27.73	27.46	27.89	29.31
	Switzerland	41.43	43.49	40.48	43.96	40.98	43.08
	United Kingdom	39.59	39.61	39.98	38.97	40.44	38.97
	United States	34.55	35.71	35.93	31.50	34.58	36.52
	OECD median	*32.70*	*33.57*	*32.97*	*31.98*	*31.91*	*33.40*
NON-OECD COUNTRIES	Brazil	26.88	28.96	26.07	26.27	26.46	30.00
	Latvia	21.94	24.60	20.26	23.65	21.89	22.87
	Liechtenstein	33.68	36.29	32.98	36.76	32.98	32.73
	Russian Federation	27.33	29.38	26.81	25.86	26.99	27.67
	Netherlands[2]	30.87	30.24	32.41	29.61	31.67	29.18

1. Japan is excluded from the comparison because of a high proportion of missing data.

2. Response rate is too low to ensure comparability.

3. The numbers in the table represent change in the reading literacy performance per unit of change in International socio-economic index of occupational status of parents.

Table 6.4b
Correlation between number of books in the home and reading literacy performance

	Combined reading literacy	Retrieving information	Interpreting texts	Reflection and evaluation	Continuous texts	Non-continuous texts
OECD COUNTRIES						
Australia	0.29	0.28	0.29	0.30	0.30	0.28
Austria	0.40	0.37	0.40	0.40	0.40	0.37
Belgium	0.34	0.33	0.35	0.34	0.35	0.33
Canada	0.28	0.26	0.28	0.28	0.27	0.26
Czech Republic	0.42	0.42	0.41	0.40	0.42	0.40
Denmark	0.35	0.33	0.34	0.35	0.35	0.33
Finland	0.26	0.24	0.24	0.25	0.26	0.26
France	0.40	0.38	0.39	0.40	0.40	0.36
Germany	0.46	0.43	0.45	0.46	0.46	0.43
Greece	0.30	0.29	0.29	0.28	0.30	0.29
Hungary	0.52	0.48	0.51	0.48	0.51	0.49
Iceland	0.27	0.25	0.27	0.26	0.27	0.26
Ireland	0.33	0.29	0.33	0.32	0.32	0.31
Italy	0.29	0.27	0.29	0.29	0.28	0.30
Japan	0.23	0.21	0.25	0.20	0.22	0.22
Korea	0.33	0.34	0.33	0.27	0.32	0.33
Luxembourg	0.43	0.42	0.42	0.41	0.41	0.39
Mexico	0.37	0.36	0.37	0.33	0.36	0.35
New Zealand	0.36	0.35	0.36	0.35	0.36	0.35
Norway	0.32	0.28	0.32	0.32	0.31	0.30
Poland	0.34	0.34	0.34	0.32	0.32	0.35
Portugal	0.39	0.37	0.39	0.38	0.38	0.38
Spain	0.39	0.38	0.38	0.36	0.38	0.39
Sweden	0.35	0.33	0.34	0.35	0.36	0.32
Switzerland	0.43	0.40	0.43	0.42	0.43	0.41
United Kingdom	0.39	0.37	0.39	0.39	0.39	0.38
United States	0.42	0.41	0.42	0.40	0.42	0.41
OECD median	*0.35*	*0.34*	*0.35*	*0.35*	*0.36*	*0.35*
NON-OECD COUNTRIES						
Brazil	0.26	0.25	0.26	0.26	0.26	0.26
Latvia	0.29	0.28	0.31	0.26	0.29	0.27
Liechtenstein	0.33	0.31	0.35	0.32	0.32	0.31
Russian Federation	0.34	0.32	0.34	0.32	0.34	0.33
Netherlands[1]	0.36	0.33	0.36	0.37	0.37	0.33

Regression of reading engagement and reading literacy performance on number of books in the home[2]

	Combined reading literacy		Retrieving information	Interpreting texts	Reflection and evaluation	Continuous texts	Non-continuous texts
	Reading engagement	Performance					
OECD COUNTRIES							
Australia	0.20	19.81	19.66	20.24	19.63	20.64	19.40
Austria	0.24	25.24	24.14	25.63	26.81	25.69	24.72
Belgium	0.22	22.17	23.61	22.16	22.97	22.60	22.48
Canada	0.22	17.67	18.04	17.98	17.84	17.86	17.33
Czech Republic	0.23	29.73	32.66	28.75	30.35	28.62	32.81
Denmark	0.20	21.85	22.22	21.31	22.53	21.94	22.73
Finland	0.23	16.90	17.85	17.33	16.90	16.82	17.90
France	0.24	23.46	24.66	23.40	24.95	24.47	22.81
Germany	0.29	33.71	32.63	32.72	37.45	35.03	32.08
Greece	0.12	19.79	21.41	17.94	22.13	20.07	20.47
Hungary	0.21	32.06	34.26	30.63	32.08	30.60	34.86
Iceland	0.21	17.96	18.24	18.23	17.18	17.88	18.57
Ireland	0.22	20.27	19.32	21.12	19.25	19.93	20.87
Italy	0.18	17.52	18.40	16.11	19.37	16.81	19.53
Japan	0.24	13.02	13.23	13.51	13.23	12.66	14.41
Korea	0.22	16.28	19.90	16.08	14.61	15.68	18.96
Luxembourg	0.18	24.31	25.96	24.33	25.95	25.92	25.56
Mexico	0.10	23.55	26.63	21.40	26.24	22.92	25.28
New Zealand	0.19	25.65	27.07	26.71	24.54	25.93	25.14
Norway	0.20	20.83	19.71	21.18	21.70	20.48	21.63
Poland	0.14	19.67	22.04	18.94	20.16	18.99	21.62
Portugal	0.17	25.39	26.84	24.07	26.22	25.31	26.10
Spain	0.21	22.04	23.55	21.36	22.50	21.22	25.04
Sweden	0.22	21.87	23.08	21.80	22.45	22.46	21.88
Switzerland	0.28	28.10	28.84	28.14	30.59	28.55	28.54
United Kingdom	0.22	25.43	25.09	25.84	24.74	25.93	24.25
United States	0.23	27.79	28.70	28.02	26.61	28.02	27.89
OECD median	*0.22*	*22.04*	*23.55*	*21.40*	*22.53*	*22.46*	*22.73*
NON-OECD COUNTRIES							
Brazil	0.18	18.12	19.14	17.69	19.43	18.36	20.07
Latvia	0.11	21.05	23.23	20.57	20.39	21.37	20.71
Liechtenstein	0.24	22.53	23.46	23.22	24.84	22.10	21.58
Russian Federation	0.10	20.61	22.89	20.27	20.59	20.28	21.91
Netherlands[1]	0.21	19.23	20.32	20.33	18.77	20.24	18.22

1. Response rate is too low to ensure comparability.
2. The numbers in the table represent changes in the reading literacy performance per unit of change in the index of the number of books in the home (see Annex A3 for definition).

Table 6.4c
Correlation between home educational resources and reading literacy performance

		Combined reading literacy	Retrieving information	Interpreting texts	Reflection and evaluation	Continuous texts	Non-continuous texts
OECD COUNTRIES	Australia	0.23	0.23	0.22	0.24	0.22	0.24
	Austria	0.20	0.20	0.19	0.19	0.19	0.21
	Belgium	0.33	0.33	0.31	0.35	0.33	0.33
	Canada	0.18	0.18	0.16	0.19	0.17	0.18
	Czech Republic	0.31	0.32	0.30	0.29	0.31	0.32
	Denmark	0.22	0.21	0.21	0.21	0.22	0.22
	Finland	0.14	0.14	0.12	0.14	0.12	0.15
	France	0.28	0.29	0.27	0.26	0.28	0.26
	Germany	0.28	0.29	0.27	0.27	0.27	0.28
	Greece	0.26	0.29	0.25	0.23	0.24	0.27
	Hungary	0.31	0.31	0.30	0.29	0.29	0.31
	Iceland	0.11	0.11	0.10	0.11	0.11	0.10
	Ireland	0.26	0.25	0.25	0.26	0.25	0.26
	Italy	0.17	0.16	0.15	0.18	0.16	0.17
	Japan	0.20	0.19	0.19	0.16	0.19	0.18
	Korea	0.18	0.18	0.18	0.15	0.17	0.18
	Luxembourg	0.34	0.33	0.33	0.34	0.30	0.31
	Mexico	0.37	0.37	0.37	0.30	0.35	0.37
	New Zealand	0.31	0.32	0.30	0.31	0.30	0.34
	Norway	0.31	0.30	0.30	0.31	0.30	0.31
	Poland	0.29	0.30	0.28	0.26	0.27	0.30
	Portugal	0.28	0.28	0.28	0.27	0.28	0.27
	Spain	0.21	0.21	0.21	0.20	0.21	0.20
	Sweden	0.15	0.14	0.12	0.16	0.14	0.15
	Switzerland	0.24	0.23	0.24	0.26	0.24	0.22
	United Kingdom	0.25	0.25	0.24	0.27	0.25	0.25
	United States	0.33	0.33	0.33	0.32	0.33	0.34
	OECD median	*0.26*	*0.25*	*0.25*	*0.26*	*0.25*	*0.26*
NON-OECD COUNTRIES	Brazil	0.33	0.31	0.32	0.32	0.32	0.33
	Latvia	0.19	0.21	0.19	0.17	0.18	0.19
	Liechtenstein	0.27	0.27	0.27	0.25	0.28	0.24
	Russian Federation	0.24	0.24	0.23	0.22	0.23	0.24
	Netherlands[1]	0.29	0.29	0.28	0.28	0.28	0.30

Regression of reading literacy performance on home educational resources[2]

		Combined reading literacy	Retrieving information	Interpreting texts	Reflection and evaluation	Continuous texts	Non-continuous texts
OECD COUNTRIES	Australia	24.07	24.55	22.74	24.42	23.64	25.57
	Austria	23.31	24.04	22.71	24.11	22.29	26.36
	Belgium	38.64	42.81	34.89	43.40	39.04	40.59
	Canada	16.71	18.18	15.50	17.67	16.32	17.63
	Czech Republic	31.69	36.48	30.36	31.26	30.05	37.60
	Denmark	22.49	22.86	22.01	22.73	22.61	24.72
	Finland	12.51	15.20	11.81	12.76	11.29	15.15
	France	28.42	32.91	27.66	28.46	29.83	28.38
	Germany	40.79	42.79	38.46	43.32	40.70	41.79
	Greece	22.91	28.11	20.18	24.08	21.61	25.49
	Hungary	30.84	34.92	28.66	30.80	28.32	35.87
	Iceland	10.67	12.89	9.95	11.23	10.84	10.49
	Ireland	23.44	24.08	23.94	22.78	23.16	25.61
	Italy	18.13	19.78	15.95	21.70	17.37	20.61
	Japan	17.96	20.03	17.36	17.42	17.38	18.75
	Korea	12.54	15.33	12.87	11.72	11.99	14.75
	Luxembourg	36.42	38.78	36.34	41.80	34.47	37.49
	Mexico	24.55	29.02	22.49	25.24	23.51	27.99
	New Zealand	31.68	34.64	31.23	31.02	30.57	34.84
	Norway	33.37	34.40	32.81	35.36	32.59	36.85
	Poland	24.82	29.04	23.67	24.60	23.95	27.55
	Portugal	31.25	33.81	29.91	30.89	31.08	31.46
	Spain	21.15	22.88	20.75	21.14	20.32	22.79
	Sweden	13.80	14.46	12.16	15.68	13.09	15.21
	Switzerland	30.12	31.71	29.60	35.79	31.30	29.94
	United Kingdom	25.63	26.61	24.57	26.47	25.65	25.72
	United States	29.06	30.35	28.92	27.94	28.75	31.01
	OECD median	*24.55*	*28.11*	*23.67*	*24.60*	*23.64*	*26.36*
NON-OECD COUNTRIES	Brazil	21.70	23.19	20.56	22.97	21.38	24.34
	Latvia	18.14	22.28	16.70	18.15	17.49	19.17
	Liechtenstein	30.35	32.97	29.23	31.37	31.50	27.31
	Russian Federation	19.91	23.08	18.75	18.98	18.86	22.25
	Netherlands[1]	33.90	39.01	35.24	31.63	34.16	36.02

1. Response rate is too low to ensure comparability.
2. The numbers in the table represent change in the reading literacy performance per unit of change in the home educational resources index.

Table 6.4d
Correlation between cultural communication at home and reading literacy performance

	Combined reading literacy	Retrieving information	Interpreting texts	Reflection and evaluation	Continuous texts	Non-continuous texts
OECD COUNTRIES						
Australia	0.31	0.28	0.31	0.33	0.32	0.28
Austria	0.26	0.23	0.25	0.28	0.26	0.22
Belgium	0.14	0.11	0.15	0.15	0.15	0.12
Canada	0.22	0.20	0.22	0.23	0.22	0.20
Czech Republic	0.27	0.19	0.22	0.25	0.24	0.21
Denmark	0.34	0.29	0.33	0.37	0.35	0.29
Finland	0.25	0.21	0.24	0.26	0.25	0.24
France	0.23	0.20	0.23	0.24	0.24	0.19
Germany	0.23	0.20	0.22	0.25	0.24	0.19
Greece	0.20	0.18	0.19	0.20	0.20	0.18
Hungary	0.17	0.15	0.17	0.18	0.17	0.15
Iceland	0.21	0.19	0.21	0.23	0.22	0.18
Ireland	0.19	0.15	0.20	0.20	0.20	0.16
Italy	0.19	0.17	0.19	0.22	0.19	0.18
Japan	0.24	0.22	0.22	0.26	0.25	0.20
Korea	0.19	0.16	0.19	0.18	0.20	0.17
Luxembourg	0.17	0.16	0.17	0.18	0.18	0.17
Mexico	0.26	0.24	0.26	0.23	0.25	0.24
New Zealand	0.16	0.13	0.16	0.17	0.16	0.14
Norway	0.29	0.23	0.29	0.30	0.29	0.26
Poland	0.17	0.15	0.16	0.19	0.17	0.14
Portugal	0.35	0.33	0.35	0.35	0.35	0.33
Spain	0.33	0.30	0.32	0.33	0.34	0.30
Sweden	0.25	0.21	0.23	0.29	0.26	0.20
Switzerland	0.24	0.23	0.27	0.27	0.27	0.25
United Kingdom	0.26	0.22	0.26	0.29	0.27	0.23
United States	0.22	0.21	0.22	0.21	0.23	0.20
OECD median	*0.23*	*0.20*	*0.22*	*0.24*	*0.24*	*0.20*
NON-OECD COUNTRIES						
Brazil	0.26	0.22	0.26	0.27	0.26	0.24
Latvia	0.16	0.15	0.16	0.16	0.17	0.14
Liechtenstein	0.22	0.20	0.23	0.23	0.23	0.23
Russian Federation	0.17	0.15	0.16	0.17	0.17	0.14
Netherlands[1]	0.27	0.24	0.28	0.28	0.29	0.22

Regression of reading literacy performance on cultural communication at home[1]

	Combined reading literacy	Retrieving information	Interpreting texts	Reflection and evaluation	Continuous texts	Non-continuous texts
OECD COUNTRIES						
Australia	30.84	29.26	31.10	32.43	32.52	27.90
Austria	24.44	22.35	23.53	28.81	25.33	22.59
Belgium	13.63	12.07	14.49	15.86	14.86	12.63
Canada	22.06	21.36	22.03	22.92	22.73	20.26
Czech Republic	21.76	20.58	20.87	25.06	21.64	22.48
Denmark	33.11	30.25	32.58	37.68	34.27	31.11
Finland	26.20	25.98	27.64	28.12	26.82	26.99
France	22.93	21.87	22.83	24.94	24.47	19.74
Germany	23.70	21.53	22.88	29.23	25.90	20.80
Greece	22.81	23.08	20.06	26.88	23.54	21.34
Hungary	18.21	18.60	16.93	20.35	17.98	18.92
Iceland	19.14	19.16	19.27	20.80	19.67	17.76
Ireland	18.68	15.22	20.21	17.97	19.58	16.84
Italy	18.85	18.15	16.95	23.20	18.52	19.59
Japan	18.40	19.03	16.43	22.65	18.81	17.57
Korea	10.52	10.70	10.38	10.81	10.74	10.87
Luxembourg	16.90	16.61	16.54	19.71	18.91	18.21
Mexico	22.02	24.03	19.87	25.11	21.74	23.69
New Zealand	16.97	15.65	17.44	18.16	17.56	15.95
Norway	29.68	25.47	30.12	32.63	29.93	29.19
Poland	16.17	16.05	15.12	20.71	17.20	14.18
Portugal	34.97	36.42	33.45	36.05	35.29	34.96
Spain	31.79	30.66	30.56	34.65	32.01	32.14
Sweden	23.93	22.52	23.09	28.57	25.53	21.54
Switzerland	27.53	26.71	28.02	30.91	28.23	28.04
United Kingdom	28.24	25.63	29.61	31.16	30.64	24.91
United States	20.66	21.52	21.12	20.60	21.79	19.72
OECD median	*22.06*	*21.53*	*21.12*	*25.06*	*22.73*	*20.80*
NON-OECD COUNTRIES						
Brazil	19.87	18.85	19.16	21.99	20.01	20.67
Latvia	16.78	17.93	15.41	19.11	18.06	16.07
Liechtenstein	21.63	21.46	21.79	25.34	22.45	23.66
Russian Federation	14.30	14.77	13.39	15.42	14.42	13.57
Netherlands[1]	22.00	22.22	23.46	21.07	23.55	18.20

1. Response rate is too low to ensure comparability.
2. The numbers in the table represent change in the reading literacy performance per unit of change in the index of cultural communication at home (see Annex A3 for definition).

Table 6.4e
Correlation between family structure and reading literacy performance

	Combined reading literacy	Retrieving information	Interpreting texts	Reflection and evaluation	Continuous texts	Non-continuous texts
Australia	0.10	0.10	0.10	0.11	0.10	0.10
Austria	0.06	0.07	0.05	0.05	0.05	0.08
Belgium	0.13	0.13	0.13	0.13	0.13	0.14
Canada	0.10	0.10	0.09	0.10	0.09	0.10
Czech Republic	0.04	0.05	0.04	0.03	0.03	0.04
Denmark	0.10	0.09	0.09	0.11	0.09	0.11
Finland	0.13	0.11	0.12	0.15	0.12	0.14
France	0.10	0.11	0.10	0.09	0.10	0.11
Germany	0.08	0.09	0.09	0.08	0.09	0.09
Greece	0.04	0.05	0.03	0.03	0.04	0.03
Hungary	0.10	0.11	0.09	0.10	0.10	0.10
Iceland	0.05	0.06	0.04	0.06	0.04	0.07
Ireland	0.11	0.10	0.10	0.12	0.10	0.12
Italy	0.07	0.08	0.07	0.06	0.06	0.08
Japan	0.07	0.07	0.07	0.05	0.07	0.08
Korea	0.09	0.09	0.07	0.07	0.08	0.09
Luxembourg	0.10	0.10	0.09	0.10	0.10	0.10
Mexico	0.05	0.05	0.03	0.05	0.05	0.04
New Zealand	0.14	0.16	0.14	0.13	0.14	0.16
Norway	0.13	0.14	0.12	0.13	0.12	0.13
Poland	0.03	0.03	0.04	0.02	0.03	0.04
Portugal	0.03	0.04	0.03	0.03	0.04	0.02
Spain	0.08	0.08	0.07	0.07	0.07	0.07
Sweden	0.05	0.06	0.05	0.05	0.05	0.06
Switzerland	0.05	0.06	0.05	0.05	0.05	0.06
United Kingdom	0.14	0.13	0.14	0.14	0.14	0.14
United States	0.27	0.27	0.26	0.26	0.26	0.28
OECD median	*0.10*	*0.09*	*0.09*	*0.09*	*0.09*	*0.10*
Brazil	0.04	0.04	0.04	0.03	0.04	0.05
Latvia	0.07	0.06	0.08	0.05	0.06	0.07
Liechtenstein	0.15	0.18	0.14	0.14	0.15	0.15
Russian Federation	0.04	0.04	0.04	0.02	0.03	0.05
Netherlands[1]	0.13	0.13	0.12	0.13	0.12	0.13

Regression of reading literacy performance on family structure[2]

	Combined reading literacy	Retrieving information	Interpreting texts	Reflection and evaluation	Continuous texts	Non-continuous texts
Australia	22.00	23.37	22.46	24.49	22.13	23.20
Austria	12.70	16.10	11.71	11.61	10.40	18.08
Belgium	33.18	37.41	30.86	36.05	32.24	36.79
Canada	21.14	22.77	19.00	21.25	19.92	22.44
Czech Republic	9.04	12.20	8.26	7.32	7.64	11.38
Denmark	19.95	21.10	18.40	23.59	18.82	24.24
Finland	25.84	24.79	25.97	29.56	24.40	29.57
France	21.45	24.61	20.56	19.36	21.22	24.82
Germany	20.50	23.51	21.48	22.87	22.60	23.53
Greece	10.26	15.93	7.15	10.55	11.36	9.41
Hungary	21.32	26.76	17.84	23.03	20.26	24.89
Iceland	10.32	12.49	7.60	12.22	8.52	14.53
Ireland	26.90	28.06	25.47	28.77	26.42	31.58
Italy	14.32	19.08	13.57	13.56	13.08	17.52
Japan	18.03	20.02	17.71	13.80	16.51	22.14
Korea	18.14	22.74	14.48	16.67	15.87	21.78
Luxembourg	23.29	26.11	21.93	28.08	26.25	27.65
Mexico	8.92	11.72	5.13	12.12	9.27	8.03
New Zealand	32.50	38.47	32.40	29.63	31.44	36.58
Norway	28.73	32.71	27.60	31.91	27.98	32.71
Poland	8.69	11.04	10.05	5.57	8.69	10.87
Portugal	7.25	9.84	7.61	6.82	9.74	5.81
Spain	15.49	17.22	13.31	15.96	14.54	17.33
Sweden	23.74	25.55	23.53	23.62	22.18	26.20
Switzerland	12.47	15.96	10.92	13.44	11.98	15.62
United Kingdom	30.09	28.70	30.01	28.77	30.64	29.02
United States	57.09	59.91	55.34	55.55	54.72	61.50
OECD median	*20.22*	*22.75*	*18.12*	*20.31*	*19.37*	*22.82*
Brazil	6.70	8.45	7.66	5.69	7.53	10.11
Latvia	14.08	15.51	16.23	11.21	13.78	16.58
Liechtenstein	36.02	45.94	32.77	36.87	34.95	36.85
Russian Federation	7.03	9.64	8.86	3.61	6.43	10.81
Netherlands[1]	30.11	34.90	29.00	28.29	29.72	31.45

1. Response rate is too low to ensure comparability.
2. The numbers in the table represent difference in reading literacy performance between students living with two parents or guardians and students living with a single parent or guardian.

Table 6.4f
Correlation of immigration status with reading literacy performance

	Combined reading literacy	Retrieving information	Interpreting texts	Reflection and evaluation	Continuous texts	Non-continuous texts
OECD COUNTRIES						
Australia	-0.05	-0.05	-0.06	-0.03	-0.04	-0.04
Austria	-0.23	-0.22	-0.22	-0.22	-0.22	-0.22
Belgium	-0.13	-0.13	-0.12	-0.13	-0.13	-0.13
Canada	-0.08	-0.08	-0.09	-0.07	-0.08	-0.06
Czech Republic	-0.02	-0.02	-0.02	-0.01	-0.01	-0.02
Denmark	-0.13	-0.11	-0.13	-0.13	-0.13	-0.11
Finland	-0.09	-0.09	-0.08	-0.08	-0.08	-0.11
France	-0.11	-0.12	-0.11	-0.10	-0.11	-0.11
Germany	-0.19	-0.20	-0.19	-0.20	-0.18	-0.19
Greece	-0.15	-0.16	-0.16	-0.13	-0.16	-0.13
Hungary	0.01	0.01	0.00	0.02	0.01	0.01
Iceland	-0.05	-0.06	-0.05	-0.05	-0.06	-0.04
Ireland	0.06	0.06	0.06	0.05	0.05	0.07
Italy	-0.04	-0.05	-0.05	-0.05	-0.05	-0.03
Japan	-0.02	-0.02	-0.01	-0.02	-0.01	-0.01
Korea[1]	m	m	m	m	m	m
Luxembourg	-0.31	-0.30	-0.31	-0.31	-0.27	-0.27
Mexico	-0.17	-0.15	-0.16	-0.15	-0.17	-0.15
New Zealand	-0.08	-0.07	-0.09	-0.05	-0.08	-0.05
Norway	-0.10	-0.10	-0.10	-0.09	-0.10	-0.10
Poland	-0.04	-0.06	-0.05	-0.04	-0.05	-0.03
Portugal	-0.02	-0.03	-0.02	-0.03	-0.02	-0.04
Spain	-0.05	-0.05	-0.04	-0.03	-0.04	-0.05
Sweden	-0.18	-0.19	-0.17	-0.15	-0.17	-0.17
Switzerland	-0.32	-0.33	-0.31	-0.29	-0.30	-0.32
United Kingdom	-0.10	-0.10	-0.10	-0.10	-0.10	-0.10
United States	-0.09	-0.10	-0.09	-0.08	-0.09	-0.10
OECD median	*-0.09*	*-0.10*	*-0.09*	*-0.08*	*-0.09*	*-0.10*
NON-OECD COUNTRIES						
Brazil	-0.03	-0.02	-0.02	-0.01	-0.02	-0.03
Latvia	-0.01	-0.03	0.01	-0.01	0.01	-0.03
Liechtenstein	-0.29	-0.30	-0.28	-0.25	-0.26	-0.27
Russian Federation	-0.01	-0.02	0.00	-0.01	0.00	-0.01
Netherlands[2]	-0.19	-0.21	-0.17	-0.18	-0.18	-0.20

Regression of reading literacy performance on immigration status[3]

	Combined reading literacy	Retrieving information	Interpreting texts	Reflection and evaluation	Continuous texts	Non-continuous texts
OECD COUNTRIES						
Australia	-16.05	-17.61	-18.36	-10.53	-13.87	-14.21
Austria	-89.33	-92.07	-86.28	-91.75	-86.18	-92.03
Belgium	-77.10	-85.84	-68.94	-83.98	-75.71	-83.93
Canada	-25.33	-26.08	-28.93	-21.14	-27.51	-21.02
Czech Republic	-22.86	-26.32	-23.04	-7.71	-16.54	-32.44
Denmark	-66.34	-61.82	-68.95	-68.95	-69.66	-62.06
Finland	-79.95	-98.11	-79.97	-77.18	-75.70	-102.91
France	-70.92	-84.65	-66.34	-65.42	-70.34	-74.53
Germany	-71.89	-78.23	-68.18	-83.44	-68.36	-74.00
Greece	-73.79	-85.45	-71.77	-74.33	-77.15	-64.81
Hungary	6.02	11.52	2.09	13.25	6.44	9.95
Iceland	-65.06	-76.33	-65.89	-64.30	-69.68	-58.37
Ireland	46.89	52.22	53.42	39.36	42.81	57.61
Italy	-42.90	-60.12	-51.50	-52.59	-53.20	-38.11
Japan	-45.92	-47.01	-34.42	-65.93	-37.03	-38.60
Korea[1]	m	m	m	m	m	m
Luxembourg	-84.26	-90.29	-86.19	-95.94	-80.90	-83.66
Mexico	-95.07	-102.96	-82.46	-112.08	-98.95	-97.55
New Zealand	-24.48	-25.70	-28.94	-15.68	-27.46	-17.82
Norway	-59.19	-61.96	-60.19	-57.48	-58.78	-66.51
Poland	-90.99	-137.45	-91.23	-83.44	-106.68	-76.88
Portugal	-20.31	-30.29	-15.83	-29.23	-19.12	-31.79
Spain	-32.82	-40.47	-31.22	-41.01	-28.11	-42.84
Sweden	-69.85	-84.11	-70.43	-60.06	-68.21	-74.27
Switzerland	-103.41	-117.36	-99.66	-104.82	-100.08	-110.23
United Kingdom	-67.92	-67.62	-64.55	-62.28	-68.55	-61.94
United States	-40.54	-46.24	-39.45	-37.28	-39.80	-44.36
OECD median	*-65.70*	*-64.79*	*-65.22*	*-63.29*	*-68.29*	*-62.00*
NON-OECD COUNTRIES						
Brazil	-67.59	-58.26	-55.18	-29.54	-59.30	-72.55
Latvia	-2.42	-8.69	2.77	-1.93	1.80	-9.09
Liechtenstein	-94.85	-108.99	-88.52	-90.25	-86.63	-89.46
Russian Federation	-5.21	-10.21	-2.45	-3.06	-2.53	-7.63
Netherlands[2]	-81.17	-102.80	-79.08	-74.90	-78.08	-87.36

1. Korea did not collect information on student immigration status.

2. Response rate is too low to ensure comparability.

3. The numbers in the table represent difference in reading literacy performance between native students and non-native students.

Table 6.5
Correlation between classroom environment characteristics and reading engagement and performance on the combined reading literacy scale

		Performance press				Disciplinary climate				Sense of belonging				Relationship with teachers			
		Perfor-mance	S.E.	Reading engage-ment	S.E.	Perfor-mance	S.E.	Reading engage-ment	S.E.	Perfor-mance	S.E.	Reading engage-ment	S.E.	Perfor-mance	S.E.	Reading engage-ment	S.E.
OECD COUNTRIES	Australia	-0.09	(0.02)	0.00	(0.02)	0.15	(0.02)	0.16	(0.02)	0.04	(0.02)	-0.01	(0.02)	0.16	(0.02)	0.26	(0.02)
	Austria	-0.08	(0.02)	-0.04	(0.02)	0.06	(0.02)	0.09	(0.02)	0.06	(0.02)	0.00	(0.02)	0.03	(0.02)	0.10	(0.02)
	Belgium	0.02	(0.02)	-0.03	(0.01)	0.03	(0.02)	0.06	(0.02)	0.08	(0.02)	0.08	(0.01)	-0.02	(0.02)	0.11	(0.01)
	Canada	-0.10	(0.01)	-0.02	(0.01)	0.13	(0.01)	0.15	(0.01)	0.04	(0.01)	0.00	(0.01)	0.15	(0.01)	0.20	(0.01)
	Czech Republic	-0.09	(0.02)	-0.06	(0.02)	0.10	(0.02)	0.09	(0.02)	0.13	(0.02)	0.04	(0.02)	0.03	(0.02)	0.14	(0.02)
	Denmark	0.02	(0.02)	0.03	(0.01)	0.08	(0.02)	0.09	(0.02)	0.06	(0.02)	0.00	(0.02)	0.17	(0.02)	0.21	(0.02)
	Finland	-0.15	(0.02)	-0.13	(0.02)	0.10	(0.02)	0.15	(0.02)	-0.03	(0.02)	0.00	(0.02)	0.12	(0.03)	0.17	(0.02)
	France	-0.06	(0.02)	-0.06	(0.02)	0.02	(0.02)	0.07	(0.02)	0.06	(0.02)	0.08	(0.02)	-0.02	(0.02)	0.12	(0.02)
	Germany	-0.11	(0.02)	-0.08	(0.02)	0.10	(0.02)	0.14	(0.02)	0.08	(0.02)	0.00	(0.02)	0.03	(0.02)	0.14	(0.02)
	Greece	0.12	(0.03)	0.08	(0.02)	0.03	(0.03)	0.10	(0.02)	0.11	(0.02)	0.18	(0.02)	-0.02	(0.03)	0.16	(0.02)
	Hungary	-0.02	(0.02)	0.00	(0.02)	0.17	(0.04)	0.17	(0.03)	0.18	(0.02)	0.15	(0.02)	-0.10	(0.03)	0.15	(0.02)
	Iceland	-0.14	(0.02)	-0.03	(0.02)	0.09	(0.02)	0.09	(0.02)	0.03	(0.02)	0.02	(0.02)	0.19	(0.02)	0.19	(0.02)
	Ireland	-0.07	(0.02)	-0.01	(0.02)	0.19	(0.02)	0.16	(0.02)	0.00	(0.02)	0.03	(0.02)	0.12	(0.02)	0.24	(0.01)
	Italy	-0.06	(0.02)	-0.04	(0.01)	0.15	(0.02)	0.21	(0.02)	-0.01	(0.02)	0.07	(0.02)	-0.05	(0.02)	0.12	(0.02)
	Japan	0.05	(0.03)	0.05	(0.02)	0.22	(0.04)	0.08	(0.02)	0.09	(0.02)	0.03	(0.02)	0.20	(0.02)	0.14	(0.02)
	Korea	0.19	(0.02)	0.12	(0.02)	0.10	(0.02)	0.10	(0.02)	0.11	(0.02)	0.11	(0.02)	0.09	(0.02)	0.14	(0.01)
	Luxembourg	0.02	(0.02)	0.00	(0.02)	0.03	(0.02)	0.07	(0.02)	0.20	(0.02)	0.06	(0.02)	-0.04	(0.02)	0.17	(0.02)
	Mexico	0.00	(0.02)	0.13	(0.02)	0.02	(0.03)	0.08	(0.02)	0.24	(0.02)	0.22	(0.02)	0.03	(0.02)	0.18	(0.02)
	New Zealand	-0.15	(0.02)	-0.01	(0.02)	0.11	(0.02)	0.17	(0.02)	0.05	(0.02)	0.04	(0.02)	0.12	(0.02)	0.22	(0.02)
	Norway	-0.11	(0.02)	-0.05	(0.02)	0.06	(0.02)	0.09	(0.02)	0.07	(0.02)	0.04	(0.02)	0.18	(0.02)	0.20	(0.02)
	Poland	0.03	(0.03)	-0.01	(0.02)	0.23	(0.03)	0.18	(0.02)	0.19	(0.02)	0.15	(0.02)	0.04	(0.02)	0.22	(0.02)
	Portugal	-0.05	(0.02)	0.06	(0.02)	0.09	(0.02)	0.10	(0.02)	0.27	(0.02)	0.19	(0.02)	-0.06	(0.03)	0.15	(0.02)
	Spain	0.03	(0.02)	0.05	(0.02)	0.14	(0.02)	0.10	(0.02)	0.06	(0.02)	0.06	(0.02)	0.08	(0.02)	0.12	(0.02)
	Sweden	-0.15	(0.02)	-0.08	(0.02)	0.12	(0.02)	0.10	(0.02)	-0.02	(0.02)	-0.03	(0.02)	0.13	(0.02)	0.18	(0.02)
	Switzerland	-0.04	(0.03)	-0.07	(0.02)	0.15	(0.02)	0.12	(0.02)	0.16	(0.02)	0.14	(0.02)	0.05	(0.02)	0.16	(0.02)
	United Kingdom	-0.11	(0.02)	-0.03	(0.01)	0.21	(0.02)	0.19	(0.02)	0.06	(0.02)	0.04	(0.02)	0.17	(0.02)	0.22	(0.02)
	United States	-0.02	(0.02)	0.10	(0.02)	0.13	(0.02)	0.12	(0.02)	0.14	(0.03)	0.05	(0.02)	0.19	(0.02)	0.24	(0.03)
	OECD median	*-0.06*	*~*	*-0.01*	*~*	*0.10*	*~*	*0.10*	*~*	*0.07*	*~*	*0.04*	*~*	*0.08*	*~*	*0.17*	*~*
	SD of correlation	*0.08*	*~*	*0.06*	*~*	*-0.06*	*~*	*-0.04*	*~*	*0.08*	*~*	*0.07*	*~*	*0.09*	*~*	*0.04*	*~*
NON-OECD COUNTRIES	Brazil	0.10	(0.02)	0.15	(0.02)	-0.06	(0.02)	0.10	(0.03)	0.15	(0.02)	0.21	(0.02)	-0.03	(0.03)	0.20	(0.02)
	Latvia	0.02	(0.03)	0.02	(0.02)	0.09	(0.02)	0.09	(0.03)	0.13	(0.02)	0.08	(0.03)	0.08	(0.03)	0.16	(0.03)
	Liechtenstein	-0.12	(0.05)	0.02	(0.06)	-0.03	(0.06)	-0.02	(0.06)	0.16	(0.05)	0.04	(0.05)	-0.01	(0.05)	0.17	(0.06)
	Russian Federation	-0.06	(0.02)	0.03	(0.02)	0.11	(0.02)	0.18	(0.02)	0.13	(0.02)	0.16	(0.02)	0.03	(0.02)	0.22	(0.01)
	Netherlands[1]	-0.10	(0.02)	-0.03	(0.02)	0.03	(0.04)	0.07	(0.02)	0.13	(0.03)	0.04	(0.02)	0.07	(0.03)	0.14	(0.02)

1. Response rate is too low to ensure comparability.

Table 6.6a
Correlation between achievement press and reading literacy performance

	Combined reading literacy	Retrieving information	Interpreting texts	Reflection and evaluation	Continuous texts	Non-continuous texts
OECD COUNTRIES						
Australia	-0.09	-0.11	-0.10	-0.07	-0.09	-0.09
Austria	-0.08	-0.10	-0.08	-0.05	-0.08	-0.08
Belgium	0.02	0.01	0.01	0.05	0.03	0.01
Canada	-0.10	-0.09	-0.10	-0.08	-0.09	-0.09
Czech Republic	-0.04	-0.04	-0.03	-0.04	-0.04	-0.03
Denmark	0.02	0.02	0.02	0.04	0.04	0.01
Finland	-0.15	-0.14	-0.14	-0.15	-0.15	-0.13
France	-0.06	-0.04	-0.06	-0.07	-0.07	-0.06
Germany	-0.11	-0.10	-0.12	-0.09	-0.11	-0.10
Greece	0.12	0.11	0.12	0.13	0.13	0.11
Hungary	-0.02	-0.03	-0.03	-0.01	-0.02	-0.03
Iceland	-0.14	-0.14	-0.13	-0.14	-0.14	-0.13
Ireland	-0.07	-0.07	-0.07	-0.07	-0.07	-0.07
Italy	-0.06	-0.06	-0.07	-0.04	-0.06	-0.06
Japan	0.05	0.03	0.05	0.08	0.05	0.05
Korea	0.19	0.17	0.19	0.17	0.18	0.18
Luxembourg	0.02	0.01	0.03	0.01	0.02	0.03
Mexico	0.00	-0.01	-0.01	0.02	0.00	0.00
New Zealand	-0.15	-0.14	-0.14	-0.15	-0.14	-0.16
Norway	-0.11	-0.08	-0.10	-0.12	-0.10	-0.08
Poland	0.03	0.04	0.02	0.08	0.04	0.04
Portugal	-0.05	-0.05	-0.04	-0.05	-0.05	-0.05
Spain	0.03	0.02	0.02	0.02	0.02	0.02
Sweden	-0.15	-0.16	-0.15	-0.14	-0.15	-0.14
Switzerland	-0.09	-0.09	-0.09	-0.09	-0.10	-0.09
United Kingdom	-0.11	-0.11	-0.11	-0.09	-0.09	-0.12
United States	-0.02	-0.01	-0.01	-0.01	-0.01	-0.01
OECD median	*-0.06*	*-0.05*	*-0.05*	*-0.05*	*-0.05*	*-0.05*
NON-OECD COUNTRIES						
Brazil	0.10	0.07	0.11	0.10	0.09	0.10
Latvia	0.02	0.01	0.02	0.03	0.02	0.01
Liechtenstein	-0.12	-0.09	-0.11	-0.08	-0.11	-0.07
Russian Federation	-0.06	-0.05	-0.06	-0.05	-0.05	-0.07
Netherlands[1]	-0.10	-0.11	-0.10	-0.09	-0.10	-0.12

Regression of reading literacy performance on achievement press[2]

	Combined reading literacy	Retrieving information	Interpreting texts	Reflection and evaluation	Continuous texts	Non-continuous texts
OECD COUNTRIES						
Australia	-10.06	-13.27	-11.40	-7.72	-10.64	-10.66
Austria	-6.39	-8.25	-6.37	-4.52	-6.44	-7.28
Belgium	1.95	1.58	0.89	5.31	3.23	1.24
Canada	-9.71	-9.64	-10.33	-8.63	-9.40	-9.94
Czech Republic	-3.41	-3.40	-2.71	-3.78	-3.22	-3.23
Denmark	2.97	3.01	2.49	5.05	4.85	0.84
Finland	-14.69	-16.24	-15.43	-15.16	-15.01	-13.68
France	-5.84	-4.46	-5.88	-6.92	-6.60	-5.55
Germany	-11.07	-10.03	-12.43	-10.60	-11.24	-10.55
Greece	11.73	11.25	10.66	14.91	12.58	11.22
Hungary	-2.31	-3.69	-2.55	-0.58	-1.55	-3.08
Iceland	-13.21	-14.93	-12.62	-13.64	-13.49	-13.05
Ireland	-7.32	-7.50	-7.16	-6.43	-7.40	-7.82
Italy	-6.31	-7.72	-6.77	-4.47	-6.06	-7.01
Japan	4.36	2.80	3.64	7.82	4.36	4.30
Korea	13.27	14.24	13.02	13.24	12.37	14.43
Luxembourg	1.48	1.28	2.30	1.18	1.47	2.83
Mexico	-0.37	-1.24	-0.29	1.73	0.04	-0.41
New Zealand	-18.04	-18.09	-17.73	-17.51	-16.89	-19.45
Norway	-11.93	-9.21	-11.74	-13.95	-11.77	-10.41
Poland	3.37	4.57	1.89	8.25	3.83	4.08
Portugal	-5.10	-5.03	-4.04	-5.15	-5.03	-4.94
Spain	2.04	1.88	1.52	1.66	1.43	2.08
Sweden	-9.58	-10.66	-8.76	-10.13	-10.15	-9.40
Switzerland	-3.41	-3.40	-2.71	-3.78	-3.22	-14.64
United Kingdom	-12.88	-13.79	-13.13	-11.07	-11.72	-1.45
United States	-1.51	-0.91	-1.39	-1.11	-1.11	-1.45
OECD median	*-5.84*	*-5.03*	*-5.88*	*-4.52*	*-6.06*	*-5.55*
NON-OECD COUNTRIES						
Brazil	8.02	6.47	8.56	8.59	7.58	8.92
Latvia	1.55	0.60	2.05	3.48	2.34	1.04
Liechtenstein	-12.31	-10.75	-11.15	-9.89	-11.33	-7.09
Russian Federation	-4.99	-5.04	-5.42	-4.33	-4.49	-6.27
Netherlands[1]	-10.38	-12.40	-10.21	-8.54	-9.86	-11.66

1. Response rate is too low to ensure comparability.
2. The numbers in the table represent change in the reading literacy performance per unit of change in the index of achievement press (see Annex A3 for definition).

Table 6.6b
Correlation between disciplinary climate and reading literacy performance

		Combined reading literacy	Retrieving information	Interpreting texts	Reflection and evaluation	Continuous texts	Non-continuous texts
OECD COUNTRIES	Australia	0.15	0.14	0.16	0.16	0.16	0.14
	Austria	0.06	0.07	0.04	0.06	0.05	0.06
	Belgium	0.03	0.03	0.03	0.02	0.03	0.03
	Canada	0.13	0.12	0.13	0.14	0.13	0.11
	Czech Republic	0.15	0.12	0.15	0.15	0.15	0.13
	Denmark	0.08	0.07	0.07	0.10	0.08	0.07
	Finland	0.10	0.09	0.09	0.10	0.09	0.09
	France	0.02	0.01	0.01	0.03	0.02	0.01
	Germany	0.10	0.09	0.11	0.09	0.11	0.08
	Greece	0.03	0.00	0.02	0.04	0.02	0.02
	Hungary	0.17	0.16	0.17	0.18	0.18	0.15
	Iceland	0.09	0.09	0.07	0.11	0.10	0.06
	Ireland	0.19	0.18	0.18	0.21	0.20	0.16
	Italy	0.15	0.13	0.14	0.16	0.16	0.12
	Japan	0.22	0.19	0.22	0.19	0.22	0.20
	Korea	0.10	0.08	0.09	0.12	0.11	0.09
	Luxembourg	0.03	0.03	0.02	0.03	0.04	0.01
	Mexico	0.02	0.02	0.02	0.01	0.02	0.02
	New Zealand	0.11	0.10	0.11	0.12	0.11	0.11
	Norway	0.06	0.04	0.05	0.09	0.07	0.05
	Poland	0.23	0.20	0.23	0.23	0.23	0.21
	Portugal	0.09	0.09	0.09	0.10	0.09	0.08
	Spain	0.14	0.13	0.14	0.14	0.15	0.13
	Sweden	0.12	0.09	0.10	0.14	0.11	0.11
	Switzerland	0.10	0.08	0.09	0.10	0.11	0.07
	United Kingdom	0.21	0.19	0.21	0.22	0.21	0.18
	United States	0.13	0.11	0.14	0.14	0.13	0.12
	OECD median	*0.10*	*0.09*	*0.10*	*0.12*	*0.11*	*0.09*
NON-OECD COUNTRIES	Brazil	-0.06	-0.06	-0.06	-0.03	-0.05	-0.05
	Latvia	0.09	0.07	0.08	0.08	0.08	0.08
	Liechtenstein	-0.03	-0.05	-0.03	-0.02	-0.02	-0.04
	Russian Federation	0.11	0.10	0.11	0.11	0.11	0.11
	Netherlands[1]	0.03	0.03	0.02	0.01	0.03	0.04

Regression of reading literacy performance on disciplinary climate[2]

		Combined reading literacy	Retrieving information	Interpreting texts	Reflection and evaluation	Continuous texts	Non-continuous texts
OECD COUNTRIES	Australia	16.69	16.08	17.31	17.58	18.15	15.03
	Austria	4.98	6.32	3.69	5.21	4.21	5.15
	Belgium	3.15	3.49	3.26	2.22	2.77	3.39
	Canada	13.28	13.21	13.36	14.36	13.62	11.86
	Czech Republic	12.37	11.61	12.84	13.26	12.52	12.75
	Denmark	9.71	8.87	9.02	12.65	9.87	10.25
	Finland	9.56	9.76	9.07	10.30	9.24	8.97
	France	1.53	0.94	1.21	2.31	1.94	0.52
	Germany	10.13	9.51	10.66	10.13	11.15	8.01
	Greece	2.96	0.47	1.95	5.61	2.25	2.26
	Hungary	16.05	16.89	15.19	18.21	16.40	16.39
	Iceland	8.90	10.31	7.59	11.26	10.14	7.21
	Ireland	15.41	15.42	15.17	16.26	16.27	14.24
	Italy	14.11	14.23	12.72	17.07	14.44	12.08
	Japan	17.15	16.99	16.8	17.77	17.04	18.14
	Korea	6.88	6.63	5.98	9.09	7.56	7.29
	Luxembourg	2.41	2.53	2.05	3.03	4.04	0.72
	Mexico	2.03	2.54	1.71	1.66	1.88	2.57
	New Zealand	12.47	11.58	12.41	13.33	13.07	12.26
	Norway	7.79	5.07	6.72	11.97	8.14	7.53
	Poland	20.88	20.74	20.69	23.34	21.7	21.0
	Portugal	10.57	11.13	9.83	12.07	11.13	10.22
	Spain	12.18	12.07	11.78	13.28	12.38	12.58
	Sweden	12.44	11.12	10.72	15.94	11.75	12.81
	Switzerland	9.81	9.09	9.06	11.60	10.78	7.83
	United Kingdom	20.10	19.47	20.34	21.34	20.85	17.61
	United States	13.17	11.36	13.92	14.21	13.22	11.68
	OECD median	*10.57*	*11.12*	*10.66*	*12.65*	*11.15*	*10.25*
NON-OECD COUNTRIES	Brazil	-5.95	-7.30	-5.81	-3.06	-5.69	-6.22
	Latvia	9.04	8.61	8.12	8.64	8.48	8.75
	Liechtenstein	-2.59	-5.80	-3.38	-2.06	-2.12	-3.82
	Russian Federation	10.06	10.47	9.31	10.36	9.72	10.25
	Netherlands[1]	2.63	3.70	1.68	1.27	2.78	3.53

1. Response rate is too low to ensure comparability.
2. The numbers in the table represent change in the reading literacy performance per unit of change in the index of disciplinary climate (see Annex A3 for definition).

Table 6.6c
Correlation between sense of belonging and reading literacy performance

	Combined reading literacy	Retrieving information	Interpreting texts	Reflection and evaluation	Continuous texts	Non-continuous texts
Austria	0.06	0.08	0.05	0.06	0.04	0.08
Belgium	0.08	0.08	0.07	0.09	0.08	0.08
Canada	0.04	0.04	0.03	0.06	0.04	0.04
Czech Republic	0.16	0.15	0.14	0.16	0.15	0.15
Denmark	0.06	0.06	0.06	0.08	0.06	0.06
Finland	-0.03	-0.02	-0.05	-0.01	-0.04	-0.01
France	0.06	0.06	0.05	0.06	0.06	0.07
Germany	0.08	0.08	0.08	0.08	0.08	0.07
Greece	0.11	0.10	0.11	0.12	0.11	0.11
Hungary	0.18	0.17	0.16	0.18	0.17	0.18
Iceland	0.03	0.04	0.03	0.02	0.02	0.04
Ireland	0.00	0.00	-0.01	0.01	-0.01	0.00
Italy	-0.01	-0.02	-0.02	0.01	-0.01	-0.01
Japan	0.09	0.08	0.07	0.10	0.08	0.09
Korea	0.11	0.11	0.12	0.10	0.10	0.12
Luxembourg	0.20	0.19	0.21	0.19	0.20	0.19
Mexico	0.24	0.22	0.22	0.23	0.23	0.22
New Zealand	0.05	0.06	0.03	0.06	0.05	0.06
Norway	0.07	0.05	0.06	0.09	0.07	0.07
Poland	0.19	0.20	0.18	0.16	0.18	0.18
Portugal	0.27	0.28	0.26	0.26	0.26	0.27
Spain	0.06	0.06	0.05	0.06	0.06	0.05
Sweden	-0.02	-0.03	-0.03	0.00	-0.02	-0.01
Switzerland	0.13	0.13	0.12	0.14	0.13	0.12
United Kingdom	0.06	0.07	0.05	0.08	0.06	0.06
United States	0.14	0.14	0.12	0.14	0.12	0.14
OECD median	*0.07*	*0.08*	*0.06*	*0.08*	*0.07*	*0.07*
Brazil	0.15	0.16	0.14	0.15	0.14	0.14
Latvia	0.13	0.12	0.13	0.13	0.13	0.13
Liechtenstein	0.16	0.15	0.15	0.15	0.15	0.17
Russian Federation	0.13	0.11	0.12	0.14	0.13	0.11
Netherlands[1]	0.13	0.12	0.13	0.13	0.13	0.13

Regression of reading literacy performance on sense of belonging[2]

	Combined reading literacy	Retrieving information	Interpreting texts	Reflection and evaluation	Continuous texts	Non-continuous texts
Austria	5.10	6.55	3.86	5.20	3.75	7.09
Belgium	9.83	11.00	8.24	11.51	9.46	10.34
Canada	3.27	3.64	2.44	4.85	3.28	3.39
Czech Republic	19.28	20.67	17.57	21.09	18.22	21.10
Denmark	5.79	5.92	5.21	7.72	5.71	6.53
Finland	-2.54	-2.24	-4.87	-1.26	-3.41	-1.33
France	5.70	6.45	5.04	6.58	5.63	6.87
Germany	8.33	8.36	7.75	9.33	8.60	7.64
Greece	11.15	11.32	10.14	14.48	11.46	11.73
Hungary	16.82	18.83	15.01	18.70	16.02	19.53
Iceland	2.06	3.81	2.14	1.76	1.68	3.38
Ireland	-0.21	0.28	-1.15	1.21	-0.62	0.22
Italy	-0.74	-1.96	-1.42	1.57	-0.47	-1.31
Japan	8.35	9.07	6.36	11.04	7.24	10.01
Korea	9.42	11.01	10.07	8.91	8.55	12.37
Luxembourg	16.64	17.49	18.10	18.26	19.34	18.81
Mexico	20.75	22.95	17.69	25.44	20.39	22.14
New Zealand	5.58	7.28	3.54	6.50	5.16	7.03
Norway	6.58	4.74	5.91	9.46	6.55	7.31
Poland	21.44	25.28	20.37	20.04	21.17	22.88
Portugal	29.41	33.23	26.85	29.85	28.90	30.61
Spain	5.37	5.67	4.26	6.06	5.05	5.52
Sweden	-2.09	-2.59	-3.00	-0.06	-2.07	-1.15
Switzerland	12.31	13.51	11.19	14.82	12.20	12.17
United Kingdom	6.26	7.09	4.86	7.63	6.21	6.11
United States	12.83	13.82	11.11	12.99	11.60	13.29
OECD median	*6.58*	*7.28*	*5.91*	*8.91*	*6.55*	*7.31*
Brazil	12.50	14.80	11.08	13.64	12.19	13.32
Latvia	16.65	17.96	15.45	18.40	16.98	17.90
Liechtenstein	13.35	14.36	12.19	14.00	13.27	14.49
Russian Federation	13.81	13.34	13.15	15.79	13.73	13.47
Netherlands[1]	13.60	14.65	14.16	13.12	13.68	13.86

1. Response rate is too low to ensure comparability.
2. The numbers in the table represent change in the reading literacy performance per unit of change in the index of sense of belonging (see Annex A3 for definition).

Table 6.6d
Correlation between student relationship with teachers and reading literacy performance

		Combined reading literacy	Retrieving information	Interpreting texts	Reflection and evaluation	Continuous texts	Non-continuous texts
OECD COUNTRIES	Australia	0.16	0.14	0.16	0.18	0.17	0.15
	Austria	0.03	0.06	0.02	0.03	0.02	0.04
	Belgium	-0.02	-0.02	-0.02	-0.02	-0.02	-0.02
	Canada	0.15	0.14	0.14	0.16	0.14	0.14
	Czech Republic	0.05	0.06	0.05	0.07	0.05	0.06
	Denmark	0.17	0.16	0.16	0.18	0.17	0.15
	Finland	0.12	0.12	0.10	0.13	0.12	0.11
	France	-0.02	-0.01	-0.03	-0.01	-0.01	-0.03
	Germany	0.03	0.02	0.02	0.04	0.03	0.02
	Greece	-0.02	-0.03	-0.02	0.00	-0.01	-0.02
	Hungary	-0.10	-0.08	-0.11	-0.10	-0.10	-0.10
	Iceland	0.19	0.17	0.17	0.21	0.20	0.16
	Ireland	0.12	0.12	0.10	0.13	0.11	0.12
	Italy	-0.05	-0.06	-0.05	-0.04	-0.04	-0.06
	Japan	0.20	0.18	0.18	0.19	0.19	0.18
	Korea	0.09	0.09	0.09	0.09	0.09	0.09
	Luxembourg	-0.04	-0.05	-0.03	-0.05	-0.05	-0.04
	Mexico	0.03	0.02	0.02	0.05	0.04	0.02
	New Zealand	0.12	0.11	0.12	0.14	0.12	0.13
	Norway	0.18	0.16	0.16	0.19	0.18	0.15
	Poland	0.04	0.04	0.05	0.04	0.04	0.03
	Portugal	-0.06	-0.05	-0.06	-0.03	-0.04	-0.06
	Spain	0.08	0.08	0.05	0.10	0.08	0.06
	Sweden	0.13	0.13	0.11	0.14	0.13	0.12
	Switzerland	0.03	0.02	0.02	0.05	0.04	0.01
	United Kingdom	0.17	0.17	0.15	0.19	0.17	0.16
	United States	0.19	0.18	0.19	0.20	0.18	0.18
	OECD median	*0.08*	*0.08*	*0.05*	*0.09*	*0.08*	*0.06*
NON-OECD COUNTRIES	Brazil	-0.03	-0.02	-0.05	-0.03	-0.04	-0.03
	Latvia	0.08	0.06	0.08	0.09	0.09	0.06
	Liechtenstein	-0.01	-0.01	-0.02	-0.01	-0.02	0.01
	Russian Federation	0.03	0.02	0.02	0.04	0.02	0.01
	Netherlands[1]	0.07	0.07	0.06	0.07	0.07	0.07

Regression of reading literacy performance on student relationship with teachers[2]

		Combined reading literacy	Retrieving information	Interpreting texts	Reflection and evaluation	Continuous texts	Non-continuous texts
OECD COUNTRIES	Australia	17.82	16.76	17.49	19.66	19.44	16.23
	Austria	2.92	5.06	1.82	2.24	1.89	3.82
	Belgium	-2.39	-2.47	-1.69	-2.77	-2.71	-2.56
	Canada	14.13	14.71	13.31	15.11	13.83	13.95
	Czech Republic	5.19	6.58	4.62	7.13	5.14	7.11
	Denmark	16.37	16.36	15.49	17.85	16.79	15.74
	Finland	12.67	14.38	11.75	13.66	12.56	12.67
	France	-2.13	-1.47	-3.12	-0.94	-1.39	-2.58
	Germany	2.78	1.77	2.34	4.50	3.25	1.79
	Greece	-1.53	-3.26	-1.58	0.26	-1.05	-1.89
	Hungary	-9.71	-8.94	-10.68	-10.59	-9.43	-11.09
	Iceland	17.25	17.30	16.65	19.52	18.44	15.97
	Ireland	12.14	13.44	10.60	12.36	11.67	12.71
	Italy	-4.47	-6.75	-4.42	-4.17	-3.99	-5.97
	Japan	16.46	17.13	14.81	18.19	16.12	17.34
	Korea	6.74	7.64	6.56	6.89	6.12	7.22
	Luxembourg	-3.02	-4.23	-2.26	-4.44	-4.57	-4.05
	Mexico	2.60	1.89	1.43	5.47	3.37	1.53
	New Zealand	15.12	14.28	14.56	16.21	14.49	15.59
	Norway	18.23	17.66	16.84	20.04	18.61	17.09
	Poland	4.51	4.41	4.72	4.05	4.56	3.69
	Portugal	-5.78	-5.71	-6.21	-3.63	-4.68	-6.94
	Spain	6.08	7.15	4.22	8.51	6.15	5.74
	Sweden	12.61	13.54	11.20	13.55	12.71	12.18
	Switzerland	2.90	2.03	1.90	5.17	3.21	1.41
	United Kingdom	17.51	17.86	16.35	19.29	17.79	16.12
	United States	18.88	19.27	19.06	19.86	18.80	18.57
	OECD median	*6.08*	*7.15*	*4.72*	*7.13*	*6.12*	*7.11*
NON-OECD COUNTRIES	Brazil	-2.58	-1.84	-3.83	-2.51	-3.18	-2.96
	Latvia	8.42	7.89	7.94	10.91	9.81	6.95
	Liechtenstein	-1.02	-1.18	-1.65	-0.68	-1.46	0.43
	Russian Federation	2.60	2.35	1.92	4.06	2.38	1.55
	Netherlands[1]	8.36	9.74	7.72	7.86	8.76	8.33

1. Response rate is too low to ensure comparability.
2. The numbers in the table represent change in the reading literacy performance per unit of change in the index of student-teacher relationships (see Annex A3 for definitions).

Table 6.7
Regression of reading engagement on selected background characteristics

		Immigration Status	Gender	Family structure	Socio-economic back-ground	Number of books in the home	Cultural communi-cation	Home educa-tional resources	Perfor-mance press	Disci-plinary climate	Student-teacher relationship	Sense of belong-ing	Time spent on home-work
OECD COUNTRIES	Australia	0.19	0.28	0.11	0.17	0.20	0.37	0.23	-0.01	0.18	0.28	-0.01	0.34
	Austria	-0.01	0.52	0.07	0.21	0.24	0.38	0.17	-0.04	0.09	0.10	0.00	0.15
	Belgium	-0.13	0.41	0.17	0.19	0.22	0.34	0.19	-0.04	0.07	0.14	0.09	0.32
	Canada	0.18	0.47	0.08	0.14	0.22	0.37	0.18	-0.03	0.17	0.22	0.00	0.30
	Czech Republic	-0.24	0.62	0.06	0.25	0.28	0.43	0.23	-0.07	0.10	0.14	0.04	0.21
	Denmark	0.18	0.48	0.07	0.15	0.20	0.41	0.22	0.03	0.13	0.21	-0.01	0.31
	Finland	0.02	0.73	0.15	0.11	0.23	0.39	0.16	-0.14	0.16	0.21	-0.01	0.35
	France	0.06	0.29	0.11	0.16	0.24	0.38	0.22	-0.06	0.07	0.12	0.09	0.40
	Germany	-0.15	0.55	0.23	0.26	0.29	0.43	0.17	-0.10	0.14	0.15	-0.01	0.26
	Greece	0.04	0.15	0.06	0.10	0.12	0.29	0.09	0.05	0.09	0.12	0.13	0.22
	Hungary	0.04	0.36	0.10	0.16	0.21	0.37	0.18	-0.01	0.15	0.14	0.14	0.36
	Iceland	-0.26	0.38	0.03	0.10	0.21	0.29	0.15	-0.03	0.09	0.19	0.02	0.20
	Ireland	0.43	0.46	0.08	0.14	0.22	0.38	0.21	-0.01	0.15	0.28	0.02	0.23
	Italy	0.14	0.36	0.07	0.15	0.18	0.36	0.15	-0.05	0.20	0.13	-0.01	0.21
	Japan[1]	-0.86	0.24	-0.08	m	0.24	0.25	0.10	0.12	0.09	0.14	0.12	0.19
	Korea[2]	m	0.03	0.11	0.19	0.22	0.21	0.20	-0.02	0.07	0.15	0.06	0.24
	Luxembourg	0.02	0.42	0.17	0.12	0.18	0.36	0.08	-0.02	0.07	0.15	0.06	0.24
	Mexico	-0.09	0.20	-0.05	0.09	0.10	0.24	0.10	0.09	0.07	0.13	0.18	0.24
	New Zealand	0.23	0.27	0.16	0.12	0.19	0.35	0.17	-0.01	0.17	0.23	0.04	0.25
	Norway	0.08	0.50	0.09	0.13	0.20	0.34	0.25	-0.07	0.13	0.20	0.04	0.22
	Poland	-0.99	0.36	-0.04	0.11	0.14	0.32	0.11	-0.01	0.15	0.19	0.15	0.28
	Portugal	0.26	0.45	-0.03	0.15	0.17	0.32	0.19	0.05	0.11	0.14	0.18	0.25
	Spain	-0.10	0.28	0.10	0.17	0.21	0.40	0.19	0.05	0.09	0.12	0.06	0.27
	Sweden	-0.12	0.44	0.14	0.14	0.22	0.38	0.14	-0.09	0.11	0.18	-0.04	0.24
	Switzerland	-0.07	0.56	0.06	0.19	0.23	0.36	0.19	-0.06	0.11	0.16	0.17	0.28
	United Kingdom	0.32	0.25	0.11	0.13	0.22	0.40	0.23	-0.03	0.18	0.22	0.03	0.33
	United States	0.13	0.35	0.11	0.13	0.23	0.37	0.17	0.07	0.13	0.24	0.05	0.25
	OECD median	*0.02*	*0.38*	*0.09*	*0.14*	*0.22*	*0.37*	*0.18*	*-0.02*	*0.11*	*0.15*	*0.04*	*0.25*
	SD of correlation	*0.31*	*0.15*	*0.07*	*0.05*	*0.04*	*0.06*	*0.05*	*0.06*	*-0.04*	*0.05*	*0.07*	*0.06*
NON-OECD COUNTRIES	Brazil	-0.52	0.52	0.00	0.09	0.18	0.30	0.16	0.13	0.11	0.18	0.20	0.27
	Latvia	0.17	0.45	0.01	0.04	0.11	0.23	0.06	0.01	0.09	0.15	0.09	0.22
	Liechtenstein	-0.02	0.46	0.25	0.21	0.24	0.29	0.31	0.04	-0.06	0.13	0.04	0.28
	Russian Federation	0.09	0.40	0.06	0.07	0.10	0.28	0.09	0.03	0.15	0.21	0.16	0.26
	Netherlands[3]	0.02	0.43	0.15	0.20	0.21	0.30	0.21	-0.02	0.07	0.19	0.03	0.18

1. Japan is excluded from the comparison because of a high proportion of missing data.
2. Korea did not collect information on immigration status.
3. Response rate is too low to ensure comparability.

Table 7.1
Regression coefficients for the student socio-economic background based on three different models

	Linear regression		Multilevel regression	
	One factor	**Multi factor**	**Within school**	**Between school**
Australia	31.7	20.0	12.2	42.7
Austria	35.2	12.7	2.3	46.0
Belgium	38.3	15.9	6.5	61.1
Canada	25.8	16.2	11.8	28.1
Czech Republic	43.3	18.9	8.0	50.4
Denmark	29.1	15.3	12.4	21.3
Finland	20.9	13.5	11.8	11.1
France	30.8	10.7	7.4	19.2
Germany	45.3	16.7	3.7	63.7
Greece	28.1	17.0	7.5	46.8
Hungary	39.2	16.8	0.7	61.8
Iceland	19.3	12.6	10.5	7.5
Ireland	30.3	18.6	13.3	40.5
Italy	26.4	14.4	3.0	54.2
Japan	m	m	m	m
Korea	14.6	4.4	-1.1	17.1
Luxembourg	39.2	17.4	10.7	53.2
Mexico	31.8	13.1	3.4	45.8
New Zealand	31.9	20.9	15.6	42.6
Norway	29.8	14.4	12.9	10.0
Poland	35.5	20.1	1.5	82.6
Portugal	38.5	11.3	7.3	20.9
Spain	26.5	9.2	3.7	18.8
Sweden	27.1	16.9	14.1	20.6
Switzerland	40.2	16.8	9.0	19.1
United Kingdom	38.5	24.6	16.7	44.5
United States	33.6	16.5	9.9	52.8
Brazil	26.1	12.6	3.3	40.7
Latvia	21.3	13.6	8.4	45.0
Liechtenstein[2]	m	m	m	m
Russian Federation	26.5	15.1	9.2	48.3
Netherlands[1]	30.0	15.1	6.5	76.4

OECD COUNTRIES rows: Australia through United States.
NON-OECD COUNTRIES rows: Brazil, Latvia, Liechtenstein[2], Russian Federation.

1. Japan is excluded from the comparison because of a high proportion of missing data.
2. Liechtenstein is excluded from the analysis because the number of schools in the country was considered too small to be considered as appropriate for the analyses of variance decomposition.
3. Response rate is too low to ensure comparability.

Table 7.2
OECD country mean within – and between-school multilevel regression coefficients

	Combined reading literacy	Retrieving information	Interpreting texts	Reflection and evaluation	Continuous texts	Non-continuous texts
Student level						
Achievement press	-3.1	-3.8	-3.1	-2.3	-2.9	-3.7
Sense of belonging	1.0	1.3	0.4	1.9	0.9	1.6
Disciplinary climate	1.4	0.7	1.3	2.3	1.8	0.8
Teacher-student relationship	1.0	1.4	0.5	1.2	0.8	0.8
Cultural communication	2.9	1.4	2.8	4.5	3.3	2.1
Reading engagement	18.5	19.0	19.5	17.7	19.5	17.3
Time spent on homework	0.2	0.0	-0.5	1.3	0.1	0.5
Education resources	3.0	4.2	2.6	2.8	2.4	4.4
Socio-economic background	8.1	8.2	8.3	7.5	7.9	7.9
Number of books in the home	5.0	5.2	5.2	5.0	5.0	5.5
Family structure	2.3	3.3	1.8	2.2	2.0	3.6
Gender	11.9	3.5	10.2	23.9	18.6	-2.5
Grade	37.3	42.1	36.3	36.1	36.3	41.0
Immigration status	-21.8	-24.3	-21.1	-20.4	-21.4	-20.8
School level						
Reading engagement	22.6	24.2	21.4	24.0	22.7	22.3
School social intake	39.8	42.9	38.7	41.0	40.4	41.8

Table 7.3
Multilevel regression coefficients for the individual characteristics of students

	Gender	S.E.	Reading engagement	S.E.
OECD COUNTRIES				
Australia	17.9	(2.8)	24.7	(2.0)
Austria	6.3	(3.2)	18.1	(1.3)
Belgium	4.5	(2.2)	18.0	(1.0)
Canada	14.8	(1.6)	24.5	(0.8)
Czech Republic	7.7	(2.4)	17.9	(1.2)
Denmark	6.6	(2.7)	29.1	(1.6)
Finland	26.0	(2.2)	30.5	(1.3)
France	10.3	(2.0)	12.3	(1.1)
Germany	4.3	(2.3)	17.9	(1.6)
Greece	18.1	(2.5)	8.9	(1.5)
Hungary	7.4	(2.3)	14.7	(1.0)
Iceland	22.3	(2.9)	31.4	(1.8)
Ireland	6.6	(3.6)	24.5	(1.5)
Italy	11.2	(2.6)	12.4	(1.0)
Japan[1]	m	m	m	m
Korea	18.3	(2.6)	12.6	(1.1)
Luxembourg	13.6	(2.7)	11.8	(1.9)
Mexico	7.6	(2.3)	9.4	(1.2)
New Zealand	28.6	(3.4)	24.6	(1.8)
Norway	19.1	(3.7)	28.9	(2.0)
Poland	-0.5	(2.9)	11.2	(1.8)
Portugal	2.0	(2.7)	13.3	(1.5)
Spain	7.7	(1.9)	14.2	(1.3)
Sweden	19.7	(2.5)	30.3	(1.8)
Switzerland	6.7	(2.1)	23.4	(1.5)
United Kingdom	13.8	(2.3)	19.8	(1.2)
United States	10.7	(3.2)	16.8	(2.7)
NON-OECD COUNTRIES				
Brazil	0.5	(2.7)	14.1	(1.4)
Latvia	25.3	(3.2)	14.7	(2.1)
Liechtenstein[2]	m	m	m	m
Russian Federation	16.7	(2.3)	10.3	(1.2)
Netherlands[3]	2.9	(2.2)	15.5	(1.7)

1. Japan is excluded from the comparison because of a high proportion of missing data.
2. Liechtenstein is excluded from the analysis because the number of schools in the country was considered too small to be included in analyses of variance decomposition.
3. Response rate is too low to ensure comparability.
Note: Values marked in bold are statistically significant.

Table 7.4
Multilevel regression coefficients for family structure, socio-economic background and immigration status

		Family Structure	S.E.	Socio-economic background	S.E.	Immigration status	S.E.
OECD COUNTRIES	Australia	5.0	(3.9)	**12.2**	(1.9)	**-29.5**	(4.8)
	Austria	-2.8	(3.1)	2.3	(1.3)	**-30.9**	(5.5)
	Belgium	**-4.5**	(2.1)	**6.5**	(1.3)	-4.7	(6.0)
	Canada	**7.0**	(1.6)	**11.8**	(0.9)	**-25.1**	(3.6)
	Czech Republic	-4.0	(2.6)	**8.0**	(1.1)	-1.4	(18.1)
	Denmark	5.1	(2.9)	**12.4**	(1.9)	**-44.7**	(7.6)
	Finland	**10.2**	(2.9)	**11.8**	(1.2)	**-61.8**	(10.3)
	France	-0.6	(2.3)	**7.4**	(1.4)	**-15.7**	(7.9)
	Germany	-4.6	(2.6)	**3.7**	(1.5)	**-23.5**	(6.3)
	Greece	0.8	(3.5)	**7.5**	(1.6)	2.1	(8.8)
	Hungary	-4.0	(2.3)	0.7	(1.1)	3.0	(7.0)
	Iceland	4.3	(3.4)	**10.5**	(1.5)	-36.5	(22.5)
	Ireland	**8.8**	(3.3)	**13.3**	(1.5)	8.7	(10.2)
	Italy	**4.9**	(2.1)	**3.0**	(1.2)	-6.2	(17.7)
	Japan[1]	m	m	m	m	m	m
	Korea[2]	-0.5	(2.9)	-1.1	(1.2)	m	m
	Luxembourg	2.4	(3.1)	**10.7**	(1.7)	**-21.5**	(4.0)
	Mexico	**-5.0**	(2.2)	**3.4**	(1.3)	**-32.3**	(8.6)
	New Zealand	**6.8**	(3.1)	**15.6**	(1.7)	**-35.8**	(4.8)
	Norway	**11.9**	(3.7)	**12.9**	(1.6)	**-41.2**	(10.2)
	Poland	-0.2	(3.9)	1.5	(1.7)	-29.8	(29.0)
	Portugal	-4.6	(2.5)	**7.3**	(1.4)	-15.8	(10.7)
	Spain	-2.3	(2.5)	**3.7**	(1.1)	-9.3	(9.2)
	Sweden	**11.9**	(2.6)	**14.1**	(1.5)	**-27.1**	(6.5)
	Switzerland	-1.6	(2.6)	**9.0**	(1.4)	**-43.1**	(4.1)
	United Kingdom	**13.6**	(2.6)	**16.7**	(1.3)	**-31.1**	(8.9)
	United States	**21.5**	(3.9)	**9.9**	(2.0)	-6.4	(8.1)
NON-OECD COUNTRIES	Brazil	-4.7	(3.3)	**3.3**	(1.6)	-59.0	(40.4)
	Latvia	-3.9	(3.7)	**8.4**	(1.5)	-5.8	(5.6)
	Liechtenstein[3]	m	m	m	m	m	m
	Russian Federation	-3.0	(2.1)	**9.2**	(1.3)	2.5	(5.2)
	Netherlands[4]	-0.6	(4.2)	**6.5**	(1.6)	**-32.0**	(8.2)

1. Japan is excluded from the comparison because of a high proportion of missing data.
2. Korea did not collect information on immigration status.
3. Liechtenstein is excluded from the analysis because the number of schools in the country was considered too small to be included in analyses of variance decomposition.
4. Response rate is too low to ensure comparability.
Note: Values marked in bold are statistically significant.

Table 7.5
**Multilevel regression coefficients for cultural communication with parents,
educational resources in the home and number of books in the home**

		Cultural communication	S.E.	Home educational resources	S.E.	No. of books	S.E.
OECD COUNTRIES	Australia	**9.2**	(1.8)	3.0	(1.7)	**4.4**	(1.2)
	Austria	1.7	(1.5)	2.2	(1.6)	**4.6**	(1.0)
	Belgium	1.0	(1.0)	2.0	(1.0)	**3.5**	(0.7)
	Canada	**3.8**	(0.8)	0.5	(0.8)	**4.9**	(0.6)
	Czech Republic	**3.1**	(1.1)	**3.3**	(1.3)	**6.9**	(0.9)
	Denmark	**10.9**	(1.6)	0.7	(1.4)	**6.5**	(1.2)
	Finland	**5.2**	(1.3)	0.3	(1.3)	**4.1**	(0.9)
	France	1.3	(1.2)	**4.6**	(1.0)	**5.2**	(0.8)
	Germany	-0.1	(1.3)	**5.0**	(2.2)	**3.9**	(1.1)
	Greece	1.7	(1.3)	**6.1**	(1.2)	**3.0**	(1.1)
	Hungary	**-3.1**	(0.9)	-0.3	(1.0)	**6.8**	(0.8)
	Iceland	**5.8**	(1.6)	-1.8	(1.5)	**7.0**	(1.1)
	Ireland	1.7	(1.4)	**4.8**	(1.5)	**6.7**	(1.1)
	Italy	**2.8**	(1.2)	0.6	(1.1)	1.1	(0.7)
	Japan[1]	m	m	m	m	m	m
	Korea	0.0	(1.1)	-0.5	(1.1)	**5.7**	(0.7)
	Luxembourg	1.3	(1.8)	**8.5**	(1.3)	**6.3**	(1.0)
	Mexico	1.4	(1.5)	1.4	(1.2)	**4.6**	(1.2)
	New Zealand	-1.4	(1.6)	**9.6**	(1.8)	**7.9**	(1.2)
	Norway	**7.2**	(1.7)	**10.3**	(1.7)	**5.1**	(1.3)
	Poland	-1.9	(1.3)	2.1	(1.3)	1.8	(1.0)
	Portugal	**5.4**	(1.1)	2.2	(1.2)	**3.5**	(1.1)
	Spain	**4.6**	(1.2)	1.7	(1.2)	**6.6**	(1.1)
	Sweden	**6.9**	(1.4)	1.3	(1.2)	**5.5**	(1.1)
	Switzerland	1.5	(1.2)	**4.8**	(1.1)	**4.4**	(0.9)
	United Kingdom	**3.3**	(1.3)	**3.6**	(1.3)	**5.6**	(1.0)
	United States	1.1	(2.0)	0.2	(1.7)	**9.3**	(1.2)
NON-OECD COUNTRIES	Brazil	2.1	(1.5)	3.3	(1.8)	0.6	(1.4)
	Latvia	**4.3**	**(1.8)**	2.5	(1.8)	**7.2**	(1.4)
	Liechtenstein[2]	m	m	m	m	m	m
	Russian Federation	0.3	(1.0)	**3.7**	**(1.1)**	**5.0**	(0.9)
	Netherlands[3]	**5.2**	(1.6)	3.3	(2.0)	**3.3**	(1.2)

1. Japan is excluded from the comparison because of a high proportion of missing data.
2. Liechtenstein is excluded from the analysis because the number of schools in the country was considered too small to be included in analyses of variance decomposition.
3. Response rate is too low to ensure comparability.
Note: Values marked in bold are statistically significant.

Table 7.6
Multilevel regression coefficients for instruction and learning variables

		Achievement press	S.E.	Time spent on homework	S.E.	Grade	S.E.
OECD COUNTRIES	Australia	**-7.7**	(1.4)	**5.2**	(1.9)	**39.9**	(3.0)
	Austria	-1.8	(1.3)	**-7.3**	(1.3)	**31.0**	(1.8)
	Belgium	-1.5	(1.1)	0.8	(1.2)	**51.7**	(2.9)
	Canada	**-6.7**	(0.8)	**3.2**	(0.8)	**46.1**	(1.7)
	Czech Republic	**-4.0**	(1.4)	**-6.3**	(1.1)	**31.4**	(2.6)
	Denmark	-1.2	(1.5)	**-7.9**	(1.6)	**32.8**	(5.2)
	Finland	**-3.3**	(1.4)	**-4.9**	(1.4)	**40.4**	(4.2)
	France	**-2.8**	(1.1)	**3.3**	(1.1)	**46.6**	(3.1)
	Germany	-1.5	(1.2)	-2.3	(1.2)	**35.0**	(1.8)
	Greece	-1.3	(1.4)	**8.5**	(1.6)	**18.3**	(3.9)
	Hungary	-0.8	(0.9)	-0.3	(1.0)	**22.5**	(1.9)
	Iceland[1]	**-7.9**	(1.5)	**-8.6**	(1.6)	n.a.	n.a.
	Ireland	**-4.0**	(1.3)	2.1	(1.5)	**24.0**	(1.6)
	Italy	**-3.5**	(1.1)	1.7	(1.2)	**32.2**	(3.0)
	Japan[2]	m	m	m	m	m	m
	Korea	**2.5**	(1.0)	0.7	(1.1)	13.4	(11.8)
	Luxembourg	-1.5	(1.6)	**-2.8**	(1.3)	**30.7**	(2.0)
	Mexico	**-3.0**	(1.3)	**2.2**	(1.0)	**29.0**	(3.0)
	New Zealand	**-8.1**	(1.8)	**3.6**	(1.6)	**54.0**	(4.7)
	Norway	**-7.6**	(1.6)	-1.2	(1.7)	42.6	(22.0)
	Poland[1]	**-3.2**	(1.2)	0.3	(1.6)	n.a.	n.a.
	Portugal	**-3.7**	(1.0)	**-3.7**	(1.2)	**53.3**	(1.7)
	Spain	-1.4	(1.2)	**5.6**	(1.3)	**70.7**	(2.2)
	Sweden	**-7.6**	(1.2)	**-11.3**	(1.4)	**70.3**	(9.8)
	Switzerland	1.5	(1.3)	-1.4	(1.2)	**44.0**	(2.9)
	United Kingdom	**-4.3**	(1.2)	**8.1**	(1.5)	**10.5**	(2.1)
	United States	-2.0	(1.9)	**7.4**	(1.5)	**37.6**	(2.9)
NON-OECD COUNTRIES	Brazil	2.9	(1.6)	0.8	(1.4)	**33.8**	(1.7)
	Latvia	-1.1	(1.4)	2.7	(1.9)	**30.8**	(3.1)
	Liechtenstein[3]	m	m	m	m	m	m
	Russian Federation	**-3.2**	(1.2)	**9.5**	(1.2)	**34.6**	(2.8)
	Netherlands[4]	**-5.8**	(1.4)	-1.7	(1.2)	**35.9**	(3.7)

1. In Iceland and Poland, the students included in the international database were attending the same grade. Therefore, grade variable is not applicable to these countries.
2. Japan is excluded from the comparison because of a high proportion of missing data.
3. Liechtenstein is excluded from the analysis because the number of schools in the country was considered too small to be included in analyses of variance decomposition.
4. Response rate is too low to ensure comparability.
Note: Values marked in bold are statistically significant.

Table 7.7
Multilevel regression coefficients for sense of belonging and learning climate

		Sense of belonging	S.E.	Disciplinary climate	S.E.	Student-teacher Relationship	S.E.
OECD COUNTRIES	Australia	-2.7	(1.5)	2.7	(1.6)	2.0	(1.7)
	Austria	1.8	(1.4)	-2.0	(1.3)	**2.9**	(1.3)
	Belgium	**2.0**	(0.9)	1.5	(1.1)	**-3.0**	(1.1)
	Canada	**-2.0**	(0.7)	**2.2**	(0.8)	**5.7**	(0.8)
	Czech Republic	**5.1**	(1.0)	1.0	(1.1)	-1.7	(1.1)
	Denmark	2.0	(1.3)	2.5	(1.4)	**4.7**	(1.4)
	Finland	**-4.3**	(1.3)	1.0	(1.3)	**5.7**	(1.2)
	France	0.4	(1.1)	-1.4	(1.2)	**-4.9**	(1.3)
	Germany	-0.5	(1.2)	-0.5	(1.4)	0.6	(1.2)
	Greece	**3.3**	(1.3)	-0.5	(1.4)	-2.2	(1.2)
	Hungary	**4.4**	(0.9)	0.2	(1.1)	**-5.8**	(1.1)
	Iceland	-1.0	(1.4)	2.1	(1.4)	**7.9**	(1.6)
	Ireland	-2.0	(1.4)	**7.8**	(1.7)	0.7	(1.6)
	Italy	-0.5	(1.1)	-0.6	(1.2)	-1.4	(1.4)
	Japan[1]	m	m	m	m	m	m
	Korea	-0.6	(1.1)	1.1	(1.1)	**2.4**	(0.9)
	Luxembourg	**5.3**	(1.4)	0.1	(1.5)	-1.0	(1.5)
	Mexico	**5.4**	(1.3)	2.0	(1.2)	0.1	(1.1)
	New Zealand	-2.0	(1.8)	-0.4	(2.0)	**5.3**	(1.7)
	Norway	-2.9	(1.7)	-2.0	(1.7)	**8.7**	(1.9)
	Poland	**3.0**	(1.3)	**5.3**	(1.6)	**-3.2**	(1.6)
	Portugal	**6.3**	(0.9)	0.9	(1.2)	-1.4	(1.2)
	Spain	-0.3	(1.0)	-0.0	(1.4)	1.0	(1.0)
	Sweden	**-2.8**	(1.3)	**2.8**	(1.3)	**5.5**	(1.6)
	Switzerland	**5.2**	(1.3)	**4.8**	(1.3)	0.1	(1.1)
	United Kingdom	-1.8	(1.2)	**7.4**	(1.5)	**3.2**	(1.3)
	United States	2.4	(1.8)	**6.2**	(1.5)	2.3	(1.8)
NON-OECD COUNTRIES	Brazil	2.2	(1.2)	**-3.6**	(1.4)	**-2.9**	(1.4)
	Latvia	0.8	(1.7)	2.1	(1.8)	-0.1	(2.3)
	Liechtenstein[2]	m	m	m	m	m	m
	Russian Federation	1.0	(1.2)	-0.9	(1.1)	-0.5	(1.2)
	Netherlands[3]	1.9	(1.3)	-0.9	(1.5)	-0.4	(1.6)

1. Japan is excluded from the comparison because of a high proportion of missing data.
2. Liechtenstein is excluded from the analysis because the number of schools in the country was considered too small to be included in analyses of variance decomposition.
3. Response rate is too low to ensure comparability.
Note: Values marked in bold are statistically significant.

Table 7.8
Multilevel regression coefficients for school characteristics

	Reading engagement at school level		Socio-economic background at school level	
	Coefficient	S.E.	Coefficient	S.E.
Australia	4.4	(3.9)	**42.7**	(3.2)
Austria	**44.4**	(3.6)	**46.0**	(3.5)
Belgium	**22.0**	(2.3)	**61.1**	(2.6)
Canada	2.1	(2.1)	**28.1**	(1.9)
Czech Republic	**37.2**	(3.2)	**50.4**	(2.5)
Denmark	**15.2**	(5.2)	**21.3**	(4.0)
Finland	**17.5**	(5.4)	**11.1**	(2.5)
France	**33.4**	(6.0)	**19.2**	(3.6)
Germany	**44.8**	(3.1)	**63.7**	(2.7)
Greece	**65.3**	(3.9)	**46.8**	(2.6)
Hungary	**35.8**	(4.4)	**61.8**	(3.8)
Iceland	8.3	(6.5)	7.5	(3.9)
Ireland	**12.6**	(4.6)	**40.5**	(2.8)
Italy	**30.9**	(6.2)	**54.2**	(3.5)
Japan[1]	m	m	m	m
Korea	**64.3**	(3.0)	**17.1**	(2.6)
Luxembourg	9.4	(8.6)	**53.2**	(4.8)
Mexico	9.8	(6.9)	**45.8**	(3.2)
New Zealand	-6.1	(4.8)	**42.6**	(3.8)
Norway	**24.2**	(7.9)	**10.0**	(4.1)
Poland	**58.9**	(3.9)	**82.6**	(2.7)
Portugal	**19.3**	(4.5)	**20.9**	(2.4)
Spain	**25.0**	(2.8)	**18.8**	(1.7)
Sweden	-2.5	(3.9)	**20.6**	(3.2)
Switzerland	**41.2**	(4.5)	**19.1**	(4.4)
United Kingdom	**11.0**	(5.6)	**44.5**	(3.0)
United States	-7.6	(6.1)	**52.8**	(4.3)
Brazil	-1.0	(3.1)	**40.7**	(2.7)
Latvia	**23.9**	(5.3)	**45.0**	(4.2)
Liechtenstein[2]	m	m	m	m
Russian Federation	**13.7**	(2.7)	**48.3**	(3.6)
Netherlands[3]	**20.5**	(3.2)	**76.4**	(3.1)

OECD COUNTRIES / NON-OECD COUNTRIES

1. Japan is excluded from the comparison because of a high proportion of missing data.
2. Liechtenstein is excluded from the analysis because the number of schools in the country was considered too small to be included in analyses of variance decomposition.
3. Response rate is too low to ensure comparability.
Note: Values marked in bold are statistically significant.

Table 7.9

Proportion of between- school variance to the total variance (ICC) in student reading literacy performance

		Intraclass correlation (ICC)	S.E.
OECD COUNTRIES	Australia	0.18	(0.02)
	Austria	0.60	(0.01)
	Belgium	0.60	(0.01)
	Canada	0.18	(0.01)
	Czech Republic	0.53	(0.04)
	Denmark	0.19	(0.01)
	Finland	0.12	(0.01)
	France	0.50	(0.01)
	Germany	0.59	(0.01)
	Greece	0.51	(0.01)
	Hungary	0.67	(0.01)
	Iceland	0.08	(0.02)
	Ireland	0.18	(0.02)
	Italy	0.55	(0.03)
	Japan[1]	m	m
	Korea	0.37	(0.02)
	Luxembourg	0.31	(0.01)
	Mexico	0.53	(0.01)
	New Zealand	0.16	(0.01)
	Norway	0.10	(0.02)
	Poland	0.62	(0.02)
	Portugal	0.37	(0.01)
	Spain	0.20	(0.01)
	Sweden	0.09	(0.01)
	Switzerland	0.43	(0.01)
	United Kingdom	0.22	(0.01)
	United States	0.29	(0.01)
NON-OECD COUNTRIES	Brazil	0.44	(0.01)
	Latvia	0.31	(0.02)
	Liechtenstein[2]	m	m
	Russian Federation	0.37	(0.02)
	Netherlands[3]	0.50	(0.02)

1. Due to the sampling methods used in Japan, the between school variance cannot be separated from the variance between classes within school.
2. Liechtenstein is excluded from the analysis because the number of schools in the country was considered too small to be included in analyses of variance decomposition.
3. Response rate is too low to ensure comparability.
Note: The results presented in this table are based on all students included in the PISA 2000 international database. The results in all other tables in this chapter are based on the students included in the multiended analysis. For the exact numbers of students included in the PISA 2000 database and students included in the multilevel analyses. For details, see Table A3.1.

Table 7.10
Intraclass correlation for PISA, IEA reading literacy study and TIMSS

		PISA	IEA/RLS	TIMSS 95
OECD COUNTRIES	Australia	0.18	n.a.	0.45
	Austria	0.60	n.a.	0.33
	Belgium	0.60	n.a.	n.a.
	Belgium (Fl.)	n.a.	n.a.	0.40
	Belgium (Fr.)	n.a.	0.40	0.47
	Canada	0.18	n.a.	0.18
	Czech Republic	0.53	n.a.	0.21
	Denmark	0.19	0.09	0.08
	Finland	0.12	0.03	n.a.
	France	0.50	0.35	0.25
	Germany	0.59	n.a.	0.46
	Greece	0.51	0.22	0.14
	Hungary	0.67	n.a.	0.18
	Iceland	0.08	0.08	0.10
	Ireland	0.18	0.48	0.45
	Italy	0.55	0.28	n.a.
	Korea	0.37	n.a.	0.06
	Luxembourg	0.31	n.a.	n.a.
	Mexico	0.53	n.a.	n.a.
	New Zealand	0.16	0.41	0.36
	Norway	0.10	0.06	0.06
	Poland	0.62	n.a.	n.a.
	Portugal	0.37	0.27	0.15
	Spain	0.20	0.22	0.16
	Sweden	0.09	0.08	0.31
	Switzerland	0.43	0.48	0.42
	United Kingdom	0.22	n.a.	0.19
	United States	0.29	0.42	0.46
NON-OECD COUNTRIES	Brazil	0.44	n.a.	n.a.
	Latvia	0.31	n.a.	0.17
	Liechtenstein[2]	m	n.a.	n.a.
	Russian Federation	0.37	n.a.	0.31
	Netherlands[3]	0.50	0.50	0.52

1. Liechtenstein is excluded from the analysis because the number of schools in the country was considered too small to be included in analyses of variance decomposition.

2. Response rate is too low to ensure comparability.

Note: The between class variance reported by the IEA/RLS could be smaller than the PISA school variance for several reasons. *(i)* The target populations are not exactly the same. For instance, in France, the school variance in PISA is affected by the structure of the education system in which secondary education is provided by lower secondary education schools (colleges) and upper secondary school (lycees). *(ii)* Sampling error. *(iii)* PISA student performance was reported using plausible values generated with conditioning according to school membership, while IEA/RLS used Maximum Likelihood Estimates which may overestimate the within-school variance so that the intraclass correlation may be underestimated.

Note: n.a. signifies not administered.

Table 7.11
Unexplained school and student variances and percentages of explained variances between and within school

		Unexplained variance		Explained variance (%)	
		Student	School	Student	School
OECD COUNTRIES	Australia	5 742.5	371.0	0.27	0.77
	Austria	3 487.9	794.1	0.18	0.84
	Belgium	3 415.7	1 545.4	0.25	0.75
	Canada	5 186.1	649.2	0.28	0.55
	Czech Republic	3 343.8	691.7	0.20	0.78
	Denmark	5 347.3	404.0	0.29	0.65
	Finland	4 514.2	703.9	0.34	0.29
	France	3 210.7	419.0	0.19	0.89
	Germany	3 536.5	895.7	0.22	0.83
	Greece	4 250.2	1 340.2	0.10	0.70
	Hungary	2 631.9	1 038.7	0.15	0.83
	Iceland	5 373.7	313.9	0.27	0.51
	Ireland	4 959.9	397.0	0.28	0.71
	Italy	3 385.3	1 762.9	0.12	0.61
	Japan[1]	m	m	m	m
	Korea	2 723.0	512.5	0.09	0.71
	Luxembourg	4 067.4	205.1	0.26	0.91
	Mexico	3 126.4	650.8	0.09	0.83
	New Zealand	6 332.1	375.2	0.28	0.76
	Norway	6 218.1	370.4	0.29	0.59
	Poland	3 366.3	1 439.5	0.05	0.74
	Portugal	3 364.9	212.2	0.39	0.93
	Spain	3 323.2	340.2	0.40	0.75
	Sweden	5 008.6	143.2	0.32	0.78
	Switzerland	3 761.6	1 276.9	0.31	0.68
	United Kingdom	5 350.8	396.4	0.24	0.78
	United States	5 452.3	425.0	0.24	0.83
NON-OECD COUNTRIES	Brazil	3 448.1	735.9	0.17	0.75
	Latvia	5 577.9	1 232.9	0.18	0.59
	Liechtenstein[2]	m	m	m	m
	Russian Federation	4 198.1	1 515.1	0.18	0.48
	Netherlands[3]	2 789.3	785.3	0.28	0.79

1. Due to the sampling methods used in Japan, the between school variance cannot be separated from the variance between classes within school.
2. Liechtenstein is excluded from the analysis because the number of schools in the country was considered too small to be included in analyses of variance decomposition.
3. Response rate is too low to ensure comparability.

Table 8.1
Labour force participation rates of 25- 65 year olds by IALS prose literacy level

	Levels 1 and 2 (%)	S.E.	Levels 3, 4 and 5 (%)	S.E.
Australia	67	(1.1)	84	(0.6)
Belgium (Fl.)	63	(1.7)	83	(1.3)
Canada	67	(4.2)	82	(4.6)
Chile	65	(1.4)	81	(2.3)
Czech Republic	71	(1.4)	85	(1.4)
Denmark	75	(0.9)	86	(1.3)
Finland	69	(1.5)	86	(0.8)
Germany	61	(3.1)	72	(1.3)
Hungary	63	(1.1)	85	(2.2)
Ireland	56	(1.7)	73	(1.3)
Netherlands	56	(1.6)	77	(1.3)
New Zealand	70	(1.9)	81	(1.1)
Norway	73	(1.5)	89	(0.8)
Poland	67	(0.7)	82	(2.2)
Portugal	71	(2.9)	90	(3.6)
Slovenia	72	(0.7)	92	(1.3)
Sweden	71	(1.7)	87	(1.1)
Switzerland	76	(2.8)	84	(2.0)
United Kingdom	68	(1.3)	87	(0.9)
United States	74	(1.7)	84	(1.3)

OECD COUNTRIES

Source: International Adult Literacy Survey, Table 3.6 (OECD and Statistics Canada, 2000).

Table 8.2
Percentage of unemployment among adults 16–65 by IALS prose literacy level

	Levels 1 and 2 (%)	S.E.	Levels 3, 4 and 5 (%)	S.E.
Australia	11	(0.8)	5	(0.5)
Belgium (Fl.)	17	(2.7)	7	(1.0)
Canada	16	(3.9)	8	(1.1)
Chile	14	(1.0)	8[1]	(1.8)
Czech Republic	8	(0.9)	4	(0.7)
Denmark	9	(1.1)	5	(0.7)
Finland	21	(1.7)	9	(0.7)
Germany	14	(1.7)	8	(1.4)
Hungary	15	(1.2)	13	(2.2)
Ireland	23	(2.9)	11	(1.9)
Netherlands	9	(1.2)	5	(0.7)
New Zealand	16	(1.7)	4	(0.7)
Norway	6	(0.8)	3	(0.4)
Poland	17	(1.1)	11	(1.9)
Portugal	15	(2.3)	9	(1.3)
Slovenia	14	(1.0)	8	(1.5)
Sweden	11	(1.2)	7	(0.6)
Switzerland	5	(0.9)	3	(0.8)
United Kingdom	16	(1.2)	9	(0.9)
United States	7	(1.2)	4	(0.8)

OECD COUNTRIES

1. Number in this cell is not well estimated.
Source: International Adult Literacy Survey, Table 3.7 (OECD and Statistics Canada, 2000).

Table 8.3
Percentage of adults aged 25-65 who are in the top 60% of earners IALS prose literacy level

OECD COUNTRIES	Level 1 (%)	S.E.	Level 2 (%)	S.E.	Level 3 (%)	S.E.	Levels 4 and 5 (%)	S.E.
Australia	26	(1.8)	44	(1.4)	51	(1.2)	58	(1.7)
Belgium (Fl.)	6[1]	(1.2)	13	(2.1)	23	(1.9)	34	(3.7)
Canada	24	(6.4)	45	(8.4)	57	(3.0)	69	(7.5)
Chile	26	(1.8)	44	(2.0)	61	(3.2)	72	(9.2)
Czech Republic	17	(2.6)	28	(2.0)	42	(2.7)	55	(4.1)
Denmark	37	(3.6)	57	(1.5)	70	(1.5)	67	(5.2)
Finland	26	(2.6)	52	(2.0)	67	(1.5)	74	(2.4)
Germany	35	(4.2)	44	(2.5)	50	(3.5)	56	(3.1)
Hungary	21	(1.4)	41	(2.2)	62	(3.7)	55[1]	(9.8)
Ireland	24	(2.6)	45	(3.8)	60	(3.0)	75	(4.0)
Netherlands	33	(4.3)	48	(1.7)	61	(1.6)	63	(3.1)
New Zealand	34	(3.0)	54	(3.1)	63	(2.3)	73	(2.3)
Norway	38	(4.6)	57	(2.3)	74	(1.2)	70	(2.3)
Poland	57	(2.1)	65	(1.5)	75	(2.6)	87	(4.2)
Portugal	52	(3.8)	59	(4.3)	75	(4.4)	74	(6.1)
Slovenia	23	(1.3)	52	(2.6)	72	(2.8)	67[1]	(8.5)
Sweden	72	(6.1)	79	(2.4)	81	(1.5)	83	(1.9)
Switzerland	46	(6.0)	59	(4.3)	72	(3.9)	71	(5.1)
United Kingdom	25	(1.9)	43	(2.2)	57	(1.7)	72	(3.0)
United States	13	(1.9)	32	(2.8)	47	(2.6)	60	(2.6)
OECD average	*26*	*(1.0)*	*41*	*(1.2)*	*53*	*(1.4)*	*62*	*(1.5)*

1. Number in this cell is not well estimated.
Source: International Adult Literacy Survey, Table 4.9 (OECD and Statistics Canada, 2000).

Table 8.4
Percentage of adults aged 16–65 participating in adult education and training during the year preceding the interview by IALS document literacy level[1]

	Participation rate	S.E.	Level 1 (%)	S.E.	Level 2 (%)	S.E.	Level 3 (%)	S.E.	Levels 4 and 5 (%)	S.E.
Australia	39	(0.7)	14	(1.2)	29	(1.2)	47	(1.2)	62	(1.5)
Belgium (Fl.)	21	(1.1)	4[2]	(1.3)	15	(2.4)	26	(1.6)	37	(3.2)
Canada	38	(1.0)	17	(6.2)	29	(2.4)	40	(2.9)	60	(2.2)
Chile	19	(1.1)	11	(1.1)	24	(2.1)	39	(3.7)	51[2]	(11.1)
Czech Republic	26	(0.9)	11	(1.9)	23	(1.2)	29	(1.9)	35	(2.0)
Denmark	56	(0.7)	25	(3.3)	44	(1.8)	60	(1.4)	70	(1.5)
Finland	57	(0.9)	19	(1.8)	44	(2.5)	66	(1.6)	78	(1.7)
Germany[3]	m	m	m	m	m	m	m	m	m	m
Hungary	19	(0.7)	8	(1.1)	17	(1.7)	31	(1.7)	44	(4.7)
Ireland	24	(2.3)	10	(2.0)	20	(2.3)	34	(2.8)	47	(4.2)
Netherlands	37	(1.2)	17	(2.3)	27	(1.6)	42	(1.8)	53	(3.1)
New Zealand	48	(1.2)	29	(2.3)	41	(2.3)	55	(2.0)	68	(1.9)
Norway	48	(1.5)	18	(2.3)	36	(2.8)	51	(1.6)	63	(2.0)
Poland	14	(0.9)	8	(1.0)	15	(1.8)	23	(2.4)	32	(6.2)
Portugal	14	(1.0)	5	(1.4)	19	(2.6)	33	(3.4)	53	(7.0)
Slovenia	32	(1.1)	14	(1.3)	37	(1.7)	59	(2.1)	61	(5.2)
Sweden	53	(1.1)	29	(5.2)	40	(2.2)	55	(1.8)	62	(1.3)
Switzerland	42	(1.1)	20	(2.7)	34	(2.2)	48	(1.4)	64	(3.4)
United Kingdom	44	(0.9)	22	(1.7)	34	(1.8)	54	(1.8)	71	(2.0)
United States	40	(1.4)	17	(2.1)	32	(1.8)	49	(1.8)	59	(3.0)
OECD average	*35*	*(0.6)*	*14*	*(0.9)*	*29*	*(0.9)*	*46*	*(0.9)*	*59*	*(1.4)*

(OECD COUNTRIES)

1. Full-time students and people with less than 6 hours of training are excluded from these estimates.

2. Number in this cell is not well estimated.

3. Germany was not included in the table because the survey did not ask about adult education and training in the same way.

Source: International Adult Literacy Survey, Table 3.12 (OECD and Statistics Canada, 2000).

Table 8.5
Mean performance and percentage of PISA students at each level of the IALS prose literacy scale

		Mean score	S.E.	Level 1 (%)	S.E.	Level 2 (%)	S.E.	Level 3 (%)	S.E.	Levels 4 and 5 (%)	S.E.
OECD COUNTRIES	Australia	281.3	(1.2)	9.3	(0.5)	35.3	(0.9)	41.4	(0.7)	13.9	(0.7)
	Austria	262.1	(0.9)	19.8	(0.6)	41.4	(0.8)	33.0	(0.8)	5.8	(0.3)
	Belgium	277.7	(1.1)	11.7	(0.8)	33.0	(0.6)	44.4	(0.9)	10.9	(0.4)
	Canada	285.6	(0.5)	5.4	(0.2)	33.9	(0.4)	47.0	(0.3)	13.7	(0.3)
	Czech Republic	268.0	(0.8)	15.3	(0.6)	41.1	(0.6)	36.6	(0.6)	6.9	(0.3)
	Denmark	266.1	(0.7)	15.5	(0.6)	43.0	(0.5)	35.5	(0.6)	5.9	(0.3)
	Finland	301.9	(0.7)	4.2	(0.2)	22.8	(0.5)	43.3	(0.5)	29.7	(0.6)
	France	272.5	(1.0)	12.5	(0.7)	40.3	(0.7)	38.1	(0.8)	9.0	(0.4)
	Germany	264.1	(1.0)	20.6	(0.7)	37.8	(0.6)	32.7	(0.6)	8.9	(0.3)
	Greece	267.7	(2.0)	18.7	(1.4)	36.5	(0.9)	34.3	(1.2)	10.4	(0.7)
	Hungary	267.1	(1.5)	15.7	(1.1)	41.5	(0.8)	36.5	(1.2)	6.3	(0.4)
	Iceland	276.3	(0.6)	12.2	(0.4)	36.8	(0.5)	38.8	(0.5)	12.2	(0.4)
	Ireland	281.2	(1.1)	8.6	(0.6)	35.4	(0.7)	43.0	(0.7)	13.0	(0.5)
	Italy	271.1	(1.0)	13.2	(0.7)	40.0	(0.8)	38.8	(0.8)	8.0	(0.4)
	Japan	287.7	(1.3)	3.2	(0.4)	31.5	(1.3)	54.0	(1.1)	11.2	(0.7)
	Korea	285.1	(0.7)	2.5	(0.2)	33.7	(0.8)	56.3	(0.7)	7.4	(0.4)
	Luxembourg	243.7	(0.5)	33.2	(0.5)	42.9	(0.5)	21.4	(0.4)	2.5	(0.2)
	Mexico	248.4	(1.1)	28.1	(1.0)	46.9	(0.7)	22.9	(0.9)	2.0	(0.0)
	New Zealand	279.7	(1.0)	10.2	(0.6)	34.9	(0.6)	41.6	(0.7)	13.3	(0.6)
	Norway	266.2	(0.9)	16.8	(0.7)	41.0	(0.6)	35.5	(0.7)	6.8	(0.3)
	Poland	268.1	(1.3)	16.5	(0.9)	39.9	(0.8)	35.1	(1.0)	8.5	(0.6)
	Portugal	258.5	(1.5)	20.2	(1.2)	45.1	(0.7)	31.7	(1.3)	2.9	(0.3)
	Spain	270.1	(0.8)	9.2	(0.5)	45.7	(0.7)	42.3	(0.9)	2.8	(0.2)
	Sweden	269.6	(0.7)	11.7	(0.5)	43.3	(0.6)	39.8	(0.7)	5.2	(0.2)
	Switzerland	273.3	(1.4)	12.8	(0.7)	38.9	(0.9)	38.4	(0.8)	9.8	(0.8)
	United Kingdom	275.2	(0.9)	10.9	(0.5)	39.3	(0.7)	40.0	(0.5)	9.8	(0.6)
	United States	272.5	(2.1)	11.1	(1.2)	41.8	(1.2)	39.7	(1.5)	7.5	(0.8)
NON-OECD COUNTRIES	Brazil	249.8	(1.1)	25.6	(1.0)	50.8	(0.8)	22.2	(1.0)	1.4	(0.2)
	Latvia[1]	261.3	(1.6)	22.1	(1.2)	39.1	(0.6)	30.8	(1.0)	8.0	(0.4)
	Liechenstein	275.1	(1.7)	10.3	(1.4)	36.7	(1.6)	44.9	(1.5)	8.1	(1.0)
	Russian Federation	265.8	(1.0)	16.4	(0.6)	42.3	(0.5)	34.6	(0.7)	6.7	(0.3)
	Netherlands[2]	288.5	(1.3)	6.1	(0.7)	29.9	(1.0)	47.0	(1.1)	16.9	(0.9)
	Average of countries participating in PISA	*267.8*	*(0.4)*	*15.2*	*(0.3)*	*41.7*	*(0.3)*	*36.3*	*(0.4)*	*6.9*	*(0.0)*

1. Sample size of this country responding to IALS items was too small to provide reliable estimates.
2. Response rate is too low to ensure comparability.

Table 8.6
Mean performance and percentage of PISA female students at each level of the IALS prose literacy scale

		Mean score	S.E.	Level 1 (%)	S.E.	Level 2 (%)	S.E.	Level 3 (%)	S.E.	Levels 4 and 5 (%)	S.E.
OECD COUNTRIES	Australia	289.0	(1.5)	5.8	(0.5)	31.4	(1.2)	45.1	(0.9)	17.7	(1.1)
	Austria	269.7	(1.3)	14.8	(0.8)	39.4	(1.1)	37.9	(1.2)	7.9	(0.5)
	Belgium	286.9	(1.5)	7.6	(0.9)	27.6	(1.0)	49.8	(1.1)	15.0	(0.7)
	Canada	293.7	(0.5)	3.0	(0.2)	27.5	(0.4)	51.0	(0.4)	18.5	(0.4)
	Czech Republic	276.1	(0.9)	10.1	(0.5)	38.7	(0.9)	42.0	(0.7)	9.2	(0.5)
	Denmark	273.7	(1.0)	11.0	(0.8)	39.9	(0.8)	41.0	(0.9)	8.2	(0.5)
	Finland	314.7	(0.8)	1.8	(0.2)	14.9	(0.6)	43.3	(0.6)	40.1	(0.8)
	France	280.8	(1.0)	8.0	(0.6)	36.6	(0.9)	43.1	(0.9)	12.3	(0.5)
	Germany	272.1	(1.2)	16.0	(1.0)	35.6	(0.9)	37.0	(0.8)	11.3	(0.5)
	Greece	278.3	(1.8)	11.6	(1.1)	35.2	(1.0)	39.2	(1.2)	14.0	(0.9)
	Hungary	275.5	(1.6)	10.7	(1.0)	38.1	(1.3)	42.2	(1.4)	9.0	(0.7)
	Iceland	288.3	(0.8)	6.3	(0.4)	31.6	(0.7)	44.4	(0.8)	17.7	(0.6)
	Ireland	288.9	(1.1)	5.9	(0.6)	30.1	(0.9)	46.9	(0.9)	17.2	(0.7)
	Italy	282.2	(1.1)	7.2	(0.6)	35.0	(0.9)	46.0	(1.0)	11.8	(0.5)
	Japan	294.0	(1.4)	1.9	(0.4)	25.6	(1.4)	57.7	(0.9)	14.9	(1.0)
	Korea	287.9	(1.2)	1.9	(0.2)	31.3	(1.7)	57.7	(1.2)	9.1	(0.7)
	Luxembourg	251.0	(0.9)	27.4	(0.8)	43.8	(0.7)	25.3	(0.7)	3.4	(0.3)
	Mexico	254.0	(1.3)	23.2	(1.1)	47.5	(0.8)	26.7	(1.0)	2.6	(0.3)
	New Zealand	289.7	(1.3)	5.8	(0.5)	30.5	(0.9)	44.7	(0.8)	19.0	(1.0)
	Norway	277.3	(0.9)	9.6	(0.6)	37.6	(0.9)	43.1	(0.8)	9.7	(0.5)
	Poland	276.8	(1.7)	10.8	(1.0)	37.9	(1.2)	39.8	(1.2)	11.4	(0.9)
	Portugal	265.1	(1.6)	15.3	(1.1)	43.4	(1.0)	37.5	(1.5)	3.8	(0.4)
	Spain	276.0	(0.9)	5.6	(0.5)	42.1	(1.2)	48.6	(1.2)	3.7	(0.3)
	Sweden	279.9	(0.7)	5.8	(0.4)	38.2	(0.7)	48.0	(0.8)	7.9	(0.4)
	Switzerland	281.4	(1.5)	8.7	(0.6)	34.8	(1.2)	43.5	(0.9)	13.0	(1.1)
	United Kingdom	282.6	(1.2)	7.7	(0.5)	34.9	(1.0)	44.0	(0.8)	13.4	(0.9)
	United States	279.1	(2.0)	7.4	(1.0)	38.8	(1.5)	44.0	(1.6)	9.8	(1.0)
NON-OECD COUNTRIES	Brazil	255.5	(1.4)	20.0	(1.2)	51.5	(1.0)	26.6	(1.4)	1.9	(0.2)
	Latvia[1]	273.7	(1.5)	13.5	(0.9)	37.6	(0.9)	37.7	(1.2)	11.2	(0.5)
	Liechenstein	282;9	(2.4)	5.9	(1.6)	34.3	(2.2)	49.8	(2.1)	10.1	(1.6)
	Russian Federation	275.5	(1.0)	10.3	(0.6)	39.3	(0.8)	40.9	(0.8)	9.5	(0.5)
	Netherlands[2]	296.8	(1.6)	3.3	(0.6)	25.5	(1.5)	48.3	(1.5)	22.9	(1.5)
	Average of countries participating in PISA	*274.7*	*(0.5)*	*10.9*	*(0.3)*	*39.3*	*(0.4)*	*40.7*	*(0.4)*	*9.1*	*(0.2)*

1. Sample size of this country responding to IALS items was too small to provide reliable estimates.
2. Response rate is too low to ensure comparability.

Table 8.7
Mean performance and percentage of PISA male students at each level of the IALS prose literacy scale

		Mean score	S.E.	Level 1 (%)	S.E.	Level 2 (%)	S.E.	Level 3 (%)	S.E.	Levels 4 and 5 (%)	S.E.
OECD COUNTRIES	Australia	274.6	(1.4)	12.5	(0.7)	38.5	(1.1)	38.3	(1.2	10.7	(0.7)
	Austria	254.8	(1.3)	24.5	(1.2)	43.7	(0.8)	28.2	(1.1	3.6	(0.3)
	Belgium	270.0	(1.3)	15.1	(0.9)	37.6	(1.0)	40.0	(1.1	7.3	(0.5)
	Canada	277.8	(0.5)	7.8	(0.3)	39.8	(0.5)	43.3	(0.5	9.2	(0.3)
	Czech Republic	259.8	(1.4)	20.5	(1.2)	43.9	(0.9)	31.0	(1.1	4.6	(0.3)
	Denmark	258.8	(0.9)	20.0	(0.9)	45.8	(0.8)	30.5	(0.8	3.8	(0.3)
	Finland	288.3	(1.0)	6.8	(0.4)	31.2	(0.8)	43.3	(0.7	18.7	(0.6)
	France	263.8	(1.1)	17.3	(0.9)	44.1	(0.8)	32.9	(0.9	5.7	(0.4)
	Germany	257.1	(1.2)	24.5	(0.9)	39.9	(0.7)	28.9	(0.7	6.6	(0.4)
	Greece	257.4	(2.5)	25.8	(1.9)	37.6	(1.0)	29.5	(1.4	7.0	(0.8)
	Hungary	259.0	(2.0)	20.6	(1.6)	44.6	(1.1)	31.1	(1.6	3.7	(0.5)
	Iceland	265.2	(0.8)	17.7	(0.6)	41.7	(0.8)	33.8	(0.7	6.9	(0.4)
	Ireland	273.9	(1.4)	11.1	(0.8)	40.6	(1.0)	39.3	(1.0	9.0	(0.7)
	Italy	260.6	(1.5)	18.9	(1.2)	44.8	(1.0)	32.0	(1.1	4.4	(0.4)
	Japan	281.4	(1.5)	4.6	(0.6)	37.6	(1.6)	50.2	(1.5	7.5	(0.7)
	Korea, Republic of	282.9	(1.1)	3.1	(0.4)	35.5	(1.3)	55.2	(1.3	6.2	(0.5)
	Luxembourg	236.9	(0.9)	38.7	(0.9)	41.8	(0.8)	18.0	(0.6	1.5	(0.2)
	Mexico	242.6	(1.4)	33.7	(1.3)	45.5	(0.8)	19.4	(1.1	1.5	(0.2)
	New Zealand	270.4	(1.4)	14.3	(1.0)	39.1	(0.9)	38.9	(1.1	7.7	(0.5)
	Norway	256.2	(1.1)	23.0	(1.0)	44.1	(0.8)	28.9	(1.0	4.0	(0.3)
	Poland	259.6	(1.9)	22.0	(1.5)	41.8	(1.1)	30.5	(1.7	5.7	(0.5)
	Portugal	251.6	(1.7)	25.4	(1.5)	46.8	(0.9)	25.8	(1.3	2.0	(0.3)
	Spain	264.5	(0.9)	12.6	(0.6)	49.0	(1.0)	36.5	(1.2	1.9	(0.2)
	Sweden	259.6	(1.6)	17.5	(0.7)	48.2	(0.8)	31.8	(0.9	2.6	(0.2)
	Switzerland	265.4	(1.6)	16.8	(1.0)	42.9	(1.1)	33.7	(1.2	6.7	(0.6)
	United Kingdom	268.2	(0.9)	14.0	(0.7)	43.1	(0.8)	36.5	(0.7	6.4	(0.5)
	United States	265.4	(2.3)	14.9	(1.6)	45.0	(1.3)	35.1	(1.7	5.0	(0.7)
NON-OECD COUNTRIES	Brazil	243.7	(1.1)	31.4	(1.3)	50.2	(1.0)	17.5	(0.9	1.0	(0.2)
	Latvia[1]	248.4	(1.9)	31.2	(1.6)	40.5	(0.9)	23.5	(1.0	4.8	(0.4)
	Liechtenstein	269.9	(2.9)	12.7	(2.1)	39.7	(2.4)	41.3	(2.4	6.3	(1.4)
	Russian Federation	256.3	(1.2)	22.5	(1.0)	45.1	(0.5)	28.4	(0.9	3.9	(0.2)
	Netherlands[2]	280.4	(1.8)	9.0	(1.2)	34.0	(1.2)	45.9	(1.6	11.2	(0.9)
	Average of countries participating in PISA	*260.9*	*(0.5)*	*19.3*	*(0.4)*	*44.0*	*(0.3)*	*32.1*	*(0.4*	*4.6*	*(0.2)*

1. Sample size of this country responding to IALS items was too small to provide reliable estimates.
2. Response rate is too low to ensure comparability.

Table 8.8
Differences in mean performance between females and males on the IALS prose literacy scale

		Mean score for all students	Mean score for females	Mean score for males	Difference between females and males	Difference as % of SD
OECD COUNTRIES	Australia	281.3	289.0	274.6	14.4	0.36
	Austria	262.1	269.7	254.8	14.9	0.37
	Belgium	277.7	286.9	270.0	16.9	0.42
	Canada	285.6	293.7	277.8	15.9	0.39
	Czech Republic	268.0	276.1	259.8	16.3	0.40
	Denmark	266.1	273.7	258.8	14.9	0.37
	Finland	301.9	314.7	288.3	26.4	0.66
	France	272.5	280.8	263.8	17.0	0.42
	Germany	264.1	272.1	257.1	15.0	0.37
	Greece	267.7	278.3	257.4	20.9	0.52
	Hungary	267.1	275.5	259.0	16.5	0.41
	Iceland	276.3	288.3	265.2	23.1	0.57
	Ireland	281.2	288.9	273.9	15.0	0.37
	Italy	271.1	282.2	260.6	21.6	0.54
	Japan	287.7	294.0	281.4	12.6	0.31
	Korea	285.1	287.9	282.9	5.0	0.12
	Luxembourg	243.7	251.0	236.9	14.1	0.35
	Mexico	248.4	254.0	242.6	11.4	0.28
	New Zealand	279.7	289.7	270.4	19.3	0.48
	Norway	266.2	277.3	256.2	21.1	0.52
	Poland	268.1	276.8	259.6	17.2	0.43
	Portugal	258.5	265.1	251.6	13.5	0.33
	Spain	270.1	276.0	264.5	11.5	0.29
	Sweden	269.6	279.9	259.6	20.3	0.50
	Switzerland	273.3	281.4	265.4	16.0	0.40
	United Kingdom	275.2	282.6	268.2	14.4	0.36
	United States	272.5	279.1	265.4	13.7	0.34
NON-OECD COUNTRIES	Brazil	249.8	255.5	243.7	11.8	0.29
	Latvia[1]	261.3	273.7	248.4	25.3	0.50
	Liechenstein	275.1	282.9	269.9	13.0	0.32
	Russian Federation	265.8	275.5	256.3	19.2	0.48
	Netherlands[2]	288.5	296.8	280.4	16.4	0.41
	Average of countries participating in PISA	*267.8*	*274.7*	*260.9*	*13.8*	*0.34*

1. Sample size of this country responding to IALS items was too small to provide reliable estimates.
2. Response rate is too low to ensure comparability.

Table 8.9
Comparison of performance on the IALS prose literacyscale between PISA students and IALS 16 to 25-year-olds by gender

	PISA 15-year-olds		IALS 16-25-year-olds	
	Males	**Females**	**Males**	**Females**
Australia	275	289	278	290
Belgium[1]	270	287	292	295
Canada	278	294	287	287
Switzerland	265	281	280	288
Czech Repulic	260	276	278	283
Germany	257	272	284	283
Denmark	259	274	279	288
Finland	288	315	304	322
Hungary	259	276	254	264
Ireland	274	289	272	283
Italy	261	282	272	278
Netherlands	280	297	291	297
Norway[1]	256	277	295	306
New Zealand	270	290	267	286
Poland	260	277	243	261
Portugal	252	265	251	270
Sweden	260	280	310	314
United Kingdom	268	283	270	277
United States	265	279	260	265
Average of countries that participated both in PISA and in IALS	*266*	*283*	*279*	*287*

OECD COUNTRIES

1. Results are not directly comparable because of differences in the representation of language groups in two surveys.

ANNEX

C

THE DEVELOPMENT AND
IMPLEMENTATION OF PISA 2000
– A COLLABORATIVE EFFORT

Introduction

PISA is a collaborative effort, bringing together scientific expertise from the participating countries, steered jointly by their governments on the basis of shared, policy-driven interests.

A Board of Participating Countries on which each country is represented determines, in the context of OECD objectives, the policy priorities for PISA and oversees adherence to these priorities during the implementation of the programme. This includes the setting of priorities for the development of indicators, for the establishment of the assessment instruments and for the reporting of the results.

Experts from participating countries also serve on working groups that are charged with linking policy objectives with the best internationally available technical expertise. By participating in these expert groups, countries ensure that: the instruments are internationally valid and take into account the cultural and educational contexts in OECD Member countries; the assessment materials have strong measurement properties; and the instruments place an emphasis on authenticity and educational validity.

Through National Project Managers, participating countries implement PISA at the national level subject to the agreed administration procedures. National Project Managers play a vital role in ensuring that the implementation of the survey is of high quality, and verify and evaluate the survey results, analyses, reports and publications.

The design and implementation of the surveys, within the framework established by the Board of Participating Countries, is the responsibility of the PISA consortium, referred to as the PISA Consortium, led by the Australian Council for Educational Research (ACER). Other partners in this consortium include the Netherlands National Institute for Educational Measurement (Citogroep), The National Institute for Educational Research in Japan (NIER), the Educational Testing Service in the United States (ETS) and WESTAT in the United States.

The OECD Secretariat has overall managerial responsibility for the programme, monitors its implementation on a day-to-day basis, acts as the secretariat for the Board of Participating Countries, builds consensus among countries and serves as the interlocutor between the Board of Participating Countries and the international consortium charged with the implementation of the activities. The OECD Secretariat also produces the indicators and analyses and prepares the international reports and publications in co-operation with the PISA consortium and in close consultation with Member countries both at the policy level (Board of Participating Countries) and at the level of implementation (National Project Managers).

The following lists the members of the various PISA bodies and the individual experts and consultants who have contributed to PISA.

Members of the PISA 2000 Board of Participating Countries

Chair: Eugene Owen

Australia: Wendy Whitham
Austria: Friedrich Plank
Belgium: Dominique Barthélémy, Christiane Blondin, Dominique Lafontaine, Liselotte van de Perre
Brazil: Maria Helena Guimarães de Castro
Canada: Satya Brink, Patrick Bussière, Dianne Pennock
Czech Republic: Jan Koucky, Jana Strakova
Denmark: Birgitte Bovin

Finland: Ritva Jakku-Sihvonen
France: Gérard Bonnet
Germany: Jochen Schweitzer, Helga Hinke, Gudrun Stoltenberg
Greece: Vassilis Koulaidis
Hungary: Péter Vári
Iceland: Einar Gudmundsson
Ireland: Gerry Shiel

Italy: Chiara Croce, Elisabetta Midena, Benedetto Vertecchi
Japan: Ryo Watanabe
Korea: Kooghyang Ro
Luxembourg: Jean-Paul Reeff
Mexico: Fernando Córdova Calderón
Netherlands: Arnold Spee
New Zealand: Lynne Whitney
Norway: Alette Schreiner
Poland: Kazimierz Korab
Portugal: Glória Ramalho
Spain: Guillermo Gil
Sweden: Anders Auer, Birgitta Fredander, Anita Wester
Switzerland: Heinz Gilomen
United Kingdom: Lorna Bertrand, Brian Semple
United States: Mariann Lemke

PISA 2000 National Project Managers

Australia: Jan Lokan
Austria: Günter Haider
Belgium: Dominique Lafontaine, Luc van de Poele
Brazil: Tereza Cristina Cotta, Maria Lucia Guardia, Maria Inês Pestana
Canada: Marc Lachance, Dianne Pennock
Czech Republic: Jana Straková
Denmark: Vita Bering Pruzan
Finland: Jouni Välijärvi
France: Jean-Pierre Jeantheau
Germany: Juergen Baumert, Petra Stanat
Greece: Katerina Kassotakis
Hungary: Péter Vári
Iceland: Julius Bjornsson, Ragna Benedikta Garðarsdóttir
Ireland: Judith Cosgrove
Italy: Emma Nardi
Japan: Ryo Watanabe
Korea: Kooghyang Ro
Latvia: Andris Kangro
Luxembourg: Iris Blanke, Jean-Paul Reeff
Mexico: Fernando Córdova Calderón
Netherlands: Johan Wijnstra
New Zealand: Steve May
Norway: Svein Lie
Poland: Michal Federowicz
Portugal: Glória Ramalho
Russian Federation: Galine Kovalyova
Spain: Guillermo Gil
Sweden: Bengt-Olov Molander, Astrid Pettersson,

Karin Taube
Switzerland: Huguette McCluskey
United Kingdom: Baljit Gill, Graham Thorpe
United States: Ghedam Bairu, Marilyn Binkley

OECD Secretariat

Andreas Schleicher (overall co-ordination of PISA and Member country relations)
Kooghyang Ro (thematic analyses)
Claudia Tamassia (project management)
Eric Charbonnier (statistical support)
Hannah Cocks (statistical support)
Juliet Evans (administrative support)

PISA Expert groups
Reading Functional Expert Group

Irwin Kirsch (Chair) (Educational Testing Service, United States)
Marilyn Binkley (National Center for Educational Statistics, United States)
Alan Davies (University of Edinburgh, United Kingdom)
Stan Jones (Statistics Canada, Canada)
John de Jong (Language Testing Services, The Netherlands)
Dominique Lafontaine (Université de Liège Sart Tilman, Belgium)
Pirjo Linnakylä (University of Jyväskylä, Finland)
Martine Rémond (Institut National de Recherche Pédagogique, France)
Wolfgang Schneider (University of Würzburg, Germany)
Ryo Watanabe (National Institute for Educational Research, Japan)

PISA Technical Advisory Group

Ray Adams (ACER, Australia)
Pierre Foy (Statistics Canada, Canada)
Aletta Grisay (Belgium)
Larry Hedges (The University of Chicago, United States)
Eugene Johnson (American Institutes for Research, United States)
John de Jong (Language Testing Services, The Netherlands)
Geoff Masters (ACER, Australia)
Keith Rust (WESTAT, United States)
Norman Verhelst (CITO group, The Netherlands)
J. Douglas Willms (University of New Brunswick, Canada)

PISA Consortium

Australian Council for Educational Research

Ray Adams (Project Director of the PISA Consortium)
Alla Berezner (data processing, data analysis)
Claus Carstensen (data analysis)
Lynne Darkin (reading test development)
Brian Doig (mathematics test development)
Adrian Harvey-Beavis (quality monitoring, questionnaire development)
Kathryn Hill (reading test development)
John Lindsey (mathematics test development)
Jan Lokan (quality monitoring, field procedures development)
Le Tu Luc (data processing)
Greg Macaskill (data processing)
Joy McQueen (reading test development and reporting)
Gary Marks (questionnaire development)
Juliette Mendelovits (reading test development and reporting)
Christian Monseur (Director of the PISA Consortium for data processing, data analysis, quality monitoring)
Gayl O'Connor (science test development)
Alla Routitsky (data processing)
Wolfram Schulz (data analysis)
Ross Turner (test analysis and reporting co-ordination)
Nikolai Volodin (data processing)
Craig Williams (data processing, data analysis)
Margaret Wu (Deputy Project Director of the PISA Consortium)

Westat

Nancy Caldwell (Director of the PISA Consortium for field operations and quality monitoring)
Ming Chen (sampling and weighting)
Fran Cohen (sampling and weighting)
Susan Fuss (sampling and weighting)
Brice Hart (sampling and weighting)
Sharon Hirabayashi (sampling and weighting)
Sheila Krawchuk (sampling and weighting)
Dward Moore (field operations and quality monitoring)
Phu Nguyen (sampling and weighting)
Monika Peters (field operations and quality monitoring)
Merl Robinson (field operations and quality monitoring)
Keith Rust (Director of the PISA Consortium for sampling and weighting)
Leslie Wallace (sampling and weighting)
Dianne Walsh (field operations and quality monitoring)
Trevor Williams (questionnaire development)

CITO group

Steven Bakker (science test development)
Bart Bossers (reading test development)
Truus Decker (mathematics test development)
Erna van Hest (reading test development and quality monitoring)
Kees Lagerwaard (mathematics test development)
Gerben van Lent (mathematics test development)
Ico de Roo (science test development)
Maria van Toor (office support and quality monitoring)
Norman Verhelst (technical advice, data analysis)

Educational Testing Service

Irwin Kirsch (reading test development)

Other experts

Cordula Artelt (questionnaire development)
Marc Demeuse (quality monitoring)
Harry Ganzeboom (questionnaire development)
Aletta Grisay (technical advice, data analysis, translation, questionnaire development)
Donald Hirsch (editorial review)
Jules Peschar (questionnaire development)
Erich Ramseier (questionnaire development)
Gundula Schümer (questionnaire development)
Marie-Andrée Somers (data analysis and reporting)
Peter Sutton (editorial review)
Rich Tobin (questionnaire development and reporting)

OECD PUBLICATIONS, 2, rue André-Pascal, 75775 PARIS CEDEX 16
PRINTED IN FRANCE
(96 2002 07 1 P 1) ISBN 92-64-09926-3 – No. 52781 2002